Three Taps of the Gavel: Pledge to the Future

THE CHAUTAUQUA STORY

by

ALFREDA L. IRWIN

Revised and Expanded

CHAUTAUQUA INSTITUTION

CHAUTAUQUA, NEW YORK

Cover: The Miller Bell Tower

Frontispiece:
Recognition Day Parades show off Class Banners and
demonstrate class loyalties. This parade is a study in sym-
bolism with the 19th century architecture in the background, the Brick Walk (signifying the walking
community), the wide variety of ages represented, and
above all, the mottoes on the Banners, giving clues to the
concerns of succeeding classes.

Photographs from the following: (Most are or now will be a
part of The Chautauqua Historical Collection.)

Harold Wagner
Gordon Mahan
Christopher Gibbs
Si Wertz
Phil Zimmer
David Naprstek
Todd Minnigh
Todd Gustavson
Kevin Lahey
Andy O'Sullivan
William J. Robbins

Todd Gustavson provided technical assistance.

The personnel of the Chautauqua Historical Collection
assisted generously in various ways: Barbara B. Haug,
Mary Ellen Foster, Margaret R. Wade, and Arthur E.
Wade with Librarian Torrey Isaac. Dr. Julia D. Marshall
and Susan Elizabeth Becka read proofs. Rosamond Olson
and Jeanne A. Anderson helped with the typing of the
manuscript.

Designed by Abigail Sturges

Quotation reprinted from "The Chautauqua Movement" by
Joseph E. Gould by permission of the State University of
New York Press, Albany, N.Y.

Library of Congress Cataloging-in-Publication Data

Irwin, Alfreda L. (Alfreda Locke), 1913-
  Three taps of the gavel.

  Bibliography:
  Includes index.
  1. Chautauqua Institution—History. I. Title.
LC6301.C5178   1987   974.7'95   86-72282

ISBN 0-941149-00-5

CONTENTS

CHAUTAUQUA INSTITUTION

SUMMER SCHOOLS

ARTS & CRAFTS . . . . Palestine Ave.—College Hill
CONNELL STUDIO (Voice) . . . . Palestine—North Gate
THE LODGE, DANCE STUDIO . . . . Hedding Ave.—College Hill
SUMMER SCHOOL DORMITORY . . . . Hedding Ave.—College Hill
HALL OF EDUCATION . . . . Hurst Ave.—College Hill
INSTRUMENTAL STUDIOS . . . . Massey Ave.—College Hill
PIANO & VOICE PRACTICE STUDIOS

Palestine Ave.—North Gate
SHERWOOD HALL (Piano) . . . . Palestine Ave.—College Hill
LINCOLN DORMITORY . . . . Palestine Ave.—College Hill
LOGAN DORMITORY . . . . 17 Vincent Ave. at Pratt
NATIONAL FEDERATION OF MUSIC
CLUBS BUILDING . . . . Near Palestine and Forest Aves.
BELLINGER HALL . . . . Hedding at Evergreen

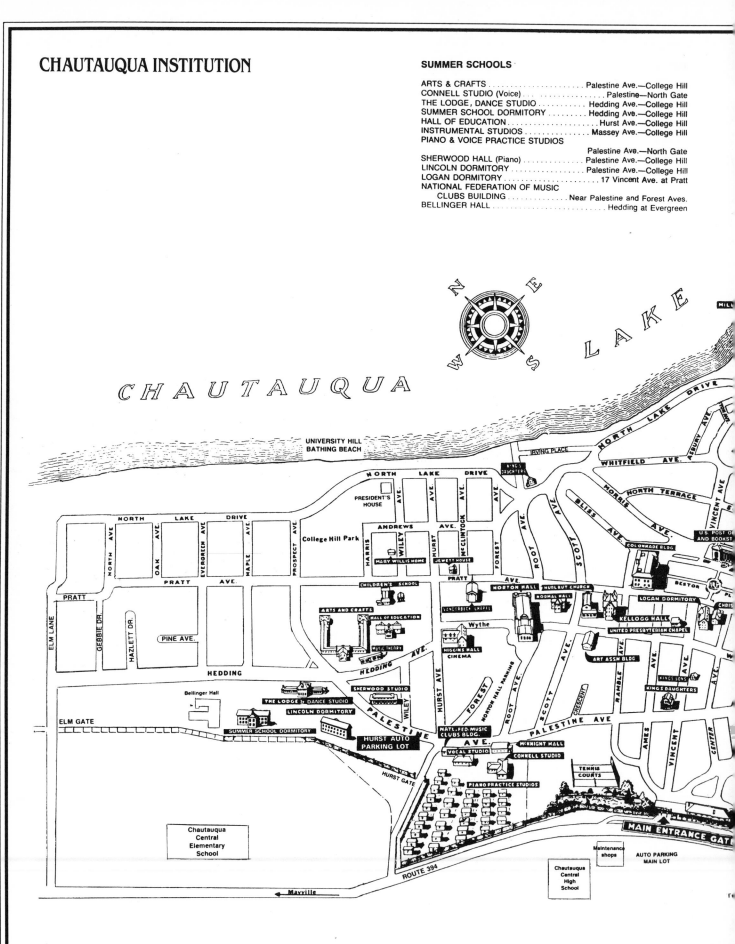

CLUBS

ALUMNI HALL . . . . Wythe Ave. at Cookman & South
ART ASSOCIATION . . . . Wythe Ave. at Scott
BEESON YOUTH CENTER . . . . Lakefront at Athletic Field
BOYS' CLUB . . . . Lakefront at Athletic Field
GIRLS' CLUB . . . . South Lake Drive at Park Ave.
SEAVER GYM . . . . Lakefront at Athletic Field
SPORTS CLUB . . . . Lakefront
YOUTH ACTIVITIES CENTER . . . . Lakefront at South Ave.
WOMEN'S CLUB . . . . 30 South Lake Dr. at Janes

SCHOLARSHIP HOUSES

JEWETT HOUSE . . . . 20 McClintock at Pratt
KINGS DAUGHTERS:
    Headquarters . . . . 34 Vincent at Palestine
    Kings Daughters . . . . 6 Irving Place
    Kings Sons . . . . 29 Vincent

RELIGIOUS BUILDINGS

BAPTIST HOUSE . . . . 32 Clark at Janes
CHRISTIAN SCIENCE HDQTS. . . . . 10 Center at Pratt
DISCIPLES HOUSE . . . . 32 Clark at Janes
EPISCOPAL HOUSE . . . . 24 Peck at Clark
EPISCOPAL CHAPEL . . . . 26 Park at Clark
HALL OF CHRIST . . . . Wythe at South Ave.
HALL OF MISSIONS . . . . Clark at Cookman
HURLBUT CHURCH . . . . Pratt at Scott
THE INTERNATIONAL ORDER OF THE KING'S
    DAUGHTERS AND SONS — IDA A. VANDERBECK
    CHAPEL . . . . Pratt Ave. near Forest
LUTHERAN HOUSE . . . . 25 Peck at Clark
METHODIST HOUSE . . . . Pratt at Bowman
METHODIST MISSIONARY HOME
                       34 Foster at S. Lake Dr.
(METHODIST) FENTON MEMORIAL DEACONESS
    HOME . . . . 21 Hawthorne Ave.
MINISTER'S UNION . . . . 25 Roberts at Bowman
PRESBYTERIAN HDQTS. . . . . 9 Palestine
PRESBYTERIAN MISSIONARY HOME
    (MARY WILLIS) . . . . 16 Wiley Ave.
UNITED CHURCH OF CHRIST HDQTS. . . . . 23 Clark Ave.
UNITED CHURCH OF CHRIST (REFORMED
    CHURCH HOUSE) . . . . 10 Pratt Ave.
UNITED CHURCH OF CHRIST (MAYFLOWER)
                        30 S. Terrace Ave.

ADMINISTRATION AND PUBLIC BUILDINGS

AMPHITHEATER . . . . Clark and Palestine
BUS STATION . . . . Main Entrance Gate
COLONNADE BUILDING . . . . Pratt and Ames
FIRE STATION . . . . Massey Ave. at Bowman
HALL OF PHILOSOPHY . . . . Clark, Cookman and Haven Ave.
HIGGINS HALL (Cinema Theatre) . . . . Wythe and Hurst
KELLOGG HALL . . . . Pratt and Ramble Ave.
LIBRARY . . . . Clark, Miller and Pratt
McKNIGHT HALL . . . . Palestine and North Gate
MILLER BELL TOWER . . . . Miller Park—Lakefront
NORMAL HALL . . . . Pratt and Scott Avenue
NORTON HALL . . . . Pratt Avenue
POST OFFICE . . . . on Bestor Plaza
PAVILLION . . . . Clark and Miller Avenue
SMITH-WILKES HALL . . . . Janes Avenue
BOOKSTORE . . . . Post Office Building

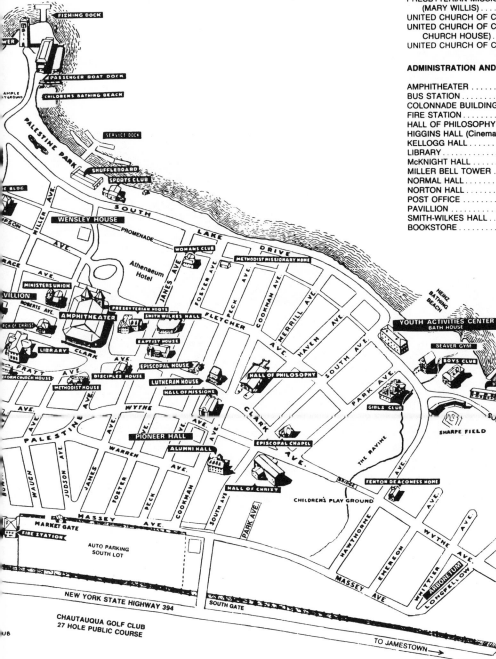

Lewis Miller   John Heyl Vincent

FOUNDERS

"WE ARE ALL ONE on these Grounds! No matter to what denomination you belong; no matter what creed, no matter to what political party of the country. You are welcome here, whether high or low. You can have a right to go anywhere you can get. (Applause) And it is something like the sample-rooms, but not in a vulgar way. You know they go to this place, and they sample this and sample that a little, and then they take whatever they like, go home, and use what they want. And so here you are welcome to go about examining the various organizations and the various things introduced to you, taking such things as you want. Believe just what you want to, what you please about them and take them with you or leave them here as you like. And you are entirely welcome to all our good things at Chautauqua. (Applause)—Lewis Miller[2]

"Born in Stark County, Ohio, in 1829. Educated at Plainfield Seminary, Illinois. Converted at fourteen. Started in the world for himself at seventeen. Apprentice to plastering business. Worked at his own trade in summer; studied in the winter. Apprentice in a machine shop. Foreman of machine department; superintendent and proprietor in the business. Continues to build reapers and farming implements generally. Inventor of Buckeye Mower—the pattern from which all modern machinery are made. His specialty is Sunday School Work. Devised Akron Sunday School room which has revolutionized S.S. architecture. Candidate on Greenback ticket for Congress years ago. For many years on Akron Board of Education. Was father-in-law of Thomas Edison. Had a lovely family and lived in the old beautiful homestead in Oak Park, Akron, Ohio." Died in 1899 in New York City following surgery.[1]

"Now the doctrine which Chautauqua teaches is this, that every man has a right to be all that he can be, to know all that he can know, to do all that he pleases to do—so long as knowing what he can know and being what he can be, and doing what he pleases to do, does not keep another man from knowing all that he can know, being all that he can be and doing all that he pleases to do. And the Christian idea of the Chautauqua movement sees that the Christian elements enters into it as one of its essential features. It is the duty of every man to help every other man to be all that he can be, know all that he can know and do all that he pleases to do under the limitations already indicated. And position in life has nothing to do with it. Well, then poverty, birth, nor color has nothing to do with it. A man is a man who has a man's motive, a man's purpose, a man's will, and who bows reverently before God that he may worship Him and gain strength to help his neighbor. That is Chautauqua."—Dr. John Heyl Vincent[3]

"Born in Tuscaloosa, Alabama, February 23, 1832. In 1838 removed to Pennsylvania. Lived at Lewisburg or at Chilisquaque, Pennsylvania. Educated at Chilisquaque public school, Milton and Lewisburg academies and at Wesleyan Institute, Newark, N.J. Licensed to preach in 1849. Traveled 'under the Elder' on the Luzerne circuit in 1851. Preached at Newark, North Bellville and Irvington, N.Y., Joliet, Mt. Morris, Galena, Rockford and Chicago 1852-1865. Founded Sunday School Quarterly in Chicago in 1865, The Sunday School Teacher and the lesson system; later became the International System. From 1866 to 1888 served the Methodist Episcopal Church as S.S. agent and Secretary. In 1888 was elected Bishop of his church. He continued to be Chancellor of Chautauqua. He retired as Bishop in 1904." He continued his speaking and writing activities. He died in 1920.[1]

PART I

THREE TAPS OF THE GAVEL

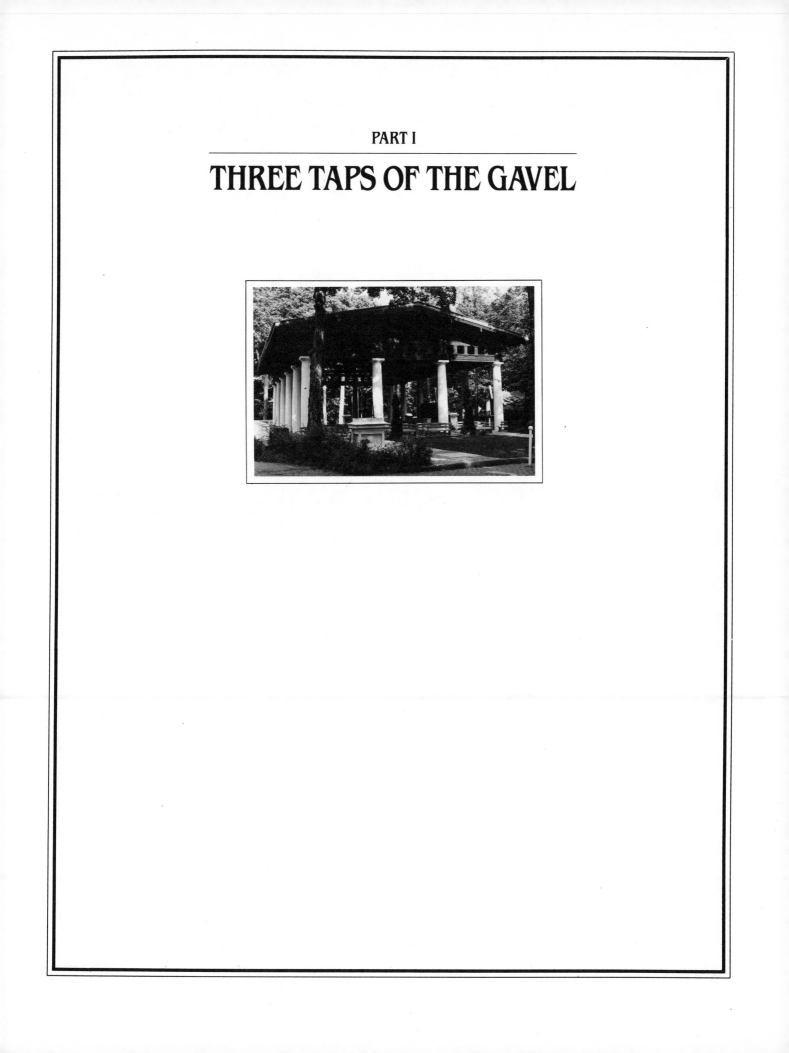

The familiar sight of sailboats on Chautauqua Lake with the Miller Bell Tower always visible
from some angle makes this particular view seem like one I saw yesterday.

INTRODUCTION

CHAUTAUQUA has been called unique even more often than she has been called beautiful.

Newcomers to Chautauqua are usually first impressed by the late 19th and early 20th century architecture. They feel that they are entering the quaint past when they see old-fashioned houses standing close together along winding, tree-lined streets.

On even a quick tour of the Grounds, however, newcomers soon become more conscious of the present, rather than the past.

There are students with their musical instruments, artists painting in the parks, boys and girls on bicycles, some men bowling on the green and others bringing in their catch of fish...There is a great deal of friendly laughter to be overheard, children's voices, a chime of bells, musicians' tuning up...

There are even some modern houses to be discovered among the Victorian oldtimers, but old and new look tended. Handsome gardens show recent planting.

Two important aspects of Chautauqua, therefore, are quickly grasped by newcomers: her tie with a quaint past, not to be denied, and her vitality in the present. Surprisingly, both aspects are rooted in Chautauqua's history, for her very beginnings in 1874 were established to meet the contemporary needs of Sunday School teachers.

While interest in the religious life motivated the first Chautauqua Sunday School Assembly, the gathering was planned to cultivate religion through education. Once started, the Assembly's educational outreach steadily increased. As it turned out, her program expanded almost immediately to meet the needs of all those who wanted to continue to learn.

Chautauqua has been fortified throughout her more than one hundred years by a sense of continuity, rooted in the determination to serve the changing intellectual and spritual needs of people from all walks of life.

One of the traditions, followed since 1904, is that the president of the Institution, or someone acting in his stead, shall open and close the summer program by delivering three taps of the gavel and making an appropriate declaration in each case.

At the 1904 opening, according to a newspaper account, General Director Scott Brown, acting for President W. H. Hickman, "stepped to the front of the platform and bearing in his hand a new gavel of olive wood from the banks of the Jordan recently presented to Bishop Vincent...He struck three resounding blows of the desk, at the same time formally declaring the season of 1904 to be opened."[4]

Following this tradition then on August 24, 1969, Dr. Curtis W. Haug, then president of Chautauqua Institution, approached the final ceremony of the season. Giving three taps of the historic gavel, he said:

"As President of the Instituion, I officially close the 96th season of this place we love (tap), of the program we enjoy (tap), and the spirit we feel (tap)."[5]

The division of "place, program and spirit" seemed very apt that night and seems equally appropriate now as we seek to examine the phenomenon of Chautauqua.

Many people have helped me as I have made this examination. I must acknowledge the initial assignment given by Dr. Haug which resulted in the first edition. I am particularly indebted to the late Margaret M. Copeland who was in charge of Chautauqua's Historical Collection for a period of some years.

As the study continued, members of the Institution's year-round staff and other Chautauquans have been most cooperative when called upon.

Succeeding administrations have demonstrated confidence in this research summary by authorizing new editions. All this I have appreciated along with the encouragement and assistance of colleagues at the Chautauqua Historical Collection. For this edition, I am particularly indebted to the University of Chicago Library for permission to refer to or publish citations from the Archives collections and to Daniel Meyer, Assistant University Archivist, Special Collections, for his assistance.

I am also grateful to Dr. Thomas A. Storch, Director of the Environmental Resources Center at the State University College, Fredonia, for the updated statement on Chautauqua Lake research activities; and to Stephen Mooradian, Senior Aquatic Biologist with the New York State Department of Environmental Conservation for information on fish and fishing in Chautauqua Lake.

I am indebted in a more intangible way to my great-grandfather, Dr. James Gallagher, who, in effect, started the Chautauqua experience for me and to my parents, Dr. and Mrs. Alfred C. Locke, who continued it. Then there are the members of my own immediate family with whom I have shared Chautauqua with the most joy, and scores of friends who have helped to make it truly a Shangri-La. Without all of them, the task would not have been undertaken.

Tree-lined streets contribute to the aura of peaceful renewal.

1

The Place We Love

SOME BASIC FACTS

CHAUTAUQUA INSTITUTION in 1986 consists of seven hundred and forty acres. Two hundred and sixteen acres lie between one and one-half miles of shoreline and one and one-half miles of iron and steel fence. (The first fence was made of wood.) These acres are usually referred to as the Chautauqua Grounds (with a capital G to indicate their special identity).

But outside the fence the Institution owns an additional five hundred and twenty-four acres. Approximately one hundred and twenty-eight acres are taken up by the Chautauqua Golf Club's eighteen-hole golf course while the remainder is being held for future development. The Whallon Farm property adjacent to the golf course contains two hundred and sixty-six acres; the Potter Road holdings about one hundred and four acres; and other separate smaller pieces round out the total acreage. The golf course enlargement will come from part of the Whallon Farm.

The property and equipment owned by Chautauqua Institution has a book value of approximately $12,800,000, while the total assessed value of non-Institution property on the Grounds is about $17,200,000.

During a summer program season of nine weeks, these facilities are used to capacity. It is estimated that seven thousand people are resident on the Grounds at the height of the season and that close to one hundred thirty thousand enter the gates during the program weeks.

Through the remainder of the year, approximately five hundred people live at Chautauqua. The Institution's main offices in the Colonnade, the Book Store, the Post Office, Hurlbut Memorial Church and Smith Memorial Library remain open year-round. Overnight accomodations and winter rentals are available.

The church and library serve as centers of winter community activity for those on the Grounds and in the environs, along with the Central School and the John W. Turner Elementary School just outside the gates. Community services, which include utilities, refuse collection, snow removal and fire protection, are provided on a twelve-month basis.

An increasing number of Chautauqua property owners are winterizing their homes and much of the new housing is accommodated to year-round living. Consequently, Chautauquans are visiting the Grounds more frequently between seasons. There is a noticeable influx of Chautauquans and visitors on weekends.

In addition, group conferences are attracted to the Grounds between seasons. The improvement of the Hall of Christ in 1967 which included central heating had made that building usable in even the coldest weather. But beginning in 1974, Bellinger Hall has provided a complete setting for group meetings. The first wing of this dormitory complex was constructed that year, but in 1984 and 1985, three more stages of the complex have been built. There are now overnight accomodations for one hundred and fifty, a cafeteria and dining room, meeting rooms and lounge areas, all under one roof.

Chautauqua Institution is a non-profit corporation. The charter, granted by the New York State Legislature in 1902, under which Chautauqua operates today, changed the previous name of "Chautauqua Assembly" to "Chautauqua Institution," and stated that the purpose and object of "the said corporation shall be to promote the intellectual, social, physical, moral and religious welfare of the people. To this end it may hold meetings and provide recreation, instruction, health and comfort on its Grounds at Chautauqua; conduct schools and classes; maintain libraries, museums, reading and study clubs and other agencies for home education; publish books and serials and do such other things as are needed and proper to further its general purpose."[6]

It must be stressed that the Assembly or the Institution never was in any sense a stock company. If there were any profits from the gate receipts, leasing or sale of lots, operation of the program or percentage payments and license fees from private business, these were invested in the improvements of buildings, Grounds and other facilities.

The Institution is governed by a twenty-four member board of trustees with an eleven-member executive committee and six executive officers. Four of the trustees are elected by the property owners.

The gate ticket, one of the unique aspects of Chautauqua, originated at the very first Assembly in 1874 when it was decided to charge an entry fee rather than take frequent collections at lectures, classes or services. This fee was sometimes referred to as a form of tuition, representing each person's share of the expense which is necessary in maintaining an educational program.

The gate ticket entitles the holder to hear concerts, lectures, other performances and services in the

Amphitheater, numerous other religious services, recitals, art exhibits and programs; to enjoy bathing beach facilities, library privileges and agreeable fellowship with people of congenial tastes.

It is true that operas and theatre productions in Norton Memorial Hall require extra payment for which reserved seating is provided; some dramatic programs in Smith-Wilkes Hall and Studio Theatre Productions in Normal Hall make small charges; and summer school courses have their own tuition fees; but financial adjustments on gate tickets are possible in some instances.

For example, people from outside the gates who have purchased opera or play tickets and intend to come for these performances only, are not required to pay the usual evening gate fee. Commuters' gate passes allow a special day rate for summer school students who live outside the Grounds.

The atmosphere of quiet enjoyment on the Grounds, one of its other unique characteristics, is almost completely the result of the gate-fence arrangement.

For the most part, the people one sees on the Grounds are those who have chosen to come for the specific enjoyment of the place, school or program. It is assumed that anyone with a gate ticket automatically becomes in his own way that special type of person known as a Chautauquan. Among these people the Chautauqua experience strikes up a strong bond winter or summer.

If there is any one characteristic that these Chautauquans have in common, it probably is the inquiring mind. All sides of public questions are open to discussion on the Chautauqua platform and tolerance of differing viewpoints is practiced as part of Chautauqua's tradition.

In addition to courses bearing college credit, there are numerous continuing education courses ranging from computer graphics to writers' workshop; hardanger embroidery to financial planning; and conversational French to calligraphy.

Whether or not more Chautauquans are conservative than liberal is open to question. At any rate, there is a climate of learning amid pleasant surroundings that nudges Chautauquans to return year after year.

To a considerable degree, Chautauqua is family-oriented. In its protected community, children are safe to go about their own activities.

Tots of three can ride to classes in a Children's School Bus, knowing that "the friendly bus driver" and school monitor will make sure that they alight at the Children's School. (They are returned in the same careful manner.) The educational and recreational opportunities for every age are satisfactory to families whose years encompass a wide span. As families gather around the dinner table at night, boys and girls can tell about their canoe expeditions at the Boys' and Girls' Clubs. (The Clubs resemble day camps.) Big sisters can report on their art or dance classes. Mothers may tell about the Exercise Class at the Sports Club or the Women's Club speakers. Fathers may even admit their golf scores. The whole family may adjourn to the shuffleboard courts after dinner if they are not going to the baseball game.

The widespread use of automobiles within the Grounds is discouraged because the narrow streets were laid out before the advent of the motor car and do not accommodate modern amounts of traffic. Since by Chautauqua tradition the pedestrian has the right of way and exercises it fully, a 15-mile speed limit is enforced.

Parking within the gates is regulated by extra fees even for property owners. Limited parking is availa-

The Pier Building was new in 1886; replaced in 1916.

ble within the Grounds while additional public parking is offered outside the gates. The effort to eliminate unnecessary use of cars preserves the unique Chautauqua quiet and safeguards Chautauqua's clear, clean air.

THE LAKE

Chautauqua's healthful climate is in large measure due to its proximity to Chautauqua Lake whose altitude is 1,308 feet above sea level. The lake has thirty-three tributaries and is also fed by run-off from the land and some springs. It is approximately eighteen miles long with an average width of one and two-tenths miles with the greatest width of two and two-tenths miles in the northern basin. The lower lake is only twenty feet deep at the most with an average depth of eleven feet; the upper, seventy-five at most with an average depth of twenty-six feet. Its water acreage is presently figured at 13,181; its area, twenty-one square miles; its shoreline, forty-one lineal miles.[7]

It lies seven hundred and thirty-five feet above Lake Erie which is only eight miles distant to the north. From the air Chautauqua looks almost like two lakes with a narrow passage between. This picture has given foundation to the belief that Chautauqua is an Indian word meaning "bag tied in the middle" or "two moccasins tied together." According to a scientific study compiled in 1937, sixty-eight per cent of the lake's volume is in the upper portion although the two halves are of about equal area.[8]

Other legends surround the name of the lake. Some say that is means "Land of the Mists" or "where one vanishes away." Some claim that it came from "Katawka," an Indian word for "one took out a fish there." There is some evidence that a tribe of Indians, the Chatakas, a branch of the Tuscaroras, came north from North Carolina to join the Iroquois and named the little lake for themselves. (Another legend says that the Indians named Fair Point "Ga-wan-ga-a," which meant "tongue of land.")

Since 1811 when the first ferry was a log raft, a ferry has carried vehicles, men and animals across the one-thousand-foot narrows about six miles south of the Grounds between Bemus Point and Stow. But a Southern Tier Expressway opening in 1982, now spans the lake with a multimillion dollar bridge, and carries most of the traffic. The ferry continues as an attraction for tourists. Present-day Chautauquans might find it surprising that the idea of a bridge across the lake is not new. As early as February 13, 1908, The Chautauqua Weekly reported such a possibility.

Chautauqua Lake's waters mingle finally with those of the Gulf of Mexico, flowing through the Chautauqua Outlet at Jamestown into the Chadakoin River, Conewango Creek, the Allegheny and thence to the Ohio and Mississippi Rivers.

One would suspect that Chautauqua Lake, higher than Lake Erie, would flow into the larger lake; but a high ridge between Mayville and Westfield forms a watershed for this part of the United States and is responsible for Chautauqua's taking the southern route while the Erie flows by way of the St. Lawrence into the North Atlantic.

According to history, the Chautauqua region was a battleground for rival Indian tribes, the Erie of the Huron and the Seneca of the Iroquois. The Senecas emerged the victors and at least some of their descendants are residing in Chautauqua and Cattaraugus Counties even today. The Treaty of 1797 compelled the Indians to give up their land around Chautauqua about 1800. When the Arcade and some cottages were built on the Grounds, it was reported that Indian skeletons and relics were unearthed, substantiating Chautauqua County's Indian lore.

Water is important to any settlement and the lake has been especially important to the Assembly. From the first, it served important transportation needs, not to mention offering food, fresh water and recreation advantages.

The lake was formerly the Asssembly's main entrance. Most of those coming from a distance arrived by rail at Mayville, Westfield or Jamestown and completed their journeys by lake steamer. This arrangement was not without adventure, especially during the first years. The two and three-deck

The Jamestown, one of the best-known steamboats on the lake.

Rustling trunks, which were necessities for early Chautauquans who came from a distance and stayed for the season

There was time for sociability in earlier days when the area behind the Pier had been cleared. There was a spaciousness to be enjoyed near the lake and boats were still bringing most Chautauquans to the Grounds.

steamers, captained by their owners, were colorful and sturdy, but they did not attempt to run on a widely accepted standard of time. Neither did the boats and railroads synchronize their schedules. There were often unexpected waits for customers. In addition, baggage which was transferred from train to steamer was not adequately marked and had to be sorted at each stop along the lake. It was a fortunate Chautauquan who landed at Fair Point with all of his own luggage. But when the Assembly was still young, it could advertise twenty boat landings a day, so Chautauquans were bound to arrive sometime and they came in "droves."

RECREATION

Today transportation on the lake is not a necessity; it is a popular pastime or sport.

The lake is busy with powered boats that tow skiers or carry fishermen. The Gadfly, a sixty-three and one-half-foot yacht offers lake tours to the public on a daily schedule. In 1976 a new excursion boat, The Chautauqua Belle, was christened for use on the lake. A steam-powered paddlewheeler, similar to those used during the first years of the Assembly, it is ninety-eight feet in length and accommodates one hundred and twenty passengers. It was built by James Webster in about a year at the Mayville Marina. The Chautauqua Yacht Club has a sizeable fleet of privately-owned sailing boats in a half-dozen classes. They race two or three times weekly, weather permitting.

In the first days of the Assembly, fishing was one of the fringe benefits of the program and still is. Some early Chautauquans after the advent of the Chautauqua Literary and Scientific Circle, proposed that the Assembly set up a course in fishing with diplomas and seals and graduation ceremonies to match the CLSC, but nothing came of it. Fishermen on Chautauqua

Lake, therefore, have gone their individual triumphant ways.

At the present time, thirty-five different fish species can be identified in Chautauqua Lake. Of this number the species angled for include: Muskellunge, Walleye, Smallmouth Bass, Largemouth Bass, Black Crappie, Yellow Perch, Blue Gill, Pumpkinseed Sunfish, Rock Bass, White Bass and Brown Bullhead. The other species are minnows or coarse fish not sought by anglers. The Muskellunge is called the King of fishes, a strong challenger of a fisherman's skill.

Years ago, the depletion of the muskie supply was feared and measures were taken to ward off the danger. Individual season limits were set at five muskies per person. The muskie season was shortened. A state regulation prevented the sale of Muskellunge in market or restaurant. Added to this was a program for artificial hatching which has grown until the present Chautauqua Lake Hatchery at Prendergast is certainly one of the largest in the country.

Statistics on the 1984 season (computed on eighteen per cent of the licenses sold and returned to the New York State Department of Environmental Conservation) reveal that eighteen hundred and sixty-one Muskellunge were caught in Chautauqua Lake. The average length was thirty-six and six-tenths inches. The Conservation Department has statistics on the Muskellunge catch as far back as 1941 and great diversity is apparent. The 1975 catch, for example, was only about half of the 1969 catch, as recorded in the first edition of this book, but it is greater than the 1974 total. The 1969 catch was one of the four largest in the records, but the 1975 average weight per fish exceeded that of 1969 by almost a full pound. These are interesting statistics for those who like to puzzle over probable causes.

Fishing licenses for residents of New York are at present $9.50; non-resident, $20.50; seven-day license, $12.50. All persons sixteen years of age or older must be licensed. To fish for Muskellunge an extra one-dollar license is required of all fishermen regardless of age. This provides the fisherman with five plastic seals, one of which must be fastened to each legal muskie kept. Licenses may be obtained at the Court House, offices of village, town or city clerks, and at some boat liveries and stores.

The Muskellunge season extends from the third Saturday in June through October 31. There is an open season on Chautauqua Lake for all weekend days during the months of January and February.

WATER SUPPLY

The Assembly's primary needs for water on the Grounds during its first years were met by a number of springs. Later, water was piped from these springs to other parts of the Grounds to make water more readily available to the growing number of cottage owners.

There was a mineral spring at the foot of Lower Bowman Avenue (near the present Sports Club) that was highly recommended for its medicinal qualities. Down near the Point the water from another spring was piped through the low-bending hollow branch of a tree to make it appear as though the tree itself were spouting water.

Later a more sophisticated water system was designed for the growing community. Water was pumped into the Grounds from the lake into a reservoir (1889) that was located high above the Grounds about three-quarters of a mile from the lake. Water from some artesian wells was also used for awhile (1887).

Nowadays, the water from the lake is pumped to the water filtration plant behind the Colonnade where it is filtered, treated and then pumped to two reservoir tanks on the hill above the Grounds. The tanks have a 300,000 and 600,000-gallon capacity, respectively. The larger tank is the newer, having been constructed in 1971. The system has the capacity to pump 600,000 gallons during twenty-two hours of pumping in a twenty-four period. Winter consumption is only 100,000 gallons per day, but peak summer demands reach 800,000 gallons per day. By pumping through the night when demand water is at a minimum, reserves are accumulated in the storage tanks so that the daily summer needs are met with comparative ease.

The Institution's central heating system which supplies heat to the Colonnade and Hurlbut Memorial Church is located in the filtration plant.

SEWERAGE DISPOSAL SYSTEM

While improvements to the community's sewer system and sewerage disposal have been made from time to time and a secondary treatment system was fully achieved in 1978, the basis of the system was designed and constructed in late 1892 and early 1893 in time for the latter season. In 1893, it was the only complete one of its kind in the United States. The Assembly Herald proclaimed on July 22, 1893: "It looks as though Chautuqua would yet enlighten America on this vital question for the sewerage question is vital."[9]

Over seven miles of sewers were laid in the '90s and soon after the grading of all avenues was completed. The trunk line of the sewer varies between twenty and twelve inches with eight-inch tributary sewers. There is not a curve in any line of the original system. Man-holes are placed at every change of grade so that should any stoppage occur, it can be found with comparative ease. The original design and construction made it possible to see from one manhole to the next in either direction. The maximum depth of the main sewers is fifteen to sixteen feet. A sewerage disposal plant was erected at the far south end of the Grounds and great care had been taken against pollution of the lake.

Prior to 1893, the Assembly had public receptacles for the collection of waste located at certain points throughout the Grounds. In spite of the simplicity of the first measures of sanitation and the large numbers of people who came to the Grounds, Chautauqua has had a record of healthful living even in the days of crowded tents and rough board cottages.

A major improvement in the sewerage disposal system was made in 1941 when a new treatment plant which used the Inhoff tank treatment methods was

Sailing is one of the most popular pastimes at Chautauqua now.

Mr. Wellman Bates is proud of his fishing catch, circa 1935.

constructed. Primary treatment was installed in 1960 with increased effectiveness achieved in 1963 through screening.

The Institution, always anxious over the lake's wellbeing, began in the '60s to plan ahead for the time when secondary treatment would be required. Step by step the Institution proceeded toward eligibility for federal and state funding for construction of a secondary treatment plant. The Utility District now figures largely in the delivery of services to the property owners and in the development of new facilities. Formerly these services were provided solely by the Institution.

By two Acts of the New York legislature in 1928 and 1934, a Utility District was created to administer the utility services to the residents of the Grounds. The land commonly known as the Grounds comprise the Utility District. The present North End was added later but the more recently acquired land across Route 394 south of the Golf Course (the Whallon Farm) has not yet been annexed to the District.

The fire hall, fire equipment, the waste treatment plant, and the water distribution system were bought or built by the Utility District and paid for by the District's taxpayers. The sewerage collection lines were owned by the Institution and the sewerage disposal plant was operated by the Institution. Service fees were charged to property owners for these services. The same was true of the water system.

During the recent negotiation for government funding, the Institution turned over the sewerage collection lines to the Utility District because it seemed more feasible for the District to manage sewage collection.

Under two referendums in 1973 and 1975, the voters of the Utility District approved the bond issue which made the construction of the secondary treatment plant possible with federal and state participation. The total cost of construction was seventy-five per cent reimbursement by the Federal government and twelve and one-half per cent by the state.

One of the prerequisites of government funding has

been the elimination of surface water from the sewage collection lines, another overall improvement which is continuing.

Added in 1985 was odor control equipment which was required by the waste treatment plant's close proximity to residential development.

The Chautauqua Utility District is governed by five elected commissioners, a superintendent and an administrative assistant.

LAKE STUDIES

One of the offshoots of Chautauqua Institution's Centennial observance was the creation of a permanent environmental studies committee. This committee in 1972 undertook the task of mobilizing Chautauquans' cooperation in protecting their environment, especially the lake. It spearheaded drives for beautification of the Grounds, enlisting old and young in anti-littering efforts. The committeee was charged with maintaining accurate, up-to-date information for the use of the administration, the board and property owners on solid waste disposal, lake management, sewage treatment, land use, highway construction and other appropriate environmental matters.

Perhaps the committee's most important step was to forge ties with the lake studies program that had already started under the direction of Dr. J Richard Mayer of the State University of New York, Fredonia College. At the committee's behest, supported by the Centennial Central Committee, the Institution made a laboratory available on the Grounds to the lake studies.

The studies expanded from year to year. Jamestown Community College faculty and students joined those from the Fredonia College and a number of scientific disciplines were drawn into the research.

The initial lake research program was funded by SUNY Fredonia, the Chautauqua County government and the Chautauqua Lake Association. Help and encouragement from the county planning department and the State Department of Environmental Conservation was also acknowledged. Part of the sophisticated equipment in the laboratory was provided by the Carnahan-Jackson Foundation. The Gebbie Foundation, the Jessie Smith Darrah Fund and the Karl Peterson Foundation, along with a few concerned citizens supported the studies financially. The five-year study (1971-1976) was the most complete study since 1937.

Chautauqua Lake research activities by the College at Fredonia are currently administered by the College's Environmental Resources Center which was previously called the Lake Erie Environmental Studies program. Dr. Thomas Storch is the director of the Center and Dr. Jimmy Winter is the associate director. Due to changes in funding following the completion of the five-year study, research activities are performed almost exclusively by the College at Fredonia. Involvement by Jamestown Community College is primarily limited to utilizing the lake environment for teaching purposes rather than research activities.

The college no longer maintains a laboratory at Chautuqua Institution, but the Institution provides the research group with facilities for docking boats and

---

CHAUTAUQUA PRESIDENTS

Lewis Miller	1874-1899
Clement Studebaker	1899-1902
Wilson M. Day	1902-1903
W. H. Hickman	1903-1906
George E. Vincent	1907-1915
Arthur E. Bestor	1915-1944
Ralph Norton	1944-1946
Samuel M. Hazlett	1946-1956
W. Walter Braham	1956-1960
J. William Carothers	1960-1963
George L. Follansbee*	1963-1964
Curtis W. Haug**	1964-1970
Oscar E. Remick	1971-1977
Robert R. Hesse	1977-1983
Daniel L. Bratton	1984-

*John A. Reed, executive vice president, summer, fall 1963
**Joseph C. Clarke, executive vice president, October, 1970 to August, 1971

storing field research equipment at the new waste water treatment plant.

Over the last ten years, funding has been provided to conduct research on specific aspects of the Chautauqua Lake ecosystem, including: the impact of the new Chautauqua Lake bridge on the lake biota; interrelationship between fish populations and aquatic weed management techniques; ecology and habitat preferences of the Walleye; and assessment of surface water quality in both lake basins. Funding for the equipment, supplies and student research stipends associated with these projects have been obtained from the Carnahan-Jackson Foundation, the Gebbie Foundation, the Clarke Memorial Trust, the Jessie Smith Darrah Fund, the New York State Department of Transportation and the New York State Legislature.

The research work conducted between 1971 and 1985 has provided an extensive data base for assessing various aspects of the lake environment. Several years of data are currently available on physical, chemical and biological components of the lake. Water temperature, dissolved oxygen, transparency, pH, heavy metals, nutrient concentrations (phosphorus and nitrogen), algae counts, and algal chlorophyll a pigment concentrations have been monitored on a temporal basis at specific lake sampling sites since the early 1970s. In addition, less extensive data have been collected on nutrient loading to the lake, lake sediments, aquatic weeds, aquatic insects and the fish community.

These data indicate that the offshore waters of the lake have not changed extensively since the first comprehensive study of the lake was conducted in 1936-1937. Water transparency and the intensity of the summer algal blooms have not deteriorated over the last fifty years; however, they do fluctuate from year to year depending on the annual loading of nutrients to the lake due to changes in precipitation. Lake water chemistry is within accepted drinking water standards and water quality is moderately hard. Despite the acid precipitation that falls in New York State, changes have not occurred in lake water pH due to sufficient alkalinity of the lake water.

Although the lake does not appear to have become more eutrophic over the last fifty years, obvious changes have occurred in some of the biota. Fish are thriving in the lake although both the muskellunge and the walleye populations are lower today than they were in the 1970s. It is uncertain whether this is due to increased fishing pressure or to unidentified changes in the lake environment. The aquatic weed communities in the nearshore waters have undergone some changes. Total weed densities are still high and most of the weed species reported in 1936-1937 are still present. However, the abundance of several of the weed species has changed.

Increases in the chloride and sodium concentrations in the lake water chemistry were in progress before the new Chautauqua Lake bridge was open to traffic. Although the causes of these increases have not been identified, feasible explanations include salting activities on roads throughout the lake's watershed and gas well drilling operations.

Research activities will continue to provide scientific information required to improve lake management

CHAUTAUQUA

"A gathering that is typically American in that it is typical of America at its best."

Theodore Roosevelt, quoted in *Chautauqua* by George William Gerwig

"Mr. Garfield, when he gave us what I think was the best solution of the mission of Chautauqua that we have had, said that all the world had been struggling all these years to get leisure hours; and he said it was left to Chautauqua to show how to use them. I think it is really its mission to show how to use leisure hours...."

Lewis Miller
Old First Night, 1889

"To those of us who saw Chautauqua in its nebulous condition in the first year, as we see it today in its 20th year, it is an evolution but like the real evolution of nature, an evolution with a mind behind it all the time. I have asked myself today, what are the root ideas in the minds of these men when this was begun. I think there were two root ideas, first, the idea of making religion more intelligent in order to make it more efficient, and second, to make mere recreation more religious and more helpful to religion, by bringing Christians more fully and heartily into it. It was to develop more of religion in the head without having any less of it in the heart."

The Rev. W. F. Crofts
Old First Night, 1893

techniques. Current work deals with assessing the effectiveness and impact of aquatic weed control methods in the nearshore waters. Special studies are under way to determine if transplanting methods can be employed to increase the pond weed species that have decreased in abundance since the early 1900s. Plans are also being formulated to study the impact of herbicides on fish populations. The hoped-for result of management-oriented lake studies is sufficient baseline data which will provide future generations with comparative data required to detect and rectify changes in the lake environment.

THE LAKE ASSOCIATION

The Lake Association is a private citizens' group that was organized in 1953 for the maintenance and protection of the lake. Under its direction efforts to remove pest weeds from the lake have been carried on by cutting, harvesting, and chemical control. The CLA, cooperating with the lake studies, has put its records into the hands of the scientists so that the effects of weed manipulation can be evaluated and the future programs wisely charged. The weed harvesting has gradually expanded. The Lake Association now has six harvesters at work throughout the summer, sometimes beginning the last week of May. They also coordinate shoreline clean-up operations. Local foundations have supported The Lake Association's capital improvements, but the contributions from an annual membership campaign provide working capital for its extensive program.

HOW DID IT ALL START?

THE FIRST CHAUTAUQUA Sunday School Assembly, formally approved by the Sunday School Union of the Methodist Episcopal Church, convened Aug. 4-18, 1874 at the present location of Chautauqua, then called Fair Point.

The Assembly leased the facilities from the Chautauqua Lake Camp Meeting Association for the first season with little intention of making it its permanent home since a protracted summer institute for Sunday School teachers was an experiment. The Assembly, however, was never in any sense of the word, a camp meeting.

The original tract at Fair Point consisted of fifty acres. It extended to the present Scott Avenue on the north and along the winding path of Palestine Avenue on the west and south. The ravine that was later trans-

formed into the Amphitheater was within the first Grounds while the site of the Hotel Athenaeum was not. East and west, the Grounds reached from the Point to the public road, approximately one-half mile.

The Assembly grew out of the association of two men, the Rev. John Heyl Vincent and Lewis Miller. The former was General Agent and Secretary of the Sunday School Union, the organization which directed Methodist Episcopal Sunday Schools. He had become Editor of the Sunday School Journal as well. (He later was elected Bishop.)

Mr. Miller was an outstanding layman in the same denomination. He was extremely interested in good Sunday Schools and general educational opportunities. He was superintendent of his own Sunday School in Akron and served on the Akron School Board, as

A park-like atmosphere developed behind the Pier Building

well. He was a life trustee of Mount Union College and president of its board when in 1870 Mount Union first offered a summer term.

In addition, he had designed a form of church architecture which was widely copied for the use of the Sunday Schools. Called the Akron Plan, it consisted of a large room surrounded by individual class rooms that could be separated by folding doors.

It is difficult for people today to understand how important the Sunday Schools needed to be in the 19th century. While the public schools were still developing, the Sunday Schools performed a significant educational work. Added to this was the renewed popular interest in education after the Civil War.

When the new idea of summer school for Sunday School teachers was discussed, Mr. Vincent suggested that it be held in Mr. Miller's handsome Akron church. But Mr. Miller had a different idea. "Let's take it to the woods," he said, thinking of Fair Point.

In spite of living in Ohio, outside the boundaries of the Erie Conference of the Methodist Episcopal Church, Mr. Miller was on the board of directors of the Chautauqua Lake Camp Meeting Association, an Erie Conference enterprise. He was thereby well acquainted with the picturesque lake and the beautifully wooded slope along its shores.

Both men envisioned the Assembly as all-denominational in spirit and performance and they were not disappointed. All of the leading Protestant denominations were represented on the first Assembly's program and among its students. Mr. Vincent's earlier cooperation with other church leaders in developing a national Sunday School lesson series made it easy for him to attract the people from denominations other than his own, while his influence through his own Sunday School publications was understandably large.

Chautauqua's location midway between New York and Chicago was an added advantage in 1874 when the Assembly wanted to attract students from all parts of the country, for Chautauqua was readily accessible by railroad. (Now its proximity to Interstate 90 makes it easy for Chautauquans to arrive by automobile since this thruway connects with the north and south I-79, the Ohio Turnpike and the New York Thruway. U.S. Route 6, another major east-west highway, may be followed to Corry or Warren, Pa. Chautauqua Lake may be reached on easy-to-be-found routes from either place. Route 394 which leads from Mayville to Jamestown and goes past Chautauqua Institution's Main Gates was formerly referred to as Route 17J. Airports at Jamestown, Buffalo and Erie, Pa. provide convenient arrival points for some Chautauquans.)

Those who arrived for the Assembly opening found that the activities were to be concentrated in the area now known as Miller Park, not far from the boat landing at the Point.

A small roofed platform faced rows of backless benches, enough for two thousand poeple. This gathering place under the sky was referred to as the Auditorium.

It was circled by tents and cottages. Mr. Vincent's tent and the general offices were located behind the platform. Lewis Miller's lots occupied the northwest

A second, larger Platform was ready for the 1876 summer.

HOW CHAUTAUQUA GREW

(Approximate)

1874	50 Acres
1876	88 Acres
1880	139 Acres
1888	174 Acres
1889	185 Acres
1900	190 Acres
1908	223 Acres
1911	303 Acres
1912	304 Acres
1916	309 Acres
1923	351 Acres
1961	455 Acres
1965	721 Acres
1981	735 Acres
1985	740 Acres

SEASONS' LENGTHS

1874, 1875	15 days
1876	24 days
1877, 1878	20 days
1879	43 days
1880	38 days
1881	47 days
1882-1884	45 days
1885	47 days
1886-1888	58 days
1889	55 days
1890	56 days
1891	55 days
1892	58 days
1893-1898	59 days
1899	60 days

Until 1976 the seasons following 1899 have never gone below 53 days nor beyond 60 days.

1964-1975	60 days
1976-	65 days

A Palestine Park lecture audience is reflected in the Dead Sea of the Model of Palestine.

corner of the park-like area at the rear of the benches. Behind the Miller lots was the first significant rise of the hill.

Dr. Vincent later wrote about the opening meeting: "The stars were out and looked down through the trembling leaves upon a goodly, well-wrapped company who sat in the grove, filled with wonder and hope.

1873—THE DECISION MADE

"One summer evening in the year of 1873," wrote George Vincent, "Lewis Miller of Akron and Dr. Vincent of New York, descended from the train at Mayville...They brought with them little luggage besides a certain 'idea' which had taken root in their minds...

"Boarding the old Colonel Philips, they began an asthmatic voyage down the lake...landed at Fair Point where several members of the Camp Meeting Association...were waiting to receive them...

"Supper over, the Grounds were thoroughly examined and Fair Point was decided upon as the local habitation of their 'idea,' which was to be developed the next season. George Vincent was nine years old when he made this trip with his father. As he jumped off the boat first, he claimed that he founded Chautauqua. Ira Miller, the eldest son, came with his father. He was 17 at the time."

Ira Miller was the father of the late Mrs. Margaret Miller Newman, well-remembered and greatly honored as a grand-daughter of Chautauqua's co-founder, Lewis Miller.

No electric light brought platform and people face to face that night. The old-fashioned pine fires...burned with unsteady, flickering flame...The white tents were very beautiful in that evening light.[10]

Up on the hill at the first Assembly was a large tent called the Tabernacle. It could accommodate most of the Assembly's audience when the rains fell too heavily through the trees of the Auditorium. It was located at the head of the present Bliss and Morris Avenues, probably in front of the Glen Park Condominiums near the northeast corner of Bestor Plaza.

Tents could be rented at Fair Point and cottagers might rent rooms. Those who did not have facilities for cooking ate at the Dining Hall, a long building of rough construction which occupied the site of the present Post Office building.

One of the more popular features of the Asssembly was a piece of construction that still attracts interest today, particularly from newcomers. This was the relief model of Palestine, showing the general contour of the Holy Land with cities, mountains, valleys and bodies of water plainly marked. The first Palestine model was laid out by Dr. W. W. Wythe, who also headed the Assembly's recreation program. But the idea was Founder Vincent's whose purpose was to give practical illustration to Biblical geography. The young minister had started his career as a teacher and had experimented with audio-visual aids when he was a pastor. His development of these aids in Sunday School teaching at Chautauqua is one of a number of "firsts" that Chautauqua can claim.

Palestine Park, one hundred and twenty feet long and seventy-five feet wide, was built along the lakefront south of the Point. It was of temporary materials the first year but has since been reconstructed, enlarged and remodeled several times. It now has a length of three hundred and fifty feet. In the beginning it was decided to use the lake to represent the Mediterranean Sea in the model, and this concept was continued. Therefore, the points of the compass are reversed. Thus, west is toward the lake, and north, toward the Sports Club. The scale of the distances is about one and three-fourths feet per mile. Through the years, it has proved a popular romping ground for children as well as geography lesson for many of all ages. Since there is increasing interest in the Middle East, Palestine Park is still a useful educational tool.

When the Assembly proved to be a success at Fair Point, the Camp Meeting Association urged the Assembly to continue there the next year and offered to add Assembly representatives to its board. After some discussion, however, the Camp Meeting Association was actually reorganized as the Sunday School Assembly Board and Mr. Miller became president of the Board, as well as president of the Assembly.

He was a dedicated and sincere Christian man with vision to match Dr. Vincent's. An astute business man, he managed the affairs of the Assembly with wisdom and skill until his death. He was financially able to help develop the facilities that were needed. Throughout his life, he was constantly reaching into his own pocket to supply needs that he found no other way to provide.

From 1874 to 1876, the Assembly operated under the charter of the Chautauqua Lake Camp Meeting Association. By an Act of Legislature May 2, 1876, however, the Association was authorized to convey its property for the sum of One Dollar to a new corporation, the Chautauqua Lake Sunday School Assembly.

In 1877 a post office was established at Fair Point, and soon after, perhaps in the same year, the community was granted permission to change its name to Chautauqua. Dr. Vincent says in "The Chautauqua Movement"[11] that application was made to the United States authorities and the request was promptly granted. Contradictory accounts of the change, however, make it diffucult to state definitely when and how it took place. Taking the name of Chautuaqua seemed a logical step since the Assembly was already making the name of the lake famous not only in this country but throughout the world.

Additional charters were granted later. Extra land under the lake along the Assembly's shoreline was granted also as the shoreline was increased.

A new educational venture, the Chautauqua School of Theology, was chartered in 1881.

By another Act of Legislature two years later, the name, Chautauqua Lake Sunday School Assembly, was shortened to The Chautauqua Assembly. In this same year Chautauqua University was chartered and a single board of trustees was authorized to serve the Assembly, the School of Theology and the University.

This divison prevailed until the Charter of 1902 combined all of Chautauqua's educational, recreational and inspirational program and its administration under the new name of Chautauqua Institution.

DENOMINATIONAL HEADQUARTERS ESTABLISHED

Congregational, 23 Clark Avenue—1882
  Rebuilt on same site—1931
  Now main headquarters for the United Church of Christ.
Methodist Episcopal, 14 Pratt Avenue—1888
  Chapel rebuilt—1955
  Now known as the United Methodist Church headquarters.
Presbyterian, 9 Palestine Avenue—1890
  Now known as the United Presbyterian headquarters.
  United Presbyterian, 18 Vincent Avenue—1891
  Original house became an annex to the St. Elmo Hotel.
Episcopal, Chapel of Good Shepherd—1894
  Present denominational headquarters, 24 Peck Avenue—1956
  Former headquarters on southwest corner of Center and Pratt Avenues.
Baptist, 15 Clark Avenue—1895
Christian Church, Disciples of Christ, 32 Clark Avenue—1896
  Brotherhood House, 28 Janes Avenue—1945
  Previous assemblage from 1884 to 1896 in the Graybiel and on the second floor of the Congregational House. Clark Avenue headquarters extensively remodeled in 1904.
Unitarian, 26 Cookman Avenue—1902
  Sold to private owner in 1962.
Lutheran, 28 Foster Avenue—1904
  Present building at Clark and Peck Avenues—1925
Fenton Memorial Deaconess Home, 21 Hawthorne Avenue—1917
  Built for United Methodist deaconesses' summer vacations.
Reformed Churches, 10 Pratt Avenue—1924
  Now under the United Church of Christ.
Minister's Union, 25 Roberts Avenue—1925
  Interdenominational residence, originally planned for clergymen and their families. Edward C. Westervelt started the idea.
Mayflower, cooperative hostel, part of the Westervelt complex, later turned over to the Chautauqua Congregational Association, now under the United Church of Christ, 4 Bowman Avenue.
United Methodist Missionary Rest Home, 34 S. Lake Drive—1925
United Presbyterian Home, 16 Wiley Avenue, 1928
  Called Mary Willis House in memory of donor's children, Mary and Willis Franks.
Christian Science, 10 Center Avenue—1949
  Chapel, 12 Center Avenue—1956

The Massey family home at Chautauqua was built at the corner of Roberts and Bowman Avenues by Hart A. Massey, whose son, Chester, and whose grandson, Vincent, followed him on the Chautauqua Board of Trustees. The basic structure of the Massey home can be recognized as part of the present Ministers Union complex. (Chester Massey was married to Bishop Vincent's half-sister.)

LET'S LOOK AROUND

THE MILLER BELL TOWER has served as a symbol of Chautauqua for many years. Since 1911 it has been a shoreline landmark. Institution letterheads and publications have carried its picture throughout the world. A little magazine about Chautauqua once bore its name. Jewelry and T-shirts have made use of its design.

Newcomers will find the Bell Tower if they leave Bestor Plaza at the north end of the Post Office and follow Vincent Avenue down the hill.

On the way they should notice the Lewis Miller Cottage which was formally designated as a Registered Historic Landmark by the United States Department of the Interior in 1966. The cottage sits cozily at the left of Vincent Avenue at the foot of the hill. A boulder has been placed at the lower outside corner of the lot to bear the official plaque of recognition.

The gray Swiss chalet-type cottage was originally painted white with raspberry trim when it was built in 1875 by Lewis Miller.[12] The Assembly was fortunate to have such a fine house in which to entertain its first illustrious guest, President Ulysses S. Grant. In those days a spacious tent occupied a platform adjacent to the cottage and a porch extended across the front of both. Because part of the wood for the cottage was precut in Akron before it was brought to Chautauqua, it has the distinction of being one of the first prefabricated houses in Chautauqua County and perhaps the nation.

This historic cottage that formerly looked out on the first Auditorium at Fair Point now has the view of Miller Park. The Auditorium was abandoned in 1882 and the open space that remained was in time named for Lewis Miller. In 1887 after a disastrous fire had leveled cottages at the lower end of the park, the Assembly Board realized that an open view of the lake would be desirable. So they bought the lots necessary to achieve this purpose and ever since, the blue of the lake may be seen through the trees of Miller Park.

There are some who refer to the Miller Cottage as the Edison Cottage, since Lewis Miller's daughter, Mina, was married to the famous inventor, Thomas A. Edison, and the Edisons later owned and occupied the Cottage. During that time, Mrs. Edison renovated the house, razed others that stood directly behind it and transformed those lots into a lovely patio and garden. At Chautauqua Mrs. Edison made an outstanding contribution as an Institution trustee and as president of the Bird and Tree Club, a forerunner of the present Bird, Tree and Garden Club. The Edisons had many interesting friends whom they entertained at Chautauqua. Chautauquans were not surprised to see Henry Ford or Adolph Ochs or other national figures sitting on the Edisons' porch.

Great excitement centered around the Lewis Miller Cottage in late July, 1929, when the 100th anniversary of Lewis Miller's birth was celebrated along with the fiftieth anniversary of Thomas Edison's discovery of his light bulb. Miller Park was brightly illuminated during that Festival of Light, as it was called.

The dedication of the Cottage on July 4, 1966 by Assistant Secretary of the Interior John A. Carver, Jr., once more focused national attention on Chautauqua and honored it as the birthplace of a tremendous idea. The plaque was received on behalf of the Miller family by Governor Charles Edison, grandson of Lewis Miller.

Continuing toward the Bell Tower through Miller Park, our path will cross South Lake Drive and we will probably find children in the Paul L. Sample Memorial

The Miller Bell Tower

Playground which was given to the children of Chautauqua in 1966 by Mrs. Sample and her daughters as a Centennial gift.

Of permanent construction, colorful and functional in design, the play equipment is a memorial to Mr. Sample, who as an active trustee and Institution vice president, had always demonstrated particular interest in Chautauqua's youth. The Playground was especially designed for younger children who are not yet occupied in Boys' and Girls' Clubs. It is close to a small lake front area near Palestine Park, commonly referred to as the Baby Beach, where the shallow water is encircled by fencing to prevent the youngsters from going into deeper water.

Perhaps it would be well to stop at the Play Area and observe the Bell Tower from this vantage point, for the Tower is sixty-nine feet tall and sixteen-foot square. It cannot be fully appreciated at close range.

The Tower's Italianate design includes the slender columns that grace each side of the open bell chamber through which the bells may be seen and heard, and the distinctive red tile roof. The Tower has a seasoned look, for it is seventy-five years old, but it undergoes periodic renewal and looks well cared-for. The plantings which surround its base were newly placed for the Centennial season.

On the day of dedication, August 1, 1911, ivy was set out in memory of Lewis Miller's son, Robert A. Miller, who had died only six days before. The ivy had been obtained from Mount Vernon by Miss Rachel Miller to plant at the Bell Tower in memory of her grandfather, Lewis Miller. But instead, Miss Rachel designated the ivy to her own father's memory as she planted it.

In 1967 the Bell Tower's chime of bells was increased from ten to fourteen so that it is more versatile and consequently, a larger repertoire is available to the bellringer. Over two hundred connections were necessary to electrify the carillon completely and centralize its action at a new console.

Three new bells were given as memorials by grandchildren of Lewis Miller; one by Margaret Miller Newman in memory of her father, Ira M. Miller; one by

Marian Nichols De Marconnay in memory of her mother, Mary Miller Nichols; and one by the late Charles Edison in memory of his mother's sister, Grace N. Hitchcock. A fourth bell that Chautauqua already possessed was also placed in the chime. Formerly this bell, marked 1878, had been housed at the bottom of the Bell Tower and rung in recent years to signify the opening of the CLSC reading year.

Another improvement was made in the Bell Tower in 1967. A new electric clock was installed and connected with the bells so that a Westminster chime rings on every quarter hour. The new clock and chime were provided by Mr. and Mrs George L. Follansbee in honor of Mrs. Follansbee's mother, Mrs. Caroline R. Barnum.

Bells have always been important at Chautauqua. The first Assembly was regulated by the Great Bell, rented from the Meneely and Kimberly Co. of Troy, N.Y. It occupied a platform near the Point. By an odd chain of circumstances, this bell now belongs to the Mayville United Methodist Church.

The Lewis Miller Cottage became a Registered National Historic Landmark in 1966.

Children make good use of the Paul L. Sample Memorial Playground.

The large Lakeview Room of the Sports Club provides a pleasant view of the boat races and other lake activity.

For the next nine years the Assembly got up, attended lectures and classes and went to bed by the tones of three bells, also located on the Point except for one year when they were brought up on the hill near the first Chapel.

Then in 1885 Dr. Vincent's fond dream of a Chautauqua chime of bells came true. The first year, even these ten bells were placed upon a large platform at the Point, but by the next year, they had found a home in the tower of a new Pier Building which had been erected on the Point to take care of the great crowds of people who arrived daily by boat. The old dock had become totally inadequate.

The new Pier Building was grand and festive in appearance. Its ticket, baggage and dock offices were located on the first floor. Tempting shops and an observation veranda occupied the second floor, while dormitory space and classrooms were located on the third floor.

But after a period of twenty years, the weight of the bells (over five tons) and the weakening effect of their movements necessitated frequent, expensive repairs to the all-wooden structure. At length, the piles beneath the building began to deteriorate. Thus a need for a sturdy bell tower became apparent and Chautauquans took this way to memorialize the man who first suggested bringing the Assembly to Fair Point.

When the traction line and motor cars were bringing more people through the Road Gate than boats brought to the Pier, and when lake steamers no longer plied the lake in great numbers, the need for the Pier Building lessened. Consequently, in 1916 it was torn down, making way for the construction of a smaller pier building that later was turned into a club house for college young people through the generosity of Mrs. Elizabeth McCreery.

Now let's follow this sidewalk along Palestine Park. (You will want to come back to Palestine Park sometime and move over it carefully to review its geography. Lectures on the Park are given here on a regular schedule and small guide books are available in the Book Store for self-help tours.) Over across the road

members of the Sports Club are bowling on the green.

Beyond us, you will see the Sports Club itself. On this side of it are the Club's shuffleboard courts. Inside the clubhouse, bridge and other games are being played by members who prefer indoor activity. Chautauquans can enjoy duplicate bridge at least twice a week in the club's Lakeview Room, a large, many-windowed room that was added in 1948.

Club personnel will welcome us and invite us to join the club for the day, for the afternoon or for the extent of our stay on the Grounds. If we ask about the club's origin, they may tell us that it began in temporary quarters in 1902 as a Men's Club. The very next year, the men converted the old electric power house and pumping station into a comfortable club house. On the outside the building still resembled a miniature English castle and was distinguished by an octagonal tower fifty feet high at one side of its main section. But inside, the club installed telephone, telegraph and stenographic services, a barber shop, shower baths, writing and smoking rooms and a reading room with metropolitan newspapers. They arranged a roof garden and a screened veranda. The Men's Club served successfully as a meeting place for business and professional men and men's groups until about 1930 when the club was dissolved.

In 1931 a new Yacht Club was formed and it used the old club house as its headquarters. Within another two years the Sports Club, an outgrowth of the lively Horseshoe Club or Quoit Club, was organized to become a recreation center for both men and women. It shared the old castle with the yachtsmen. Shuffleboard and lawn bowling were added to the club's activities and the membership grew dramatically. A new club house was finally achieved in 1942 and the old power house disappeared. The Yacht Club moved to new quarters.

Looking up the hill from the Sports Club, newcomers will see a large frame building which they will recognize at once as the famous Hotel Athenaeum, the largest hotel on the Grounds. Every feature of this edifice from the Widows' Walk on the tower to its long windows and the thirty-foot pillars at the front testifies to its 1881 vintage and to its gracious old-time hospitality. (The narrow topmost tip of the tower was removed some time ago.)

Let us walk up the hill for a closer look. This green and white residence on our right as we go up Bowman Avenue was formerly The Windsor, a private guest house. In 1966, however, it was a Centennial gift to the Institution by its owner, Mrs. Nina T. Wensley, an active member of the Board of Trustees. It was renamed The Wensley by the Institution and is used to house program guests.

The natural stone patio on our right as we turn toward the Athenaeum is called Founders' Glen. Plaques honoring the two founders have been placed there. It has been a pleasant place for Chautauquans to stop to rest on their way up the hill or just to sit and enjoy the view of the lake. New drainage and a new sandstone floor were recently installed, along with a sitting wall and two flower beds. The Charles Edison Fund provided this beautification. A new brick walkway leading from the Glen to the Amphitheater, also called the Amphitheater Handicapped Access Walk, was named in memory of Mr. Charles Heinz and Mrs. Louise Heinz Lockhart by their children, Charles and Louise Heinz. The rustic bridge nearby was named in memory of Sara Elizabeth McCracken Peters through the gifts of Mr. and Mrs. Henry B. Suhr, Jr. Mr. Suhr is a grandson of Mrs. Peters.

In 1970 beautiful nightime illumination in a variety of colors was arranged for this area at the rear of the Amphitheater. The rustic bridge on the upper side of the Glen, the Founders' Fountain and the lovely plantings take on new grace at night in this designed lighting which was a Centennial gift of Mr. and Mrs. George L. Cornell in honor of Mrs. Cornell's mother, Mrs. Pearl A. Pierce. The lighting has been enhanced recently through the continued generosity of Mr. and Mrs. Cornell. The rustic bridge, replaced in 1973 and the middle section raised and partially rebuilt at the time of the Amphitheater restoration, carries a large amount of foot traffic between the slopes of Bowman and Palestine Avenues.

The Athenaeum was preceded by the Palace Hotel, a half-tent, half-frame structure that had been used first at the 1876 Centennial Exposition in Philadelphia. It was moved to Chautauqua the next year and functioned admirably for several years. But as the Assembly grew in prominence, Mr. Miller and some other men of Chautauqua realized that the Assembly needed a large first-rate hotel. Consequently, they organized a stock company to construct the Athenaeum.

HIRAM PRATT CLEARING THE LAND

Hiram A. Pratt had been appointed by the Camp Meeting Association to be in charge of the Grounds. He was later commended for the skillful way he marked and felled the trees as he cleared the land for a meeting site and cottage-building. One of Chautauqua's principal streets, Pratt Avenue, was named for this early Chautauquan.

THE CHESTNUT STUMP

A bit north of the center of the present Miller Park there lies a cement-covered shrubbery-encircled stump. It is the huge chestnut stump on which rested the first speaker's stand at the Assembly.

In the early 1900s, Mrs. Thomas A. Edison, Lewis Miller's daughter, took over the care of this historic stump and preserved it by having it encased in cement. She placed a plaque there to remind Chautauquans of the giant chestnut's contribution to the first Assembly.

A story is told that the well-known gospel song writer and song leader, P. P. Bliss, sat on the stump one day listening to Dr. Vincent preach. The new platform had been erected in 1876 and then moved nearer the hill, so the abandoned stump offered a convenient seat to the song leader. As he sat there, he was so inspired by the words of the preacher, that he composed the words and music for "Hallelujah, What a Savior!" And at the close of the sermon, he sprang from the stump to sing his new composition.

Planning began in 1880 and according to Dr. Hurlbut, the foundation was begun. But the main building of the hotel was accomplished in the spring and early summer of 1881. Some reports say that it was completed by a large crew of workmen in ninety days in time for an August 2nd opening. How "complete" it was we cannot know, but it rapidly filled with guests. The Athenaeum was one of the first buildings on the Grounds to have a limited number of electric lights, and one of the first hotels anywhere to be lit by electricity.

In 1882 a reception honoring Lewis Miller was held in the hotel parlor and a deluxe edition of Longfellow's "Collected Poems" was presented to him as a token of appreciation by his fellow-Chautauquans. They recognized the building of the Athenaeum as one more example of Mr. Miller's wisdom and foresight.

The hotel offers one hundred and sixty rooms with bath (following the rehabilitation-restoration). An annex was added to the hotel in 1924 and a new electric Otis elevator was installed. A second-floor passageway between the annex and main structure forms an intriguing archway over Janes Avenue. The spacious dining room is noted for its cuisine as well as its two-dessert menus.

Look back now toward the lake! That small curve in the shoreline near the Sports Club used to be called Tranquil Bay and served as an embarkation point for small boats. The old Palace Hotel used to advertise "plenty of rowboats available for guests."

There's something quaint and comfortable about the large rockers on the porches, but let's go inside. The smell of wood burning in the fireplace is very pleasing and we don't wonder that the wicker chairs in front of it are filled. The chairs clustered in tete-a-tete groups in the spacious lobby are inviting. The wooden registration desk with its self-decoration is original to the hotel. The Victorian wall shelves near the dining room entrance are especially handsome and useful, too, as we see from the collection of possessions that guests have placed there temporarily as they arrive from the lecture before lunch.

The Athenaeum has been called *La Grande Dame,* presiding with imposing grace over the lake front. The top part of the tower was removed circa 1923.

Turning to the large double doors on the left, we catch our first glimpse of the large Parlor on the lake side of the hotel. It is dramatically Victorian with its dressy lace curtains at the long windows and its over-all patterned carpet on a royal blue background. The touches of yellow, white, green and coral in the carpet reappear in the light yellow of the painted wicker, all of which has served the hotel since the early 1900s, and in the lightly-patterned upholstery and pillows. This gracious room adapts easily to receptions, recitals, dinners, committee meetings, bridge parties and weddings. The parlor's oak fireplace was refinished during the restoration of the hotel (1983-1984). It is frequently used when the weather is cool. The oak leaves and tendrils which are carved across the face of the mantle are assumed to have been the choice of Lewis Miller whose home in Akron was named Oak Place.

The parlor had been previously redecorated in 1969 as a memorial to Mr. George Hukill, the gift of his daughter, Mrs. Arthur R. Leeds. Mr. Hukill was one of the early Chautauqua leaders. The brass and crystal chandeliers which she chose for the parlor are still in use there. Mrs. Leeds was an interior designer and had previously redesigned the hotel dining room and lobby.

Now let's continue up Palestine Avenue. Remember that this was the southern limit of the Grounds in 1874!

This large brick structure on our left is the United Presbyterian Headquarters, the first brick buiding to be erected on the Grounds. (The second was The Assembly Herald printing plant at the head of Bowman Avenue. It is now an apartment house.)

The refreshing Japanese garden beyond the Presbyterian House is the Carnahan-Jackson Memorial Garden, a Centennial gift in 1969 by Mrs. Clyde L. Carnahan in memory of her husband and parents, Mr. and Mrs. Alvin C. Jackson. Given as "A quiet spot for all Chautauquans," it provides a beautiful and restful corner at the edge of the busy Amphitheater.

Another memorial garden at the rear of the library may be seen if we turn right and proceed along the outside of the Amphitheater fence. This is the Mrs. Joseph H. Roblee Memorial Garden, a Centennial gift in 1967 by her daugher, Mrs. Eugene R. McCarthy. During her lifetime, Mrs. Roblee had worked consistently for the beautification of the Chautauqua Grounds. This garden, completed in 1968, beautifies the library building as well as the Amphitheater area.

If we enter the garden and sit a few moments, we see that we are across from the CLSC Veranda, the headquarters for the current year's CLSC activities. Here on the Veranda of this Institution-owned residence, newcomers may join the CLSC reading program or at least learn what the CLSC is. At 1:15 p.m. each Friday of the season, the Veranda serves as the platform for an open discussion period, called the Sidewalk Session. Usually it is the week's morning lecturer who answers questions. The chairs placed in front of the Veranda are almost always filled. Many Chautauquans choose to listen, ask questions or speak their views from the neighboring garden. (Smith-Wilkes Hall is used during inclement weather.)

We also notice the red brick structure between the Veranda and the Amphitheater. It was build in 1931 as the Congregational Headquarters on the site of the first Congregational House (1882), but since denominational union with Reformed Churches, it is now the main building of the United Church of Christ at Chautauqua. On our right is the spacious white frame building belonging to the United Methodists. This area behind the Amphitheater, including the Roblee Garden, was referred to long ago as Chapel Park because the first Chapel built in 1876 primarily for the use of year-round Chautauquans remained in this vicinity for many years.

The restored Athenaeum has its long veranda open to allow easy access to the spacious lawns below.

The rockers are part of the 19th century ambience.

The Parlor with its new decoration welcomes smaller or larger groups who need an attractive and spacious meeting-place.

The carved oak leaves on the fireplace may reflect Lewis Miller's prefer-ence for the mighty oak. His Akron home was called Oak Park.

The Carnahan-Jackson Memorial Garden gives quiet enjoyment to all Chautauquans.

Nately Ronsheim, CLSC Director, stops in the Roblee Memorial Garden with her arms full of newer and older CLSC books. She is wearing an heirloom dress and hat for an historic Recognition Day. The CLSC Veranda is just ahead across the Brick Walk.

Smith Memorial Library was given to Chautauqua in 1931 by Mrs. A. M. Smith Wilkes in memory of her father and mother, Mr. and Mrs. Henry Sumner Smith. Let us walk toward the front of the building where we can better appreciate its Neo-Georgian Revival architecture and its situation on the southern edge of Bestor Plaza.

The library belongs to the Chautauqua-Cattaraugus (Counties) Library System and remains open throughout the year. Mrs. Torrey Isaac is the present librarian. The 1984 report shows a circulation of 41,495 volumes; total books, 24,575. The collection has expanded to include video tapes and a video tape player, given to the library by the Friends of Smith Memorial Library; audio tapes of operas given by the Chautauqua Opera Guild; other audio tapes of music

as well as lectures and sermons; and audio tapes of children's stories. The Friends of the Library also contribute other services to the library, including hosting the annual Library Day celebration and building a photo lab for use by the Historical Photographs Collection. Smith Memorial Library is busy during all the year. It is greatly appreciated by summer Chautauquans and between seasons, it provides weekly programs of music, films, talks and demonstrations, as well as a place for informal study classes. Book delivery is made to shut-ins; records and listening facilities are available; art prints are circulated; coffee is available for patrons.

The Chautauqua Historical Collection, primarily located on the first floor of the library, is a resource that is constantly in use. A complete file of Chautauqua newspapers and other Chautauqua publications, letters and documents form the main section of the Collection. Oral tapes, Board minutes, scrapbooks, histories of Chautauqua organizations, books written about Chautauqua or by Chautauquans, unpublished dissertations, histories of independent Chautauquas, CLSC book selections from 1878 onward are among the holdings which attract researchers.

On the upper floor of the library, summer school courses are taught. During the Centennial year historical exhibits were arranged in the large central area as well as in one of the rooms. Since 1974 a portion of the Historical Collection has been placed upstairs. Memorabilia of the Miller and Edison families, the Bestor Collection and keepsakes of the building's donor, Mrs. Smith Wilkes, now form a permanent exhibit. The Charles Edison Fund has contributed and helped to establish the Mina Edison Collection at Chautauqua in the Heritage Room.

In the basement of the building a children's library is well patronized. It was decorated in a circus theme in 1968. Lively elephants, lions, giraffes and horses cavort around the walls, painted there by Maritza Morgan, Chautauqua's resident artist, who made the paintings her Centennial gift to the Institution. The circus theme was suggested by the wooden toy animals belonging to Col. William Kenneth McKnight, given by his children to the Children's Room and still displayed in a glass case near the fireplace. The animals had been given to the Colonel in 1894 when he was a small boy. New furnishings and equipment for this room were provided at the same time by Mrs. Clyde L. Carnahan. Through a Second Century Campaign gift by Envirogas, Inc., the children's library has been named The Willard F. Clarey, Sr. Children's Library.

The library's staff room has been furnished and decorated in memory of Helen Theurer by her family and friends. Mrs. Theurer had been Director of the CLSC (1966-1971) and was a former president of The Friends of Smith Library.

Through the years Smith Library has proved to be a very useful building. While Library Day is celebrated each year and planned by The Friends of the Library to call attention to the library's importance, the day-to-day use of the library by its patrons demonstrates its significance at Chautauqua. The spaciousness of the main reading room allows the winter programs to be held in one end of the room with enough space for the winter storage of an Institution grand piano, thus making possible musical programs with visiting artists. In the past, the wide steps and entrance were borrowed by the High School Club for the crowning of its King and Queen while hundreds of Chautauquans watched from the Plaza. Perhaps its most dramatic service came in 1961 when it became the Institution's administrative offices during the reconstruction of the Colonnade.

Many years ago on the site of Smith Library, a large CLSC Building faced Clark Avenue. Large pillars on the front and side gave a classic appearance to the building. It contained an assembly hall with seats for three hundred in addition to the offices of the CLSC and part of the time, the Book Store. The building was given in 1890 by Dr. Theodore L. Flood and George E. Vincent who were publishers of the CLSC books and The Chautauquan, a monthly magazine. Winter residents later used the assembly hall as a gymnasium and basketball court.

Beside it on the corner of Miller and Clark Avenues stood the museum, Newton Hall, which was new in 1881. The first one thousand dollars for this hall was given by Lewis Miller's brother, Jacob, who named the new building for his wife. The museum was soon filled with an amazing number of artifacts from Egypt, Palestine and the Moslem countries, including a mummy that was on loan from Mount Union College. Newton Hall was later used for many purposes even—believe it or not!—a movie house.

Here we are back at the Plaza, having made a relatively short circle to visit only a few of Chautauqua's landmarks.

This lovely village square was named Bestor Plaza to honor one of its distinguished presidents, Dr. Arthur E. Bestor. Dr. Bestor served as president longer than any other and four years longer than the first president and co-founder, Lewis Miller. In addition, before suc-

Occupying the center of Chautauqua's community life, Bestor Plaza is known and used by everyone. The improvement of this open space with the fountain sculpture in the center was a memorial to Dr. Arthur E. Bestor. Smith Memorial Library, built in 1931, is shown nearby.

Close-up of the sculpture which pictures the Chautauqua ideals of MUSIC, ART, RELIGION AND KNOWLEDGE.

In the first part of the century, the Plaza landscaping was quite different. The Pergola on the right was built in 1907.

The CLSC Building with Newton Hall behind was a predecessor of the Smith Library site.

ceeding President George E. Vincent in 1915, he had completed ten years as assistant general manager and then general manager. So his influence upon Chautauqua spanned almost a full forty years. When he first came in 1905, he was a lecturer in the Extension Department of the University of Chicago. During his lifetime, he became known internationally in the field of adult education. Under his presidency Chautauqua proved its ability to move with the times. Its schools continued to grow, its facilities to expand and its cultural impact to maintain national proportions. Dr. Bestor's platform manner was widely recongized as a hallmark for presiding officers and through the Town Meeting of the Air, which he moderated, his voice became known to many Americans who had never seen Chautauqua. He was a genuinely friendly man who allowed himself time for conversation with passing Chautauquans as he made his way from his office to the Amphitheater. It was a natural tribute, then, to name this "central park" for a man who had traversed it so constantly and so pleasantly for so many years.

The Plaza formerly looked quite different. In early maps it is referred to as a grove, a concourse, or Summit Park. An accurate model of Jerusalem, arranged by Dr. W. W. Wythe and his daughter, was set on the Plaza near Pratt Avenue between Center and Miller Avenues. The Children's Temple sat diagonally from the present Dean's Oriental Bazaar which was originally built in 1889 as the Assembly Herald Building. Later it became the Institution's Administration Building. From 1911, it has been used commercially. The Children's Temple had been built in 1878 by Lewis Miller for the especial use of the Children's Class under the Rev. B. T. Vincent and Frank Beard, but its Akron Plan assembly hall was adaptable to other Chautauqua programs. The Children's Temple was removed in 1911. Also, in the early days, a "business block" occupied the middle of the Plaza. Rows of small frame buildings housed shops and even the post office on an extension of Vincent Avenue which ended at Clark Avenue. Fire razed these flimsy structures in 1904 and by the next summer the first Colonnade appeared and became the business center of the community. Kellogg Hall, which had been built on the northeast corner of the "business block", survived the flames and was moved to its present site. The landscaping of the northern part of the Plaza near the Colonnade was arranged through a special gift from a member of the Chautauqua Board of Trustees, N.T. Arnold of Ridgeway, Pa.

Now, Bestor Plaza is a meeting place for young and old. Its open space, green grass and shade trees give comfort and pleasure to those who use it. The memorial fountain with its four-sided shaft is usually encircled by children and young people. The fountain design illustrates Chautauqua's emphasis on Religion, Knowledge, Music and Art. At night as one stands near Smith Library and looks across the Plaza at the lighted pillars of the Colonnade, it seems as though this view, in addition to that of the Bell Tower, could suitably symbolize Chautauqua.

BUILDINGS DIRECTORY

Alumni Hall—Wythe Avenue between South and Cookman Avenues. Built in 1892 by CLSC Classes 1886-1895. First called Union Class Building. The first few CLSC classes had built their own class buildings, but the prospect of each succeeding class having a special home began to seem impractical. The Assembly gave the land for Alumni Hall and it has served as headquarters for all CLSC alumni. The second and third floors were not entirely finished at the time of its opening, but work was carried on from year to year. The third floor was refurnished as a dormitory for the use of the Chautauqua Summer School in 1946-47. The second floor is used for class rooms and contains an apartment for the resident host and family, while the first floor accommodates programs, luncheons, receptions and class meetings. The CLSC Alumni Association has its offices there.

Amphitheater—General program center below Clark Avenue between Bowman and Palestine Avenues. (See pages 33-41, 135, 140, 155).

Arcade—Former historic public building now privately owned. On south side of Miller Park below Simpson Avenue. When it was built in 1891, its $10,000 cost was second only to that of the Athenaeum Hotel. The top floor was first used by Mr. Sherwood for his piano instruction and recitals. At one time there was a tea room on the second floor. Later the second and third floors were used as dormitories. The first floor housed shops. The Chautauqua Book Store was located there for a period. The Arcade was reconditioned in 1967 in preparation for the Centennial. Sold by the Institution in 1985. Exterior restored to conform to National Historic District Guidelines. Interior contains condominiums.

Arts and Crafts Quadrangle—Faces Pratt Avenue between Prospect and Harris Avenues in the general area known as College Hill. Designed by the eminent art educator and artist, Henry Turner Bailey, the building's first section was erected in 1909. A large College of Liberal Arts Building was formerly located on Pratt Avenue near Prospect Avenue. It appeared in time for the 1887 season to take care of the growing classroom needs and served until 1919 when it was razed. The arts and crafts classes had met in various places and were centralized in what was called a "Village" near the Main Gate and tennis courts in 1900. The Village consisted of eight buildings and two tents. The program was very popular when it began. It even extended through the winter for at least one year because there were few places where instruction in so many crafts was offered. The Quadrangle is sometimes referred to as the Art Center for it contains studios for arts and crafts. The center court of the Quadrangle overlooks the lake. The Henry Turner Bailey Studio in the Arts and Crafts Quadrangle was so named during the Second Century Campaign through gifts by the artist's family.

Art Association Galleries—Wythe Avenue between Ramble and Scott Avenues. This building was erected in 1891 as the College Chapel for approximately $2,000. It had a seating capacity for four hundred and fifty. In addition to serving as a chapel and lecture room, it could accommodate other group meetings. It was used for children's Sunday School classes between 1891 and 1910 and for some period by the Girls' Club. The Chautauqua Commons dining room was moved there from the second floor of the Colonnade in 1910 and operated until 1933. From 1934 to 1943, the building was used as a rehearsal hall for operas and plays. In 1944, W. R. Thompson opened a cafeteria, continuing until 1956 when the Institution made the building available to the Chautauqua Art Association. Through the generosity of Mr. and Mrs. Arvid J. Kling, it was remodeled to become a gallery and Art Association headquarters. It also contains an apartment for a resident assistant. This and other

The Arcade was built in 1891. This early picture shows that the Chautauqua Book Store was located here before it was moved to the Colonnade. The Arcade is now privately owned. The exterior has been restored to adhere to historic guidelines while the interior has been converted to condominium use.

major improvements were made by Mr. and Mrs. Paul L. Norton.

Athenaeum Hotel—Below the Amphitheater. Built in 1881. (See pages 19-21, 138, 154, 164, 165, 177).

Bath House—At Heinz Beach on South Lake Drive near South Avenue. First floor contains beach dressing rooms and life guard headquarters; second floor originally a gymnasium named for Jacob Bolin. It was used by the Columbus Boys Choir which held summer sessions at Chautauqua from 1944 to 1957. The building was reconditioned in 1965 and dance department studios were subsequently located there. Presently, the Youth Activities Center is using the facility.

Beeson Youth Center—On the lake front below Sharpe Memorial Field. Built in 1968 as a memorial to Mr. and Mrs. Charles Beeson (Charles and Ruth Anne) by members of the Beeson family and friends. Mr. Beeson was a member of the Board of Trustees at the time of his death. The new building replaced the Athletic Club Building which had been erected in 1905 following the 1903 organization of the Athletic club. It offered a private dock for members, storage area for shells of the Chautauqua crews and members' small boats, four bowling alleys, lockers and lounge areas at a time when recreation facilities were being centered at the south end of the Grounds. Croquet and roque courts were also moved there. The new building meets present needs: Headquarters for the Boys' and Girls' Clubs, staff apartments and rooms for indoor games and crafts. The emphasis on the new building in on YOUTH.

Bellinger Hall—Slightly east and north of the Summer Schools Dormitory. Ground breaking was held August 11, 1973; first occupancy, during the 1974 season; second wing ready for occupancy, 1984; two more phases, open in 1985. First unit of this six-phase complex was the only new building construction during Chautauqua's centennial year. It was built, furnished and equipped by funds from the Gebbie Foundation, at a cost of approximately $338,000. When the total complex is built, it will represent an investment of approximately $3 million, provide dor-

mitory space for 250 students and dining facilities. It will be adaptable to conferences and ski weekends between seasons. Bellinger Hall was named in honor of the late Mrs. Geraldine Gebbie Bellinger, a former Institution trustee. During her lifetime Mrs. Bellinger was not only a generous and devoted Chautauquan, but she was also a private benefactor of many students and artists. William Parker, representing the Gebbie Foundation at the ground breaking, stated that Miss Marion Gebbie and her sister, Mrs. Bellinger, "would be the first ones to approve this investment." The Gebbie Foundation was created from the estates of the sisters. Bellinger Hall was designed by J. Scott Lawson, a Rochester, N. Y., architect and a Chautauquan of long standing. The dormitory's exterior of brown stain shingles with white trim blends easily with that of the existing summer school buildings while its comparatively low profile combines pleasantly with the more modern residences nearby. Blaisdell Brothers of Jamestown were the building contractors.

Boys' Club—Beyond Seaver Gymnasium on South Lake Drive. Contains Boys' and Girls' Clubs' activities center. Built in 1899 through the liberality of N. F. Clark of Oil City, Pa.

Children's School—Pratt Avenue between Hurst and Harris Avenues. Built in 1921. Additions made in 1926, 1947 and 1969; a large open porch, in 1975. During the Second Century Campaign gifts by Mr. and Mrs. George L. Cornell provided new improved bathrooms, hot water, relaid brick walks, new flooring, painting and carpeting. Other gifts to the Children's School were given by Mr. and Mrs. H. A. Steindler. Kindergarten was included early in the Assembly program along with instruction for kindergarten teachers. Nursery School education was pioneered at Chautauqua. Morning sessions are now held daily, Monday through Friday, throughout the season for children from two and one-half through six years old. Children are divided into groups according to development and skills. They are encouraged to learn through play under skilled supervision. In recent years, a pre-Club program has been initiated for older children (ages 5 and 6) who have previously attended Children's

Bellinger Hall, a valued resource for student housing or year-round Conferences.

School. The children in this group stay through the lunch hour until 2 p.m. They have swimming instruction, group games, handcrafts and field trips. Visiting hours each Friday morning give parents and Chautauquans an opportunity to see the school in operation, understand its philosophy and become acquainted with one another.

Cinema Theatre—Wythe Avenue at Hurst Avenue. This building was formerly Higgins Hall. (See Page 28). A full program of current films is shown here for approximately eleven or twelve weeks each summer. The selection of films is discriminating and the response of the public has been enthusiastic. Although the Institution does not operate the Cinema, the movies that are shown are looked upon as another program option for Chautauquans.

Colonnade—Faces the Plaza. Large concrete pillars give the Colonnade its gracious, imposing appearance. Administrative offices located on the second floor. Present Colonnade is the third on the same site. First one razed by fire when it was not yet four years old (October, 1908); second one, 1961. President J. William Carothers earned Chautauquans' gratitude and respect for his leadership during the rebuilding of the Colonnade. Largely through his management, it was completed in time for the 1961 season, only five months after the fire.

Connell Memorial Studios—Beyond McKnight Hall toward the highway. Built in 1939 in memory of Horatio Connell whose death in 1936 concluded twenty-one years as head of the vocal Department of the Chautauqua Summer Schools. Contains three studios for vocal instructors.

Girls' Club—Faces Seaver Gymnasium on South Lake Drive. Contains Girls' Club activity headquarters and rooms for indoor games, programs and projects. Built in 1902.

Golf Club—On the west side of Route 394 across from the Grounds. In 1977 two new structures were built adjacent to each other to replace the original club house which was heavily damaged by fire in the early morning of June 14, 1976. The larger building includes the dining room and kitchen facilities and space for group meetings or social functions. It is winterized and available for rental throughout the year. The other building is used primarily by the golfers. It contains the pro shop, a small lunchroom and locker area. The original clubhouse was made possible through an initial gift of $10,000 by S. I. Munger in 1920 and was opened in 1921. Unfortunately Mr. Munger did not live to see the completion of the building. In 1924 the club house was enlarged by Mrs. Munger and Mrs. Myrtle B. Wilcox and redecorated two years later by Mrs. Munger. During the '60s, the Mungers' daughter, Mrs. George N. Aldredge, refurnished the clubhouse again as part of her Centennial gift to the Institution. Golf began at Chautauqua as early as 1896 when a small course was laid out at the rear of the main college building (Pratt Avenue near Prospect Avenue). It extended west toward the highway and north from the Bicycle School (Root and Palestine Avenues) to the fence. In 1914 a nine-hole golf course was opened on the Chautauqua Farm where the Agriculture Camp had been operating. More land was pur-

The Hall of Christ was set higher than the other buildings nearby so that it could dominate the area. Also, its background of woods and trees was felt to be an appropriate reminder that early Christians worshipped out-of-doors. The architect said that he designed the building as a place where spiritual truth could be taught irrespective of creed or denomination. He envisioned it as a building for all Christians in the broadest sense of the word.

chased to the south in 1921 and three years later in 1924, the golf course was enlarged to 18 holes. A new watering system for tees and greens was installed in the fall of 1975 and a new barn to house equipment was also built. Additional nine holes with opening expected in the spring of '87.

Hall of Christ—South Avenue facing Wythe Avenue. Dedicated in 1909. Completely renovated in 1967. Maintenance endowed through the Second Century Campaign. This building represents one of the fondest dreams of Bishop Vincent and was designed to provide not only a memorial to the Christ, but also a center for the study of His Life and Work. The Hall of Christ is a stone and brick edifice, designed by Architect Paul J. Pelz who also designed the Library of Congress in Washington, D. C. The renovations in 1967 were a Centennial gift from Mrs. Robert D. Campbell of Pittsburgh, Pa. in memory of her husband who had had a particular interest in the Chautauqua Department of Religion and its program. Mrs. Campbell was an active member of the Chautauqua Board of Trustees at the time and is now an honorary member. There is comfortable seating for two hundred and fifty in the main hall which now has an acoustical ceiling, modern lighting, carpets and new decoration. Central heating was installed. Two smaller rooms on the first floor have been designated for the Gould Bible collection and as the Kenneth H. Hitchcock Memorial Room. Excavation made possible two additional large meeting rooms, a kitchenette, and rest rooms on the lower floor. The lower floor has been named the Campbell Room. New interior furnishings were added in 1967 through a gift from the Gebbie Foundation. The Hall of Christ's setting symbolizes the high position Dr. Vincent gave to the inspiration of Jesus Christ throughout the life of Chautauqua.

Hall of Education—Wythe Avenue between Hurst and Harris Avenues. Two wings of this building were small cottage-type classroom buildings, Annex A and Annex B, built in 1884 on Pratt Avenue facing Harris Avenue, set near the proposed site of the Col-

Normal Hall was built by students of the Normal Course for Sunday School Teachers, for whom the Assembly was first convened.

lege of Liberal Arts Building, completed three years later. Moved to present location in 1900 when a middle section was built to join the two small buildings. First known as the Hall of Pedagogy.

Hall of Missions—Cookman Avenue between Wythe and Clark Avenues. Contains headquarters for Department of Religion, class and conference room and staff aparatments. Built in 1924. The Class building of the 1884 CLSC Class was razed to make way for this building. A statue of St. Francis of Assisi was given in 1933 by the Globe Club and placed at the Clark Avenue side of the hall. Statue is the work of Ruth Sherwood, daughter of William H. Sherwood, first head of the Chautauqua Piano Department. Children of the Globe Club brought stones for the fountain, imitating St. Francis of Assisi who by his own hands, collected stones to rebuild the churches of Europe. This hall has been marked by a bronze plaque designating its listing on the National Register of Historic Places. It was the first building to be completely restored through a gift to the Second Century Campaign.

Hall of Philosophy—Clark Avenue between Cookman and Haven Avenues. Completed in 1906. Restored through gifts to the Second Century Campaign. (See pages 42-46, 85).

Higgins Hall—Built and dedicated in 1895, the gift of State Senator F. W. Higgins of Olean, and his sister, Mrs. F. S. Smith of Angelica, N.Y., in memory of their father, Orrin Trall Higgins. Higgins Hall was designed as a lecture room with adjoining library, kitchen and parlor. The smaller rooms could be opened into the larger lecture hall to give greater seating capacity. At the dedication, Bishop Vincent said that the hall was to be used for the programs of young girls at Chautauqua, but it was used for many different programs, including art exhibits, recitals and play productions. Perhaps its most dramatic occasion was the formal breakfast that was given there in honor of President Theodore Roosevelt in 1905. His address in the Amphitheater that followed was one of his first major statements after having been elected to his own full term as President. Used now by the Cinema Theatre. Air conditioned.

Hurlbut Memorial Church—Built in 1931 and named for one of the most beloved Chautauqua figures, Dr. Jesse L. Hurlbut. Dr. Hurlbut supervised the Normal Courses, beginning in 1875, taught the Adult Bible Class and assisted with CLSC. He succeeded Dr. Vincent as editor of the Methodist Episcopal Sunday School Publications. He wrote one of the most definitive histories of Chautauqua, "The Story of Chautauqua," and is well-known as the author of "Story of the Bible" for children, a book which is still in print and in paperback. Dr. Hurlbut celebrated fifty years at Chautauqua in 1924. He died in 1930. Hurlbut Church serves as the community church for year-round residents in the vicinity, as well as on the Grounds. It functions under the United Methodist Church and observed the fiftieth anniversary of its church building in 1980-1981. The congregation's centennial was marked earlier (1977). The Methodist House and Higgins Hall had served as meeting places for the congregation at different periods following the disuse of the old Chapel. First plans for Hurlbut Church located it on Pratt Avenue facing the Plaza.

Jewett House—Corner of Pratt and McClintock Avenues. Built by Mrs. A. H. Jewett in 1886 as a residence for self-supporting young women, teachers and others who wanted to study at Chautauqua. Still used as a residence by the Summer School.

Kellogg Hall—Corner of Pratt and Ramble Avenues. First located at the corner of Vincent and Pratt Avenues when Vincent Avenue extended through the Plaza to Clark Avenue and was lined with small shops. Only slightly damaged in the fire that took those shops in 1904, a misfortune that led to the building of the first Colonnade. Kellogg Hall was moved to its present site in 1905. The new location contained adjoining space for a kindergarten play area. In addition to the kindergarten, the hall housed the WCTU headquarters, and on the second floor, the handcraft classes for women. The first floor now holds the Summer School offices during the season, including the registration office; and the second floor, classrooms. The building was extensively renovated in 1971, but was completely restored during the Second Century Campaign. Since then, the third floor could be used again for dormitory rooms. The hall was given in 1889 by Mr. James H. Kellogg of Troy, N. Y., in memory of his mother, Anne M. Kellogg. The original uses of the hall represented the interest of Mrs. Kellogg in children, opportunities for women and the WCTU.

Lincoln Dormitory—Near Sherwood Studio and the Lodge on Palestine Avenue. This spacious dormitory is compatible with the external features of neighboring buildings, but it is completely modern in its interior design. It was given as a Centennial gift in 1966 by Mrs. John C. Lincoln in memory of her husband, a dedicated Chautauquan for over seventy years.

The Lodge—Hedding and Palestine Avenues near the Arts and Crafts Quadrangle. Built in 1912 as an Emergency Hospital by Dr. William S. Bainbridge, Dr. Jay W. Seaver and Dr. James A. Babbitt, it functioned in cooperation with the Institution. The building has since been used by the Summer School as a residential facility. In 1986 major reconstruction provided the

Chautauqua School of Dance with a dance studio in one wing of the Lodge and an office, costume shop and locker room on the first floor of the center wing. The remainder of the building has been upgraded for continued use as a summer school residence. Two additional dance studios were constructed in an extension of the building at the rear. The small building that has provided faculty apartments behind the Lodge has been moved nearer Sherwood Hall. These improvements and new dance studios are made possible through a grant from the Carnahan-Jackson Foundation.

Logan Dormitory—Corner of Pratt and Vincent Avenues, facing Bestor Plaza. Earlier was private home of a Martin Family. Bought in 1918-1919 by the National Board of the YWCA, facilitated by a gift from Mrs. Lewis H. Lapham of New York. For many years it functioned as the YWCA Hospitality House and after 1922, operated under the local board's supervision. In 1965 in conformance with a national YWCA policy, the organization's Chautauqua real estate was sold to Mrs. Harry A. Logan, Sr., of Warren, Pa., then a member of the Chautauqua Board of Trustees. (Mrs. Logan was later made an honorary trustee.) Mrs. Logan presented the property to the Institution as a Centennial gift. The building has been used as a dormitory for Summer School students and was named for the donor. A large drawing room on the first floor serves as a meeting place for groups and classes. This beautiful addition to the original home was given by Miss Rannie Webster in 1931. Mrs. Logan completely restored, renovated and refurnished Logan Dormitory as part of her Second Century gift to the Institution. The work was completed in 1981.

McKnight Recital Hall—Palestine Avenue near Root Avenue. It is used for recitals and for rehearsals of the Chautauqua Music School Festival Orchestra and other groups. It was built in 1953 in memory of William A. McKnight by his widow.

National Federation of Music Clubs Building—Near Palestine and Forest Avenues. It was given in 1963 by the Northeastern Region of the NFMC as an additional practice house for music students.

Normal Hall—Pratt Avenue at Scott Avenue. Built in 1885 by the Normal Alumni, consisting of graduates of the Normal Classes for Sunday School teachers. The Normal Classes were the foundation of the Summer School. Their first instruction sessions were held in tents near the Auditorium, which was located in the area now known as Miller Park. The Normal Department later held classes in a big tent on the site of Normal Hall. The building is now used by the Theater School and the Studio Theatre. Normal Hall is another one of the Institution's historic structures which was "saved" and restored during the Second Century Campaign.

Norton Memorial Hall—Pratt Avenue between Root and Forest Avenues. This hall was built in 1929 by Mrs. O. W. Norton as a memorial to her husband and her daughter, Ruth. The project was guided by her son, Ralph, who later became president of the Institution. It represents the family's interest in music and the arts. It is used for the presentation of operas in English, plays, chamber music concerts and for occasional extra programs or meetings. It is said to have been the first monolithic concrete building constructed east of the Mississippi River. It is in the art deco style. During the Second Century Campaign, the Hall has had restoration. The roof was replaced; public rest rooms were renovated; stage door enlargement, window restoration, exterior painting, stage machinery and electrical replacement were also completed, along with an interior design.

Octagon Building—Wythe Avenue and Cookman Avenue. Built by Pittsburgh (Pa.) CLSC members in 1885 for their use at Chautauqua. It was acquired by the CLSC Classes of 1883 and 1885 in 1889 as their class building. Now owned by the Institution and used for Writers' Workshop sessions and other small classes.

The Pavilion—Occupies the site of the former Refectory which was built in 1946 when the Plaza was improved and the Pergola removed. The Pergola, an open-air ice cream parlor and merchant stand, was

Norton Hall, the home of the Chautauqua Opera Company. For many years it was also the home of the Cleveland Play House Summer Theatre and now provides playing space for the new Chautauqua Conservatory Theater.

The Octagon Building was ready for the summer of 1885.

built in 1906 and located in the northeast corner of the Plaza. It was both a gathering place for Chautauquans and a thoroughfare. When it was gone, the Plaza was extended to include that corner. A refectory, meaning a dining hall in a college or institution, proved to be rather an exalted name for the place where Chautauquans bought their ice cream cones, but the neat red brick building was an attractive addition to the Plaza area. Further changes came in 1972 when Welch Foods, Inc. assumed management of the Refectory. (See page 63). Now operated by the Chautuaqua Hotel Corporation.

Pioneer Hall—Cookman Avenue above Wythe Avenue. Built in 1885-1886 by the first class to graduate (in 1882) from the Chautauqua Literary and Scientific Circle. Members called themselves "The Pioneers." The building contains many mementoes of early Chautauqua. It is open to the public after CLSC Round Table programs each Thursday afternoon during the season. It was formerly maintained by the Class of 1938, but now is cared for by the Class of 1963. This building has never been wired for electricity, so when it is open after the CLSC Vigil each year, visitors must examine the mementoes by candlelight.

Post Office—Faces Bestor Plaza on Clark Avenue. In addition to postal department facilities, it contains the editorial and business offices of the Chautauquan Daily, the Institution's mailing and supplies headquarters, the 55-Plus Weekends Office and, in the basement, the famous Chautauqua Book Store. At one time the print shop and bindery of The Chautauqua Press were located in this building. The Post Office was new in 1909.

Road Gate—Main entrance to Chautauqua, often referred to as the Main Gate. The handsome pillared brick building was constructed in 1917 at a cost of $40,000 by the Chautauqua Traction Company. It contained the Traction Company's waiting room, ticket office, baggage, freight and express services, as well as entrance and exit lanes for automobiles and a Chautauqua gate ticket office. It still houses the entrance

and exit lanes for automobiles and the main Institution ticket office; all are open twenty-four hours a day. On big program nights, there is an auxiliary ticket window to take care of the demand. The Main Gate contains the manager's office, the parking office which takes care of parking that exceeds one day, the Opera and Play ticket office, the Hospitality and Information Office which also offers help with accommodations, the Lost and Found and the Farmers' Market (open Monday through Saturday).

Seaver Gymnasium—Beyond the Bath House and Public Beach on South Lake Drive. Built in 1890 to house an active gymnastic school. It honors Dr. Jay Webber Seaver who was prominent in the development of the School of Physical Education. A Yale professor, he taught physiology at Chautauqua, and headed the school after Dr. Anderson, its founder, left in 1904. Building now used for youth activities during the daytime when the clubs are in session. Available other hours for adult recreational activities.

Sherwood Studio—Palestine Avenue beyond Hurst Avenue. It was built in 1912 to memorialize William H. Sherwood, the first head of the Piano Department of the Music School. It is used for piano instruction, master classes and recitals. It was reconditioned in 1966 by Mrs. Rena Munger Aldredge as part of her Centennial gift. During the Second Century Campaign, the Munger-Aldredge Recital room of Sherwood Studio was named in memory of Mrs. S. I. Munger and Mrs. George N. Aldredge through gifts of Mrs. Samuel A. Shelburne, a daughter of Mrs. Aldredge, who remembers the interest of her mother and grandmother in recitals, teachers and students at Sherwood Hall.

Smith Memorial Library—Miller Avenue facing Bestor Plaza. Built in 1931 by Mrs. S. M. Smith Wilkes (See pages 22, 23).

Smith-Wilkes Hall—Below Clark Avenue between Janes and Foster Avenues. Given by Mrs. A. M. Smith Wilkes in 1924. According to Dr. Bestor at the time of dedication, it was to be considered as the permanent home of the Bird and Tree Club (now the Bird, Tree and Garden Club), but is used for many other purposes. It accommodates small and large audiences and has excellent acoustic qualities. Mrs. Smith Wilkes made a provision that the Bird and Tree Club should occupy the auxiliary rooms, including a kitchen on the lower floor. Mrs. John C. Lincoln improved the kitchen and public rest room facilities in 1969 as a special gift to the club and the Institution. The year before, in 1968, the club had planned and dedicated the Grace Lincoln Newbury Terrace at the rear of the hall. Mrs. Newbury was a former president. The first landscaping the club provided behind Smith-Wilkes Hall was a memorial to another former president, Mrs. William K. McKnight. In 1974, an enlargement of the Smith-Wilkes Garden with additional landscaping was given by Eleanor McKnight Haupt in memory of her mother,Mrs. McKnight. In the 1885 map of Chautauqua this block is referred to as Wild Wood Park.

Sports Club—South Lake Drive at lower Bowman Avenue. (See page 18).

Strings Studio—Massey Avenue at Miller Ave-

The Chautauquan and The Assembly Herald Building was erected in 1889 on the site of the first Chapel which was conveniently moved near the corner of Pratt and Bowman Avenues.

nue. This brick structure has an unmistakable turn-of-the century look. It was constructed in 1900 as an electric plant. The first electric power house was built on the lake front in 1893 and was soon too small for the growing demand for electricity. Even in 1903, the "new plant" needed an addition. The building now holds studios for the instructors in strings, while the rear of the building houses Grounds equipment for the maintenance department.

Summer School Dormitory—Between the Lodge and Bellinger Hall. Built in 1924. Houses Summer School students. Mr. and Mrs. L. P. Clawson gave $2,000 toward its construction. Improvements made through the Second Century Campaign.

Vanderbeck Chapel—(Ida A. Vanderbeck Chapel) Pratt Avenue near McClintock Avenue. Though not strictly a public building, this charming small chapel is shared with others by the International Order of the King's Daughters and Sons. This group maintains an active scholarship program and brings to the Grounds each year outstanding students from many parts of the country and abroad. The Order maintains three dormitory houses. Its students take part in the Chautauqua Summer School as well as the Order's own program. Many of these students have talents that they share by appearing on programs at club or denominational house meetings throughout the season. This chapel was built in 1963 and named for an outstanding Order leader. The international offices of the Order were moved to Chautauqua following the 1972 season and occupy the first floor of Benedict House, 34 Vincent Avenue.

Veranda—Clark Avenue near Amphitheater. It was purchased by Chautauqua in 1900 to be an annex to the Administration Building. The Assembly Herald offices and other publication offices were moved there. (See page 20).

Women's Club House—South Lake Drive next to Hotel Athenaeum. Built in 1929 on the site of the former club house. This building now on the National Register of Historic Places. As early as 1882 Chautau-

qua women were meeting under the leadership of Emily Huntington Miller. In 1889 a Woman's Club was formed with Mrs. Miller as president. The Club was affiliated with the General Federation of Women's Clubs from 1896-1974. (Changed its name from Woman's Club to Women's Club.) It is regarded as a national organization whose members come from every state and many foreign countries. An extremely active club, it is well-known for its support of scholarships and for high quality twice-weekly programs through the Chautauqua season. The club has a number of departments and activities so that it attracts women of all ages and interests.

Youth Activities Center—Located in Bolin Gym.

LIFE AT CHAUTAUQUA

"Now we aver that at Chautauqua (admitting, of course, exceptions to the rule) the people live in a condition of great mental excitement. A great museum of sights, a perfect tempest of musical sounds, a whirlwind of ideas, a deluge of thoughts, all this storm beating upon the machinery of the human intellect, straining its wheels, clogging its spindles, forcing the shuttle of its loom to fly with incredible swiftness, in weaving a web of thought so intricate and of ever-changing pattern and hue,—all this being admitted, our question becomes one of grave concern. We do not know positively whether this place was selected, in which to perform these mighty miracles of thought, because of its unlimited supply of the raw material, but we are quite sure that there is no place in America where the question, "What shall we eat?" can be more readily or satisfactorily answered.

"The flour and potatoes, from the gravelly ridges of the lakeshore; the beef and lamb, butter and cheese, cream and milk, of its beautiful and fertile hill pastures; its poultry and eggs; and then that specialty of Chautauqua, the Chautauqua Lake pickerel, taken daily from those pure waters, are sufficient assurance that we have at Chautauqua whereon we may build the answer to our question . . ."

R.M. Warren
Chautauqua Sketches

Dr. William N. Jackson, director of religion at Chautauqua, is shown at the pulpit during the ecumenical Sunday morning worship service August 24, 1986. The console of the Massey organ is brought out into full view for the Sunday service.

2

The Program We Enjoy

AT THE AMPHITHEATER

"Is THERE ROOM for one more?"

This is the question frequently asked on big program nights at the Chautauqua Amphitheater when six thousand try to crowd into the pit and side sections while another thousand wait around the rim, hoping to see an opening somewhere. (The Amphitheater is "comfortably filled" by an audience of fifty-six hundred. Bleachers at the rear accommodate another five hundred.)

The Amphitheater is Chautauqua's most amazing structure, for it can change its make-up and play many roles.

It serves as the home of the Chautauqua Symphony Orchestra whose more than seventy chairs about fill the fifty-two-foot-wide platform.

After a Saturday night's concert, the chairs and conductor's podium disappear. The stage crew lowers the Christian flag from the ceiling so that it may hang above the platform. The crew brings out a pulpit, two chairs for the ministers, and voila! The Amphitheater is a church.

On Sunday afternoons it becomes a concert hall again for soloists' recitals, chamber music ensembles or the Chautauqua Music School Festival Orchestra.

Then in the evening, it turns back into a church for the famous Chautauqua Sacred Song Service.

On Monday morning large black velour curtains on metal frames will be moved into place on the platform to make a pleasant background for the morning speakers.

Two chairs are centered behind the speaker's stand. A grand piano is rolled out. Now the Amphitheater is ready for the regular 9:30 Devotional Hour. But at 10:45, the piano will be rolled behind the curtains and the Amphitheater will become strictly a lecture hall.

During the afternoon on an average day, if there is no orchestra rehearsal, a dance company or a visiting soloist may be practicing. No matter who it is, Chautauquans are free to wander quietly in and out, to enjoy a few minutes or an hour of listening. Many Chautauquans double their money by attending both rehearsals and concerts.

Children, too, are sometimes captivated by the music and stop to listen while they munch their ice cream cones. If they're well indoctrinated in Chautauqua ways, they will stay on the fringe because no eating (or smoking) is permitted in the venerable open-air auditorium. Most children and adults probably just

"A RARE INCIDENT"

"Dr. Vincent, Monday night, stated to the vast congregation that one of our keen-eyed, strong-handed policemen captured Saturday night a couple of young men who had brought to Fair Point a large square box filled with bottles of whiskey. The whiskey they had kept, but had sent the young men home. But whiskey at Fair Point was as much out-of-place as Satan among the sons of God. The question then was: What shall be done with the whiskey? It was voted that J. B. Gough and Francis Murphy (leading temperance lecturers) be a committee to dispose of it. After some minutes they appeared upon the platform in their shirt sleeves, Mr. Murphy having a shovel upon his shoulders. They reported that they had decided that the monster should be killed and buried. Mr. Gough then delivered a sort of funeral oration, holding a bottle in his hand. He let it fall upon the platform, and down came the shovel in Murphy's strong hands upon it, breaking it into a thousand pieces. And thus the bottles were disposed of. The spirits fled and the fragments of glass were buried out of sight."

The Chautauqua Daily Assembly Herald
August 8, 1877

Dr. Karl A. Menninger, a Chautauquan for many years, has been a frequent lecturer in the Amphitheater and in other halls on the Grounds.

"overhear" the afternoon music as they hustle by.

The wide range of tastes among Chautauquans has encouraged the program department to provide great variety while holding to its "best talent" tradition.[13]

The Amphitheater's first predecessor, called the Pavilion, came into being in 1877 when the Tabernacle tent (See page 14) was moved to this ravine. The natural half-bowl of land was cleared and fitted with benches which faced a platform.

Then in 1879 came the first real Amphitheater, all wooden, with posts that blocked the view of many and a flat roof that was too noisy when it rained. It was a great improvement over the Pavilion, however, and was well within the Assembly's budget since its total cost was only $4,500.

The present Amphitheater was constructed in 1893 at the unbelievable cost of approximately $26,000. It is covered by a trussed roof and supported by only twenty steel columns so that most seats give an unobstructed view of the platform. Shorter wooden pillars meet the edge of the roof around the rim. The choir loft provides seats for three hundred and fifty and Chautauquans may sit there for concerts, thereby getting a closer look at the working conductor and musicians. The overall wood construction provides exceptionally fine acoustics for musical performers.

The Amphitheater stage and choir gallery were enlarged in 1907 when the Massey memorial organ was installed. Even then, however, the stage extended into a circular front section which somewhat limited program presentations. Later this situation was corrected when the stage was "squared off" and thus enlarged.

The new organ was given in memory of Hart A. Massey by the Massey family of Toronto, Canada. Mr. Massey had served as an Assembly trustee. The organ was designed with four manuals of sixty-one notes each with a pedal of thirty-two notes. (Three generations of the Massey family served a total of fifty-two years on the Board of Trustees.)

At the time of the organ's installation, it was necessary to construct a fireproof organ chamber which was provided with steel curtains that can be lowered when the organ is not in use to protect it from the damp air. Beneath the chamber is a basement seven feet high with concrete flooring. Steam heat connections for keeping the organ at an even temperature throughout the year were installed, but are no longer used. An auxiliary lighting system for the Amphitheater is also located there.

Seven years after the organ was placed in the Amphitheater, Mr. Chester D. Massey provided some additions: two new stops, new motor bellows for the tremolos, renewal of every valve, repairing of combinations, pistons and the replacement of the electrical connections. Small improvements were made in 1918 and 1920. By 1928 it was necessary to install a new console along with new mechanical and electrical systems, and new generators. But is wasn't until 1972 that the organ was given a complete cleaning and renovation. The gift of an anonymous Chautauquan made possible this major task which was planned and executed under the supervision of Robert V. Woodside, Chautauqua's official organist.

It was an amazing project. The reed pipes were removed and sent to the factory for revoicing. Other pipes were washed with soap and water and replaced after the chests in which they are set were vacuumed and mopped. In addition to obtaining small new parts for the organ, three new sets of pipes were included in the improvements. The pitch of the organ was brought to A-440 which enables it to be combined more successfully with the orchestra and a new console was chosen. Mr. John Schleigh who installed the 1928 console and who had been running the organ since 1965, was in charge of the work. The powerful instrument thus achieved new flexibility, exactitude and color in its 65th year and in time for the Institution's Centennial.

Above the Amphitheater ceiling is rafter space with a catwalk that leads to the control booth and to the clusters of Amphitheater ceiling lights whose bulbs must be changed from above.

The original Pavilion and both Amphitheaters have performed a great service by fostering the community

AMPHITHEATER NAMED

Dr. James M. Buckley, prominent minister and editor of the Methodist Episcopal Church, appeared on the Chautauqua Platform the very first year and for more than forty years thereafter. One of his regular program features was a "Question-Drawer." According to reports, there were few questions that he could not answer. He was able to think quickly and enjoyed a remarkable memory. He was serving as editor of The Christian Advocate, a Methodist Episcopal publication, part of this time.

The story is told that when Dr. Buckley came for the first time into the imposing structure which had replaced the Pavilion in the ravine, he surveyed it thoughtfully and then said to Dr. Vincent, "This is a genuine Amphitheater!"

The name must have appealed to Dr. Vincent. He immediately adopted it. The Amphitheater, properly written with a capital "A," became the most important meeting place for Chauatauqua's program events and services.

The first Amphitheater in 1879 had "fairly comfortable" seats for five thousand and many posts!

spirit of Chautauqua, which some say is akin to college spirit. It has been in the "Amp" that Chautauquans have caught much inspiration from one another as well as from the programs, and garnered information to carry to their home communities and responsibilities. They still do.

Beginning with the very first Assembly, the "best talent" has been sought and this is the reason that the term "Chautauqua platform" has become a synonym for good, informed speaking.

Before radio and television and the era of supermass communication, the Chautauqua platform provided a forum for the free discussion of important issues that needed to be heard by large numbers of people. Audiences of six thousand were not easy to come by in those days.

Controversial questions were debated or their opposing sides presented in successive lectures. While the Assembly opened its platform to divergent strains of thought, it did not sponsor opinions or causes. Stern and stirring lectures early urged the pros and cons of

Woman Suffrage. Labor and management argued their cases. Before the United States entered the first World War the issues involved in that European conflict were analyzed from French, German and English standpoints. The current problems of world hunger, literacy, overpopulation, the inner city and human rights have all been realistically taken apart on the Chautauqua platform.

A letter from Woodrow Wilson in the Chautauqua Historical Collection gives a significant assessment of Chautauqua's philosophy and platform practice. Writing to Mr. George Creel of the wartime Committee on Public Information concerning the proposed speaking campaign to provide information to the citizens, he said, "Your suggestion of Mr. Arthur E. Bestor, president of Chautauqua Institute, to direct this work is excellent. You are fortunate to be able to enlist one who has been so intimately connected with a great American educational institution devoted to popular instruction without prejudice or partisanship."

During the Second Century Campaign the Amphitheater was completely restored and prepared for its next century of service. It received new structural supports, a new roof, new sound and lighting systems, painting, reconditioned pipe organ, installation of equipment for the hearing impaired and an expanded porch. New internal backstage restructuring and facilities were achieved for the improvement of program presentations for the comfort of the artists. More than $2.2 million was spent to safeguard the future of this historic treasure.

In spite of television's place in today's world, the Chautauqua platform still provides a significant forum. Chautauquans enjoy hearing national leaders in person, asking them questions, receiving immediate answers and shaking hands with them afterward. Because the audience is drawn from all parts of the country, speakers are often challenged by widely separated viewpoints during question-and-answers.

The Amphitheater has hosted Presidents of the United States, Marian Anderson's farewell concert, the Mormon Tabernacle Choir, the late Robert F.

Van Cliburn rehearses for one of his first performances at Chautauqua.

Albert Stoessel is shown with the Chautauqua Symphony Orchestra (probably sometime in the 1930s), an orchestra which he organized and directed until his death in 1943.

Kennedy in a Meet-the-Press program, Van Cliburn before and after he won the Tchaikovsky Award in Moscow and a host of other celebrated guests.

It has also been enjoyed for sentimental occasions. The annual Old First Night (Chautauqua's birthday party) is celebrated there. It has seen larger, more gala events, such as the Golden and Diamond Jubilee Anniversary Pageants.

On one memorable CLSC Recognition Day evening, August 21, 1889, the annual CLSC banquet was held in the pit of the Amphitheater. Six hundred and fifty CLSC graduates sat down to dinner while the galleries were filled with other Chautauquans who came later to hear the banquet program.

In 1969 the Institution arranged television sets on the stage so that Chautauquans could watch man's first step onto the moon, an historic moment always to be remembered. In 1974 they witnessed President Nixon deliver his resignation address while Ferrante and Teicher waited to complete their concert. The next day in the Amphitheater they heard and watched President Ford's inauguration.

No Chautauquan who was present will forget the First Day Ceremony of the Chautauqua Movement Commemorative Stamp on August 6, 1974, the Centennial year.

Chautauqua has been called the "grand-daddy" of all musical festivals in this country. It happened naturally as Chautauquans responded to the needs of one decade after another. Indications are that music will become even more important in Chautauqua's future.

Music permeates the Grounds!

Sherwood Studio at the north end of Palestine Avenue resounds all day with piano sounds: lessons, practice, interpretation recitals and master classes, extending into the evenings.

The village of piano shacks, little brown shingle houses that look like tourist cabins near the north gate and fence is rented to capacity all day, every day, throughout the summer.

McKnight Hall, Connell Studio, Hurlbut Church, the Theory Building and the Ensemble Buildings are all used for rehearsals and lessons. Even out under the trees one may see a string quartet at work. The Music School Festival Orchestra and the Chautauqua Youth Orchestra have regular practices.

Three hundred and seventy-seven music students were registered for instruction in 1985 and over $105,000 was awarded in two hundred and fourteen scholarships.

If you go past Smith-Wilkes Hall between 6:15 and 8 p.m. many evenings you will hear the Chautauqua Choir rehearsing for its Sunday services. (On Monday evenings, it will probably be the Regional Choir at work on its special program. You may recognize the music from a well-known oratorio.)

Norton Hall where the operas are performed has its own share of rehearsals, for both singers and orchestra must prepare four productions each season.

The denominational groups and other clubs make good use of the abundance of talent on the Grounds. The Chautauqua Women's Club sponsors Talent Recitals during the season to support its extensive scholarship work. By participating in these programs, music students receive valuable experience in addition to giving pleasure to others.

Most people, however, think of the Amphitheater programs when "music at Chautauqua" is discussed, and first of all, the orchestra. Chautauqua's own symphony was a long time in coming. Before that, an excellent Meadville (Pa.) Band, Rogers' Band and an orchestra organized by Henry B. Vincent served the Assembly's instrumental needs.

In 1909 the New York Symphony Orchestra under Walter Damrosch gave an afternoon concert at Chautauqua. Their return engagement in 1910 was considered "a highlight."

During Music week in 1914, Victor Herbert's orchestra performed daily with Mr. Herbert, himself, conducting. Then for the next three years the Russian Symphony appeared at Chautauqua for a week each season. A French military band performed during Music Week in 1918, but in 1919 the New York Symphony returned, preparing the way for the next year's big coup when it was announced that the New York orchestra would remain six weeks, giving at least five concerts each week.

Hearing the orchestra that many times in one season convinced Chautauquans that they wanted as much symphonic music as they could fit into a summer's program. Thereafter, except for 1922 when the Detroit Symphony was engaged for a series of fifteen concerts, the New York orchestra came every year through 1928.

In this latter year, the New York Symphony and the New York Philharmonic became one orchestra, requiring Chautauqua to make a change also. As it turned out, many of the former New York Symphony members continued to come to Chautauqua and with some others, formed the nucleus of a brand new organization, the Chautauqua Symphony Orchestra.

Albert Stoessel became the first conductor of the new orchestra and musical director of the Institution, continuing in both capacities until his death in 1943. Stoessel had been appearing at Chautauqua since 1921 with the New York Symphony Orchestra (except for 1922) and was influencing the growth of Chautauqua's musical program all during those years. He had succeeded Walter Damrosch as conductor of the New York orchestra, was enjoying a wide reputation as a violinist and was becoming recognized as a composer, as well. In 1928, in the absence of H. Augustine Smith, he had also directed the Chautauqua Choir.

Mr. Stoessel drew outstanding young talent to Chautauqua and also gave increasing prominence to American-born music. The orchestra became the foundation of Chautauqua's musical program, furnishing the complement of the opera orchestra, a new development in 1929, and even providing the accompaniment for the Sacred Song Service.

Stoessel was one of those credited with interesting Mrs. O. W. Norton in the building of a concert hall that could also be used for operas and plays. (See page 29).[14] Once this edifice, Norton Hall, was assured, he launched into the creation of the Chautauqua Opera Association.

Chautauquans' taste for opera had been growing since 1926 when the Rochester Opera Company presented six operas in English in the Amphitheater. They had previously heard opera in concert form and operatic literature in recitals and had enjoyed dramatic readings and plays on the Amphitheater stage. Now they were delighted with the prospect of having an opera hall and an "opera season."

Another innovation was beginning to flourish at Chautauqua, radio broadcasts of orchestra programs. They began in a limited way in 1927 over Station WLBW in Oil City, Pennsylvania, and later became nationwide.

Norton Hall's facilities also encouraged the growing interest in chamber music at Chautauqua. Mischa Mischakoff, who came to Chautauqua with the New York Symphony as its concertmaster in 1926, organized that same year the Mischakoff String Quartet which, in turn, became the nucleus for the Chamber Music Society. This Society gave three public recitals in Smith-Wilkes Hall in 1928 and two private musicals in the Norton home at the invitation of Mrs.

Ralph H. Norton. The new hall proved to be an excellent setting for chamber music concerts and they continued until 1981 under an endowment established by Mr. and Mrs. Norton.

The combination of Stoessel as conductor and musical director, Ernest Hutcheson and Horatio Connell as teachers and artists, not to mention Mischa Mischakoff and the outstanding choral leaders and artists, set the climate for a musical program at Chautauqua that not only attracted large audiences, but superior performers and students, as well.

Albert Stoessel had completed the 1943 programming and had arranged for soloists and guest conductors before his sudden death on May 12, 1943. So the season of 1943 was, in a sense, still a Stoessel season. William Willeke, who had conducted the New York Symphony for half of its first six-week stay at Chautauqua, conducted the orchestra for part of the season, along with Dr. Howard Hanson, Director of the Eastman School of Music, and Vladimir Golschmann, Conductor of the St. Louis Symphony Orchestra.

The next year Franco Autori became the second regular conductor of the Chautauqua Symphony Orchestra. Autori, a native of Italy who had become a naturalized citizen, had attracted attention in this country for his work in Buffalo where he had trans-

The Mischakoff String Quartet (1942) included: Reber Johnson, violin; Georges Miquelle, Cello; Nathan Gordon, Viola, in addition to Mischa Mischakoff.

SHARING NORTON HALL

Professional repertory theatre was established in 1930.

The story is thought to be true that Frederic McConnell, director of the Cleveland Play House, was vacationing at Maple Springs in 1929, when he came across the lake to see what was going on at Chautauqua. He found that there was a new Norton Hall. Soon after he proposed to Dr. Bestor that theatre join opera in the regular use of the new hall.

The idea was accepted and the Cleveland Play House began summer performances at Chautauqua the next year. During many of these years the Play House also conducted a summer theatre school. 1980 was the final year for the Cleveland Play House at Chautauqua.

A full Amphitheater with Franco Autori on the podium. Autori conducted the Chautauqua Symphony Orchestra from 1944 through 1952.

Sergiu Comissiona was named Music Director and Principal Conductor of the Chautauqua Symphony Orchestra in 1976.

formed a Federal Music Project into a community-supported orchestra. At Chautauqua, Mr. Autori continued the Stoessel policy of programming works along with the standard repertoire and of presenting soloists of wide acclaim. In 1946 the Student Orchestra performed the Saturday morning concerts series, thus relieving the "big" symphony from some of the rigors of its demanding schedule. The year of 1952 was Autori's last season at Chautauqua.

His successor was Walter Hendl, Conductor and Musical Director of the Dallas Symphony Orchestra, and one of the rising young talents to come to the fore following World War II. In 1958 Hendl left Dallas and became Associate Conductor of the Chicago Symphony Orchestra with his former mentor, Dr. Fritz Reiner. In 1964, upon the retirement of Dr. Hanson as head of the Eastman School, Walter Hendl was selected as the new Director.

At Chautauqua Hendl continued the program interest in both the monumental works of the symphonic repertoire and in contemporary music. He continued the Pop concerts and the presentation of distinguished soloists. Knowledgeable, painstaking, imaginative and alert to current trends, Hendl set high standards for himself, the orchestra and the audiences. He sometimes appeared as piano soloist with the orchestra, in artists' recitals and as pianist with the String Quartet. During 1962 and 1963 he added to his Chautauqua and Chicago duties, those as Artistic Director of the Ravinia Festival and Musical Director of the Caramoor (N.Y.) Festival. In 1966 he served on the jury for the Third International Tchaikovsky Piano

Contest in Moscow and in 1967, in a similar capacity for the Schubert Competition in Vienna.

Hendl remained as conductor and musical director at Chauauqua until 1972 when a period of ill health caused him to resign from both his Eastman and Chautauqua positions. His improving health enabled him to appear as a guest conductor from time to time at Chautauqua and he has resumed an active career.

Following Hendl's resignation, the Institution engaged a succession of guest conductors. At length, in November, 1975, the Chautauqua Board of Trustees approved the appointment of Sergiu Comissiona as Music Director and Principal Conductor of the Chautauqua Symphony Orchestra, its fourth principal conductor in a forty-six-year span. Maestro Comissiona was Director of the Baltimore Symphony Orchestra at the time and had made guest appearances at Chautauqua during the 1975 season.

He was born in Bucharest, Rumania, where he had become a violinist and also made his conducting debut. His experience included posts in Rumania, Israel and Sweden before he assumed his Baltimore duties in 1966.

The concerts programmed during Comissiona's first season at Chautauqua were well-received. Ten guest conductors appeared during the summer and the total number of concerts were advanced from twenty-one to twenty-four. The size of the orchestra exceeded seventy members.

Chautauquans reacted positively to the new music director's style and interpretation and welcomed him warmly to their podium. The Maestro continued as

Maestro Walter Hendl, Conductor of the Chautauqua Symphony Orchestra 1953-1972, invited Van Cliburn to appear as soloist with the Orchestra before the young man entered and won the Tchaikovsky Competition. Van Cliburn has appeared six times at Chautauqua.

Varujan Kojian became Music Director and Conductor of the Orchestra in 1981.

Wilbur de Paris and his Dixieland Band broke new musical ground at Chautauqua.

Principal Conductor through 1979 and since that time has appeared regularly as a guest conductor.

In 1981 Varujan Kojian became the Music Director and Conductor of the Orchestra, remaining through 1984. In the intervals between the appointments of Music Directors, guest conductors and programs were decided upon with the help of the Program Department and the Concertmaster, Millard Taylor.

In times past, the program director designated one or two weeks as Music Weeks. But in recent years when the orchestra has been in residence for six or seven weeks and has given more than twenty concerts, every week might be called Music Week.

The Chautauqua Symphony Orchestra has been affected by economic pressures of the time. Some of its former members of long standing were obligated to remain with their winter orchestras on a twelve-month basis because major orchestras began negotiat-

OLIVE WOOD DESK

The small desk made of olive wood that the current President of Chautauqua sometimes uses when he is making announcements on the Amphitheater platform was first used by Bishop Vincent at the beginning of the 1893 season, the same year that the Amphitheater was new.

The Bishop had long wished for a speaker's stand made of olive wood from Palestine. The Institution's Secretary, W. A. Duncan, knew of this desire, and when he was traveling in Europe in 1892, ordered such a desk. It was delivered, happily enough, just in time for the next season.

ing their contracts in this way. The identity of the Chautauqua Symphony Orchestra has remained intact, however, and for the most part a seven-week schedule of three concerts a week has been continued.

In addition to the orchestra concerts the Amphitheater hosts other outstanding events some of them with popular appeal. There may be Metropolitan opera singers, military bands, jazz or rock groups, television personalities, distinguished foreign artists and orchestras (Yehudi Menuhin and the Bath Festival Orchestra, for example), composers and guest conductors. The day the Mormon Tabernacle Choir sang two concerts, afternoon and evening, there were thirty thousand people on the Grounds, it is claimed, the biggest single day's attendance since Theodore Roosevelt's fourth visit in 1905.

While Paul Whiteman drew enthusiastic applause when he presented his band in concert during the 1939 season, it was not until 1960 that Wilber de Paris and his Dixieland Band brought real jazz to the Chautauqua stage. This innovation was received so wholeheartedly by Chautauquans that similar attractions have been programmed ever since. Ella Fitzgerald and Al Hirt both appeared during the season of 1968 and it was difficult to say which snarled traffic more as the eager crowds arrived at the Main Gate.

The founding fathers used music from the first not only as an accompaniment to worship and Sunday School methods, but also as entertainment.

On the very first evening of the Assembly after the opening service, there was Music on the Lake. Singers and instrumentalists boarded a small steam yacht and anchoring off-shore, parallel to Palestine Park, played

"THE EVE OF BATTLE"

"This is the eve of the great mental and moral conflict which is to take place in this pleasant grove. Ignorance, shams and errors of various kinds are to be assailed by facts, logic, experiments, eloquence and song. Science, morality and revelation are to be the open and fair fields of action. Already some of the Titans are on the Grounds...The fact is two weeks at Fair Point during the Assembly will put into one's lifetime the ordinary experience of years..."

The Chautauqua Assembly Daily Herald
Thursday, July 27, 1876

and sang while hundreds on shore listened to the melodies and even joined in on the choruses. It is little wonder that Chautauquans were thrilled to be at Fair Point in spite of the inconveniences of tent living.

The Assembly's song leaders were among the best. P. P. Bliss, W. F. Sherwin, Ira D. Sankey and C. C. Case. Miss Mary A. Lathbury who is famous for her hymns, "Break Thou the Bread of Life" and "Day is Dying in the West", was present almost every summer during the early period. One season she presented five new hymns to Chautauqua.

Dr. H. R. Palmer headed the School of Music when it was more formally organized in 1889 and served as Musical Director for the Assembly. He was followed by Alfred Hallam who served from 1902 to 1919. Under Mr. Hallam's leadership, significant growth in the music program was apparent, especially in the field of choral music. William C. Bridgman succeeded Alfred Hallam for one year.

In 1921 H. Augustine Smith began a seven-year term as Musical Director of Chautauqua. Under Smith, pageantry was combined with sacred music to furnish deeply religious and dramatic programs. He wrote and directed Chautauqua's Golden Jubilee Pageant. He developed regional choruses, combining them with the three-hundred-voice Chautauqua Choir to achieve some noteworthy musical productions.

After Mr. Smith left Chautauqua, Mr. Stoessel was given the title of Musical Director and supervised to some extent all of the departments of music. Following his death, however, the opera, the choir, the orches-

"NOTES BY THE WAY"

"It would be a popular movement at Chautauqua this year if Dr. Vincent would so arrange the programme that the people could have say three or four hours relaxation from public service each day. It has been a common complaint in previous years that there was too much cramming with lectures and special services. Since we are to have a Council of Reform this year, let the work of reform begin in the programme."

The Chautauquan Daily Assembly Herald
May 10, 1877

Free speech at Chautauqua apparently allowed even the idolized Dr. Vincent to be criticized!

tra and the School of Music became separate divisions, each with its own director.

Alfredo Valenti who had shared the development of the Chautauqua Opera Association with Mr. Stoessel, became General Director and remained until his retirement in 1958. Julius Rudel of the New York City Center Opera followed for one year. John Daggett Howell then headed Chautauqua opera through 1965 when Leonard Treash was appointed. Mr. Treash was Artist Voice Teacher and Director of Opera at the Eastman School of Music. Following his resignation during the season of 1980, Cynthia Auerbach became the Artistic Director of the Opera Company.

Choir directors who followed Mr. Stoessel, were: R. Lee Osburn, 1929 and 1930; Walter Howe, 1931-1948; Harrison Potter, 1949-1951; Cecil Stewart, 1952-1958; Paul Christiansen, 1959 and 1960; Richard Paige, 1961-1967; W. William Wagner, 1968-1971; Robert V. Woodside, 1972-1978; Edward Polochick, 1979 and 1980; Phillip Carey, 1981; Phil Aley, 1982-

Organists who have not only accompanied the Chautauqua Choir, but given recitals in the Amphitheater (and most of them have also taught organ at Chautauqua), include: I. V. Flagler, 1885-1903; Percy J. Starnes, 1904, 1905; Henry B. Vincent, 1906-1924; Hugh Porter, 1925-1929; Walter Howe, 1930; Hugh Porter, 1931; George William Volkel, 1932-1955; Robert V. Woodside, 1956-1968; Gerald S. Crawford, 1969; Raymond H. Ocock, 1970, 1971; Robert V. Woodside, 1972-1978; Doris H. Eicher, 1979—   .

Perhaps the Sunday morning church service in the Amphitheater, one of Chautauqua's most unique gatherings, captures best the truth about the overall program. In this service several of the prime elements of the Chautauqua experience are noticeable.

First of all, the service is ecumenical, as Chautauqua services have always been. The large numbers of people of many faiths who participate give a distinct character to the service.

Second, the practice of religion, traditionally the foundation of all other activities at Chautauqua, is reaffirmed at this service. The founders' philosophy of the non-separation of the sacred and the secular— "all things to the Glory of God!"—is openly acknowleged again each week.

Third, the music so important throughout Chautauqua, reaches excellence in this service not only when the choir sings , but also when the organ swells to double forte and the congregation rises together to join in the singing of the Doxology and the hymns.

It is in this setting that the Chaplain of the Week begins his ministry. Clergymen from many parts of this country and abroad are invited to serve for one week at a time, preaching daily, sometimes teaching, often counseling and mingling informally with Chautauquans during their stays. Chautauqua's sensitivity to social change was evident in 1975 when Dr. Cynthia C. Wedel, a former president of the National Council of Churches, was invited to Chautauqua as a Chaplain of the Week, the first woman so to serve. There have been more women taking worship leadership roles since then, not only as Chaplain, but as layleaders during the Sunday services. Women are also active in the Religion Department's lecture program.

AT THE HALL
OF PHILOSOPHY

THOSE PEOPLE who are hurrying along the Brick Walk in friendly groups of six or eight are going to a lecture in the Hall of Philosophy.

The Brick Walk is a Chautuqua colloquialism for Clark Avenue and since cars are not allowed there, pedestrians often fill to capacity the twelve-foot-wide avenue. Clark Avenue extends from the Colonnade to the Hall of Christ. (Vincent Avenue from Massey Avenue in front of the Main Gate to the Plaza is also a Brick Walk of similar proportions.)

The Hall of Philosophy is located beyond Cookman Avenue within calling distance of the Hall of Christ, Alumni Hall and the Hall of Missions. It is an outdoor auditorium of Grecian design that can accommodate audiences of approximately one thousand. Its first purpose was to serve the Chautauqua Literary and Scientific Circle, but it has become equally important to other segments of the Chautauqua program.

The Hall is built on the upper slope of an entire block which was part of St. Paul's Grove, an open section of the Grounds which Bishop Vincent set aside for

the use of the CLSC a week after he had announced his celebrated reading plan on Aug. 10, 1878.

The present Hall still has the grove atmosphere, for handsome trees and shrubbery encircle it. Even the best of lectures is enchanced by the natural beauty of the setting. Of course, where there are trees, there are usually birds. So any program in the Hall of Philosophy is apt to have some competition from these natural songsters.

The year after the Chautauqua Literary and Scientific Circle was initiated, a white wooden outdoor meeting hall, similar to the present structure, arose in St. Paul's Grove. Called the Hall of Philosophy, it was surrounded by the tall standards on which the "Athenian fires" were burned for special CLSC occasions. Busts of Plato, Socrates, Goethe, Shakespeare and others occupied the main pillars, looking down on the Hall's inspired gatherings.

In 1892, close by, a fountain made of natural stone was constructed by the Pioneer Class on its tenth anniversary. On the day of dedication, ivy from almost

The first Hall of
Philosophy.

every state in the Union and some foreign countries was planted around it. Extra lighting was installed later by the CLSC Class of 1888 and other improvements were made by other classes, especially on their tenth anniversaries.

But after a period of years, this first hall began to deteriorate and it was decided to replace it with a building of more durable materials, though still in the Classic spirit.

First plans, however, proved to be too grand for the money at hand, especially as prices kept rising while construction was delayed. Therefore, consistent with Chautauqua's pay-as-you-go policy, adjustments on materials were agreed upon to lessen the cost. Even so, the new hall could not be completed at once, and the ingenious Chautauquans used the foundation and floor under a tent roof for their meetings. In fact, even the floor was not ready for the first of the 1904 season. Consequently, meetings scheduled for the hall were held in the grove of trees behind the Hall of Christ site, in a manner not unlike the first meetings in the Auditorium in Miller Park. The Hall was completed in 1906.

The new Hall was set at a slightly different angle from the first to correspond better with its lower entrance on Fletcher Avenue. Its balustrade was reconstructed in 1925 through Old First Night gifts. Its masonry and roof were reconstructed and its wooden parts repainted in 1965 from the General Centennial Fund.

At the present time, the Department of Religion schedules 2:15 p.m. lectures in the Hall of Philosophy Monday through Friday. The Women's Club meets there at 3:30 p.m. The traditional Sunday evening Vespers Service, originally a CLSC service, meets at 5 p.m. (Bishop Vincent wrote the order of service which is still followed.)

In addition to these regularly scheduled meetings,

"As a Power. . .after the Civil War. . .Chautauqua has been more potent in uniting the people of our own country than any other influence."

About Chautauqua
Emily Raymond

"Chautauqua must be kept in close and sympathetic connection with the great currents of national life. It must be a center from which the larger and more significant movements may gain strength and intelligent support."

President George E. Vincent
Annual Report, 1909

other groups and classes meet there occasionally. Recognition Day Commencement is held there as it has been since 1882 when eight hundred of the more than one thousand and seven hundred graduates were present. Some years the Friends have used one corner of the hall for early Sunday Morning Meetings. Recently, a Scandinavian Day observance drew a Standing Room Only crowd as the center benches were moved back to accomodate a program of folk dancing.

An anonymous donor during the Second Century Campaign made possible major improvements to the Hall of Philosophy: the repair of the interior mosaics; repair of concrete columns, aprons and base of the building; the repainting of the benches; the modernization of restrooms, exterior and interior painting and staining; and the restoration of roof stenciled designs.

Newcomers may be asking, "What is the CLSC?" Put very simply, it is a year-round home reading program.

The Hall of Philosophy with its outdoor setting attracts lecture audiences, but the aesthetic impact of the structure compounds their study experiences.

Chautauquans find the Hall of Philosophy a pleasant place in which to encounter ideas that are relevant to their non-vacation world.

EDITORIAL NOTE

"Bring the boys and girls to the Assembly. They may spend half their time climbing trees or boating on the lake and may not listen to many learned lecturers, but they cannot avoid seeing and hearing many things which will tend to improve their minds and shape their destiny in life. They well see that on the whole, life may be made something good and grand."

The Chautauqua Daily Assembly Herald
May 10, 1877

Still pertinent today! What better way for children to learn the love of music than by hearing it frequently, consistently as they come and go past rehearsals or concerts in the Amphitheater even if they never go in and sit down! Much good is simply "absorbed" at Chautauqua when no one is looking!

ANOTHER FIRST

It may not be generally known that the formation of the National Woman's Christian Temperance Union in November, 1874, resulted from a meeting of women held at Fair Point during the first Sunday School Assembly.

The Assembly took place after a vigorous and prayerful campaign against the sale of liquor had been carried on in Ohio, as well as in nearby Fredonia and Jamestown in Chautauqua County. Hundreds of women had been drawn into the crusade.

During the Assembly, these Ohio leaders and others counseled together and set November as a time for a convention to be held in Cleveland for the purpose of uniting the efforts of women from all states in the cause of temperance.

The call was signed by Mrs. Emily Huntington Miller, Secretary of the Chautauqua Meeting. (Mrs. Miller later became the first President of the Chautauqua Woman's Club.)

Women from sixteen states attended the founding convention in Cleveland. The National Woman's Christian Temperance Union, the name of the new organization, was headed for many years by Miss Frances Willard. Miss Willard had been persuaded to resign as Dean of the Women's Department of Northwestern University to become the WCTU's first president. She was the first woman to have full Platform status at Chautauqua and appeared there frequently. Miss Willard worked not only for temperance reform, but also for woman suffrage.

The idea for the CLSC had been in Dr. Vincent's mind for some time and at the end of the 1877 season, he promised his fellow-Chautauquans a surprise announcement the next summer.

True to his promise, he made the explanation of his idea in the Pavilion on a Saturday morning in early August. He hoped that a few would be interested, but there were more than a few. The Pavilion was so crowded that the side curtains had to be lifted, and over seven hundred people signed up for the CLSC within three days.

Dr. Vincent's aim was "to promote habits of reading and study in nature, art, science and in sacred and secular literature."[15] Twenty to forty minutes a day was projected as liberal allowance for CLSC reading to complete one year's course. He wanted many who had been deprived of formal education to acquire "the college outlook"[16] and those who had attended college to progress through programmed reading. He outlined a four year cycle which would give a successive yearly emphasis on English, American, Continental European and Classical history and literature.

"Knowledge promotes power," Dr. Vincent reminded his friends[17] at Chautauqua, and many wholeheartedly responded to this ambitious thought. The first announcement also proposed that members could be in touch with professors during the off-season months and make periodic reports to them. This plan was a forerunner of the correspondence courses which were later carried on under the Chautauqua University banner.

A monthly magazine, The Chautauquan, a literary and home magazine, was established in 1880 by Dr. Flood, editor of the Assembly Herald. With the wide circulation of The Chautauquan, the number of textbooks to be printed for the CLSC could be reduced since the magazine carried both required and supplemental readings for CLSC members as well as articles of general interest.

The first books in the CLSC courses were regular trade editions. In 1878, some of the books were Chautauqua textbooks and later many of the books were written especially for the CLSC and printed at Chautauqua.

In addition to its home reading, the CLSC eventually developed Round Table discussions of their books as part of the summer program while lectures on coordinate CLSC themes were included in the general Assembly program.

The reading circles were organized all across the country and even beyond both oceans; members found it easier to read and study in groups than to pursue their courses alone.

Miss Kate F. Kimball, executive secretary of the CLSC from 1878 until her death in 1917, kept in touch with the circles and directed the nation-wide growth of the program. Ida M. Tarbell, too, developed a considerable correspondence on behalf of the CLSC during her years on the staff of The Chautauquan. Miss Tarbell annotated the CLSC readings in the magazine for the benefit of readers without access to libraries and answered questions sent in by the Circles.

At the present time, Nately Ronsheim serves as CLSC Director. Several basic books are selected from year to year by the director along with extra books that may be purchased at a special price and used for credit toward graduation. Innovative summer programming has brought seminars and mini-courses in addition to Round Tables and Sidewalk Sessions so that the entire CLSC program has been strengthened. The CLSC was one hundred years old in 1978.

Chautauquans often claim that the CLSC was the first book club in America since it makes book selections for its members and gives them special purchase rates. For a short period there was actually a Chautauqua Book of the Month Club which flourished under that name and apart from the CLSC, apparently for those who wanted books other than the standard CLSC selections.

Dr. Vincent admitted that there were many who started the four-year course who didn't finish it, but even if they read a portion of the books, he felt confident that they had been in that measure helped. He insisted that the self-discipline learned in home study was as great a benefit as the accumulation of knowledge. It is estimated that over a million readers have been enrolled for various periods of time in the CLSC.

The classes of the CLSC have possessed a strong sense of "belonging," the same sort of loyalty that was felt by the Normal alumni for the Assembly.

While widespread educational, social and communications changes within the United States make the appeal of the CLSC less dramatic than in former years, there is still a camaraderie among the current classes that supports the general feeling of loyalty to Chautauqua. This camaraderie serves as one more tie to the place that is already beloved.

It is appropriate to have the Hall of Missions and the Department of Religion Office which it houses, close to the Hall of Philosophy and to the Hall of Christ, for these buildings are all used in connection with the Department of Religion. The hall is listed on the National Register of Historic Places.

There are accommodations there for the Director of the Department of Religion, the Chaplain-of-the-Week, the Religion Department lecturer and the staff.

Since many ministers have been connected with the development of Chautauqua, it is impossible to mention all those who have taken major roles. There are scores of college presidents, bishops, missionaries and theological professors of many faiths who have contributed to both platform and classes in the strong presentation of religion, its history, theory and "weekday power."

Dr. Jesse L. Hurlbut was a source of strength to Dr. Vincent from the second year of the Assembly. He supervised the Normal Classes, assisted with the CLSC, taught the Adult Bible Class each Sunday afternoon, lectured in Palestine Park and on the platform. He appeared at the other independent Chautauquas and sometimes managed their programs and studies. He attended Chautauqua for fifty years and in 1921 recorded his memories of its growth in a book, "The Story of Chautauqua."

In this book Dr. Hurlbut tells about the establishment of the Daily Devotional Hour in 1882 by Dr. Benjamin M. Adams at Bishop Vincent's request. Afterward (and we are not sure when "afterward" was)

The Hall of Missions

WHAT IS CHAUTAUQUA?

"Chautauqua is a force, developing the realities of life in the consenting personality."

George E. Vincent

CLUB PROGRAMS

The greater share of Chautauquans, it is safe to say, are of a gregarious nature and consequently, have organized themselves into interest groups with their own activities. These clubs have become increasingly important, since they bring additional program talent to the Grounds and share it with other Chautauquans, increasing the overall variety in the daily schedule. The Clubs' projects for raising money for worthwhile causes, such as scholarships, Old First Night and beautifying the Grounds usually provide pleasurable pastimes for many other Chautauquans, as well as themselves.

The list of clubs changes from time to time as Chautauquans themselves do, but at present, the following clubs have regular schedules and programs: The Women's Club; the Bird, Tree and Garden Club; the CLSC; the Sports Club; the Chautauqua Circle of the Daughters of the American Revolution; the Boys' and Girls' Clubs; the Golf Club; the Tennis Association; the Yacht Club; the Youth Activities Center; and the Art Association.

All of these clubs are available to the public under their own prescribed rules consistent with the nature of each group. Many are the good times that are shared by Chautauquans through club activities and meetings. Newcomers may watch for announcements in The Chautauquan Daily concerning all of these clubs. Even those Chautauquans who are on the Grounds for a short time may join or attend Women's Club meetings, for example, or those of the Bird, Tree and Garden Club, both of which have excellent and well-publicized programs each week of the season.

NEWSPAPER "IN THE WOODS"

The Chautauqua Assembly Daily Herald made its appearance in 1876, the third season of the Assembly. It was a private enterprise with Dr. Theodore L. Flood as editor and Mr. Milton Bailey of Jamestown, publisher. Dr. Flood continued as editor until 1899 and became the publisher in 1880.

The name of the newspaper was changed to The Chautauquan Assembly Herald in 1878 and to The Chautauquan Daily in 1906. After Dr. Flood's retirement, the Assembly became the publisher.

The Daily is one of the most unusual in the country, since it appears for only the weeks of the Chautauqua season and is written "in the woods" some miles from its printing shop. Because it carries the news of the Chautauqua program, its columns often contain firsthand accounts of national and world leaders or outstanding artists who are visiting or performing on the Grounds.

The newspaper's 100th anniversary was observed during the 1976 season. Historical supplements were included in the ten Saturday issues, each covering a decade of Chautauqua reporting. The Bird, Tree and Garden Club planted a tree in the Arboretum in honor of The Daily's birthday. Former staff members and business employees gathered with the 1976 staff for a reunion picnic.

The Chautauqua newspaper has served as a proving ground for many young writers who have gone on to find journalistic or literary careers. Ida M. Tarbell is one of the most famous authors to have spent an apprenticeship with the Chautauqua publications.

The Garden Statue of St. Francis of Assisi at the Hall of Missions

a weekly chaplain was named to preach on Sunday, at the Daily Devotional Hour and sometimes to teach or lecture. "The greatest preachers in the American pulpit have spoken at this service (the Devotional Hour). . .," Dr. Hurlbut declared.[18] This chaplain-of-the-week plan is still followed.

The School of Sacred Literature and the Chautauqua School of Theology also served to support the religion emphasis at Chautauqua. In 1896 when the former school had increased its faculty, Professor Shailer Mathews was listed as a new faculty member. Dr. Mathews became increasingly important to Chautauqua. He organized and directed the Department of Religion from 1912 to 1933 and served as an Institution Trustee from 1914 to 1937. Dean of the Divinity School of the University of Chicago, he brought high credentials to his combined religion and education responsibilities at Chauatuqua. Other outstanding clergymen succeeded him. Dr. Herbert W. Blashfield was listed as Secretary of Religious Program through 1942. Dr. Alfred E. Randell was named Religion Department Director in 1944. (He had been Secretary of the Department in 1943.) He served through 1958 when he was followed by Dr. Henry Smith Leiper. Dr. Leiper continued through 1967. Dr. Herbert Gezork assumed the leadership in 1968, serving until the close of the 1972 season. Dr. Alton M. Motter was designated as Acting Director of the Religion Department in 1973 with Dr. Loew coming in 1974. Dr. Loew served ten years, retiring at the end of the 1983 season. He was followed by Dr. Wiliam N. Jackson. These Department of Religion directors with their wide acquaintances among preachers, teachers and scholars throughout the world, have drawn to Chautauqua excellent thinkers and speakers. Consequently, the Department's program has been both inspirational educational, and consistent with Bishop Vincents' goals: the best talent and pan-denominationalism.

IN THE SUMMER SCHOOLS

WHILE A NEWCOMER may have caught a glimpse of college young people on the beach or in the Plaza, he has not seen a true cross section of Chautauqua students until he has visited Kellogg Hall just before the Summer School begins. In the airy rooms of this old building there is a furor of registration which aptly illustrates the breadth and appeal of the Chautauqua Summer School.

There are high school students who are coming to study music and play in one of the School's orchestras; there are graduate music students who have followed a favorite teacher to his summer studio. There are students in art and dance, beginning with those who seem so very young, and including those with more years of study. There are those who have come for the Writers' Workshop and parents who want to arrange tutoring for their children. There are sometimes doctors and lawyers who may want to study piano or gourmet cooking while they are on vacation. Over 1,900 students were enrolled in 1985 in the overall Summer School program, not counting the Boys' and Girls' Clubs and the Children's School.

Section 2 includes: Open Enrollment courses, Special Studies and Youth Activities.

The study of music follows an expected pattern with both class and individual instruction available and recommended. Art, dance and theater instruction is given in a classroom environment. Short-term registration is possible although most serious students come for the entire period. The Art Center is open for eight weeks. The School of Music and the School of Dance extend for seven weeks. In the Theater School, the Conservatory Theater Company (for ages 19 and up) continues for eight weeks while the Studio II section (for ages 16-18) completes its work in seven weeks.

Extra benefits of Chautauqua study are found in the opportunities to enjoy symphony concerts, artists' recitals, operas, plays, art exhibits and dance programs. Contacts with performing artists and outstanding individuals from all walks of life are possible and become a catalyst in the learning process.

There are fifty-nine faculty members in the School of Music; twenty-eight at the Art Center; four in the School of Dance; and seven in the Theater School. Four foreign countries were represented in the 1985 faculty: England, Japan, Canada and Australia.

Chautauqua's School of Special Studies consists of over one hundred courses which range in length from one-day workshops to nine-week classes. Planned to satisfy the vacationer's interest in short-term learning experiences often in untried, stimulating areas or skills, these courses provide opportunities for lifelong learning and are consistent with Chautauqua's tradition of popular education. At Chautauqua education is a vacation/recreation activity. The Special Studies Courses might include: Career Decision-Making; Shorthand in One Week; Personal Computing Potpourri; Introduction to Word Processing; Ballroom and Line Dancing; Chess Made Easy or For Advanced Players; Golf Clinics; Creative Crochet; Flower Arranging with instructions on specific needs, such as making a Williamsburg Wreathe or decorating your church; writing for Publication; American Sign Language; Creating Wellness; Antiques; Pierced and Cut Lampshades and Painting the Oriental Way. There are foreign language studies and tutorial arrangements possible. There are Special Studies Courses for all ages.

Besides State University of New York, Fredonia College credit for music workshops, many Chautauqua Summer School courses in music are approved by the New York State Department of Education Office of Non-collegiate Sponsored Instruction. These courses are toward undergraduate credit and are approved as recommended toward Regents College Degrees which are granted full accreditation by the Middle States Association of Colleges and Schools. Chautauqua credit hour equivalencies are based on their specific recommendation. Students must declare their desire for credit recommendations at the time of enrollment. It is the home school's option to accept, reject or alter the credit recommendation. Students should contact their college regarding acceptance.

There are a number of aspects of the Chautauqua System of Education that are noteworthy. The Schools' curriculums are flexible, always changing to meet the demands of the times, always seeking to be relevant. A brief history of the course offerings and the mechanics of study at Chautauqua will substantiate the claim.

The Normal Classes with which and for which the Assembly began in 1874 were a sign of those times. They had been organized within most Protestant denominations to give Sunday School teachers learning that was similar to that of the Normal Schools which prepared public school teachers for their work.

The sessions at Fair Point were designed to be intensive and thorough study periods alternated with relaxation and entertainment. Very little had been done in this country up to that time in the development of summer schools, so the Chautauqua Assembly was pioneering when it organized vacation study.

After the first year, the founders recognized that the same principles of good Sunday School teaching and administration could not be studied forever by the same people, although they believed that there is always variety in the study of the Bible. Consequently, in the second year of the Assembly, they made some changes in the teaching of Sunday School methods, continued Bible study and added the study of Hebrew; in the third year, they added New Testament Greek; and in the sixth year, 1879, Latin, German, French, Oriental languages and Anglo Saxon. The School of Languages, under which these studies were offered, was the first formal beginning of a separate Chautauqua Summer School. It must be added that kindergarten instruction had been available previously and was continued, becoming more "scientific" from year to year.

A Teachers' Retreat was held for public school teachers during that summer in 1879 with outstanding educators from leading universities as lecturers.

The next year the School of Languages and Teachers' Retreat were united and the summer school program was enlarged. The National Education Association had its annual meeting at Chautauqua, an event which implied national recognition of Chautauqua's educational work.

Year by year new departments were added. Instruction in the use of the microscope and telescope was one of the early innovations. The Chautauqua School of Theology and a system of correspondence courses were initiated in 1881. Instruction in music theory began. (The correspondence courses were an out-

growth of Dr. Vincent's ideas concerning the CLSC. While two other attempts had previously been made in correspondence teaching, Chautauqua's efforts in this line became better known. The still-functioning International Correspondence Schools of Scranton, Pa., did not begin until 1891, ten years after Chautauqua first offered this type of education.)

Dr. William Rainey Harper joined the faculty in 1883 as an instructor in Hebrew. He was then a professor in the Baptist School of Theology in Morgan Park, Illinois, and was said to be a dynamic teacher, capable of arousing a class to its best efforts.

With the receipt of a new charter from the State Legislature in 1883, Chautauqua gathered together its various educational programs under a new designation, Chautauqua University. Eventually all the academic subjects were listed under the College of Liberal Arts. In 1887 Dr. Harper was made Principal of the College of Liberal Arts. In this position, he made an outstanding contribution to the growth and worth of the Chautauqua Summer School. In 1891 he was accorded the high honor of being invited to become the first president of a reestablished institution, the University of Chicago.

Despite his new responsibilities, he remained in a place of leadership at Chautauqua through 1898. (In 1895 the Chautauqua Summer School had been again reorganized under Dr. Harper.) Even after 1898, however, he appeared on the Chautauqua platform. Into the development of the new university in Chicago, he took ideas that had been worked out at Chautauqua: summer, correspondence and extension courses.

In 1886 the School of Physical Education was formed under the direction of Dr. W. G. Anderson of the Adelphi Academy in Brooklyn. The growth of this school was dramatic and continued for decades, eventually joining the New York Universtity program which was developed at Chautauqua in the nineteen twenties.

When Dr. Vincent was elected a bishop in the Methodist Episcopal Church in 1888, his son, George E. Vincent, was made Vice Principal of Instruction at Chautauqua to assist his father. Ten years later George Vincent was to become Principal and assume an even larger role in the supervision of Chautauqua's educational system, both the school and the platform. He became president of the Institution in 1907.

In the year 1888 another new venture was tried, a University Extension series, a plan whereby successive lectures on a subject were given in communities throughout the country by lecturers who were sent out by Chautauqua University. Syllabi were printed and distributed, and printed questions were to be answered at home and returned to the lecturer for his correction and comments. University credit was given for these courses when they were completed satisfactorily.

In 1889 the School of Music was formally established with instructors in all departments and Dr. H. R. Palmer named as General Director of Music. Palmer had come part-time to Chautauqua as early as 1879, working with William Sherwin and C. C. Case, but with Sherwin's death, Dr. Palmer assumed more responsibility. He remained in a position of leadership until 1901. During his tenure, the fame of Chautauqua

Creativity at the
Children's School

as a music center spread; its quality of music education increased; and its faculty had sufficient attainment to appear as performers on the Assembly program. One of the musicians who lent considerable prestige to Chautauqua's music was William H. Sherwood who came to head the piano department the same year in which Dr. Palmer became Music Director. Sherwood came every summer until his death in 1910.

Following Dr. Palmer, Alfred Hallam headed Chautauqua music for the next eighteen years. During this period, choral music was emphasized, instruction in public school music was expanded and the musical offerings were generally widened. Instrumental instruction was gradually extended. Hallam attracted good teachers and performers and may have been responsible for the New York Symphony Orchestra's entrance into Chautauqua.

H. Augustine Smith served as Musical Director during most of the twenties. During his seven years some notable achievements are recorded. His gift for pageantry and large choral productions was outstanding. The residency of the symphony orchestra lifted the entire music program to a new plane. The performance of opera in English in the Amphitheater in 1926 was a landmark event. The summer of 1927 was Mr. Smith's last season.

Albert Stoessel directed the overall musical program at Chautauqua in 1928, but he was not officially appointed Director of Music until the following year. As director, he oversaw the School of Music as well as the orchestra program and the opera productions. Following his death, Evan Evans, who had been head of the Vocal Department since 1937, assumed the Directorship of the Music School. He held both positions until his death in 1954, but 1953 was his last summer at Chautauqua. After Mr. Stoessel's death, the orchestra and opera, like the Music School, functioned separately and have continued to do so.

Julius Huehn of the Eastman School of Music succeeded Evan Evans and remained as Music School Director until 1960 when illness caused him to resign. Dr. James Yannatos was acting Director in 1964 and Director for the next two years. He was followed by Dr. Evan Whallon who occupied the post for five years (1968-1972). While there have been some years when the Music School functioned directly under the Summer School head, in 1972 Robert V. Woodside combined these responsibilities in a special way. As longtime official organist and pipe organ teacher and with his other extensive music experience, Mr. Woodside was well able to give direction to the School of Music, as well. Nathan Gottschalk is the present Director.

Even in the early '90s, the educational tools that were being utilized at Chautauqua were not widely used elsewhere. However, as the full-time universities began to adopt vacation study, correspondence and extension work, Chautauqua changed its own emphasis. It doffed its pioneering garb and sought its next role in the emerging American educational drama.

The use of "University" was dropped from Chautauqua's school brochures in 1892 and the term "Chautauqua System of Education" was coined. The power to

Painting in the Quad

grant degrees, which had been sparingly used, was voluntarily relinquished in 1898.

After the turn of the century, the Chautauqua Summer School concentrated most of its promotion on professional courses for public school teachers, the music courses and cultural studies of a broad nature.

One surprise was the coordinated Arts and Crafts program which was launched in 1900 and drew much enthusiasm since few places offered instruction in so many crafts. Furniture-making and carving were skills that attracted students who remained during the winter and "Chautauqua Furniture" came on the market after the winter sessions.

Another noteworthy development was the Library School under Melvil Dewey, New York State Librarian. This School continued until World War II and later was reactivated by Syracuse University and later by the University of Pittsburgh.

During the early 1900s, Summer Institutes for teachers were held. Courses that teachers completed at Chautauqua in these Institutes were recognized for credit on teachers' certificates in New York State and by other New York schools. College credit courses at Chautauqua were successively offered by New York University, Syracuse University, the State University of New York, Fredonia, and the University of Pittsburgh. The change of one university relation to another reflects again Chautauqua's responsiveness to changing conditions. In 1975 a new broad credit equivalency service was devised. (See Page 47).

Even a short history of the Summer School should include the names of those who carried leadership from time to time in this most unusual Chautauqua System of Education.

During George Vincent's term as Institution president (1907-1915), he was assisted in the supervision of the Summer School by Scott Brown, Arthur E. Bestor and Percy H. Boynton. The latter had been active as Secretary of Instruction, but was made Principal in 1913, serving through 1916. He was followed by Dr. Elmer B. Bryan, president of Colgate University, who remained for two years. The burden of the Chautauqua Summer School proved too heavy for Dr. Bryan when added to his Colgate responsibilities. After his resignation, Mr. Bestor, who had succeeded George Vincent as President, became Principal of Instruction,

The practice shacks are small rehearsal rooms for students or anyone who wants to practice musical skills.

as well. President Bestor had a number of valuable assistants so that the Summer School continued to be strong. Among them was Charles E. Peirce who later became Institution Secretary. Mr. Peirce served as Acting Dean and as Secretary of Instruction from 1927 to 1937. Elsie Hartzell was Registrar from 1940 to 1950.

Ralph McCallister assumed responsibilities in connection with both the education and program departments in 1944, eventually becoming vice president for these two areas. He had come to Chautauqua at a time when Chautauquans were shocked by the death of their beloved Dr. Bestor, but it was generally agreed that he carried on the high quality of school and platform program which Dr. Bestor had maintained. Mr. McCallister resigned in 1961. Mrs. Ruth Skinner Hutchins served as Registrar of the Summer School from 1950 through 1961.

Dr. Helen M. Overs and the late Dr. Ruth Ranson each directed the School for two years and one year, respectively, before Joseph C. Clarke came in 1964. Mr. Clarke became vice president for education, remaining until 1970 when he resigned. Under his leadership, the Summer School made orderly progress and the scholarship program continued to grow. Lincoln Dormitory was built during Mr. Clarke's term of office and other significant planning for the future was explored. So great was the confidence in Mr. Clarke that he was selected and persuaded to serve as executive vice president of the Institution in the interim between Dr. Haug's resignation and Dr. Remick's inau-

---

"Chautauqua is an idea, embracing the 'all things' of life—art, science, society, religion, patriotism, education— whatsoever tends to enlarge, refine and ennoble the individual, to develop domestic charm and influence, to make the nation stronger and wiser, and to make Time and Eternity seem to be what they are—parts of one noble and everlasting whole."

John H. Vincent
in the Introduction
A Reading Journey Through Chautauqua
by Frank Chapin Bray

---

guration as President. Mr. Clarke was greatly honored by Chautauquans for contributing his service to the Institution for another year after having just resigned from the supervision of the Summer School. He was made an honorary trustee of the Institution and continues to serve in this capacity.

Burdell F. Cotten directed the Summer School for one year. Then in late 1971, Mr. Woodside became Assistant to President Remick, for Education. In this position, he developed the School's curriculum, expanded the workshop format that Chautauqua had pioneered, and increased the variety of Special Interest or Enrichment Courses. With his own background in music, he was aware of the music students' needs for ensemble experience as well as individual lessons and made both these opportunities part of each student's program. Thus, there was a new emphasis on chamber music. He structured a new Preparatory Division so that younger, less experienced music students could find appropriate instruction and ensemble work. In 1975, however, Mr. Woodside was made vice president and assistant secretary of the Institution, shifting his responsibilities from the Summer School to the general program.

Dr. Joseph V. Totaro was named Dean of Educational Services in August, 1975. He served until January 1, 1977. He continued as Professor of Education at SUNY-Fredonia while he was Dean at Chautauqua.

Jean Quinette, who became year-round Summer School Secretary in 1964 and later was named Registrar and Assistant to Dean Totaro, has occupied the position of Coordinator of the Summer Schools since 1977. Marcie D. Larson was Summer School Registrar from 1974 to 1976.

In May, 1980, Richard R. Redington was appointed Director of Education, Youth and Recreation in a newly-defined position that unified programs of education and recreation for both youth and adults. In the fall of 1983, Mr. Redington was named Vice President of Education, Youth and Recreation.

Throughout the changing of leadership roles, however, Chautauqua's basic educational attitudes and beliefs have continued. It has always offered intensive instruction for the specialist, the serious student who is working toward a specific goal, and also courses of a more popular nature for general enrichment. The latter courses have appealed to vacationers who want to keep busy but not work too strenuously.

Chautauqua has believed that "education ends only with life," and has encouraged adults to continue purposefully the learning process. For this reason, the planned CLSC reading is considered an important part of the educational effort at Chautauqua, even today.

The Chautauqua System of Education has also coupled knowledge and skills with the goal of service, urging Chautauquans to fit themselves for some good work for the benefit of society.

In a report which was printed as part of the Year-Book of 1895, Chancellor John Heyl Vincent points out Chautauqua's "complete cooperation among the educational factors of society," and states the philosophic goals of the total educational program at Chautauqua.

"If the scholars and the people are to come together," Dr. Vincent wrote, "the various agencies which each represents must be utilized in a common aim . . .Chautauqua has from the first put great stress upon this cooperation of agencies in education: the home, the weekday school, the Sunday School, the pulpit, the pastorate, the lyceum, the press and whatsoever besides can in any way make for the uplift of humanity as a whole."[19]

He builds the case for the sacredness of all parts of life, an attitude that does not separate religion from life. He says, "People who have been impressed with the thought—the radical thought—that Chautauqua is a distinctive educational institution should not be allowed through any emphasis placed upon its entertainment on one hand, or its rigidities of class discipline on the other, to imagine that the religious and spiritual mission of Chautauqua has been overlooked. Chautauqua is nothing if not religious. It is denominational. It is undenominational. It is not so much

ROLLER COASTER

A roller coaster with five hundred feet of track was a new attraction at Chautauqua in 1885, and properly or not, it was advertised as "good for the health." While not much is known about this structure and how it came to Chautauqua, announcements refer to its location at the northwest corner of Hurst and Palestine Avenues near the Skating Rink which occupied the intersection of Scott, Root and Palestine Avenues. The Skating Rink was the site of the first Physical Education classes and once served as the location for the thriving Bicycle School.

SECRET OF SUCCESS

"Chautauqua seeks to adapt itself to the wants of the time. It tries to be flexible and supply whatever it sees needed."

George E. Vincent
speaking in 1901
Scrapbook III, p. 78.

undenominational as pan-denominational. It is so religious that it embraces with breadth of liberality all religions . . .

"It is religious, but it does not forget the religiousness of all legitimate pursuits and studies. It believes rather in an informing force of life than a formal cult . . ."[20]

"As in the past, so in the future," the Bishop continued, "it must be the purpose of Chautauqua to maintain both branches of its service at their maximum of effectiveness. The scholastic work must attract the specialist, and the popular work must continue to reach the people . . ."[21]

Apathy, the enemy of education, has been the target of Chautauqua's effort. An atmosphere of "seeking" has been engendered naturally. Joy in learning and the ambition to accomplish more has proved to be the contagion Chautauqua has spread indiscriminately.

The young men in the School exhibited teamwork and drill. There were rowing teams, "serious" baseball with Alonzo Stagg from Yale as an assistant and professional studies in physical education. Croquet, roque, tennis and golf were introduced early because recreation was a fundamental part of the Chautauqua experience.

AMONG THE DISTINGUISHED VISITORS AND PROGRAM FIGURES THROUGH 1976

United States Presidents
Ford, Gerald R., July 30, 1965
  Face the Press
Garfield, James A. 1880
Grant, Ulysses S. 1875
Hayes, Rutherford B. 1889
Hoover, Herbert
  out of season, May 25, 1922
McKinley, William, August 23, 1895
Roosevelt, Franklin D.
  1917, 1919, 1929, 1936
Roosevelt, Theodore
  1890, 1894, 1895, 1905, 1914 (Oct.)
Taft, William 1904

Presidential Candidates
Bryan, William Jennings
  July 6, 1907 August 16, 1912
Goldwater, Barry, July 4, 1961
Hughes, Charles Evans
  1907 (paid $55.06)
Kennedy, Robert, August 6, 1965
  Face the Press
Landon, Alf, August 26, 1936
Muskie, Sen. Edward
  August 12, 1966
Rockfeller, Nelson 1958, 1962
Romney, George, August 4, 1967
Smith, Al 1926 (Paid $360)
Stassen, Harold 1958, 1967, 1973, 1974
Thomas, Norman
  1933, 1936, 1948, 1952
Wallace, Henry
  Secretary of Agriculture 1934
  (later Vice President)

The following are some of the distinguished visitors at Chautauqua:

Musicians
Akiyama, Kazuyoshi
Altsculer, Modest
Anderson, Marian
Antoine, Josephine
Atkins, Chet
Autori, Franco
Ax, Emanuel
Bacon, Katherine
Ballard, Earline
Bampton, Rose
Barab, Seymour
Barrere, Georges
Basie, Count
Bates, Leon
Bender, David
Berberian, Ara
Berlin, Patricia
Bible, Frances
Bimboni, Alberto
Bond, Carrie Jacobs
Borge, Victor
Bower, Beverly
Boxer, Harold
Britton, George
Bothers Four
Brott, Boris
Brown, Elaine
Brown, Les
Brown, Les and Band of Renown
Brubeck, Dave and Quartet
Buckley, Emerson
Bybell, Patricia
Bye, Erik
Carlyss, Earl
Case, C. C.
Case, Richard
Charry, Michael
Chautauqua Symphony Orchestra
Christiansen, Dr. Paul
Christopher, Russell
Cliburn, Van
Coci, Claire
Cole, Frances
Columbus Boy Choir

Comissiona, Sergiu
Connell, Horatio
Conradi, Austin
Costa, Mary
Craig, Patricia
Craighead, David
Criz, Henry
Crooks, Richard
Cumming, Robert
Dame, Donald
Damrosch, Walter
Darrenkamp, John
Daugherty, Lee
Davidson, John
Dello-Joie, Norman
Detroit Symphony Orchestra
di Virgilio, Nicholas
Dobbs, Mattiwilda
Downs, Olin
Duchin, Peter
Dufft, Carl E.
Eberly, Ray
Eckerberg, Sixten
Ellington, Duke
Erskine, John
Esch, Beverly Dame
Evans, Evan
Everly Brothers
Farrell, Eileen
Faull, Ellen
Feliciano, Jose
Ferrante and Teicher
Fiedler, Arthur
First Piano Quartet
Fiske Jubilee Singers
Fitzgerald, Ella
Fox, Virgil
Freeman, Ruth
French Military Band
Friml, Rudolph
Friskin, James
Friskin, Rebecca Clarke
Gallagher, Gil
Galvany, Marisa
Gaul, Harvey
Gershwin, George
Glazer, Frank
Golschmann, Vladimir
Goodwin, F. A.
Gordon, Marjorie
Gordon, Nathan
Grainger, Percy
Greenwell, Gean
Gutche, Gene
Hallam, Alfred
Hampton, Lionel
Hanson, Howard
Harness, William
Harth, Sidney
Harvard Glee Club
Harvuot, Clifford
Hayes, Roland
Hempel, Freida
Hendl, Walter
Henderson, Skitch
Herbert, Victor and Orchestra
Herman, Woody and Orchestra
Hinderas, Natalie
Hines, Jerome
Hirt, Al
Hollander, Lorin
Horne, Marilyn
Howe, Walter
Huehn, Julius
Huffman, Herbert
Hutcheson, Ernest
Inoue, Michi
Irving, Robert
Iturbi, Jose
James, Sonny
Janiec, Henry
Jepson, Helen
Johanos, Donald
Johnson, Reber
Jones, Betty
Katims, Milton
Kenny Rogers and the First Edition
Kenton, Stan
Kilby, Muriel
King Family
Kingston Trio
Kness, Richard
Kohanski, Paul
Kolar, Victor
Krachmalnick, Jacob
Krall, Heidi
Krebiel, Dorothy
Kullman, Charles
Lane, Louis
Lathbury, Mary

Lebrun, Louise
Libling, Max
Listemann, Bernhard
Lloyd, David
Lombardo, Guy and Orchestra
Lovett, Julia
Lymann, Howard
Madeira, Jean
Marlowe, Jeffry and Ronald
Marsh, Ozan
Mason, Marilyn
Matushevski, Voytek
McCrea, John
McGovern, Maureen
McKnight, Ann
McKuen, Rod
McPartland, Marian
Meier, Johanna
Meister, Barbara
Melton, James
Mendelssohn Choir of Pittsburgh
Menuhin, Hephzibah
Menuhin, Yehudi
Mercer, Ruby
Merrill, Robert
Miquelle, Georges
Mischakoff, Mischa
Mitchell, Howard
Mitropoulos, Dimitri
Montgomery, Dr. Merle
Moog, Dr. Robert A.
Moore, Grace
Moore, Melba
Mormon Tabernacle Choir
Moye, Eugene
Murphy, Edward
Neeley, Marilyn
Nero, Peter
New York Brass Quintet
New York Symphony Orchestra
New Zealand Band
Neway, Patricia
Norman, Jesseye
North Carolinians
Olefsky, Paul
Oliver (William Oliver Swofford)
Palmer, Horatio, R.
Patacchi, Val
Paul Winter Consort
Peebles, Joan
Pellerite, James
Peters, Roberta
Phraner, Leighton
Pierce, Billie
Pierce, DeDe
Pittsburgh Symphony Orchestra
Porter, Hugh
Potter, Harrison
Preservation Hall Band
Quilico, Louis
Raitt, John
Rochester Opera Company
Rose, John
Rose, Leonard
Roy, Will
Russian Symphony Orchestra
Ruttenberg, Marian
Samaroff-Stokowski, Olga
Sankey, Ira D.
Savoia, Rosa
Schein, Ann
Schermerhorn, Kenneth
Schickele, Professor Peter
  (P.D.Q.Bach)
Schoenberg, Arnold
Scruggs, Earl
Serendipity Singers
Shankar, Ravi
Shearing, George
Sherwin, William
Sherwood, William
Skram, Knut
Slatkin, Leonard
Smith, H. Augustine
Smith, Norwood
Sorel, Claudette
Sousa, John Philip
Sozio, Peter
Spaulding, Albert
Speaks, Oley
Spitalny, Phil and Orchestra
Steber, Eleanor
Steigerwalt, Gary
Steinberg, William
Stellman, Maxine
Stoessel, Albert
Swann, Frederick
Swarthout, Gladys
Sze, Yi Kwei
Tennesseans

Terry, Warren Lee
Thibault, Conrad
Thomas, John Charles
Thomas, Michael Tilson
Thompson, Hugh
Tibbett, Lawrence
Torkanowsky, Werner
Tucker, Richard
U.S. Air Force Band
U.S. Army Field Band and Chorus
Uppman, Theodor
Ushioda, Masuko
Valenti, Alfredo
Varga, Lazio
Vincent, Henry
Vitale, Joseph
Volkel, George
VonSauer, Mme. Angelica
Walker, William
Warfield, William
Washburn, Charles
Weaver, John
Whiteman, Paul and Orchestra
Whittemore and Lowe,
  duo piano team
Wild, Earl
Wilkins, Frederick
Williams, Roger
Willeki, Willem
Woodside, Robert V.
Willson, Meredith
Welk Orchestra and soloists
  without Lawrence Welk
Yeend, Frances
Zinman, David

Dancers
Adair, Tom
Bonnefoux, Jean-Pierre
Carow, Joe
d'Amboise, Jacques
Danilova, Alexandra
Hendl, Susan
Kent, Allegra
McBride, Patricia
Pittsburgh Ballet Theatre
Richardson, Naomi
Shawn, Ted
Villella, Edward

Distinguished Visitors at Chautauqua
Abbott, Lyn
Aberdeen, The Marquis of
Aberdeen, Lady
Adams, Alexander G.
Adams, Maude
Addams, Jane
Adebo, Chief S. O.
al Farugi, Dr. Isma'il R.
al Farugi, Lois Lamya
Alvarez, Dr. W. O.
Anderson, Dr. Jesse
Angell, James B.
Angell, Sir Norman
Anglin, Margaret
Anthony, Susan B.
Aptheker, Dr. Herbert
Babson, Roger
Bach, Marcus
Bailey, Maj. Gen. Charles J.
Baker, Dr. Robert
Balchen, Bernt
Bangs, John Kendrick
Baldwin, Hanson
Barnes, Dr. Ronald
Bauer, Marion
Baumbach, Jonathan
Beale, Ambassador Oliver H.
Beard, Frank
Beaver, James A.
Bell, Alexander Graham
Bennett, Dr. Thomas R. II
Berger, Victor L.
Bestor, Paul
Bethune, Mary McCleod
Birren, Dr. James E.
Bjerro, Jens
Black, Hugh
Bolling, Dr. Landrum
Booth, Dr. Edward Prince
Brewster, Dr. Kingman, Jr.
Brogan, D. W.
Brooks, Dr. Henry
Brooks, Phillips
Brown, Gordon
Brown, Dr. Noel J.
Bryce, Lord
Buckley, Dr. J.M.
Bunche, Ralph

Burgess, John W.
Burton, Dr. Richard
Buttrick, Dr. David
Buttrick, Dr. George A.
Byrd, Admiral Richard E.
Cadman, S. Parkes
Campbell, Dr. Anne
Campbell, Dr. Ernest D.
Canham, Erwin
Catt, Carrie Chapman
Chang, Sr. Chentung Lieng
Chang, Dr. Chun Ming
Chase, John P.
Church, Col. Samuel H.
Ciardi, John
Clemenceau, Georges
Clemenceau, Mme. Georges
Clews, Henry
Coe, Dr. Chalmars
Colby, Bainbridge
Colvin, D. Leigh
Commager, Dr. Henry S.
Comstock, Anthony
Conwell, Russell H.
Cosby, Bill
Cousins, Norman
Cuomo, George
Daly, Dr. Mary
Davenport, Marcia
Davis, The Rev. Evelyn
Dean, Vera Micheles
Dewey, John
Dewey, Melvil
Dietz, Dr. David
Dirksen, Congressman Everett M.
Dixon, Jeane
Doremus, Prof. R. Ogden
Doty, Arthur M.
Doty, Robert M.
Drummond, Henry
Dubos, Dr. Rene
Duff, Sen. James H.
Earhart, Amelia
Edison, Gov. Charles
Edison, Mina Miller
Edison, Thomas A.
Ehrensvard, Dr. Goestra
Eielson, Carl B.
Eliot, Charles W.
Engle, Paul
Fallows, Bishop Samuel
Fedje, Dr. Raymond N.
Ferguson, Charles W.
Ferre, Dr. Nels F. S.
Filene, Edward W.
Fine, Benjamin
Finley, Dr. John H.
Finlay, Dr. Terrence J.
Fiorato, Hugo
Fish, Hamilton
Fishbein, Dr. Morris
Fisher, Irving
Fiske, John
Fitzgerald, Scott
Flemming, Dr. Arthur S.
Ford, Henry
Fosdick, Dr. Harry Emerson
Foster, Lawrence
Francis, Robert
Franck, Dr. Frederick
Frank, Glenn
Fuertes, Louis Agassiz
Garlin, Hamlin
Gezork, Dr. Herbert
Goldberg, Dr. Martin J.

Goncharoff, Dr. Nicholas T.
Goodell, Sen. Charles E.
Gordis, Dr. Robert
Gordon O. O.
Graziphene, Dr. Leonard R.
Green, Dr. and Mrs. Elmer
Greenfell, Dr. Alfred
Grewe, Ambassador Wilhelm
Guy, Dr. William V.
Guyer, Congressman Tennyson
Hale, Edward Everett
Hammond, Mrs. John Henry
Hapgood, Norman
Harbord, Maj. Gen. J. C.
Hastings, Congressman James F.
Hayward, Dr. Beresford
Hazelton, Dr. Roger
Heath, Dr. Douglas H.
Henning, Edward B.
Hertz, Dr. Richard C.
Higby, Wayne
Hirschberg, Dr. J. Cotter
Hodes, William
Hofgren, Ambassador Daniel W.
Housman, Dr. Russell
Howe, Julia Ward
Hoyt, Dr. Kenneth
Huffmann, Dr. John A., Jr.
Hughes, Charles Evans
Hunter, Dr. Howard E.
HuShih, Ambassador
Jackson, Dr. Blyden
Jackson, The Rev. Paul G.
James, Dr. William
Janeway, Eliot
Janeway, Elizabeth
Jefferson, Joseph
Jerome, William Travers
Jones, The Honorable William Bowdoin
Jorden, Dr. Clarence
Joyce, Dr. Bruce
Judd, Dr. Walter
Kagawa, Dr. Toyohiko
Keating, Sen. Kenneth
Keller, Helen
Kennedy, Charles Rann
Kennedy, Ethel
Keohane, Dr. Robert O.
Kimbrough, Emily
Kipling Rudyard
Klein, Herbert
Kniker, Dr. Charles
Koppel, Ted
Krupsak, Lt. Gov. Mary Anne
Kuhn, Margaret E.
Kuo, James K. Y.
LaFollette, Gov. Robert M.
LaKing, Ambassador George R.
Lawrence, David L.
Laubach, Dr. Frank
Leach, Henry Goodar
Lee, Everett
Lee, Ivy L.
Lewis, Fulton
Lindbergh, Charles A.
Lindsay, Mayor John V.
Lindsay, Veghel
Lindsay, Judge Ben
Loew, Dr. Ralph W.
Logan, John A.
Logue, Edward J.
Lonaeus, Gunnar
Lundine, Congressman Stanley
MacGowan, Kenneth
MacInnis, Dr. Donald E.

Makowski, Mayor Stanley
Malik, Dr. Charles
Malone, Ted
Mamadouwane, Deputy Minister Bocar
Manion, Dr. Clarence
Marney, Dr. Carlyle
Marshall, Thurgood
Marty, Dr. Martin E.
Martz, Professor Marshall S.
Massey, Chester
Massey, Hart
Massey, Raymond
Massey, Vincent
Matthisen, Edith Wynne
Mayer, Dr. J. Richard
McCarthy, Eugene J.
McConnell, Bishop Francis J.
McCord, Dr. David
McCullough, Joseph
McDonald, James G.
McMillan, Donald
Menninger, Jeanetta
Menninger, Dr. Karl A.
Menninger, Dr. Robert G.
Menninger, Dr. W. Walter
Menninger, William C.
Midttun, Harold Swanoe
Mitchell, Dr. Broadus
Mitchell, James P.
Mitchell, John R.
Montagu, Ashley
Moritz, The Honorable Bernard
Morrison, Kathleen
Morrison, Dr. Theodore
Morton, Robert R.
Musmanno, Michael A.
Mustin, Burt
Naguib, Mustafa
Nash, Bernard E.
Nason, John W.
National Band of New Zealand
Newbigin, The Rt. Rev. Leslie
Newman, Dr. Leslie
Nichols, Bishop Roy C.
Niebuhr, Reinhold
Niemoeller, Dr. Martin
Ochs, Adolph S.
Oliver, Dr. Covey T.
Ordway, Dr. Frederick I.
Overstreet, Harry and Bonaro
Page, Thomas Nelson
Pahk, Induk
Palmer, A. Mitchell
Pannell, Dr. Anne G.
Pearson, Drew
Peary, Mrs. Admiral Robert
Pennybacker, Mrs. Percy
Perkins, Frances
Persell, The Rt. Rev. C. B., Jr.
Peters, Dr. John L.
Peterson, Roger Troy
Phelps, Dr. William Lyon
Phillips, Ellis L., Jr.
Phillips, Kathryn Sisson
Phelan, Dean Thomas
Pike, Dr. James A.
Pollard, Dr. W. G.
Potter, Bishop Henry C.
Pound, Roscoe
Proxent, Senator Jess J.
Priest, Ivy Baker
Prior, Harris K.
Proudfoot, The Rev. James D.
Pyle, Howard
Ramsey, Sir William
Read, Dr. David H. C.
Read, Leonard E.
Reischauer Ambassador Edwin O.
Reuther, Victor
Rhode, Mrs. Owen
Riis, Jacob A.
Riley, James Whitcomb
Rivercomb, Senator Chapman
Robert, Gen. Henry M.
Robinson, Bishop Harold Barrett
Rockefeller, John D., Jr.
Rockefeller, Gov. Nelson A.
Rohde, Ruth Bryan
Roosevelt, Franklin D., Jr.
Roosevelt, Mrs. Franklin D.
Rountree, Martha
Rowan, Carl T.
Ruttenberg, Stanley
Sarg, Tony
Schultz, Douglas C.
Scribner, Dr. Harvey
Scott, Governor Robert W.
Seaman, Sir Owen
Selden, David
Semple, Robert B., Jr.

Gov. George Romney

Sergio, Lisa
Shafer, Gov. Raymond P.
Shapley, Dr. Harlow
Shaw, Anna Howard
Sittler, Dr. Joseph
Smith, William
Smith, Kitty Miller
Snowden, Mrs. Philip
Sochatoff, Dr. A. Fred
Sockman, Dr. Ralph W.
Somerset, Lady Henry
Spicer, Mrs. Donald
Stagg, Amos Alonzo
Stanley, Mrs. Herman
Stassen, Gov. Harold E.
Steckel, Ned
Steimle, Dr. Edmund A.
Stoessinger, John
Stokes, J. G. Phelps
Stone, John Timothy
Stone, Melville E.
Stransky, Father Thomas
Sullivan, Dr. Leon
Summerall, Gen. Charles P.
Swaim, Dr. J. Carter
Taft, Lorado
Talmadge, DeWitt
Tannenbaum, Rabbi Marc H.
Tarbell, Ida M.
Taylor, Gen. Maxwell
Thai, Vu Van
Thomas, Lowell
Thompson-Seton, Ernest
Tooze, Mrs. Fred J.
Torrini, Rudolph E.
Trueblood, Dr. Elton
Van Slyck, Philip
Vanderlip, Frank A.
Vaughan, Bishop Benjamin
Nool Young
Viereck, Dr. Peter
Wadsworth, Sen. James W.
Wallace, Lew
Walsh, Frank P.
Warshofsky, Fred
Washington, Booker T.
Washington, Mayor Walter
Webb, Bunyan
Wedel, Dr. Cynthia C.
Weeks, Edward
Wells, Dr. Kenneth D.
Wessell, Dr. Nils Y.
White, Dr. Paul Dudley
Whitlock, Brand
Wicker, Tom
Wickersham, George W.
Widdemer, Margaret
Wiggin, Kate Douglas
Wilkins, Sir George Hubert
Wilkins, Roy
Willard, Frances E.
Wilson. Charles E.
Wilson, Gov. Malcolm
Win, U, Ambassador
Winograd, Arthur
Woelfkin, Cornelius
Wolsey, Rabbi Louis
Woollcott, Alexander
Wood, James N.
Wright, Dr. Austin

Dr. Garra L. Lester, Chautauqua's community physician for more than 40 years, receives the Chautauqua Salute and a Plaque of Commendation at Old First Night in 1977. Vice President Woodside was presiding.

Rudolf Friml waves back.

3

The Spirit We Feel

ON JULY 23, 1967, Chautauqua paid host to a remarkable composer-pianist, Rudolph Friml. Five months after his appearance at Chautauqua, Mr. Friml was to celebrate his ninetieth birthday. Those in the audience knew this and appreciated the significance of his long and productive life. Many of them had been humming his tunes for decades.

There was, therefore, an air of affectionate expectancy when Dr. Haug came on stage to introduce Mr. Friml. President Haug ended his introduction by inviting the members of the audience to greet their guest with the Chautauqua Salute.

At the moment the short-statured, quick-stepping Mr. Friml entered the stage, the Amphitheater became a "moving" picture of waving white handkerchiefs.

True to his outgoing personality, Mr. Friml whipped out his own handkerchief and waved back with obvious delight.

Honor and appreciation had made a complete circle! This is one aspect of the Chautauqua Spirit.

The Chautauqua Salute is in itself an explanation of the Chautauqua Spirit.

It was in the Auditorium in the Grove on the afternoon of August 15, 1877, that Mr. S. L. Greene, a deaf man who was also unable to speak, appeared before the Assembly. He was from Ontario, Canada. With the assistance of a reader, James Hughes, also from Ontario, who presented Mr. Greene's introductory statements and explanations, Mr. Greene demonstrated the motions which represented certain words. Then Mr. Greene began his own "reading" of certain scriptural passages, including Christ Stilling the Tempest and The Lord's Prayer.

So vivid was his communication that the audience spontaneously applauded. Dr. Vincent was quick to realize that Mr. Greene could not hear this voice of approval. He suggested instead that Chautauquans wave their white handkerchiefs.

Ever since, this Salute of white handkerchiefs has been reserved for the highest praise that a Chautauqua audience wishes to bestow. By tradition, it is never given except at the invitation of the President of the Institution although there have been some spontaneous exceptions.

At the closing exercises in 1880, Dr. Davidson from Cleveland, rose from the audience and asked that the Chautauqua Salute be given for Dr. Vincent and it was done.

At the program on Recognition Day, August 22, 1888, a rainbow salute was given Bishop H. W. Warren, Commencement orator. People waved not only their white handkerchiefs, but also their Recognition Day programs which were printed on colored paper. This kind of a salute was given to Miss Kimball and others on different Recognition Days.

On Old First Nights after Lewis Miller's death (1899) a moment of silence was always observed in the founder's memory. In 1904, however, Bishop Vincent asked Chautauquans to observe the moment in a different way. He asked them to stand and raise their handkerchiefs reverently for a moment and then slowly lower them as a more visible expression of honor and memory.

When the first Chautauqua Salute was given, Dr. Hurlbut had described it as "white lilies dancing under the leaves of the trees. . ."[22]

For this reason, the silent raising and lowering of the handkerchiefs as a memorial is called "The Drooping of the Lilies." Both Salutes are entered into with the same pride and sincerity and one can sense the Spirit of Chautauqua on these occasions.

Chautauqua's first community bus which began to operate in 1962 was well-named The Spirit of Chautauqua, because it moved throughout the Grounds from day to day, a visible sign of the intangible "spirit."

The Spirit of Chautauqua served a great need, saving valuable time and energy for busy Chautauquans. It transported children to the Children's School and oldtimers up the hill; it helped residents on the edges of the campus keep their appointments and those who had stayed too long at the beach to get the dinner started on time; it offered a special 6:30 p.m. tour with commentary so that new and old Chautauquans could learn about the history of the Grounds; it provided special evening service to the Norton Hall performances with "home deliveries" to one's door. The first daytime fare was only ten cents so that many were observed riding the bus six times a day. Inflation raised the fare to fifteen cents. Now riding the buses around Chautauqua is a free service for the comfort of everyone, but most of all, an inducement for Chautauquans to refrain from driving private cars.

In the beginning bus service at Chautauqua was realized in the way most improvements are, by the generosity of one or more Chautauquans who recognize a need. In this case, it was Mrs. Elizabeth McCreery, a former member of the Board of Trustees.

For a long time, Mr. Charles E. Peirce, secretary of the Institution, had hoped for some form of public transportation especially since the use of private cars on the Grounds needed to be curtailed. About 1960 Mr. A. F. Hickman, president of the Sports Club, articulated the need of his club members for easy access to transportation up and down the hill. After considerable study, Mr. Hickman was convinced that a bus was the answer. When Mr. Peirce discussed the matter with Mrs. McCreery and she heard the estimated cost figure, she quickly agreed to supply the amount. For ten years Mr. Hickman supervised the annual bus maintenance and reported that income from fares usually balanced expenses.

It was Dr. John A. Reed who won the bus-naming contest in 1962 with his entry, The Spirit of Chautauqua. It was also "Doc" Reed, as he was affectionately known all during his days as Old First Night Director, who asssembled the original commentary which was given on the 6:30 p.m. tour.

Instead of just one bus, the Institution in 1986 operates seven electric-powered trams and four buses (two regular-sized buses and two mini-buses). Effort is made to set the routes to satisfy the needs of the public so that those who live on all parts of the Grounds can easily find a bus that may be expected to reappear every twenty minutes.

The evening tour bus is scheduled only several times each week. For that informational tour, a fee of $2.00 is charged.

Some mid-morning or afternoon when you are riding the bus, ring the bell and alight at the Boys' and

The Gingerbread Cottage

Girls' Clubs near Sharpe Memorial Athletic Field. If you will walk to the waterfront or to the baseball diamond or into Beeson Youth Center, you will see young Chautauquans in action with plenty of enthusiasm and competitive vigor. In their shining eyes, their spontaneous jumping up and down, their screams and groans as games wax and wane, you will see their enjoyment of Chautauqua, their "spirit."

If you ever witness these youth on Old First Night when they run down the aisles of the Amphitheater singing "Onward, Boys' Club! Onward, Girls' Club!",

Former WCTU headquarters at Chautauqua is now the Rogers' family home.

you will feel the thrill of seeing into Chautauqua's future.

Perhaps you are one who feels the Chautauqua Spirit at the Chautauqua Symphony Orchestra concerts. Sometimes the night is especially beautiful, the orchestra inspired, the numbers well-combined. On such nights as you leave the Amphitheater, you are exhilarated by the new insights you've experienced, and above all, by the yearning to make your own expression of them. This exhilaration and this wanting to reach out is part of the total Chautauqua experience and Spirit. It explains why so many Chautauquans return as often as they can. As David Morton wrote in The Chautauquan Daily, July 16, 1952: "They come, indeed, in response to one of the oldest impulses that we know: man's instinct to return again and yet again, to that which is the presence and source of the best that he has known."

The Chautauqua Spirit may be sensed as one views the homes of Chautauquans. The vacation homes that began to appear soon after the start of the Assembly reflect not only their period of American life, but also their owner's personal attachment to "the place" they loved.

At 34 Janes Avenue, The Ginger Bread Cottage, as Miss Pauline Fancher has called it, was in the Carrier family for four generations before Miss Fancher purchased it in 1962. This doll-size house was built in 1891, if not before, on a tent platform. It demonstrates folk art and may be referred to as American Gothic. Miss Fancher has partially winterized the house so that it may be enjoyed beyond the summer months. It is one of the most photographed spots on the Grounds. Coming upon it unexpectedly, one might believe he

had trespassed into the Victorian Age of the fairy tale locale of Hansel and Gretel. The quaint carving, the cozy upstairs porch that hides under the main roof all contribute to the cottage's charm.

The John S. Rogers' family home at 32 South Lake Drive was already in existence in 1895, according to the earliest record of Chautauqua homes that is presently available. It was probably built before that, however, since lake front property was developed early in the Assembly's history and 32 South Lake Drive is located just beyond the Athenaeum Hotel (1881).

The Chess family owned this home before the WCTU bought it in 1925. At that time the Frances E. Willard Memorial Window that had been installed in the WCTU Room in Kellogg Hall was moved to the new lake front headquarters. After the James G. Haller family purchased the property in 1946, the Willard Window was moved once again, this time to the national WCTU home in Evanston, Illinois. Mr. and Mrs. Rogers obtained the property in 1974.

The gables in this house, its tower, its decorative bargeboards and paired columns furnish another example of American folk art at Chautauqua. Farther south at 40 South Lake Drive, the large white frame house on the northwest corner has the distinction of having housed two of Chautauqua's presidents, Dr. W. H. Hickman and Judge W. Walter Braham. This house, too, represents an expansive era in American society when families enjoyed porches and leisurely gatherings.

The house next door, 38 South Lake Drive, has been in the Hukill family for over ninety years. Early in this century, the Hukill home underwent a modernization of its front exterior; early pictures show its first porch and abundance of carpenter's lace.

The Braham family home and the Hukill family home beyond, are both historic Chautauqua homes of the early period and are still enjoyed by members of those families.

The Carnahan home on North Lake Drive reflects its era at Chautauqua.

North of the Hukill home is the Bishop's Garden, the name given to the garden which occupies the former site of Bishop Vincent's combined cottage-tent home. This Garden becomes more and more beloved by Chautauquans for its natural beauties are well-tended and its location on the lake front makes it highly accessible. Bishop Vincent's granddaughter, Elizabeth Foster, recently gave a sculptured plaque of her grandfather which was installed in the Garden.

Modern Chautauquans have also been expressing their love for Chautauqua by building attractive, usable homes whose architecture reflects present-day living patterns. There is surprising variety in these more recently built homes along the North Shore. A ride on the bus takes one through this newer section.

The Carnahan residence on North Lake Drive has an interesting design. The varying levels of the roof on different parts of the house indicate how the architect had fitted the structure to the decline of the terrace toward the lake. Its modern functionalism has been made to look comfortable and inviting and the lawn which surrounds it gives a feeling of space and vacation pleasure.

In 1985 a new official summer residence for Chautauqua's President and his family was built on North Lake Drive beside College Hill Park. When it was completed there proved to be much that was appropriate, even special about this home that would serve Chautauqua Presidents for years to come. Its location was "inspired"—in "Old Chautauqua" but not far from a newer residential section. Set on the rise of the hill, it affords almost as many unobstructed views of the lake as it has windows and porches. In turn, it becomes a focus for boaters as they look toward shore. Dramatic exterior elements draw attention to the house: the Chippendale rose stain of the wood with contrasting and detailed touches of burgundy and cream; the inviting but surprising gazebo that finishes the north side of the rear porch; the Colonial blue front door that dominates the spacious front porch; and the dormers

of the second floor which give a clue to the five-bedroom capacity. The first floor interior has been planned to have an abundance of public space so that there may be a feeling of openness and hospitality, especially during official functions. A large dining room is adequate for large buffet dinners; a sizable foyer and living room opening on each other and leading to the porches, provide plenty of elbow room for guests. The kitchen is large enough for family sit-down eating or as a base for caterers. Scott Lawson, celebrated Chautauqua architect, is credited with the design of the house, collaborating with Dr. and Mrs. Bratton and Trustee Robert B. Osburn to achieve Chautauqua's needs.

To Mrs. Bratton goes large credit for thoughtful details that distinguish the house and give it the aura that it deserves as the official residence. Chautauqua antiques which were not being used elsewhere, plus "attic finds," as Mrs. Bratton calls them, have been refinished and combined to give an "Eastlake oak" theme. To find a mantle that suited the house, however, took scouting trips to several barns and then a miracle of restoration and adaptation. Wallpaper, of course, carpets, china, beds, linen and two tables had to be new purchases. Her awareness of the uniqueness of Chautauqua fueled her determination to help make this house "very special." She thinks the best compliment came from a man who was looking for the President's home, but couldn't find a new house on North Lake Drive. "Then I knew we had achieved our goal. The house looks as though it has always been there. It is compatible to Chautauqua and to its own location."

Perhaps no single episode in Chautauqua's history reveals the Spirit of Chautauqua as poignantly as the financial crisis of 1933-1936. The way the Institution's extreme danger was faced and conquered by the Spirit at work clearly demonstrated the Bishop's ideal of "weekday power."

Because of the effects of the national Depression, attendance at Chautauqua had diminished, money surpluses from five seasons had disappeared and operating deficits had piled one on top of another. In addition, expenditures for improvements, though some of them were of a self-liquidating nature, had carried the Institution deeper into debt at an inopportune time.

By the time that the season of 1933 had closed, there was no money even to pay the accumulated interest, and Chautauqua faced the prospect of being taken over by her creditors. Chautauqua's liabilities had reached $785,512.[23]

The Chautauqua Trustees at length petitioned the Court for a receivership and on Dec. 21, 1933, a wise judge placed Chautauqua in the hands of two friendly responsible men, Alburn E. Skinner, chairman of the Board of Trustees, and Dr. Charles R. Haskin, Chautauqua's resident physician.[24]

Most Chautauquans hadn't realized that disaster was so close, and when the news spread, they still could not believe that the Institution, as they had known it, might cease to exist.

Once the first shock was over, however, the Chautauqua Spirit began to assert itself, proving that it was more than poetic fervor. Chautauquans began a daring attempt to save their "beloved friend."

First of all, a group of Pittsburghers whose hearts bore allegiance to the Miller-Vincent tradition, led by Samuel M. Hazlett, an attorney, pledged the receivers that they would underwrite the cost of the 1934 program.[25]

(In spite of the fact that the 1934 season resulted in a net gain of $17,000, Chautauqua's debt climbed in 1934 to $819,956 as the receivers discovered additional liabilities, bad assets, bad accounts receivable and more accrued interest.)

The Pittsburgh group, aided by other Chautauquans, next organized an independent corporation, the Chautauqua Reorganization Corporation, and began raising money to clear away Chautauqua's debt.

They purposed to "acquire all claims against Chautauqua by purchase, by gift or any other means so that by the end of three years it would be the sole creditor of Chautauqua Institution."[26]

Mr. Hazlett became the president of this corporation and with other dedicated Chautauquans concentrated on constructive efforts to save the Institution. The corporation promised the creditors that it intended to pay off the indebtedness dollar for dollar. The character of Chautauqua's people, its greatest asset, was listed as proof that this impossible task could be done. Three years for a miracle!

The audacity of these leaders intrigued their fellow-Chautauquans in spite of widespread discouragement. Chautauquans responded as best they could and as often as they could, though personal finances continued to suffer from the Depression's pinch.

An imaginative way was found to dramatize the appeal. Each Chautauquan was asked to buy back a particular spot on the Grounds that memory made dear to him. A map of Chautauqua was erected on the Plaza and as contributors purchased small or large areas, the map recorded them.

Members of the Bird and Tree Garden Club "sold" Chautauqua's beautiful trees to stimulate more contributions to the fund. Little strips of metal, noting the purchases, were tacked to the trees.

Members of the Women's Club "sold" seats in the Amphitheater as Chautauquans remembered dear friends whose company they had enjoyed there.

Cottage owners were asked to pay an assessment of twenty per-cent of the assessed valuation of their properties thus purchasing the land which they had originally leased for the erection of their vacation homes. Mr. Hazlett oversaw the necessary changes in the Institution's Charter which would authorize the purchase of leases and the issuance of property deeds.

The people in the vicinity were reminded of how much the Institution had meant to them in added business. Friends of Chautauqua far and wide were alerted to the need and were asked to be generous. The Chautauqua Trustees led the way in giving.

The President's home was built in 1985, but follows the style of vacation homes built earlier in this century, fitting unobtrusively into its setting.

When the last check came in on the next to the last day of the 1936 season, two blasts of the fire siren signified the victory. People laughed and cried when they realized that the unbelievable task had been accomplished. What Dr. Bestor called "a second Old First Night" was held. Special stunts and fireworks on the lake front were enjoyed.[27]

Following the tremendous effort, the Chautauqua Reorganization Corporation carried out its plan to put Chautauqua on a firm financial basis so that never again would it be in real danger.

For this purpose, the Chautauqua Foundation was incorporated. Entirely independent of Chautauqua Institution, the Foundation is chartered to receive gifts and legacies, to invest the funds it accumulates for the purpose of undergirding the Chautauqua program and its facilities.

The late Walter C. Roberts was the first president of the Chautauqua Foundation. He was followed by Harold F. Reed who resigned in 1967. John D. Hamilton succeeded Mr. Reed and served until 1971 when Richard H. Miller became the Foundation's president.

Endowment under Foundation ownership reached $11 million at current market values at the end of its fiscal year, June 30, 1986. From the investment income and on a formula adopted by the Foundation Board in 1972, the Foundation provides an annual payment to Chautauqua Institution consistent with the Foundation's original purpose. Specific portions of the Chautauqua program as well as certain Summer School scholarships function under endowments through the Foundation. Efforts are made to add to endowment capital not only through new gifts, but also through

---

NATIONAL SOCIAL ROLE

At a kindergarten mothers' meeting at Chautauqua in 1895, Mrs. Theodore W. Birney appeared on the program, speaking on behalf of the need for a National Congress of Mothers. By February, 1897, enough interest had been aroused throughout the country that a meeting was convened in Washington, D.C., for the purpose of organizing such a Congress of Mothers. It later became the Parent-Teacher Association, the PTA.

In 1895 the spirit of the country was ready for an organization of parents, suggests Bonaro W. Overstreet, who co-authored the history of the PTA with her husband. "It was natural for parents at Chautauqua to discuss this need," says Mrs. Overstreet, "and natural, too, for them to give support or even leadership to the new organization as it developed on state and local levels."

Chautauqua through the years had proved to be a place for effective idea-exchange. With many Chautauquans in leadership roles in different parts of the country, ideas discussed at Chautauqua were and still are taken back home at the end of the summer to be advocated or tried at the local level. What Mrs. Emily Huntington Miller, the first president of the Chautauqua Women's Club, said of that club can be said of the total Chautauqua programs: "Its aim is to reach, through representative women (or men) gathered at Chautauqua, a large number of communities in different parts of the country, arousing them to an active interest in the vital questions pertaining to home and social life."[30] This is Chautauqua's unparalleled opportunity, her unexaggerated claim to a national social role.

wise investment management. In the present climate of rising costs, the importance of the Foundation's support of the Institution has increasing significance.

Dr. Hazlett who spearheaded the drive to save Chautauqua was elected President of the Institution in 1946 and served until his death in 1956. But nine years before he became President, Chautauquans honored him for his astute and dedicated work on behalf of Chautauqua. The first $50,000 received by the Chautauqua Foundation on Old First Night, 1937, was designated as the S. M. Hazlett Honorary Endowment. In addition, a "Thank You" Book was made and presented to him. Everyone who had made a contribution placed his name in the book. He had also received an honorary doctorate from Waynesburg College in 1939.

The forward to the book of gratitude reads, as follows:

"To give tangible expression of the warm feeling of gratitude that we Chautauquans have for those of the group who have through steadfast leadership and courage led Chautauqua up from the Valley of Despair, this book is made. Every name in it is placed there in sincere tribute to the men and women who have brought Chautauqua back; and as he is the leader and representative of those who accomplished this stupendous task, this book is affectionately dedicated and presented to Dr. Samuel Hazlett . . . Each page will be headed 'We Thank You' and every name recorded in it will be there because of the real feeling of every true Chautauquan . . ."[28]

One of the highlights of the '70s was the installation of Dr. Oscar E. Remick as the Institution's thirteenth president.

Following the resignation of President Curtis W. Haug in September, 1970, a presidential search committee spent many hours and much effort in finding the person best fitted to lead Chautauqua into its second century.

On April 17, 1971, the Board of Trustees, following the committee's recommendation, elected Dr. Oscar E. Remick to be Chautauqua's next President. Dr. Remick was then serving as Vice President of Assumption College in Worcester, Massachusetts, where he also served as Academic Dean and Professor of Religious Studies. In Dr. Remick were combined administrative abilities, intellectual achievement, participation in the education community and knowledge of the interrelations of religion and culture.

Great expectations preceded Dr. Remick's arrival on the Grounds in mid-season, 1971 and great ceremony attended his formal acceptance of the presidency on Aug. 1, 1971, at a Sunday morning service.

Mr. Richard H. Miller, great-grandson of the first Chautauqua President, and the current chairman of the Board of Trustees, made the formal investiture of Dr. Remick with "the powers, privileges, authorities and responsibilities of the Presidency of Chautauqua Institution. ."

As Dr. Remick stepped into the lectern and accepted the historic gavel, the large audience arose in a spontaneous gesture of respect and honor. It was a moment when the Chautauqua Spirit was deeply moving.

CENTENNIAL CELEBRATION

Evan Whallon conducts the Chautauqua Symphony Orchestra at a Centennial season concert.

IN 1974, Chautauqua's 100th birthday was observed. This anniversary gave another generation of Chautauquans an opportunity to express their devotion to Chautauqua. The impetus and direction of the celebration came from Chautauquans themselves, working closely with Dr. Oscar E. Remick, their new President.

Upon taking office, Dr. Remick recognized immediately that planning for the Centennial should begin promptly. Instead of turning to professional planners, he chose a lifelong Chautauquan, Miriam S. Reading, to head the Centennial Central Committee. Other active Chautauquans with diversified skills and interests were invited to serve. Fine cooperation was developed between the administration and the committee and careful consideration was given to the committee's ideas by the Board of Trustees. The meshing of staff and volunteer efforts laid the groundwork for a successful celebration, but it was the enthusiastic participation of hundreds of Chautauquans that made the Centennial memorable. The spirit of Chautauqua was widely shared.

Ten years before, a campaign had been launched to provide improvements to the Grounds and buildings, so that Chautauqua's physical facilities and appearance would be adequate for a centennial observance. (References to Centennial gifts appear elsewhere in this book.) In addition, the first edition of "Three Taps of

the Gavel" was brought out in 1970 for the purpose of stimulating interest in Chautauqua's history with the idea that a more detailed history would be written for the Centennial year.

The actual planning for the celebration, however, began in January, 1972, when the first meeting of the Central Committee was called. Before the day's deliberations were concluded, the philosophy of the observance had been thoroughly discussed and sub-committees had been formed. A sizable start had been made!

It was generally agreed that day, and later formally affirmed, that while appropriate recognition of the past should be made during the Centennial year, emphasis should be placed on Chautauqua's role in the present and future. Chautauqua's tradition of relevance and flexibility must be honored, the Committee declared. This, in itself, was an indication of the aliveness of the Chautauqua Spirit.

The large book on Chautauqua was commissioned by the Board of Trustees at about this time and Dr. Theodore Morrison set to work on his research with publication anticipated for 1974.

Quite unexpectedly, one of the sub-committees, the environmental committee, soon assumed permanent stature. The long range values to be gained from protecting the environment, especially the lake, were seen to be a continuing concern for Chautauquans far beyond the centennial year. The Centennial Central Committee recommended that the Institution recognize this priority by establishing a permanent environmental committee. The Board of Trustees' authorization for such a committee was followed by presidential appointments.

A description of the work of this committee may be found under the section of this book, The Place We Love, page 10. By selling recycled notepaper, beginning in 1972, the committee was able to buy new refuse cans to support their anti-littering campaigns, to hire a special Grounds cleanup man during the Centennial Year, to promote awareness of the importance of beautification and to contribute to the lake studies. The notepaper carried Jane Nelson drawings of Chautauqua scenes which made the paper easily saleable, as well as appropriate for the occasion.

Another immediate development of the Central Committee was its determination to apply for a Chautauqua Centennial commemorative stamp.

On behalf of this effort, the Central Committee accepted the offer of cooperation from the Reuben E. Fenton Philatelic Society of Jamestown whose knowledge and experience were helpful. A Centennial subcommittee, headed by Mrs. John F. Tim, Jr., also was appointed and worked diligently to collect signatures on petitions which would accompany the application for a commemorative stamp. Dozens of Chautauquans, as well as Jamestown philatelists, wrote to their national legislators for support and circulated petitions, some in far distant states so that the national appeal of the Chautauqua stamp could be demonstrated.

In the end, it was the Chautauqua Movement, itself, that was honored since a stamp cannot be issued to commemorate an institution or a municipality. (This is the established policy of the Citizens' Advisory Stamp Committee which makes the stamp selections.) Mrs. Mary Margaret Jamieson, the committee's executive secretary who handled the First Day Issue at Chautauqua, gave Dr. Remick much credit for his personal presentation of the stamp request in Washington.

While some were disappointed that the stamp design highlighted the rural implementation of the Chautauqua Movement and did not show an Institu-

tion scene, the stamp nonetheless carried the name of Chautauqua around the world along with the message that the Movement began in 1874, Chautauqua Institution's founding date. The Committee rejoiced that the Chautauqua, N.Y. Post Office was chosen for the First Day issue which was set for the day of Old First Night, the first Tuesday in August, when Chautauqua's birthday is celebrated. This day, August 6, 1974, became the focal point for Centennial fervor. Not only did the Post Office gear itself for the tremendous task of handling First Day Issue orders, but the Institution began planning to entertain official visitors and to provide suitable ceremonies.

News of the stamp through philatelic journals and through the national press focused attention on the 100-year old Institution. People whose only contact with Chautauqua had been through the now extinct traveling Chautauquas, learned that the originator of the Chautauqua System of Popular Education was still alive and doing well. Parts of the country which had established independent Chautauquas dug into their histories to reestablish long untended ties with the Institution.

Obtaining the commemorative stamp is one of the best examples of the manner in which the entire Centennial effort was carried on. The work of countless Chautauquans, the knowledgeable help of the neighboring Philatelic Society in Jamestown and the official support of Dr. Remick and his administration dovetailed effectively to achieve the dreamed-of goal. That it was a long-held goal was proved in Washington where records showed that an application for a commemorative stamp had been received there at the time of Chautauqua's 75th anniversary.

Still another exciting result of a Centennial subcommittee's work occurred in 1973, the year before the Centennial. On July 21, 1973, the Chautauqua Grounds within the gates were officially added to the National Register of Historic Places. This was the culmination of intensive work for a brief year and a half. Miss Pauline Fancher, then librarian of Smith Memorial Library, led the Historic Sites Subcommittee and a large corps of volunteers in preparing the information on each property within the gates, assembling the accompanying pictures and making the proper applications at the precise time required. Dr. Remick, upon becoming President, had made initial inquiries concerning historic recognition and had indicated to the Centennial Committee that seeking designation would be an appropriate project.

State Senator Jess J. Present, who was the main speaker when the Certificate of National Recognition was received, said that in addition to the honor of being so designated, Chautauqua could now enjoy the advantages of being eligible for certain funds and programs on a grant basis and protected from condemnation by government agencies for alternate uses of its land. At that time, he said the Chautauqua Grounds comprised the largest New York State Registered Historic Place. Senator Present was introduced by Chautauqua's Board Chairman, Mr. Miller. Steven Levy, Assistant Deputy Director of the New York State Historic Trust, who had made Chautauqua's presentation to the boards in Albany and Washington, formally presented

The First Day Cover, The Chautauqua Stamp

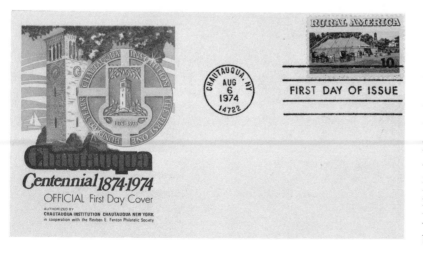

the certificate to Dr. Remick. In response, Dr. Remick described the excitement with which news of the recognition had been received. He acknowedged the help of Chautauqua's representatives in Albany and Washington and the presence that day of Mr. William Taylor, Chairman of the New York State Council of Parks and Recreation. He affirmed that Chautauqua would be faithful to this greatest responsibility, "To preserve our heritage...We, too, must build!" he said. "We accept the past and a greater future."

Achieving historical designation in 1973 allowed Chautauqua to enter its big year of celebration with its cultural significance officially proclaimed.

Another development in 1973 contributed to the anticipation of the Centennial season. This was the transformation of the Refectory into a turn-of-the-century Refreshment Pavilion and Old Fashioned Store by Welch Foods, Inc.

The Welch locations in Disneyland and Disney World had led the company to recognize the appeal of nostaligia. Since Welch's began in 1869 and Chautauqua, in 1874, their histories are framed in almost identical years. The two enterprises had been neighbors since 1897 and there is evidence that Bishop Vincent, himself, influenced Dr. Welch to relocate his business in Westfield. Indeed, Dr. Welch was an active Chautauqua trustee for approximately fifteen years, beginning in 1908. As R. Craig Campbell, president of Welch's observed, "Welch's has always had high admiration for the Chautauqua Idea and Welch employees through the years have been Chautauquans...We're grateful that the Institution has allowed us to be a part of Chautauqua."

Especially enjoyed was the Pavilion's awninged outdoor patio where Chautauquans sat and talked while they refreshed themselves and indulged in the pastime of watching their fellow-vacationers. The young waiters in their striped shirts and arm bands and the waitresses in their puff-sleeved blouses and patterned aprons added to the early-1900s atmosphere. No effort was spared by Welch's to make the Pavilion authentic in period design and gracious in its atmosphere. The psychological effect upon Chautauquans was subtle, but strong. They began to look anew at their own Victorian-or-before homes and appreciate what they had. They began readying them for the next year's anticipated entertaining.

The year of 1973 saw much other activity as the subcommittees carried forward as much of their work as possible before the members would separate for the winter.

The Centennial flag competition was held and the design in blue, green and white by Mrs. Helen Kazalunas of Mayville, N.Y., was selected. By the next summer the design had been transformed into beautiful flags which flew at the Main Gate, at the Amphitheater and at President Remick's home.

The Centennial medallion design was accepted and the appropriate subcommittee, headed by Mrs. Dan W. Cook, set to work to have the medallion properly minted in bronze and silver and to obtain for sale, pins, pendants and other keepsakes which reproduced the medallion design in miniature. The Summer School's sculpture instructor, a Chautauquan of long standing, H. Richard Duhme, Jr., had prepared the medallion design for the committee. Mr. Duhme was also a member of the Central Committee. The Institution ordered medallions to serve as awards of recognition during the Centennial year, and afterwards, as leadership awards.

Mrs. Norman G. Jacobs and members of her Heritage Subcommittee alerted Chautauquans to the historical exhibits that were being planned for next year and gathered promises of loans of family heirlooms and museum pieces from cooperating Chautauquans. The largest exhibit was arranged on the second floor of the library and it served to point up the need for an adequate Chautauqua museum. Many other historical exhibits were developed throughout the Grounds. Some were changed from week to week. Miss Fancher, librarian of Smith Library at the time, was actively involved with the memorabilia at the library, especially those items received from the Charles Edison Fund.

In June, 1973, two presidents share the honors of cutting the ribbon for the official opening of Welch's Pavilion. R. Craig Campbell, President of Welch Foods, Inc., is shown at the left with Dr. Oscar E. Remick, President of Chautauqua Institution.

Miriam Reading, the Centennial Central Committee Chairman, shows the winning Centennial flag design, created by Helen Kazalunas.

Dr. Hanson receives a Centennial Medal at the "Merry Mount" performance with Opera Director Leonard Treash and Dr. Remick applauding.

Another subcommittee, chaired by Mrs. George L. Cornell, prepared Walking Tour Guides for the use of Centennial visitors. This project was sponsored by the Friends of Smith Memorial Library, and proved very helpful. Mrs. Frank G. Karslake, granddaughter of one of Chautauqua's most illustrious early leaders, Dr. Julius King, spearheaded the effort to tape Chautauqua's oral history. She secured fellow-Chautauquans to share their memories of former days, outstanding events and personalities so that the personal reports of Chautauqua's history could be preserved. This committee is another one that is continuing to work.

In May of the Centennial year, Chautauqua Institution was paid another honor which reaffirmed its relevance in the modern world. It received one of the annual awards for distinguished contribution to the Arts from the New York State Council on the Arts. In ceremonies at the Albright-Knox Gallery in Buffalo, Governor Malcolm Wilson made the presentation, citing Chautauqua's "sustained activity as a performing and visual arts center of national importance." Dr. Remick accepted the award, paying tribute to those who had labored at Chautauqua in the Arts in the context of education. He summarized Chautauqua's goals: cultivation of human creativity to be used for the service of mankind.

While the Central Committee and its subcommittees were working on projects, Dr. Remick had been structuring a 1974 program that would, in itself, be a Centennial celebration.

One of the highlights proved to be a world premiere of "Philip Marshall," an American opera by Seymour Barab. The Institution had been considering the possibility of a commissioned opera for the Centennial when "Philip Marshall" came to its attention. The work appealed to Leonard Treash, General Director of the Chautauqua Opera Association, and because its story concerned the post-Civil War period, it was appropriate for a celebration of Chautauqua's 1874 beginnings. Barab had not only composed the music, but written the libretto, as well. Having already established a reputation for popular one-act operas, he had written "Philip Marshall" as his first three-act opera.

The world premiere was thus secured for Chautauqua and presented on July 12, in Norton Hall with Theodor Uppman of the Metropolitan Opera Company in the title role and the composer in the audience. The production was sponsored by the New York State Council on the Arts. It was conducted by Wolfgang Schanzer and staged by Whitfield Lloyd-Schanzer. It drew reviewers from a distance: Allen Hughes from the New York Times, Ruby Mercer from Opera Canada and Robert Cumming from Music Journal.

Another opera production had sentimental overtones which were in keeping with the anniversary spirit. This was the final opera of the season, "Merry Mount," with its composer, Howard Hanson, conducting. Dr. Hanson had been an active Chautauquan for many years.

Both Seymour Barab and Howard Hanson received Centennial Medallions in honor of their works and their participation in the Centennial observance.

Dr. Remick cooperated with another Centennial subcommittee to arrange a morning lecture series which was centered around the needs and roles of older citizens in American society. "The Coming of Age: A Celebration" brought outstanding speakers to the Amphitheater platform: Edward Weeks, Senior Editor of The Atlantic Monthly Press; Dr. Karl A. Menninger of the Menninger Foundation; Mrs. Margaret E. Kuhn, National Convener, Gray Panthers; Roy Wilkins, Executive Director, NAACP; and Erwin D. Canham, Editor Emeritus, The Christian Science Monitor. Dr. Carl S. Winters moderated the panel discussions in the afternoons. Interesting resource people were invited to participate in these discussions which proved lively and demonstrated the importance of the committee's concerns for Chautauqua's responsibility in this area.

The committee has since followed up its interest in older citizens by planning at least three "winter" program weekends per year. Called "55-Plus Weekends," the two-day programs have attracted growing numbers of people who are fifty-five years of age or more. Some of them are coming to Chautauqua for the first time. Thought-provoking lectures and discussions center around a specific weekend theme and evening entertainment is scheduled. The activities are held at Bellinger Hall where meals are served and accommodations provided. Dr. Helen M. Overs, a member of the subcommittee and a year-round Chautauqua resident, has been in charge of arrangements, assisted by others in the winter community. Mrs. Miriam Reading, chairman of the subcommittee, underwrote part of the original cost to get the program underway with the Institution's continuing help.

There was so much variety within the Centennial summer that any Chautauquan could easily find an event to captivate his interest and participation. Many organizations or groups of co-workers sponsored reunions.

A Centennial Ball after the Saturday night concert on August 3 drew hundreds to the Hotel Athenaeum drawing room where Dr. and Mrs. Remick and Mr. and Mrs. Miller led the Grand March to the music of Peter Duchin and his orchestra. There never had been anything quite like that at Chautauqua and old and young joined in the spirit of joy and pride in the place they loved. Chautauqua was 100!

Over sixty boats sailed in the Centennial Yacht Club Regatta during the first weekend in July. Bronze Centennial medallions, mounted in wooden plaques, rewarded the winners in flying Scot, C-Scow, Lightning and Sunfish classes. A barbecue dinner and barn dance was also planned for the visiting sailors. Many Chautauquans participated in the Regatta by watching the races.

A traditional Vesper Service was held one Sunday evening in Miller Park to memorialize the first services held in the open auditorium near the Point. Chautauquans had been asked to dress in old-fashioned costumes that day and there were some at that service in authentic Chautauqua heirloom dresses. An extra gesture of friendliness was extended by families who reside around Miller Park. They served refreshments on the Arcade veranda following the service.

E. A. Smyth was in charge of a committee that invited Chautauquans to submit slides for a new Chautauqua slide presentation that people could borrow to show for programs at home.

Mrs. Ned Heinzerling and her committee who had been entrusted with decorating the Grounds for the Centennial were busy all summer accepting compliments for their efforts and for the manner in which they inspired others to beautify their own properties. There were hanging baskets of flowering plants and vines around the Main Gate and public buildings, but also on almost everyone's porch. Landscaping appeared in new places, some arranged by the committee; some, by individuals. Along the lake side of the Athenaeum Hotel, the message, "Centennial, 1874-1974," was spelled out in plants on a long bed that was constructed so that it could be "read" from the road below. The Bird, Tree and Garden Club revived an old Chautauqua custom of awarding ribbons to houses and gardens that had been noticeably improved and beautified or possessed some unique feature. The ribbons were awarded on July 24 (Lewis Miller's birthday) from a horse-drawn buggy.

The Publications subcommittee had commissioned

MEDALLION RECIPIENTS

1974
Jack Danziger, orchestra member of longest service, 56 years, July 3.

Seymour Barab, composer and librettist for "Philip Marshall," July 12.

New York State Governor Malcolm Wilson on Governor Wilson Day, July 27.

Mischa Mischakoff, Chautauqua Symphony Orchestra Concertmaster, 1926-1964, July 30.

Walter Hendl, Chautauqua Symphony Orchestra Conductor and Musical Director, 1953-1971, July 30.

Miriam S. Reading, Centennial Chairman, Old First Night, August 6.

George L. Follansbee, former Institution President and Vice President, August 6.

Judge W. Walter Braham, former Institution President, in absentia, August 6.

Curtis W. Haug, former Institution President, in absentia, August 6.

Howard Hanson, distinguished Chautauquan, educator, composer and conductor of "Merry Mount," one of the operas of the Centennial season, August 19.

Dr. Garra L. Lester, beloved Chautauqua physican, at a local celebration of Dr. Lester's extended years of service, August 28.

1971—Leadership Award and Medallion
John D. Hamilton, Vice Chairman of the Executive Committee of the Board of Trustees, former Chautauqua Foundation President, Old First Night, August 5.

1978—Medallion
Richard H. Miller, for outstanding leadership during seven and one-half years as Chairman of the Chautauqua Board of Trustees. Old First Night, August 1.

1985—Medallion
Howard G. Gibbs, following his retirement as Chairman of the Chautauqua Board of Trustees, 1985. Presented formally in the Amphitheater July 12, 1986.

Patricia McBride and Jean-Pierre Bonnefoux are shown in performance August 10, 1974. Jean-Pierre Bonnefoux is now the Artistic Director and Principal Teacher for the Chautauqua School of Dance.

President Remick receives from F.X. Biglin, the Regional Postmaster General, a Commemorative Stamp Album celebrating the issuance of the Chautauqua Movement Stamp at Chautauqua, August 6, 1974.

Chautauqua's artist in residence, Maritza Morgan, to draw the pictures for a Centennial coloring book for children. She drew the history of Chautauqua in the spirit of the title she chose, "Chautauqua, I Love You," delighting both adults and children. The Daily celebrated the Centennial by bringing out a forty-page historical issue on Stamp Day and announcing the sale of bound copies of the season's Dailies. These publications matched in spirit the handsome Centennial program book, created in a period design by Charles R. Tranter and all of them are now treasured mementoes.

CENTENNIAL GOALS

When asked how the demands of the 20th and 21st centuries differed from those of the past, Mrs. Miriam S. Reading, chairman of the Centennial Central Committee, commented on the changing patterns of leisure time, the imminence of the 12-month school year and increased longevity.

"These must make us consider more extensive use of the facilities here on the Grounds. However, with any changes that we consider, we must maintain those values which are so vital a part of Chautauqua—the friendliness, the quiet, intimate atmosphere, the importance of the individual, the chance for growth and enrichment in every aspect of the human life. Diversity of age, geography and belief have been and must continue to be, our strengths—all within a scale that is manageable. Intellectual and moral courage, a desire for excellence in all aspects of our program—these continue to be our goals as we enter our second century. . .

"The thinking that typified the early Chautauqua days showed remarkable perception of man's needs—intellectual, cultural, religious and physical. It further recognized a responsibility to society. If we, in 1974, can rededicate ourselves to this same perception of man's needs, and meet them in a manner consistent with the framework of the last part of the 20th and the 21st centuries, we shall be paying the best possible tribute to those men and women of such insight in Chautauqua's past. . ."

The Chautauquan Daily
July 21, 1972

The new book on Chautauqua by Theodore Morrison, "Chautauqua, A Center for Education, Religion, and the Arts in America," was chosen as a CLSC book. It is the largest, most extensive history of Chautauqua and has been produced by the University of Chicago Press. Dr. and Mrs. Morrison were guests of the Institution for a week in July and Dr. Morrison addressed the CLSC and autographed books.

The appearance of Dr. Remick on the Today Show the day before the stamp was issued focused the attention of millions of Americans on the uniqueness of Chautauqua. There was growing anticipation of August 6, Stamp Day and Old First Night combined, and indeed it turned out to be the memorable day that Chautauquans had pictured.

The sun shone brightly as if it were giving a blessing to the festive atmosphere. A red and white striped tent had been set up in front of the Post Office for the sale and cancellation of stamps. Another less flamboyant "depot" had been installed in the Hotel Athenaeum lobby, and the Jamestown Post Office's mobile unit was stationed at the Main Gate. There were thousands of stamps processed with the first day issue cancellations and thousands more that were dispatched to collectors and dealers. There were 50,000 stamps sold that day in the Post Office alone.

The program at the Amphitheater at 11 o'clock was "an affair of State," with the Chautauqua Symphony orchestra lending its prestigious presence. The playing of the 1812 Overture and Sousa's Stars and Stripes Forever in a pre-ceremony concert, set the tone of dignified excitement. The Amphitheater, itself, was profusely decorated with red, white and blue bunting and the Colors were presented by members of the Four Armed Services as the proceedings began. Victor A. Murphy, Chautauqua postmaster, gave the welcoming remarks. F. X. Biglin, Regional Postmaster General, Eastern Region, United States Postal Service, presented the main address and the Commemorative Stamp Albums. Julia Lovett, Chautauqua's Affiliate Artist, sang God Bless America. The director of the Department of Religion, Dr. Ralph W. Loew, pronounced the invocation; and the chairman of the board of trustees, Richard H. Miller, the benediction. Dr. Oscar E. Remick, President of the Institution, served as Master of Ceremonies and both his words and manner added to the significance of the occasion. For Chautauquans with great love for "this place" and great confidence in its future, the ceremony seemed to be the crowning event of the first one hundred years and the anticipation of what might come during the second century. The day's official guests were entertained at a reception in the President's home and at a luncheon program in the Hotel Athenaeum.

The day was full of music. Skitch Henderson returned to Chautauqua to conduct the orchestra in an afternoon concert. The oldest town band in the United States with continuous existence, from Franklin, Pennsylvania, played on the south end of the Plaza at 5 p.m. The Music School Festival Orchestra and the Studio Band played at the birthday party, Old First Night.

Old First Night proved to be in Dr. Remick's words "a great, blessed family evening" with everyone taking some part. Recognition Medals were awarded to three former Presidents and to Miriam Reading, Centennial Central Committee chairman. The Play House presented an amusing historical skit that was largely based on material from the early Assembly Heralds. There was the largest Old First Night attendance in recent years, at least. The community gift that was received set a new record and cake was served to all who would stand in line.

While high moments and supremely organized events had marked the day, happily there was also plenty of that Chautauquaesque enjoyment of the good, clean air, the garden atmosphere, family, friends, and the comparatively small experiences that give character to any period of time.

An example of genuine Chautauqua Spirit is to be found in the official Centennial Scrapbook in Smith Memorial Library. It was compiled by a member of the Centennial Central Committee who volunteered to do it when the suggestion was made that a scrap book should be kept. It took hundreds of hours, for many Chautauquans had responded to George L. Follansbee's requests for clippings about the Centennial. Well-known as a lifelong Chautauquan and the grandfather of two seventh-generation Chautauqua children, George has always served the Institution whenever and wherever he could. He even stepped in as President one summer when he was needed. His gift of the Centennial Scrapbook to the Historial Collection is a priceless one.

There were some who feared that the year after the Centennial would see a marked letdown from the high spirits of the 100th anniversary, but such was not the case. The Centennial program had attracted many new people who now considered themselves Chautauquans and wanted to return. In mid-season, Vice President Woodside in a Daily interview stated that the Summer Schools, Norton Hall and the Golf Course were all ahead in their attendance records from mid-season of the year before. He added that gate attendance figures were also building.

"Most people who come to Chautauqua want to come back and do so at one time or another," he said to The Daily. "What we have here is so unique that it draws people . . . I feel that we have made a very vital approach to our second century."

A dramatic announcement in the Second issue of the 1975 Daily had set the tone for the season and the new century.

It was announced that the Gebbie Foundation of Jamestown had awarded Chautauqua Institution a challenge grant of $1 million which it would make available on the basis of one dollar for every three dollars which Chautauqua would raise from private sources over a five-year period. The terms of the grant specified that the Gebbie Foundation would give $200,000 per year for five years if Chautauqua met certain fund raising goals (averaging at least $600,000 per year), and, if Chautauqua also met all of the other requirements: To operate without a deficit in each of the five fiscal years of the grant period; to build a reserve fund of $600,000 so that by 1980 the Institution would have accumulated substantial financial resources toward planning its future seasons; by September, 1977, to eliminate all long and short-term

indebtedness for borrowed funds; and from October 1, 1977 through September 30, 1979, not to incur any indebtedness for borrowed funds.

As Dr. Remick made the announcement, he pointed out that the Foundation's gift, plus the $3 million which Chautauqua would raise, should put the Institution's regular operations and programs on a sound footing. He said that the $4 million objective was a first step in a larger program of development, to be announced later, through which additional funds would be sought for endowment growth and physical plant renovations and additions.

"The Gebbie Foundation's challenge grant is a magnificent expression of faith in the future of Chautauqua Institution," Dr. Remick declared. "It will provide tremendous incentive in strengthening Chautauqua for its second century of service."

On Old First Night, 1975, the thrilling total of $505,530 was recorded on the big scoreboard in the choir loft. Hundreds of gifts, big and small represented widespread belief in Chautauqua's future. Two large $100,000 gifts helped swell the total at the end of the evening: One from the Carnahan-Jackson Foundation and one from an anonymous donor. The audit for the fiscal year ending Sept. 30, 1975, established that the amount needed to qualify for the Gebbie Grant payment had been achieved and that the Institution had operated without a deficit. The first year of the challenge had been met; private gifts totaled $631,754.

In 1976, the effort was successful again. The Institution had conducted its affairs through the 1975-1976 fiscal year without having to make short-term loans and again had operated without a deficit. In addition to the $707,196 gifts which were Gebbie-eligible, other gifts to the Institution amounted to $384,034, making a grand total of $1,091,230. Chautauquans, themselves, could scarcely believe that they were reaching annual giving in such unprecedented amounts.

Another outcome of the 1975 season which was destined to become widely supportive of the Chautauqua uniqueness was the documentary film, "The Chautau-

The Children's School gives an eloquent Centennial birthday wish! President Remick and School Director Joan Smith look on admiringly.

Rebecca Richmond

qua Experience." Since its release in June, 1976, it has been shown throughout the country and acclaimed by critics, as well as viewers-at-large. So far, it has won two awards.

The film was produced by Forney Miller Associates of Ambler, Pa. Miller and his associate, Art Ciocco, spent more than the number of weeks they had planned at Chautauqua, so intrigued did they become by their subject-matter. They approached their topic subjectively and in their final opus gave much more than a catalogue of Chautauqua offerings. Chautauqua is interpreted in the film through people's widely differing participation in a host of activities. Almost dance-like in its grace and movement, it seems to catch the essence and spirit that is still alive within the time-hallowed gates.

At the beginning of the 1976 season, Dr. Remick reported to Chautauquans a few of his speaking engagements on behalf of Chautauqua. The invitations indicated a growing awareness both in this country and abroad that the Chautauqua idea is still unique, still universal in its appeal.

In Washington, D.C., he addressed the Cultural Affairs Officers from all the Embassies on the unusual combination of religion, education and the arts at Chautauqua.

In Norway, he spoke to government ministers, artists, Lutheran and Catholic clergy and cultural groups on the living relationship between the arts and religion that has taken form at Chautauqua.

In Scott's Bluff and Chadron, Nebraska, he took part in two days of a two-week revival of the Tent Chautauqua under the aegis of the University of Nebraska, speaking on the history of Chautauqua, as well as its outreach.

All year, too, the Institution president had been flying back and forth to New York City where he was taking an active part in the work of the New York State Council on the Arts.

President Remick said, "As I have had these extended experiences, I become more and more convinced of the richness of the human family and more and more aware of being a citizen of the world. Peoples of all nations have both diversities of culture and traits in common, and the interchanges are important. Sometimes our Chautauqua experience is so precious to us that we want to build a tent to contain it, but we must open this experience to the world and carry on the daring catholicity of spirit which Lewis Miller and John Vincent had...I am intensely moved by the belief that Chautauqua is on the verge of a new significance by virtue of its values."

Dr. Remick frequently urged Chautauqans in the future to be not only typical of America at its best, as President Theodore Roosevelt had said, but also to be typical of the world at its best.

Though six months later Dr. Remick was to resign to take up educational duties elsewhere, during his presidency he had articulated bold dreams for Chautauqua and stirred others to action, as well. Chautauqua had been well launched into its second century and Chautauquans, themselves, were eager for the future.

When it comes to interpreting the Chautauqua Spirit, however, a poet can do it more succinctly than anyone. For many Chautauquans, words of Rebecca Richmond express "the spirit we feel" with the most eloquence.

Mrs. Richmond was the author of five books about Chautauqua and one book about a famous Chautauquan. Through her efforts, after the end of World War II, there was resumed the Bell Tower Scholarship Program which each year brings two students from England to study at Chautauqua. The cooperative exchange with the English Speaking Union had been initiated by Dr. Bestor and interrupted by the war. It was Mrs. Richmond who edited the little magazine about Chautauqua, The Bell Tower. It was she who provided the greatest impetus for the Writers' Workshop at Chautauqua, having earlier organized the Chautauqua Poetry Circle and Sandwich Poets. She had great hopes (and fears) for the place she loved so much.

TO CHAUTAUQUA— MOMENT OF FAREWELL[29]

By Rebecca Richmond

Sometimes I wish that I could love you less
For when the summer ends and I must go,
Almost it is a rending of my soul.
You are a part of me and I of you.
Some other moment I shall sit apart
To count the many reasons for my love—
The varying beauty under summer clouds
Of rippling water, of ravine and grove;
The quick light-hearted friendliness
We breathe in with the air, the joy
Of learning, peace of wisdom—yes,
Another time I'll meditate on these.
But not today. Today
I only know I leave you.
And I am silent with too much to say.
I shall remember lovely, little things—
I shall hear echoes on far city streets—
Sometimes I wish that I could love you less.

PART II

PLEDGE TO THE FUTURE

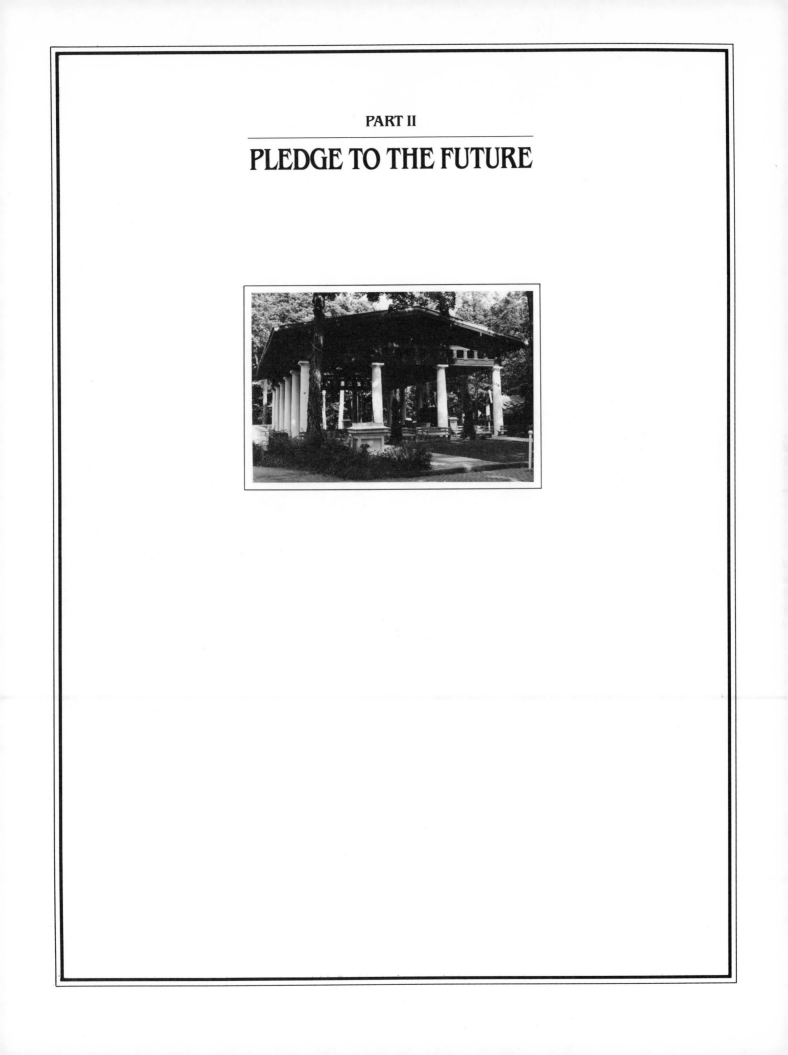

The restored and improved Amphitheater probably captures most completely the impact of the Second Century Campaign, and the new commitment to the future which has been made by both old and new Chautauquans. The dedicatory plaque is attached to the Boulder that may be glimpsed in front of the iron fence near the upper center of the picture.

INTRODUCTION

DANCING OUR PLEDGE
TO THE FUTURE

MEMORIES are usually made vivid by feelings. So I don't wonder that I remember Chautauqua's Centennial Ball in a distinctly personal way: stepping into a favorite long dress, adjusting my dangling earrings prior to starting the walk to the Hotel, stepping along Chautauqua streets in evening dress and high heels, a maneuver especially cumbersome that night as I tried to keep up to daughters and sons-in-law.

The music had already begun to push through the ordinary stillness of ten o'clock as we came down the hill above the Athenaeum veranda where familiar Chautauquans had already claimed rocking chairs so that they could watch the steady flow of arriving friends. There was an aura of hilarity—a party version of Old First Night fervor. Even Chautauquans who were not well-acquainted exchanged waves and smiles. There was perhaps some anticipation of what was to come the next week. Dr. Remick was to appear on the Today Show Monday morning to tell the whole country about Chautauqua and its Centennial. Then on Tuesday the Chautauqua Stamp would be issued and the Centennial would be officially celebrated all day and evening. But at the moment, there was frank delight in the occasion of the Ball, astonishment over everyone's being so dressed up and a warm feeling of "the Chautauqua family." This was scarcely an event for outsiders.

The fact that the Ball was a "first" added to the merriment. Never before had this 1881 wooden floor been called upon to bear the weight of dozens of dancers. Indeed, in 1881 dancing would not have been allowed or planned in the first place.

The underpinnings of the parlor had been strengthened before the season began in a conscious effort to provide for this very night. A great deal of other planning had gone into the arrangements. Most of the 700 tickets had been sold the summer before or through the winter issues of The Chautauquan. All were completely spoken for by July 9th of the Centennial season. Peter Duchin's Band had been secured for the Athenaeum party while a group called "Weekend" was to play in the Hall of Philosophy for those "under twenty-five."

When the Grand March started under the direction of George Follansbee, the President of the Institution and the Chairman of the Board with their ladies, clasped arms and marched forward. In the excitement everyone else fell in behind. The leaders couldn't circle back because of all the enthusiastic followers. But who cared that the Grand March couldn't proceed in order? There were just too many people for the size of the room and the crowded confusion was a gauge of the pride and joy everyone was feeling.

Punch was being served from an elegantly laid table in the lobby. Mrs. Richard W. Talbot, Sr., granddaughter of former President Samuel M. Hazlett, was chairman of the Ball. James Eckstein was costumed to portray Lewis Miller and was pictured during the evening with Kim Arnn, great-granddaughter of that cofounder of Chautauqua.

Those who came early were fortunate because they could dance freely before the parlor became overcrowded. The Band provided music in a variety of styles: the Samba, the Fox Trot, the Charleston, the Waltz and Rock with variations. Younger dancers mingled with older, especially as the evening progressed because the "Weekend" failed to appear. The Duchin music thus began to attract the youth away from the records which were being substituted in the Hall of Philosophy, along the path which the committee had bordered with luminaries between the Hall and the Hotel.

Rain began to fall near midnight and Chautauquans gradually began to scatter for their homes. We came up through the Amphitheater to save our clothes abit, but we didn't really worry about getting wet. We had had an evening to remember.

What would happen to Chautauqua after the Centennial Ball, I wondered. Such exuberant unabashed love for Chautauqua had been shown by so many. We all seemed to have *danced* our pledge to the future. Would we remember it after the Centennial summer? Where would all this love of Chautauqua go?

The story of the next few years gives at least part of the answer.

The Chautauquan Building in Meadville, Pa., where the
magazine and some of the CLSC books were published.

1

Continuity Through Change

CHANGE and continuity are two forces which have an astonishing kinship at Chautauqua. Sometimes they appear to be at odds, but periodically it becomes apparent that change and continuity at Chautauqua are identical. People recognize this when they say lightly, "The more things change at Chautauqua, the more they remain the same." They are usually referring to changes in administration, so the easiest way to trace Chautauqua's continuity is through the changes of its presidencies.

Lewis Miller, co-founder and first President, was also referred to as the President of the Board of Trustees. He served in both capacities for twenty-five years and it is not difficult to believe that the development of the original two-week Assembly into a University bore the marks of his leadership. The effects of his steady guidance for a quarter of a century can still be sensed in the character of Chautauqua's survival in a changing society. The strength of his influence was directly felt the last year of his life and immediately afterward during a period of major reorganization. Stability had been established by the example of the first leaders and it was strengthened by those who followed and by the total Chautauqua experience. Nonetheless the summer and fall of 1898 might be viewed as a time when a proposed "radical change" threatened continuity.

In the first place, the idea of adapting the camp meeting tradition to Christian education came without question from Lewis Miller. From a copy of a handwritten letter and notes from Mr. Miller to Dr. William Rainey Harper, we read a description of the evolution of the idea which resulted in the first Assembly and the Chautauqua that was to come.

Mr. Miller wrote: "This conception came to me like an invention comes to a person. This conception came to me at a camp meeting which I attended at Canton, Ohio in August, 1871. My mind turned at once to J. H. Vincent whom I loved and respected because of his enthusiastic and aggressive Bible study and Bible Lesson System and general development of educational interest as the only man I knew would work such a scheme successfully. When the opportunity came, I mentioned the scheme to him. He considered it a wild, impractical visionary camp meeting scheme. By persistent effort of two years as opportunity would serve and a final all day's talk on a famous and memorable all day's carriage drive laying before him in great detail

the plan or idea, his aversion to grove meetings and doubt about making the scheme a practical success was overcome..."

"On our return to my home, the Bishop and I fixed up preliminary programs and after several meetings completed a plan sufficient to lay before the Sunday School Board in New York as set forth in the first Bulletin."[1]

Lewis Miller continues: "In the book written by Bishop Vincent called *The Chautauqua Movement,* he gave me entirely satisfactory credit in these words, 'The success of Chautauqua must especially be gratifying to Lewis Miller, Esq. The Chautauqua Assembly is one of the fruits of his thoughtful and earnest life...' "[2]

The Miller letter to Dr. Harper continued to identify the goals and characteristics of the new enterprise. "The original scheme was a Christian education resort which should change... from an evangelism idea to Christian development, when all phases of modern civilization should be made to give recognition to true Bible development, that modern civilization was Christian civilization. That pleasure, science, and all friends of true culture should go side by side with true religion. To develop such a scheme and give it the strength to gain a place in the thoughts of the various phases of society, it requires the cooperation of the different denominations and educational interests."[3]

The visit to Fair Point on Chautauqua Lake by Mr. Miller and Mr. Vincent prefaced the October meeting of the National Sunday School Board, and their joint agreement on the suitability of the Chautauqua Lake site set the stage for the organization of the enterprise.

From Dr. Jesse L. Hurlbut in his volume, *The Story of Chautauqua,* we are reminded that the first Assembly was held not by Miller and Vincent independently, but "under the sanction and direction of the Sunday School Board of the Methodist (M.E.) Church." The Normal Committee of that denomination's Sunday School Union, for whom John Vincent was corresponding secretary, "was charged with the oversight of the projected meetings."[4]

The Normal Committee consisted of J. H. Vincent, the Rev. H. M. Simpson. secretary, the Rev. J. C. Thomas, J. Bentley and A. G. Newman. Moreover, the part of the Chautauqua Lake Camp Meeting Association must not be minimized. On August 16, 1873, the lot-owners of the Association had ratified the use of the Grounds for the proposed Assembly, and the Sunday School Union's acceptance of the Assembly idea, according to Vincent, was in response to a formal request by the executive committee of the Camp Ground Association.

The Normal Committee named Lewis Miller president of the proposed Assembly and John H. Vincent superintendent of instruction. One of the goals was to obtain the best talent in the country to assist with the Assembly.[5]

The spirit of cooperation which attended the founding of Chautauqua must have been one of the reasons for its success. We read that for almost a whole year efficient committees were hard at work. The operation of the Assembly had been divided into six departments: instruction, entertainment, supplies, order, recreation and sanitary. Most of the committee heads were from the Erie M. E. Conference. One was from Lewis Miller's home city of Akron.

The official report of the first Assembly prepared by the Rev. G. L. Westgate for the Sunday School Union, shows that three M. E. Bishops, three editors in addition to Vincent, three college or university presidents and other professors, Sunday School leaders and preachers from the main Protestant denominations appeared on the program. Two women, one a college professor,were also included. On the eleventh day of the Assembly, Vincent, himself, said that there had been one hundred seventy-eight ministers and one hundred twenty-five superintendents, but no man could number the Sunday School teachers who had participated. The response might be taken as a gauge of Miller and Vincent's combined influence nationally not only within their own church, but among other denominations.

The story of the Assembly's early growth into permanence is briefly told on pages 5-20 of *Three Taps of the Gavel.*

Much progress ensued during the first decade. Lewis Miller was quick to supply needs that he saw or to fulfill wishes expressed by Dr. Vincent. (Later Vincent was to say that he had given little attention to the financial condition of Chautauqua, trusting implicitly to the wisdom of the Board.)

Mr. Miller met the first year's deficit, and in time, found other men of wealth who would join him in supporting Chautauqua one way or another. Some would take positions on the Board. Some would assist Miller in providing buildings. Sometimes Miller's credit enabled the trustees to obtain loans and mortgages. Hurlbut gives an eye-witness account of Miller's attention to the details of Assembly life. He states that while Miller was able to take part in but few of the exercises, he and Vincent corresponded during the year about programs. The Assembly's educational goals were foremost in Miller's thinking. For a number of seasons he brought his Normal Class from Akron to study at Chautauqua and he served as Superintendent of the Sunday School during the first Assemblies. Hurlbut says that that task would be "like organizing a new school of fifteen hundred members every Sunday, on account of the constant coming and going of students and teachers."[6]

At the time that Chautauqua was getting started,

W.A. Duncan

Kate F. Kimball

Lewis Miller was president of the trustees at Mount Union College and he had also been serving on the School Board in Akron. He was well-equipped by practical experience in these positions to make decisions about educational matters and he was attuned to the concept of popular education which was to evolve at Chautauqua.

An example of his judgment may be seen in his counsel which Vincent accepted to have CLSC readers follow a simultaneous reading plan. All readers in any one year would read the same selection of books, but current readers would not necessarily have to read the books already read by their predecessors, as Bestor explains.[7] All readers, however, would eventually cover four years of reading centered successively on English, American, Continental-European and Classical subjects.

Correspondence learning was included with the reading plan during the first years. Members answered questions based on the prescribed books and articles or wrote paragraphs on coordinated subjects. Sharing written work and discussions, local Circles carried on their programs and kept in touch with CLSC headquarters, partly through The Chautauquan Magazine which included some of the required readings, a section for Circle reports, program guides and annotations on the readings.

The outreach of Chautauqua's education program took many paths. Until the optimism and expansionism of the times is remembered, it seems astonishing that these Chautauquans were unafraid to try new methods, unafraid to fail and unafraid to succeed. Their first concern was answering people's needs. As one sees the new features which were added year by year, one begins to sense the extent of their confidence.

A School of Theology, for example, was established to meet the needs of pastors who could study briefly at Chautauqua (or not at all) and carry their course work by correspondence. At the time correspondence study had been minimally tried elsewhere and was considered innovative.

As Chautauqua settled down into a steady growth and both founders became more involved with their individual careers, it was necessary to rely on others to assume larger Chautauqua responsibilities.

Amos K. Warren enjoyed the confidence of Mr. Miller in the position of Assembly Secretary and Superintendent of the Grounds. It was to Mr. Warren that Lewis Miller entrusted the building of the Athenaeum Hotel. After Mr. Warren's death, W. A. Duncan of Syracuse became Secretary and managed Chautauqua's practical affairs and records, remaining in this position until after Mr. Miller's death. It was through Mr. Duncan that Ellis G. Hall was brought to Chautauqua as the architect of many of the public structures which were built between 1885 and the turn of the century. (The Pier Building, the Electric Plant that became the Men's Club, the Arcade, the Presbyterian and Methodist Episcopal headquarters and the Seaver Gymnasium were his designs. He worked with Mr. Miller in designing the new Amphitheater and served as the superintendent of its construction.)

Miss Kate F. Kimball was the young woman whom

Dr. Vincent engaged to help with the CLSC correspondence that began to inundate him once the Reading Circle idea spread from state to state. Brought in on almost a temporary basis, the young woman soon proved her potential, progressing naturally from record-keeper to executive secretary; from an arranger of graduations to one of those who influenced the selection of books.

Dr. Hurlbut came the second year and for fifty years in all, helping first with the Normal Course for Sunday School teachers and later with the CLSC and in countless other ways.

Another person who came to Chautauqua at Vincent's behest to fill a special need and who remained for fifteen years was Dr. William Rainey Harper. There is no doubt that Dr. Harper's service at Chautauqua (detailed in *Three Taps of the Gavel* on page 48) proved to be even more valuable than Dr. Vincent would have imagined.

There are some who like to infer that John Vincent was extremely canny in signing up the promising young Baptist scholar, Dr. Harper. They think Vincent feared that the Baptists who had established a Christian resort across the lake at Point Chautauqua, or some other group might attempt a dynamic program that would be competitive with Chautauqua, and that it might occur to them to engage Dr. Harper.

However that may be, there is evidence that the two men met by appointment on a train "somewhere between Chicago and St. Louis" and came to an understanding about "sharing" Chautauqua.

While Vincent was shrewd to recognize Harper's abilities, Vincent, himself, was not without a national reputation and must have been equally intriguing to the younger man. During their meeting while Vincent was explaining the unusual educational program that was developing at Chautauqua, the basis was laid for a long, sincere friendship between the two men. Evidence of Harper's feeling for Vincent appears at the close of the article already referred to in The Outlook. Dr. Harper wrote: "No man ever heard Bishop Vincent speak without respecting him. No man ever came into close touch with him without loving him."[8]

In 1883 when the various departments of Chautauqua seemed to need a new "umbrella" under which to function, an application was made for a new charter as a university. When the charter was granted, Lewis Miller became President of the University, but the decision to name Dr. Vincent as Chancellor was delayed at Vincent's own suggestion. At last at the Annual Meeting in 1885, Vincent made recommendations for a reorganization which were immediately enacted by the Board.

There would be five main departments of the University.

The first, The Chautauqua Assembly, would include the summer meetings at Chautauqua, the Sunday School Normal Department, The School of Languages (CSL) and the Chautauqua Teachers' Retreat (CTR).

The second department would be the CLSC.

The third, The Chautauqua School of Liberal Arts (CSLA) (which had been known as Chautauqua University), with powers as designated in the charter.

The fourth, The Chautauqua School of Theology (CST) with purposes and powers as in its charter.

The fifth would be The Chautauqua Press. (For the first time The Chautauqua Press was established as part of the university.)

Three committees would be appointed to cooperate with the Chancellor in the management of the departments. There would be one committee on the Assembly; one on the CLSC, CSLA and the CST; and one committee on The Chautauqua Press.

The Superintendent of Instruction (Vincent) would hereafter be known as the Chancellor of the University. The Chancellor's duties would be: to arrange and conduct the Chautauqua Assembly; to engage speakers, teachers, leaders of music and such other assistants as the program might require; to conduct the affairs of the CLSC, the CSLA and CST; to submit to the Board each January a statement of the expenditures in the several departments during the previous year and an estimate of probable expenses for the ensuing year.

The income from the general membership fees in the CLSC, in the CLA and in the CST, with such annual appropriations as may be made by the Board to these departments, should constitute their funds respectively, out of which all expenses of these departments shall be paid annually. *The surplus in these departments should be paid to the treasurer of the Assembly Board.*

This last provision, however well-intentioned, was to figure in the 1898 dilemma.

The report of that meeting printed in the March, 1885 Chautauquan under the heading, "The Trustees Reorganize Chautauqua,"[9] seemed to enlarge the duties of Dr. Vincent as Chancellor, although perhaps it was only an official re-statement of the duties he was already performing.

We see specific mention of the reelection of Lewis Miller as President from year to year and presume this constitutes the precedent for the current Board policy to elect or reelect the President of the Institution annually.

The close cooperation between President Miller and Chancellor Vincent was expected to continue and reference to it appeared in print from time to time.

As the organization at Chautauqua was becoming more complex, Dr. Vincent's duties within the church intensified. It was natural then that he should turn to his only son, George, for extra help that he could rely on without fail.

The summer after George was graduated from Yale (1885), he began substituting for his father on the platform. His rapid delivery and natural wit caused Chautauquans to come early so they would not miss his program announcements. After his father was elected Bishop (1888), young George became Vice-Principal of Instruction, thus working closely with Dr. Harper, and about the same time we read of his taking charge of the publication of books for the Chautauqua Press.

In a report in the March, 1889 Chautauquan, the listed responsibilities of the Book Director, George Vincent, included circulars and advertisements. It showed that Col. Elliott F. Shepard of the New York Mail and Express had been printing George's columns

Dr. Jesse L. Hurlbut

Dr. William Rainey Harper, Principal of the College of Liberal Arts

Dr. George E. Vincent

Dr. T.L. Flood

on popular education, and that George had prepared Advance Numbers of The Assembly Herald and other advertisements for Chautauqua and the CLSC.[10]

In 1890 Flood took Vincent into partnership and the Chautauqua-Century Press was formed to produce the CLSC Course and other books. Vincent actually served as Book Editor in this arrangement. It was in 1890 that the CLSC Building was built and given to Chautauqua by the new partnership. Flood, who had been the first editor of The Chautauqua Assembly Daily Herald, had become its publisher in 1880, the same year in which he established The Chautauquan Magazine. Later Flood was to add book production, principally for the CLSC.

George Vincent also became increasingly helpful to Dr. Harper, as Dr. Harper's supervision of the College of Liberal Arts became more demanding and the status of the College began to rise. After Dr. Harper's first year in direct management of the College, many able professors were attracted to Chautauqua and the reputation of the College was thereby enhanced. Dr. Harper's own return to Yale Divinity School as Professor of Semitic Languages reflected well on Chautauqua. Inevitably Harper's influence at Chautauqua extended beyond the College to the popular educational program of the Platform.

After he became President of the new University of Chicago in 1891, Dr. Harper continued his relationship with Chautauqua, so close were his ties of loyalty not only to Chautauqua, but to the concept of mass education which he found there. It is little wonder then that George Vincent followed Dr. Harper to the University of Chicago for his graduate work, and that after he earned his doctorate, he joined the faculty there.

It is interesting to contemplate the characteristics of Lewis Miller, John Vincent and William Rainey Harper and to notice that they shared similar capacities for hard work, optimism, idealism and a certain winsomeness that drew supporters to each of them. As Lewis Miller attracted men of Christian purpose and wealth to Chautauqua and John Vincent seemed able to unite those of widely separated views and positions, Dr. Harper attracted both professors and students to this college or university "in the woods."

Joseph E. Gould summarizes in *The Chautauqua Movement* the demands Harper fulfilled for the summer university. As Principal of the College of Liberal Arts, it was necessary for him to secure "fifteen department heads and one hundred or more teachers, preparing sections for over two thousand students, planning a curriculum to include language and literature, mathematics and science, music, art, physical culture and practical art." Gould says that he edited the catalogue, supervised the publicity and helped secure program events and formulate policy.[11]

But the thirst for learning which Harper saw in the rank and file at Chautauqua must have been an inspiration to him. His own love of learning and the desire to share the rewards either through teaching or administration were a mark of his own personality and emotional strength.

While all of the students may have numbered 2,000, as Gould estimates, the University students who were working toward degrees in April, 1886 were approximately 295 persons, according to Professor R. S. Holmes, registrar. The students were scattered geographically, representing thirty of the states, the District of Columbia and the Provinces of Ontario and Quebec. The numbers were "about equally divided" between the sexes.[12]

In the July 26, 1889 issue of The Assembly Herald, a report states that "450 students are enrolled in the College of Liberal Arts... The classes now organized are not sufficient to accommodate the increasing numbers and others will be formed at the end of this week in German, Latin, Hebrew and Greek."[13]

The collegiate atmosphere is amusingly described in a paragraph in the same issue where it jokes about how many professors, students and visitors are there from Yale. "Universities and colleges all over the country are represented here, though no one institution in such large numbers as Yale," the report says. "Many professors from our best universities and colleges teach at Chautauqua during the summer..." The writer goes on to observe that some institutions "noticeably Harvard, Amherst, the University of Wisconsin and the University of Michigan are appreciating this demand and are establishing within their walls summer schools...."

Statistics for 1890 for the College of Liberal Arts and the Schools of Sacred Literature show a total of 622 students. "Of these more than three hundred are teachers," states The Assembly Herald on July 26th. The students represent various geographical sections, as follows: New England, 50; Middle Atlantic States, 280; Central States, 190; Western States, 40; Southern States, 45.

The period between 1889 and 1892 was especially demanding for Dr. Harper and Chancellor Vincent for another reason. They decided to adapt university extension courses to Chautauqua's year-round offerings. Dr. Vincent had seen the University Extension Movement in England and thought it was a perfect plan for Chautauqua. Harper agreed, along with Dr. Herbert B. Adams of Johns Hopkins, who was teaching at Chautauqua in the summer.

By the fall of 1889, Chautauqua had a roster of professors who would be available as lecturers in communities across the country. These lectures might be of general interest or valuable to students who would sign up for credit, do written work and have personal guidance from the lecture-teachers by correspondence. It was one more way to reach the citizenry-at-large with learning. About 1892, however, it is said that Chautauqua began to realize that it could not be a full-year university. Established schools had profited from watching Chautauqua. With their own forward thinking, they had developed and enlarged their entire curricula and included summer courses. Chautauqua, therefore, continued only to maximize its original specialty of summer study, although even as late as 1900, there is evidence that credit for completed course work was granted to a faithful student by Chautauqua University.

Even when the title of "University" was dropped from the brochures and the Chautauqua System of Education was used as an overall description of the courses (1892), the quality of the faculty remained high. Yale, Wesleyan, the University of Nebraska, Wells, Boston, Hamlin, Northwestern and Chicago Universities were among the schools represented on the faculty.

In the description of the courses for the coming summer in The Chautauquan, June, 1895, this statement was made about the College of Liberal Arts: "Its standards of scholarship are high, its work being done under a charter granted by the Legislature of the State of New York, annual reports being submitted to the regents of the State University."

Vincent had sensed quite early that the College of Liberal Arts could never be put on a financially paying basis. "Yet it is of great importance to our work as a whole," he said in 1889.[14]

He continued candidly: "To many, Chautauqua has been and still is a superficial institution for giving a very large number of people a very thin veneer of spurious culture. But by establishing and supporting the College of Liberal Arts we disprove this assertion by showing that we know how to set a standard of thorough scholarship. It is very appropriate that the popular Assembly exercises should be made the virtual source of endowment for the College of Liberal Arts, which as it comes better to be understood, will gain in numbers and influence."

Lack of endowment was no doubt a factor in the changing educational patterns at Chautauqua.

The demands of Lewis Miller's own business affairs were increasing as the '90s brought more and more diversity into the lives of other Chautauqua leaders. Some negative forces developed. Dr. Flood, for example, who had been a constant factor for Chautauqua since 1875, developed other active interests, including politics. He even ran (unsuccessfully) for Congress from his home district in Pennsylvania. Along the way, he brought his son, Ned, into a management role with the Chautauqua publications and at about this time complaints about The Chautauquan and CLSC books began to surface. In 1893 the Bay View Association established its own reading circle, book list and magazine. The strength of the CLSC organization began to decline after Dr. Vincent was elected Bishop. Daughter Assemblies were either ignored or served by volunteers in a way that resulted in their smaller CLSC enrollments. "The uniqueness of Circle membership vanished," says Dr. Charles R. Kniker, in his volume, "CLSC 1878-1914, An Historical Interpretation of An of An Educational Piety in Industrial America."[15] Dr. Kniker specifies that in addition to an out-moded curriculum that was followed after 1890, the rise of new leisure activities, the extension of formal schooling and increasing urbanization were among the external forces threatening the CLSC.

This may have been the reason that Dr. Harper began to study the problem of the CLSC and to search for an answer that would save the Bishop's beloved brain-child and also strengthen the growing university of which he was president.

He found a willing ally in Dr. Flood who was anxious to divest himself of his publishing business.

When Harper's "Solution" was first made known to Dr. Vincent, he looked favorably upon it. Afterwards,

and at a crucial time, he withdrew his support.

We can imagine his first openness to any idea proposed by his good friend. He completely respected Dr. Harper. We can appreciate that there were benefits in the plan that he could see immediately: benefits to his longtime friend, Dr. Flood, and to his own son, George. The Bishop was quite aware of the problems with the CLSC and he must have been sorely perplexed about its future. In addition, Harper's plan held the promise that with the new plan Dr. Vincent could continue the same relationship he had always had with the CLSC. Later, however, the total effect on Chautauqua was a question he could not resolve. The year of 1898 was a testing time for Vincent, Miller and the Chautauqua Movement.

There are three different statements which are connected with Harper's "solution" which was indeed a plan to move the reading circle and the publishing interests from Chautauqua to Chicago.

The first, called Chautauqua Propositions, declared that the CLSC and the publishing interests would not (in the future) make any contributions toward the support of the Assembly.[16]

A supporting paragraph explained that the present situation of the CLSC was due in large part to the way the CLSC money which should have been used for organization and development had been turned over to the Assembly.

(The statement that the money derived from the CLSC should have been devoted to quality control and development of this important aspect of the work, harks back to the 1885 organization.)

Harper believed that the Assembly must be reorganized so that it could depend on its own income. His suggestion for doing this was in centralization of management and reduction of expenses, popularizing the work and broadening the constituency. An increase in gate fees was urged. (All of these recommendations were startling, if not explosive in their implications for the Assembly.)

Returning to the publication interests, the statement said that this part must be a subsidiary of the educa-

College of Liberal Arts Building was ready for the 1887 season. It was affectionately called "the Moorish Barn," for obvious reasons. Unfortunately, it was allowed to deteriorate and was razed in 1916.

tional side of the work. To do this the Chautauqua-Century Press and The Chautauquan must become the property of the CLSC and the CLSC must become incorporated as an institution not for profit. The CLSC thus organized and endowed must work with the various Chautauquas, with colleges and universities and with other reading clubs.

The new corporation would be named The Chautauqua Institute. It would be organized with Chicago as its headquarters. It would "include the CLSC, receive from the Chautauqua University, The Chautauquan and the Chautauqua-Century books and goodwill; (and) the Institute of Sacred Literature."

The "organization would include a Board of Trustees of nine men to whom should be entrusted its business affairs. . .; a council of educational experts to whom should be entrusted the selections and approval of all publications; and a faculty of teachers who would prepare its publications and train its lecturers."

The Chautauqua Institute's first purpose would be the "encouragement of good reading." Its work would be "conducted in cooperation with Chautauqua Assemblies. . ., with certain colleges and universities" and "with reading associations already organized."

A vigorous effort would be made to secure endowment for the Chautauqua Institute, but it would be maintained meanwhile by its fees and by special gifts.

In a second detailed statement concerning the Chautauqua Institute, the coordination and combination of all private reading circle and home study enterprises in the United States was anticipated as well as all of the publishing of books and periodicals for the home reading market.

It was further suggested that books published for various levels and interests of reading circles would be placed on the open market as well, and an appeal would be made to the general trade.

The "Starting Point" of the project was the acquirement of the CLSC as an organization, the purchase of The Chautauquan and the Chautauqua-Century Press, contracts or franchises, goodwill, subscription lists, copyrights, plates, etc. (The contract between the present proprietor and the Chautauqua management is to expire Jan. 10, 1906. The Chautauqua-Press has a list of sixty books in its catalogue.)

The future extension of the reading circle would be developed through the more than sixty Chautauqua Assemblies which could become influential centers for the movement.

A stock company with capital of $500,000 was part of the plan. No part of the capital would be used for equipping a manufacturing plant. Printing and bookmaking would be done by contract. A monopoly of the reading circle business was anticipated and with the Chautauqua CLSC demand as a center core of the business, "a profitable outcome seemed certain. . . ." "The elimination of the present menace of competition and widely scattered effort in reading circle work would make possible the reduction of prices and fees, thereby increasing the enrollment of readers and rendering larger profits certain," the prospectus said.[17]

A third paper was a draft of an agreement to be signed by a contributor (to the Fund) for the general purpose of distributing the results of literary, scientific and biblical investigation, with the understanding that:

1. The work provided for by the income of said fund shall be done under the name of the Chautauqua Institute, said Institute to be incorporated under the laws of the State of Illinois, with a Board of Directors who shall be selected by Bishop John H. Vincent and the donor, and who shall perpetutate themselves in accordance with the terms of the charter. The headquarters of the Institute shall be in the city of Chicago.

(This may have been devised originally for the interview with Miss Helen M. Gould for the solicitation of an endowment gift.)

2. That the said Institute shall assume and develop the work of the Chautauqua Literary and Scientific Circle upon such terms as may be agreed upon with the Board of Trustees of the Chautauqua Assembly.

3. That Bishop John H. Vincent shall sustain the same relationship to the Chautauqua Institute which he now sustains to the Chautauqua Literary and Scientific Circle and the Chautauqua Assembly.

4. That The Chautauquan and the Chautauqua-Century Press publications now owned by private parties under a contract which operates for ten years to come, shall be transferred to the Board of Trustees of the Chautauqua Institute on the following conditions:. . ."

(Dr. Harper had laid out equitable procedures in great detail, thus illustrating his direct way of dealing with problems or projects.)[18]

There were some other provisions in his specific proposal that are of interest, however: That the magazines, journals and books used by said Institute in the prosecution of its work should be published by the University of Chicago Press upon such terms as might hereafter be agreed upon, said Press acting as agent for the Institute;

That the income of said fund should be used for the purpose specified except that in the discretion of the trustees the sum of $50,000.00 might be used as capital in the transaction of business, with a provision that a sinking fund should be established for the replacing of this amount, the same to provide $2,000.00 a year for twenty-five years;

That the Extension Division of the University of Chicago be associated with the work of the Chautauqua Institute in such a way as might best promote the efficiency of both.[19]

That the Chautauqua Trustees would transfer their goodwill and the goodwill of the system of Chautauqua Assemblies in the United States and throughout the world in so far as it lay within their control, and that the Chautauqua Institute should associate with itself the Chautauqua Assemblies in so far as may be practicable.

There were doubtless those at Chautauqua who believed that Dr. Harper would make a good president when Lewis Miller might choose to retire and the young educator could not have been unaware of the position of respect which he occupied at Chautauqua. Perhaps this knowledge gave him the courage to draw up the plan which he admitted in a letter to George Vincent was "radical." He knew he had the support of Dr. Flood and his son, Ned, who hoped to work with the Institute in Chicago. George was discouraged enough with Dr. Flood to be favorably inclined toward the plan. Both he and Dr. Harper felt that their presentation had won the Bishop's support. (JHV letter of May 3, 1893; "The CLSC could not suffer by the plan and I am satisfied that Dr. Harper is all right.")[20]

Dr. Harper, wasting no time, looked for someone who might want to invest money in the plan. He found a Mr. Conkey who offered to put in $50,000.00. Dr. Flood objected to that amount, saying that he would not consent to the business going to Chicago on any less than $100,000.00 paid up working capital because that amount would be needed to put agents into the field and to carry on a successful propaganda movement. Indeed, he was persuaded that the capital stock of the new company should be twice that, of which $100,000.00 would be cash. He added that he had more than $50,000.00 invested in the business in Meadville in buildings, machinery, money etc., "that we do not expect to load up this new transaction with."[21]

In an earlier letter the same month (March 2, 1898), Dr. Flood had written to Dr. Harper enthusiastically: "The impression...is this: That we would have a combination of the Chautauqua reading circle movement and assemblies—the greatest movement of the kind in the world—yourself and the Vincents and Mr. Conkey, a great capitalist with a tremendous printing house already organized to do the work in the most economical way at the lowest prices...We are not looking for a Sunday School man or a reformer...We are looking for a successful business man and he seems to measure up...

"Therefore, I am in favor of it and am ready to join hands with you and Dr. George E. Vincent and Bishop Vincent in bringing it about...I am well satisfied that if Bishop Vincent endorses it, we can go to the Chautauqua trustees.and they will approve it without any trouble..."[22]

Another step in the development of funds may be found in a request from Miss Helen Miller Gould for $25,000.00 as a gift to the Chautauqua Institute. The purpose of this gift is listed in a letter from Dr. Harper to Miss Gould. It states that the gift would purchase for the Institute The Chautauquan Magazine and its rights from Dr. Flood.[23]

In her reply a week later, July 2, 1898, she indicates that Bishop Vincent had joined Dr. Harper in the gift request and that the first sum mentioned to her had been larger. "Were it not for other interests and obligations, I would gladly promise the full amount mentioned...," she says. She puts among the conditions of her gift that a permanent endowment of $100,000.00 be raised before January 1, 1899, and that her name be withheld until the full amount is raised.[24]

A handwritten letter to President Harper from George Vincent, June 7, 1898, explains the basis for his discouragement with Dr. Flood and the way the CLSC was heading. It served as a further encouragement to Dr. Harper to proceed.[25]

By August 3, 1898, George Vincent was able to report to Dr. Harper on the Board's first reaction to the plan which apparently had been already submitted for consideration. Dr. Harper was remaining in Chicago partly it is assumed because of responsibilities there

and partly because he did not want to exert undue personal pressure on the Board.

George reports that the Board has delayed action for two weeks because the "radical" plan was difficult to understand fully.

The objections George summarized:

"1. Taking the heart out of Chautauqua in removing the CLSC from the control of the Chautauqua Board to a distant and unrelated group of trustees...."

"2. A feeling that the endowment was not for the Assembly but for another institution, and that it would be giving away without any return a source of revenue up to the present, something which might be maintained as a loss in the future, for the sake of the general good...."

"3. A reaction on Chautauqua of the popular conviction that one of the most characteristic elements had been transferred to other auspices."

"4. The popular conviction that a heretofore democratic institution would come under the auspices and control of capital." (This was the suggestion of Senator Higgins, a Chautauqua trustee.)

"5. Mr. Duncan's contention which he made very vigorously, that such a transfer would impair the value of the bonds and would be resented by all Property holders at Chautauqua."

"6. If the fund is to be raised for Chautauqua, why not have the Board of Trustees, reorganized, if necessary, made the trustees and have the thing administered by Chautauqua for Chautauqua?"

George admits that answers to all these objections "readily occur to the minds of those who support the measure."

Then he brings in the name of Mr. Day who was to become quite influential during the few years of change that were imminent. Mr. Day, a trustee from Cleveland. Ohio, apparently felt some compromise could be reached, whereby the end would be secured without divorcing the CLSC from Chautauqua. He suggested that the Chautauqua Board be reorganized and another sort of administration guaranteed and that the endowment fund be raised for the Chautauqua Board.

George urges Dr. Harper to consider compromise, cooperating in the accomplishment of the goal without sacrificing the unity of Chautauqua. He calls on his "deep and genuine interest" in Chautauqua.

Before closing, he reminds his good friend of the delicacy of his own position. "I am trying as honestly as I can to do the best thing for Chautauqua irrespective of the best thing for me."

Concerning Miss Gould's proposed gift, he quotes Mr. Miller's opinion that Miss Gould's letter reveals that "the conditions had been laid out for her, and therefore there was no reason to believe that if other conditions were laid out for her, she might not accept them."

Then he urges Dr. Harper to be present at the next Board meeting. "Mr. Day says that if you do not want to give the impression of pushing things through, that you ought not to stay away. And the general desire of everybody is to have you at the next meeting and have a full and thorough discussion of the whole matter. The Board are in the position of honestly wanting to

Wilson M. Day

do the best thing, and if they can be convinced that this is the best thing, they will vote for it. There is no captious opposition. So far there is only a desire for more light."[26]

A reply from Dr. Harper contained agreement that it was wise for the Board to delay a final decision. Opposition on the Board is only natural and inevitable, he said. However, he came out strongly for the basic premise of his plan:

"The very essence of the whole plan is to separate the CLSC from the New York Chautauqua. This is vital. Nothing can be done on a large scale until this is accomplished. The CLSC has been bled for the sake of Chautauqua and Chautauqua has lain down on the CLSC, and for this reason failed to do many things which otherwise she would have done and which she will immediately do if separated from the CLSC. That the idea of the CLSC should succeed during the next twenty-five years, it is necessary to be in a position to make combinations. This is the only possibility of success. Joined with the New York Chautauqua, this will be impossible. The CLSC or better the Chautauqua Institute of which the CLSC becomes a part, will be in a position as a separate institution to come into relationship with other Chautauquas and other institutions. It would be no easier in the future than it has been in the past to secure the co-operation of other Chautauquas and other institutions if the CLSC should continue to be connected with Chautauqua."

He felt there was no danger to Chautauqua, that he had already raised the question of the bonds and it was shown that relief from the CLSC as a certain amount of regular expenditure meant that the matter ought not to be a serious one.

He said he could not ask Miss Gould to change the conditions of her gift. He would not object to someone else presenting her with a new set of conditions.

If his plan was not to materialize, he told George another association similar to the CLSC would be organized in Chicago. It was to avoid this and to perpetuate the name of Chautauqua that he had devised the plan and the name Chautauqua Institute.

In addition to his own view that Mr. Miller had always opposed the CLSC, he told George that the Bishop's attitude was even more serious. He says: "Before we obtained the promise from Miss Gould, he informed me absolutely that he proposed to withdraw officially from Chautauqua. This was reiterated again and again before the meeting of the committee, the reasons, of course, being evident. Now, he maintains that the adoption of the report of this committee will compel him to withdraw; in other words, his ground has entirely shifted. I cannot help but feel that his position is unreasonable, but of course, you understand that I am not willing for a single moment to antagonize his wishes in this or any other matter."

But he assured George that he was willing to assist the future development of Chautauqua provided he could see that matters were in a shape that would warrant the supposition that development would be possible.[27]

It was shortly after this that word was received of the death of Theodore Miller in the Battle of San Juan Hill and the adjourned meeting of the Board of Trustees was postponed until after the funeral services would be conducted in Akron.

The funeral arrangements were delayed because Theodore's body was in quarantine in New York. In the meantime, the Chautauqua committee had undergone considerable change of sentiment.

According to a letter from George Vincent to Dr. Harper, Mr. Day was "in favor of Chautauqua autonomy and consolidation in Cleveland and of raising money to secure control of The Chautauquan and publications. . . ." Mr. Skinner, treasurer, had altered his position, in favor of securing the result under Chautauqua auspices rather than under the Chicago Plan. But if the Board would choose to do nothing, he would favor the original scheme (Harper's). Mr. Thomas seems to have weakened in his support of the Committee's report. Mr. Rockwell is stiffer than anyone in standing by the report. He puts the chief confidence in your judgment of the matter.

"I understand that other trustees, for example, Short, Jesse Smith, Duncan, Robert Miller and Lewis Miller are openly antagonizing the proposition.

"Father's attitude remains unchanged. He feels that he was subjected to very severe pressure at our last conference and my heart smites me in some measure for my share in it. He at once telegraphed Mr. Day that there were obstacles to the Cleveland plan, and that it would better be reconsidered or modified. Father has adopted a position of absolute neutrality. He will not oppose the Chicago plan, nor will he advocate it. He will acquiesce in it if it is deemed best by the Board, and in the absence of any other plan he regards it as probably the best available scheme."

George continued by saying that a Chautauqua autonomy plan and the Chicago plan would probably both be presented and should be discussed thoroughly. Again, he urges Dr. Harper to come and underlines that request by adding the names of Mr. Skinner and Mr. Rockwell as others who advise his presence. Along the way, the suggestion that the Chautauqua Institute Board contain some members of the Chautauqua University Board received unenthusiastic approval from Dr. Harper, but is mentioned again by George as the "best thing in sight."

A postcript to George's letter records the fact that Mr. Skinner has read the letter and thinks it is a true account of the way things stand.[28]

Five days later George wrote another letter to Dr. Harper. In it he encloses a general plan that had been formulated by Mr. Day and Mr. Skinner. Unfortunately the copy of the Plan has not been preserved with the letter. But it probably contained the elements of the changes that were to come.

"We went yesterday to Akron to the funeral of Theodore Miller. Everything passed off very smoothly. Father in the memorial address, quite outdid himself. I think it was the best thing I ever heard him do. He had prepared very carefully, and I never knew an address to be more delicately fitted to the occasion. Everybody was delighted, and the family greatly gratified. I think the personal relationships have never within a dozen years been so satisfactory as they are today. Of course whether there is any element of permanency in it remains to be seen.

A picture of some of the early Board members taken on the steps of Normal Hall, probably 1897 or 1898. Chester Massey is in the middle of the second row. Mr. Duncan, Dr. Vincent and Lewis Miller are easily identificable on the front row. W.H. Shortt of Youngsville, Pa., on the right in the top row, was one of the Board members to oppose Dr. Harper's plan for the CLSC.

Another timely note was added: "The season is holding up very well;—contrary to my expectation, the three extra days are proving a success."[29]

We have no record of the Board meeting so heartily anticipated, but it is apparent the Chicago plan was not adopted and that other changes were to take place over a period of months.

Reference to an implied coolness between the founders' families and the use of a time frame of "a dozen" years causes speculation over the cause. Could it have been connected with the University and John Vincent's emerging prominence as Chancellor and then his election as Bishop?

On November 10, 1898 George Vincent wrote to Dr. Harper a letter that must have been difficult for him to write in view of his conflict of loyalties.

"I just received permission last night to tell you what has been kept a secret heretofore. I did not feel at liberty to disclose it in our interview on Monday.

"Ten days ago father and Mr. Day saw Miss Gould and explained to her the change of plan in detail. She seemed to prefer the plan of autonomy and unity and promptly promised to give $25,000.00 provided that $25,000.00 more could be raised and she extended the time limit. The money is to be for Chautauqua endowment. Mr. Day believes in supporting the summer schools by endowed chairs and swinging the publishing end as a business proposition. He is arranging to borrow money for the purchase of The Chautauquan and the books.

"I hope we may have the proposed interview at an early date."[30]

Approximately three months later Chautauqua experienced a severe setback in the death of Lewis Miller, its president, at a time when other momentous changes were already in motion.

There is some suggestion in one letter from Dr. Harper to George Vincent and in another to Mr. Day that Dr. Harper greatly regrets the misunderstanding that developed between him and the Chautauqua Board and that it might have been avoided.

To George, he writes: "If I had received this letter (the copy of the letter of your father to which you referred in our conversation), the whole matter would have assumed a different form. I should have been able to answer the question asked in the latter part in the affirmative. As a matter of fact, I myself had written about the same time, to you, a letter which granted that the dismemberment of Chautauqua was a thing no longer to be considered, in view of your father's feeling...The whole question is whether it is not too late to mend the situation."[31]

He thanks Mr. Day for the "full and kind statements which you have made in your letter of June 30, (1899)." But Dr. Harper had already said that he felt his assistance at Chautauqua was no longer needed.[32]

As early as May 31, 1899, he had acknowledged with cold politeness a letter received from John Vincent the fall before. He closed with a request that Dr. Vincent present his (Harper's) resignation to the Chautauqua Board at the next meeting.[33]

By August 4, 1899, he put into motion a plan of organized University Readers and University Reading Groups which would function as a fourth division under the Extension Department of the University of Chicago. Writing to Professor James, he outlines the general plan embodied in the Chautauqua Institute Proposal. In the final paragraph, he refers to the fact that Professor James will be working on this plan with Mr. Flood. Thus, we assume, that Ned Arden Flood was already working in Chicago with the University. The Flood interests at Chautauqua were to be terminated with the September, 1899 issue of The Chautauquan.[34]

Even in 1899, the story of Dr. Harper's resignation from Chautauqua became a "big story" in metropolitan newspapers. Some journalists charged that an attempt by Rockefeller and/or the Baptists to take over the Chautauqua Movement had been foiled. Headlines included: "Methodists Outwit Baptists;" "Holy War—Methodists Knock Out Baptists."[35]

The articles included the interpretation that the defeated proposal would have made Harper the virtual head of the Chautauqua Movement.

Hostility to the Chicago plan brought to the front

Clement Studebaker

Wilson M. Day of Cleveland on whose proposition it was decided that all the departments except the Assembly should be centered in Cleveland.

(The unsuccessful launching of the Chautauqua Institute to save the CLSC seems to explain Dr. Harper's later lack of acknowledgment of Chautauqua at the University of Chicago, a fact that Gould notes.)[36]

Dr. George E. Vincent was elected to take Dr. Harper's place at the head of the collegiate department. Mr. Day became General Manager, superintendent of the Grounds and treasurer. Clem Studebaker of South Bend, Indiana, who had been first vice president became acting chairman of the Board and was elected permanent chairman in August, 1899.

A letter from Dr. Harper to Thomas E. Will of Manhattan, Kansas, answers some of the charges that had been made in the press. Dr. Harper says, in part:

"A more absurd statement could not have been invented than the statement that the Standard Oil Company of Mr. Rockefeller or the University of Chicago desired to get control of the Chautauqua Movement. As a matter of fact, the trustees of the University and Mr. Rockefeller have for years made every effort to persuade me to break my connection with Chautauqua on the ground of my health and my duties connected with the University. I make this suggestion because I am sure you desire to publish only the truth...."[37]

For the record, it might be well to reproduce a copy of Bishop Vincent's letter to Dr. Harper which is undated and which may be the letter Dr. Harper says he wishes that he had received before it was too late. The letter reads, as follows:

"My dear Dr. Harper:

"It is impossible for me to carry out the concession which I made under unreasonable pressure when we last discussed the Chautauqua problem. I cannot be neutral or indifferent to a consummation I have foreseen and feared for years, and against which I have faithfully and forcibly, again and again protested.

"I honor you. I have received many kindnesses at your hands. I believe that you have been honorable throughout. If I were in your place, I should feel as you do; but I must protest against the dismemberment of Chautauqua. I cannot help myself. Your plan would be agreeable to me for several reasons, and immediately better for George. It would relieve me of much anxiety; but I have my Church work, many old Chautauquans and the future of Chautauqua itself to take into consideration. I dare not, even by silence, permit what appears to me a serious damage to the interest I have loved and served for a quarter of a century, in which my personality is intimately involved.

"Why will you not remain to help Chautauqua as Chautauqua? This I shall be happy to have you do; but I ought not, I cannot consent to the separation of its interests. Faithfully yours, J.H.V."[38]

Was this the question Harper said he could have answered in the affirmative?

The twenty-sixth annual meeting of the trustees of the Chautauqua Assembly was held at the Hollenden Hotel, Cleveland, Ohio, January 11, 1900. Fifteen of the twenty-four trustees answered to roll call. Bishop Vincent sent his regrets in a letter to Mr. Studebaker along with extremely gracious words of congratulations on the success that was "crowning" the Chautauqua Movement in all its departments. He especially commended the Board on the recent issues of The Chautauquan.

From the report of Mr. Studebaker, the acting president of the Board of Trustees, the reorganization of Chautauqua's work had evidently already taken place although the vote on revision of the by-laws was yet to be adopted at that meeting.

According to the reorganization, the general administration was now centered in the Executive Board. Much power had been given to this Board and to the respective heads of the departments of instruction and administration. Hence, many meetings and frequent consultations had been held, Studebaker said. System, efficiency and economy had all increased as a result, he continued.

The season of 1899 was the 25th season. "The Program was unusually rich and symmetrical," he said, "The summer school showed the high-water mark of attendance and the general health, order, and good-will was highly gratifying."

Mr. Studebaker said that the Assembly would not, however, be in a position to prosecute its great educational work as it should until the endowment fund would reach at least a half a million dollars. He hoped that the fund "so auspiciously begun by friends of Chautauqua, would be followed up."[39]

Reports of the Popular lectures and entertainments were given along with the Schools. In an appended report by Miss Kimball, an increase of more than 50 per cent in the CLCS class enrollment of 1903 over 1902 was shown. There had been an increase of 25 per cent in new circles, as well. There was a slight reduction of price for the CLSC course; the required books were cut to four with a closer relationship between the Course and the Magazine. There was a list of special courses for graduate students. The series of articles in the Magazine were planned so that they might form the basis for literary club programs. This was an apparent attempt to enter a different market beyond the families of Circle members.

The "working force" at Chautauqua included Wilson M. Day, Cleveland, chairman of the executive board and general manager. Mr. Day was a former newspaperman and was president of the Cleveland Printing and Publishing Co. He was also a member of the Board of Allegheny College. Perhaps his election to the Board at Chautauqua might have come about through an acquaintance with Lewis Miller in Akron when Day was an editor of the old Akron Beacon. Day was also a son of a Methodist minister of the Erie Conference. At any rate, his presence on the Chautauqua Board at a time of transition made him a candidate for the post of interim leader. It appears that he had agreed to give several years to the endeavor. From his credentials, he seems to have been well-prepared to oversee the restructuring of the Chautauqua Press and it was logical for him to move it to Cleveland.

He selected William S. Bailey to be publications director. Bailey was a son of the first publisher of the Chautauqua Assembly Daily Herald, Milton Bailey. Although he was from Jamestown, Bailey moved to

Cleveland with the Chautauqua interests.

Frank Chapin Bray of The Literary Digest was made Editor of The Chautauquan and its quality noticeably improved immediately. He remained with The Chautauquan until it merged with the Independent, and during that time it achieved some interesting innovations. Some of its series of articles were reissued as books, and the magazine, itself, was offered at one point as a reading course in combination with such important daily newspapers as The Detroit Journal, the Toledo Blade, the Cincinnati Post and the Los Angeles Express. Pets and Animals, the publication of the Junior Naturalist Clubs organized in cooperation with Cornell University's Nature Study Department, was produced by the Chautauqua Press under Bray who also wrote a popular book, "A Reading Journey Through Chautauqua." (Often quoted from this book are Bishop Vincent's introductory paragraphs which define Chautauqua.) The magazine's art work also improved when Bray became editor. Lewis Buddy is listed as Art Editor and presumably must be given credit for the cover designs and illustrations that attract the interest of art historians today.

Bray had been brought to Chautauqua when he was a boy and had an early relationship with Chautauqua publications, having been first a newsboy and later a typesetter for Dr. Flood.

The merger with The Independent paralleled changes within the CLSC and within the magazine publishing climate in the country. For a time Bray continued to be the Chautauqua Editor with The Independent. During Bray's term at Chautauqua, the Institution also began The Chautauquan Weekly and there was attempted briefly The Chautauquan Weekly Newsmagazine. The Chautauquan Weekly resumed with the merger of The Chautauquan with the Independent and continued through 1933.

In a paper on "The Role of Chautauqua in Adult Education" written in 1948 by William S. Bailey, he recalls that the subscription list of The Chautauquan was pitifully small when Chautauqua assumed ownership, testifying to the magazine's lessening appeal under Flood.[40]

A. W. McCoy of Meadville became Editor of The Assembly Herald which was renamed The Chautauquan Daily in 1906.

George Vincent was listed in the work force as Principal of Instruction. His assistant was Scott Brown who was also a faculty member at the University of Chicago. When Wilson Day would leave his administrative post at Chautauqua, Scott Brown would be named as "Director." Arthur E. Bestor, came in 1905 from the same university as an assistant to Scott Brown.

J. F. Hunt was director of buildings and Grounds; George W. Rowland, chief of sanitary, fire and repair service.

According to the revision of the bylaws enacted January 11, 1900,[41] a five-member executive committee would carry on the general executive work. It was composed of the chairman of the board, the principal of instruction, the president of the board of trustees, the treasurer of the board of trustees and the secretary of the board of trustees.

The overall work was divided between the department of instruction and the department of administration.

The department of instruction "embraced" summer schools, home reading, and popular lectures and entertainments.

Administration contained the subdivisions of publications, buildings and Grounds, extension, and accounting/finance.

In addition to the expected duties of a Principal of Instruction, George Vincent was charged with shaping the general literary work of Chautauqua, selecting the CLSC books, overseeing the general policies of The Chautauquan and all educational work.

The chairman of the Executive Board was responsible in both broad and specific terms for the financial functions and interests of the Assembly, to cooperate with the Principal of Instruction on all publishing interests and "propaganda movements." He was to devote especial attention to securing permanent endowments and gifts of buildings.

Thus may be seen how continuity was maintained during a strong test of Chautauqua's purpose and leadership, with the Chautauqua Board of Trustees responding valiantly as the loss of the first president-founder had to be faced and the 25th anniversary needed to be celebrated.

There even seemed to be an aura of progress as the season of 1900 approached. The south allotment had been surveyed and avenues bearing the names of American poets and authors had been laid out. Building lots in this section were larger than ordinary Chautauqua building lots. According to a May, 1900 brochure, Lowell Avenue descended by an easy grade to Lake Drive which now followed the lake shore from

Front cover, The Chautauquan, 1907

The Library School was developed under an outstanding educator in that field, Melvil Dewey. Dewey was an active trustee and quite involved with the building of the first golf course.

the northern to southern extremities of the Grounds. The new iron bridge across the ravine leading to the south allotment would now permit a complete circle of the Grounds either by carriage or on foot. The laying of the cornerstone for the Hall of Christ was announced for sometime during the coming summer. A new and ample supply of pure drinking water had been secured through the sinking of an artesian well located on a high hill west of Chautauqua. From this well through a new system of pipes water was to be carried to public drinking and supply fountains in various parts of the Grounds.

Clement Studebaker, who had been drawn to Chautauqua by his fellow-industrialist , Lewis Miller, died approximately two years after assuming the full leadership role (November, 1901). Meanwhile, his son had joined the Board of Trustees and he remained active for many years. Mr. Day succeeded briefly to the presidency before asking to be relieved of Chautauqua responsibilities.

The first Colonnade had graceful curving outdoor steps to the second floor. The store fronts were in keeping with the period.

Actually, a great deal had been accomplished during Mr. Day's active management. The literary interests were improved; the business affairs were carefully looked after with a stronger emphasis on the Board's role. A modern electric power plant was built; the Hall of Christ was designed and begun; an overall architectural and landscaping plan for the Grounds was undertaken; the Hall of Education was built; and Chautauqua University formally dropped university status to become Chautauqua Institution, combining its various aspects more appropriately under a new State charter and establishing its corporate structure.

In addition, the stage was set for the election of a new chairman of the board, Dr. W. H. Hickman. Dr. Hickman would come in June, 1903 from the chancellorship of DePauw University although the formal election would not take place until August, confirming an arrangement ratified by letters from all the trustees. A descendent of two prominent Virginia families, Dr. Hickman was a graduate of DePauw from which he also had his Doctor of Divinity degree. He was formerly president of Clarke University in Atlanta. He was a member of the North-West Conference of the Methodist Episcopal Church and had served his denomination in a number of important ways.

The intricacies of the search for a newcomer to serve as board chairman are not clear, but the quality of the candidate could not have been higher. His experience as a university president emphasized the educational aspect of Chautauqua. Dr. Hickman, indeed, added greatly to the prestige of Chautauqua, for he was a gifted speaker and represented the Institution on many occasions throughout the country.

He had strong management skills. In 1904 when the stores burned along the part of Vincent Avenue which then extended through the Plaza, he successfully supervised the building of the Colonnade, raising money for it and other projects. During Dr. Hickman's administration, however, Scott Brown functioned as General Director of business affairs.

It is a matter of interest that after his first summer at Chautauqua, Dr. Hickman submitted a preliminary blueprint of his responsibilities relating to the "larger life" of the Movement.

First, he wanted to bring Chautauqua expenditures fully within the limits of its income.

Second, he hoped to clean up all debts except the bonded debt.

Third, he intended to complete the buildings that had been started and push with vigor the Commercial Block enterprise (the Colonnade).

Fourth, he wanted the strongest men in the country on the Board of Trustees, men who would not only serve, but who could and would give largely to the various phases of the larger life of Chautauqua.

"Successful administration along these lines will bring a certain enthusiasm, a certain widespread confidence in the stability and divine mission of Chautauqua. Conditions once obtained will make it easier to go to the outside world for endowments, betterments of properties, and bonded debt paying; but lacking these conditions, no man can hope to do much with the outside world." He added that the 1904 season had been successful and that the outlook was full of hope.[42]

In 1905, however, Dr. Hickman began telling the Chautauqua trustees that he did not wish to continue more than another year. He had been asked to become the pastor of the First Congregational Church in Jamestown and he was sincerely drawn to the pastoral relationship. The Colonnade opened in 1905 at least in part. The lower stores were occupied as the upper floors were completed. The structure was not formally accepted by the Board until 1906 when the landscaping of the Park near the new building had also been completed.

Dr. Hickman entered into a contract with Chautauqua concerning the amount of time he would give to the Institution in the off-season months during 1906, spending most of this time in church work in Jamestown, while spending full-time at Chautauqua during the season.

Then at the Annual Meeting of the Board of Trustees Oct. 30, 1906, Dr. George E. Vincent was elected President of Chautauqua Institution. This action, in effect created a new office, since Dr. Hickman had been elected President of the Board, not President of the Institution. Both Mr. Studebaker and Mr. Day had also been presidents of the Board, but all of them have been referred to as Presidents of Chautauqua and are so listed.

Dr. Hickman had strongly urged the election of Dr. Vincent, who then began his presidency at the beginning of the new year, 1907.

The state of Institution affairs following the season of 1906 seemed most satisfactory. There was great reason for confidence.

Dr. Hickman reported the completion of the Hall of Philosophy, except for the Athenian Lights, at a cost of about $16,000.00. The old hospital had been remodeled with new furnishings installed at a cost of $850.00. Twelve hundred feet of new wrought iron fence had been put up and pledges for about six hundred feet more had been secured. Difficulties with contracting parties for work on Auli Christi were reported, but the enclosure of the structure could not long be delayed, Dr. Hickman said. The sale of seventeen lots during the year for $5,700.00 was reported.

As Principal of Instruction, George Vincent said that the general average of excellence in the program of 1906 had never been equalled.

Among other things, he mentioned that the Institution was represented at the International Congress for Popular Education at Milan by Professor Andreas Baumgartner of Zurich.

The Board was anticipating the installation of the Massey Pipe Organ in time for the 1907 season.

If there ever was a time that continuity seemed reaffirmed by the Trustees at Chautauqua, it was at the election of George Vincent as President. He had grown up at Chautauqua, fulfilled whatever assignments were given him, completed his preparation for a professional career in education and excelling there, had remained faithful to the Chautauqua movement. He was a worthy successor.

It is interesting that while George Vincent had been a professor of sociology at the University of Chicago,

Dr. W.H. Hickman

The post office was new in 1909.

A Junior Orchestra was organized in the summer of 1943 by Edward Murphy of the Summer Schools' staff. It has grown substantially in size and quality through the years until now, as the Music School Festival Orchestra under Dr. Nathan Gottschalk, it plays in the Amphitheater in addition to the Chautauqua Symphony Orchestra. A second Youth Orchestra for younger students is also growing in performing experience.

he was made Dean of the Faculties of Arts, Literature and Science there in 1907, the first year of his Chautauqua presidency.

But other signs of continuity were working for Chautauqua. Dr. Hickman remained as a member of the Board of Trustees, after resigning as president. Ira Miller and Clement Studebaker, Jr., remained active Board members after the deaths of their fathers. Other Board members continued in office for a number of years, assuring the integrity of Chautauqua goals. Furthermore, John Vincent was still active to varying degrees from year to year. He was still called "Chancellor" and was often on the platform, although he had resigned from the Board of Trustees in 1902.

Chautauqua had also proved resilient in a social climate that was plagued by economic swings that could be devastating. It seems remarkable that Chautauqua was able to go from year to year without losing out to the financial uncertainty of some periods.

When George Vincent became President, the prospects were favorable overall. Arthur Bestor, who had been assistant to Scott Brown, became Director.

The enrichment of the popular educational program followed the Institution's aims and physical improvements continued, as well.

The year of 1909 was a noteworthy example. The new Colonnade had burned the October before, but a replacement was provided by the next season. 1909 also saw the building of the first section of the Arts and Crafts Quadrangle and the Post Office. Most thrilling of all was the completion of the Auli Christi (The Hall of Christ). This was also the year when Walter Damrosch brought the New York Symphony Orchestra to Chautauqua for the first time. The musical program was increasing in both quality and quantity under the leadership of Alfred Hallam.

Four years after George Vincent became President of Chautauqua, he also accepted the call to be President of the University of Minnesota. This development added prestige to Chautauqua but placed even more responsibility on young Bestor, although Vincent was known for his organizational ability and his capacity for hard work. (His training under Harper could not but have strengthened those personal qualities.)

Dr. Bestor is shown with longtime Chautauquan, Alf Landon when the latter was running for President of the United States and speaking at Chautauqua. (1936)

President Roosevelt delivered his famous "I hate war" speech at Chautauqua.

It is well worth mentioning that at the University of Minnesota Vincent inaugurated a circuit of "University Weeks," a modified Chautauqua. Programs included lectures by members of the faculty on many subjects, concerts by the glee club, debates by members of the debating societies, plays by the dramatic club, talks to business men at luncheons and to women's clubs in the afternoons.[43]

Arthur Bestor was not a complete stranger to Chautauqua work when he came in 1905 to assist Scott Brown. He had been an undergraduate at the University of Chicago when Dr. Harper was still heading the Chautauqua System of Education. Hs had been enrolled in class under Dr. George Vincent. His father, moreover, the Rev. 0. P. Bestor, had made it a part of his pastoral work to found CLSC Circles in towns in which he served.

Bestor graduated from the university in 1901 with an enviable record which included election to Phi Beta Kappa. After graduation he went to Franklin College in Indiana to teach for two years before returning to Chicago for graduate study and as a lecturer in political science in the Extension Division of the University. It is interesting that Dr. Harper's implementation of the extension course idea was continuing and did continue for some time. Indeed, Bestor, himself, remained as an Extension lecturer with Chicago until 1912 when duties at Chautauqua began to require most of his attention.

As Director of Chautauqua, Bestor had ample opportunity to learn how the diversity of Chautauqua must be handled so that program, schools, facilities and finances would mesh into a unified operation.

Board members continued during the Vincent presidency to participate as policy-makers. They could see that changes in the highway at Chautauqua's new front door were imminent and that there was need for improvement. The Board could envision the benefits to be derived from an improved highway which would bring more people to Chautauqua. So they began to plan and as opportunity presented itself, they purchased extra land. They knew that the trolley company would not spend money for a station if adequate

space were not available. The State and County Highway officials wanted to improve the highway, but the design would call for partial relocation. The purchase of the Prendergast Farm seemed imperative. Later the Prendergast Farm provided space for the golf course which brought an entirely new constituency to Chautauqua. Some land at the north end had also become available earlier and thus a considerable investment had been made.

But in 1914 just at the time that Chautauqua was hoping to begin to realize an estimated $150,000 return on its investment, international events and finally World War I intervened. While the market for vacation home sites was adversely affected, the State and County did, indeed, build a brick highway in front of the Institution's entrance and the Chautauqua Traction Company built a handsome brick Traction Station which became in 1917 the gateway into the Grounds.

Meanwhile, in 1915 George Vincent resigned as President of Chautauqua to become the President of the Rockefeller Foundation. Arthur Bestor was elected to succeed him at Chautauqua and a revision of the bylaws eliminated the office of director. George Vincent was named Honorary President of Chautauqua.

In 1919 Mr. Bestor also assumed the direct supervision of the summer schools when E. B. Bryan, President of Cogate University, gave up his Chautauqua position after serving for two years. (See page 49)

Through the person of Arthur Bestor, Chautauqua's continuity was to receive strong support. He remained in the presidency until his death, serving the Institution in different positions for approximately forty years; twenty-nine, as president. His thorough knowledge of Chautauqua was put to good use.

As might be expected, Dr. Bestor had an understanding of Chautauqua's unique fiscal position, which he stated well in successive annual reports to the Board. He was able to lead the Board and the Chautauqua constituency into a Half-Million Comprehensive Plan following World War I in hopes that Chautauqua might regroup its financial forces and face the future in a stronger position; eliminate interest payments and build up endowments.

A young Arthur Bestor came to Chautauqua as Assistant Director.

Governor Alfred E. Smith spoke at Chautauqua in 1926 and was accompanied on his visit by the Speaker of the New York State Assembly J.A. McGinnies of Ripley.

George Gershwin spent the summer of 1925 at Chautauqua, composing a commissioned work which became "Concerto in F". Ernest Hutcheson, shown with him, was head of Chautauqua's Piano Department in the School of Music.

Ralph H. Norton, seventh Chautauqua President

Ralph McCallister, Vice President, Program and Education, 1946-1961

During the presentation of the Comprehensive Plan,[44] the financial history of the Institution was summarized. It showed that beginning with 1892, there had been no liabilities, but by 1895, $94,000 of asset liabilities had been incurred. (The installation of a sewer system and the building of a new Amphitheater in 1893 may have been responsible. Also, an economic depression was generally experienced in 1893.) In 1900 further liability was incurred. (The purchase of the publishing interests took place at this time and the south allotment was developed.) During the first decade of the new century other major building projects were undertaken although a pay-as-you-go policy was followed as much as was possible. Then came the preparations for the Main Gate improvements.

John D. Rockefeller was persuaded to offer a 20 per cent matching gift as part of the $500,000 Comprehensive Plan. The first year of the Campaign was full of zest and more than half the goal was reached. The Campaign was officially closed in 1921 without total success but with much benefit reported and strict pledges of future financial management given, especially to the cottage owners.[45]

Dr. Bestor's years as President saw a creativity that matched the history of the times and the first years of Chautauqua. As Dr. Arthur E. Bestor, Jr., pointed out in a tribute to his father in The Chautauquan Daily August 4, 1944, Dr. Bestor possessed the ability "to grasp the real issues of American life and thought" during a period of change. He was able to build a program that maintained Chautauqua's "cultural and spiritual leadership."

Improvement of physical facilities kept pace with the enrichment of the program because Board members and President shared the same value-judgments. An expenditure such as that for the water filtration plant, however, was considered a matter of necessity.[46] When the 1929 world Depression came, Chautauqua faced bankruptcy and suffered acutely from disbelief and despair.

The major details of that crisis appear in *Three Taps of the Gavel* on pages 58-60. The toll of physical energy which was exacted from the leaders as they battled against great odds for Chautauqua's survival cannot be measured for the most part, but in 1944, sudden illness struck down President Bestor after a tremendously strenuous week which included besides constant travel, conferences with trustees and three Commencement addresses. Among other people he had seen were Ralph Norton, chairman of the board, and Ralph McCallister who was to become the new director of program and education at Chautauqua. In a letter to his children describing his week, Dr. Bestor wrote: ". . . .one of the finest things that I have ever done for Chautauqua has been to have an important part in securing his (Ralph Norton's) interest initially and in developing it over twenty years. I realize I have only a part in this but it has been somewhat important. . ." [47]

When Dr. Bestor died, Mr. Norton was persuaded the next summer to accept the Presidency of the Institution with Samuel M. Hazlett, president of the Chautauqua Reorganization Corporation (CRC), acting as his Executive Vice President. There were some,

including Mr. Norton, who would have preferred Mr. Hazlett to succeed Dr. Bestor, for Mr. Hazlett served as Acting President in the first few months following Dr. Bestor's death. But Mr. Hazlett had made a promise that he would complete the work of the CRC before he would leave it. He therefore remained at his main task but assisted Mr. Norton with administrative duties. Two years later Mr. Norton resigned partly for reasons of health but at a time when he felt confident that Mr. Hazlett could accept the added responsibility. Mr. Hazlett was elected in August, 1946.

While Mr. Norton was President, he instituted and provided liberally for the improvement of the Plaza as a memorial to Dr. Bestor. His efforts on behalf of the project (officially approved by the trustees), were a witness to the great friendship that had existed between the two men.

Mention must be made of Ralph McCallister and of his contributions to Chautauqua, beginning in 1944. Shortly before Dr. Bestor's fatal illness, Mr. McCallister had been selected as a professional in adult education to be engaged to ease the work load of the President. As Director of the Adult Education Council of Chicago, Mr. McCallister was well-qualified to function in both the education and program departments. Before he had actually begun his Chautauqua work, however, Dr. Bestor became ill. With Dr. Bestor's sudden death and the situation so shockingly changed at Chautauqua, Mr. Norton and a number of the Chautauqua trustees met with Mr. McCallister again. They asked him to complete the schools' and program plans for the summer and carry them through. Mr. McCallister recalls being introduced to his first Chautauqua audience by Mr. Hazlett and then presiding in the Amphitheater all summer. After a successful season, Mr. McCallister was appointed to a new position, Director of Program and Education. By this time Mr. Norton had been elected President.

It had been made clear to Mr. McCallister from the beginning that he was to report directly to the Board. This arrangement continued even after Mr. Hazlett became President and Mr. McCallister was named Vice President for Program and Education. As time went on, according to McCallister, the tenor of the Board seemed to be changing. When new members were chosen, emphasis seemed to be laid on qualifications related to their business careers. This trend was not to be wondered at when the events of the '30s were painfully remembered and post-World War II social conditions were understood. But Mr. McCallister began to fear for the educational, artistic and cultural values that might become subordinated to business interests. Budgetary issues and priorities of the Institution became points of debate. McCallister affirmed that Chautauqua should be "business-like," but not "like a business."

McCallister has stated that he felt at home at Chautauqua "in the creative tradition stemming from Miller, Vincent (both Vincents), Harper, Shailer Mathews and to some extent Bestor and found there an opportunity to serve some of my highest aspirations as a professional leader in continuing and adult education, and as a fosterer of the arts and recreations."[48]

There were many accomplishments. He succeeded

in obtaining three grants from the Fund of Adult Education which had been established by the Ford Foundation. Thousands of Chautauquans took part in this program that was very close to the Institutions's core purpose.

Under Mr. McCallister's aegis, Syracuse University began offering summer courses for university credit at Chautauqua (1954), when New York University chose to end its thirty-year affiliation with the Institution.

While justifiable emphasis has been laid on Mr. Hazlett's great efforts to maintain Chautauqua's operation when it was facing liquidation to achieve the final victory, his performance as president must not be taken for granted.

During his ten years in office, he administered Chautauqua with the high level of efficiency that had marked his CRC presidency. Those who worked with him tell also of his patience, courage and his sincere religious commitment. Certainly the record of Chautauqua's resurgence after the '30s testifies to his leadership.

As a President, he had strict ideas about the necessity for individual Chautauqua departments to balance their budgets. He stressed the religion department and the summer schools as the basic Chautauqua programs. His pet enthusiasm was youth. He advocated programs that would draw and hold the youth at Chautauqua. The High School and College Clubs first flourished under his presidency. He wrote Chautauqua's Diamond Jubilee Pageant. He made frequent speeches and traveled to visit Chautauqua Societies. Although he lived in Tarentum, Pennsylvania, he came to Chautauqua each month during the year and was a vigorous President while continuing the practice of law.

After Mr. Hazlett's death during the summer of 1956 at Chautauqua, Judge W. Walter Braham, vice president, succeeded to the presidency and served for four years.

The continuity of the Institution and the community was thus preserved as the leadership was selected from within the Board of Trustees. The post-war era with its frank enjoyment of the material blessings of peace was conducive to a vacation complacency. Nonetheless, Mr. McCallister on the lecture platform tried to direct attention to the major problems of the time and see that they were explored by leaders of thought and action. He frequently focused on individual countries, inviting ambassadors to be guests of the Institution and interpreters of their countries. There was an attempt to understand the workings of the United Nations. He brought into focus the Civil Rights issue. Unfortunately, the fears generated by the Joseph McCarthy probes even touched Chautauqua at times and Mr. McCallister was thought by some to be inviting too many speakers viewed as "liberals." But Mr. McCallister was forward-thinking in entertainment, as well. It was he who first brought New Orleans jazz to the Amphitheater and ballet to the concert stage.

Judge Braham was a winter resident of New Castle, Pa., and a distinguished member of the Pennsylvania Bar. He was retired from the Bench, but was still extremely busy in his profession. He was an historian by avocation and lectured frequently both at Chautauqua and elsewhere. For some time he had taught Chautauqua's Adult Bible Class. In 1960, however, Judge Braham made known his desire to retire, stating that he thought it was time for Chautauqua to have a year-round resident manager-president.

So another Chautauquan, although not a member of the Board, was voted in as President. He was J. William Carothers, selected, it appeared, because of his extensive experience in business. He had just retired as an executive from the Baltimore Gas and Electric Company. He was, indeed, a direct, let's-get-things-done kind of President.

One of the first staff vacancies to occur in the Carothers' presidency was created by the death of Gerald Lynch who had been treasurer since 1937. Curtis W. Haug, YMCA secretary in Jamestown, was recommended to fill the vacancy and was subsequently appointed. Haug was a personable young man who had attracted the attention of Board Chairman Cyril T.M. Hough and other trustees from Jamestown.

Meanwhile, a rift had been gradually developing between Vice President McCallister and some members of the Board. It may have represented a philosophical difference over Chautauqua's cultural and educational goals. At any rate, the new President with his management style widened the rift so that Mr. McCallister resigned rather suddenly in early January, 1961.[49] Mr. Haug was named acting program director almost immediately and after the 1961 season was elected vice president for program.

Early January brought another shocking event. A tragic fire gutted the Colonnade and took the life of one of the third floor residents. In this critical situation, Mr. Carothers exhibited outstanding leadership as he guided the rebuilding and spoke out confidently that the new building would be ready for the coming season. He established administrative offices in Smith Memorial Library, moved quickly to have the Colonnade site cleared, contracts let and the work carried forward without delays. His work in industry helped in a number of aspects of Chautauqua management. He was interested throughout his presidency in improving the physical functioning of the Institution. He negotiated the transfer of the Chautauqua telephone exchange to the Jamestown Telephone Co., considering it advantageous to Chautauqua.

There was much that was frustrating to President Carothers as he tried to turn a summer educational facility into a modern operational model that he could identify with. It was perhaps too much of a career-shock for him to come from a modern utility firm to the management of a place as unique and diverse as Chautauqua, even though he was used to vacationing there.

During Mr. Carothers' presidency the CLSC experienced a low point and made an upturn. During 1960 and 1961, CLSC had functioned without a director and some people thought that the Institution might decide that it had outlived its time. Dr. Frank C. Laubach, as has been mentioned, inspired CLSC alumni to express themselves on Recognition Day, and whether or not this led to the appointment of a director in 1962 is not clear. But CLSC began to take on new

Samuel M. Hazlett served ten years as President.

Judge W. Walter Braham succeeded Mr. Hazlett.

President J. William Carothers

George L. Follansbee, Acting President, Summer, 1963

Dr. John A. Reed, Executive Vice President, Summer 1963

Margaret Miller Newman, daughter of Ira M. Miller, granddaughter of Lewis Miller, speaks at the dedication of the new bells in the Miller Bell Tower in 1967. Mrs. Newman gave one of the bells in memory of her father.

Dr. Curtis W. Haug as he prepared to strike Three Taps of the Gavel for the last time, August 30, 1970.

life again. Another good omen in 1962 was a two-year subsidy received from the Ford Foundation to help with costs of hiring young opera singers. The next year the Martha Baird Rockefeller Fund for Music subsidized the first of three Mozart productions under George Schick.

In spite of Mr. Carothers' business accomplishments and his selection for the presidency by a business-oriented Board, there seemed to be a growing lack of cooperation between the Board and the President. Perhaps Mr. Carothers' health was also a factor in his decision to resign in May, effective June 15, 1963. In his letter of resignation, he said, "Because of my deep feeling for Chautauqua, it has been a satisfying experience to be helpful to the Institution at a time of crisis and gratifying to leave it in a sound and promising condition." The trustees agreed that he was leaving the Institution in a sound financial position. Mr. Carothers remained a full-year resident of Chautauqua until his death, May 1, 1969 , and his family continues to be a part of Chautauqua. A plaque denoting his service in rebuilding the Colonnade was placed there by his family July 1, 1971, on the l0th anniversary of its re-opening.

Vice President George L. Follansbee became Acting President in the summer of 1963, but because he could not give his full time to the position, Dr. John A. Reed, Old First Night Director, was asked to serve as Executive Vice President. (George Follansbee was President and Headmaster of Shadyside Academy in Pittsburgh at the time.) These two men, both of them Chautauquans for many years, gave to the community a valuable sense of continuity as they worked together that summer. John Reed was on duty every day. George Follansbee spent long weekends at Chautauqua and conducted staff meetings each Monday morning before his return to Pittsburgh.

All this time, Curtis Haug was proving himself to be a programmer with both flare and discernment. When first approached about the presidency, he said, "No. I like what I'm doing." Later he said, "Yes, if I can do the program, too."

Thus, Chautauqua returned to the idea of having the President be more than a manager. In the mode of George Vincent and Arthur Bestor, Curtis Haug became a popular presiding officer, never needing a note even for lengthy introductions. His most significant contribution came through the department of popular education as it was played out in the Amphitheater. He chose single and often popular musical events that brought large audiences to Chautauqua: Marian Anderson's Farewell Concert and the Kingston Trio when those young men were at the height of their first acclaim. The most noteworthy perhaps was the Mormon Tabernacle Choir which appeared in two concerts in one day, one of which was recorded for the Choir's regular broadcast. The lecture program was stimulating enough to satisfy most vacationing Chautauquans with occasional refreshing highlights: John Ciardi, Tom Wicker, a Meet the Press Format with Gerald Ford and Bobby Kennedy on two succeeding Friday nights. (Presiding Newsman was Lucian Warren.) There was the ever-resilient Ashley Montagu, the investments lecturer Julia Walsh, foreign affairs com-

mentators, popular science lecturers and a lifelong Chautauquan, Dr. Edwin Prince Booth, who for a number of years made historical biography on the platform both dramatic and literary.

Haug, himself, was a strong president in that most decisions had to pass through his office. In spite of this, he seemed readily available to all Chautauquans as well as to staff-members. It has been suggested that "not as much was going on at Chautauqua" then, but actually there seemed to be alot on the griddle. For example, Chautauqua enlarged its land ownership by 266 acres with the purchase of the Whallon Farm in 1965.

One of the significant events for the Institution during Dr. Haug's presidency took place June 30, 1970 when for the first time, Chautauqua Institution's status as an institution exempt from real property taxes under the laws and Constitution of the State of New York was established by a unanimous opinion of the Appellate Division of the Supreme Court. Four years of litigation had preceded the 1970 decision. Assessments for five years, 1966-1970, were involved with the Town, County and School District participating. The Institution recovered $145,000 in the outcome of the Court action. Eighty-one parcels were stricken from the assessment rolls upon the grounds that they were either totally or partially exempt.

About ten years before an expected celebration of the Institution's Centennial, a development plan was set in motion so that buildings and Grounds would be improved for the observance. Lincoln Dormitory was built in 1966. The same year the Miller Cottage was designated as an Historic Landmark. The Hall of Christ was completed and improved in 1967; Miller Bell Tower improvements included new bells and a new Westminster chime and clock; and the Arcade was renewed. The Beeson Youth Center was built in 1968. The Athletic Field had been named in 1965 for Dr. Albert H. Sharpe, outstanding physical education and Boys' Club director at Chautauqua. Several memorial gardens and additions to other gardens were established during this period.

In the midst of this preparation for the Centennial, President Haug resigned to become the managing director of the Van Wezel Performing Arts Hall in Sarasota, Florida. It was September, 1970. There was still time for a new president to be chosen who could give guidance to the 100th anniversary.

Shortly before this took place the continuity of Chautauqua's founding principles seemed to receive welcome reenforcement when Lewis Miller's great-grandson, Richard H. Miller, was elected to the Board. Mr. Miller said that he was glad to join the Board for he had a natural affection for Chautauqua and felt a responsibility because of his great-grandfather. In addition, he had the conviction that Chautauqua was uniquely capable of taking leadership in reactivating value concepts and pioneering new ways of transmitting them from generation to generation.

In September he was appointed chairman of the committee who would search for a new president and two months later at the annual meeting, he was elected Chairman of the Board. When a new president was

finally elected, it was Chairman Miller who made the formal investiture.

The rationale of the committee's search was explained by Chairman Miller in an article he prepared for The Chautauquan Daily.[50] He said that it was decided first to seek a person who could serve as both president and program director. It was thought that a president would have the maximum opportunity and authority to provide direct and creative leadership in programming.

Since education permeates the Chautauqua experience, it was expected, Miller said, that a president should have a strong orientation toward education and especially adult education; that he should have broad cultural interests and be an active churchman. He should have public speaking skills and administrative abilities; he should have some experience in financial development.

The final choice of Dr. Oscar E. Remick was not made until late March or early April, 1971. He was elected by the trustees April 17, 1971 and came in late July, shortly before his installation which took place August 1 at a 9:30 Sunday morning service in the Amphitheater.[51]

Dr. Remick seemed to meet all of the qualifications agreed upon by the Committee. He was a Baptist clergyman who was presently vice president, academic dean and coordinator of academic affairs at Assumption College in Worcester, Massachusetts. He was thus a teacher, a churchman, an administrator and an ecumenical leader. He was the first Protestant minister to have joined the theological department of a Roman Catholic College. He was not yet 39 years of age.

When he stepped into the pulpit on August 1, 1971, and undertook his presidential responsibilities, he affirmed:

"I accept the challenge of the presidency, highly determined that the visions of the founders will be expanded to embrace new perceptions of what it means to be a Servant of God in the service of man. . . ."[52]

It had a familiar and a reassuring ring.

Lincoln Dormitory was built by Mrs. John C. Lincoln in memory of her husband, giving the Summer Schools under Joseph C. Clarke a much-needed resource.

Dr. Remick receives the gavel at his induction as President of Chautauqua. Richard Miller is shown at left with Dr. Remick, Dr. Herbert Gezork, Director of the Department of Religion, and Joseph C. Clarke, Executive Vice President.

The "sweet nostalgia" of Old First Night was epitomized
in the fanciful, icing-ladened cakes on-stage. (1977)

2

Search for a Successor

WHILE CHAUTAUQUANS in their winter homes were busy with preparations for Christmas in December, 1976, a significant change in the fortunes of the Institution was taking place. Dr. Oscar E. Remick had decided to accept the deanship of the performing arts and a professorship in philosophy at the Fredonia College of the State University of New York. His formal resignation from the presidency was dated Dec. 24, 1976. The loss of a president was not the good news expected from the new year. Understandably it brought a certain amount of anxiety to Chautauquans who liked to think of this dream-of-a-place as a constant in a changing world.

Those who knew of Dr. Remick's enjoyment of a full-year academic environment and his love of teaching were not exactly surprised by his leaving. During his years with the Institution he had been teaching part-time at the nearby Fredonia College and had also accepted Christian Education responsibilities at the First United Presbyterian Church in Jamestown. He seemed to thrive on active involvement with "educating," perhaps assuming that the stimulation from teaching and dealing with students made him a better administrator. In addition, since coming to Chautauqua his personal participation in the arts had been expanded. He had been appointed to the New York State Council on the Arts and had proved to be an active member. Furthermore, he was foreseeing an even greater role for himself in this vital part of today's culture.

His intellectual examination of Chautauqua's relationship with the arts in the context of education resulted in new statements of Chautauqua's unique potential in the present and in the future. These he expressed in part in the Epilogue to the Centennial volume of Chautauqua history written by Theodore Morrison.[1] He appeared on many platforms in this country and abroad where he articulated the significance of man's creativity and dignity.

"A center for fullest human enrichment without the arts would be incomplete," he wrote, "as would a center for the arts without concern for human enrichment. Chautauqua's dedication and commitment to both the arts and the enhancement of life are among its most significant characteristics."[2]

However, Dr. Remick's days at Chautauqua were not altogether easy. He had brought with him an objective viewpoint. With his capacity for bold thinking, he had stirred Chautauquans to both positive and negative reactions. His ideas appeared too astonishing to some. Perhaps after five and one-half years, he felt that one of his main missions had been accomplished—to challenge self-complacency and *status quo* thinking at Chautauqua. At any rate, the intensity of his life commitment and the range of his concerns could not allow him to extend his time in the presidency.

He could be proud of his leadership through the Chautauqua Centennial. In close cooperation with Board Chairman Richard H. Miller, he had participated in the initiation and first success of the Gebbie Challenge so that Chautauqua's fiscal condition had been improved while he was president. Through its example, the combination of a strong president with a strong chairman had achieved fuller participation by board members and an evolutionary staff reorganization. A year-round Vice President for Development had replaced the traditional Old First Night Director and a Vice President for Program had been appointed. A Dean of Educational Services was a designated position for a year and a half when it was changed to Coordinator of Summer Schools.

In an address to the Property Owners Association in the summer of 1977, Mr. Miller called Dr. Remick "an extraordinary president," and he said that objective historical writers had already stated that Dr. Remick's presidency had marked a whole new era at Chautauqua. "The sense of intellectual and spiritual excitement that Oscar Remick brought on these Grounds renewed our own joy in ourselves and confidence in the Institution..."[3]

Members of the Board of Trustees took Dr. Remick's resignation seriously, accepted it and moved ahead with planning for the coming season. Chairman Miller announced that Robert V. Woodside, vice president for program, would assume day-to-day responsibilities and authority for internal administration.

A committee of trustees had been appointed by Mr. Miller in November for the purpose of studying the Chautauqua Presidency. This committee he now used as the basis for a presidential search committee. He added two non-trustee members. The committee comprised: Miriam Reading, chairman, William C. Rittman, Gertrude Shelburne, Jeffrey Simpson, Samuel Price, Edward P. Boyle and John W. McCredie, Jr.

A diligent search for a new president was begun almost immediately. The position was advertised in appropriate journals. Chautauquans' own suggestions were received and studied. Talks were carried on with foundations, government officials and elected representatives of the Chautauqua area. Staff-members were also not overlooked.

The committee decided against using a professional search firm because of the difficulty outsiders would have in understanding the nature of the Institution and its needs. Using the Chautauqua Challenge as a guide, the committee rewrote the Presidential job description. For the benefit of the candidates, the committee prepared its own resume of Chautauqua's historical background, its present functional structure and its resources, as well as its financial needs.

A brief analysis of the changes in society-at-large prefaced five exploratory questions which were addressed to all candidates. Through their responses, candidates had an opportunity to communicate their ideas concerning Chautauqua's role as a center for the arts, education and religion. Likewise the committee had an opportunity to assess candidates. Emphasis was placed on the years ahead.

Approximately one hundred and twenty serious applications emanating from twenty-eight states and three foreign countries were placed before the committee. Each was carefully considered and interviews were scheduled when there seemed to be even a remote chance that the applicant might be right for Chautauqua. Differences in experience, age, sex and color were represented among the applicants along with varying careers, specializations and skills.

Individual committee members would conduct initial interviews with the applicants from their own areas. The task of exchanging information as a committee was made more difficult by the severe winter weather. Although they worked steadily the members proceeded cautiously, no doubt grateful that no deadline had been given them. Thus, in spite of their almost constant activity, the season began with still no announcement of a new President. During the season, final candidates were invited to come to Chautauqua. But the prospect of deciding on a President and then having that successful candidate be able to work out the details of acceptance within the time-frame of a season, became increasingly dubious. Indeed, the Search Committee Chairman, Miriam Reading, made a frank report to the Property Owners Association on August 20, 1977, outlining the committee's procedures and the seemingly distant prospects of an immediate conclusion to their efforts.

Chautauquans are thinking, seeking, articulate people for the most part. Furthermore, while often critical of "the way things are going at Chautauqua," they are intensely loyal and defensive when Chautauqua is criticized from the outside. As many of them viewed the seemingly successful 1977 season, they asked the natural question, "Why can't we have one of our own as President? Why can't the man who has been in been in charge since February continue as President?"

Bob Woodside had been a Chautauquan for approximately thirty-seven years. He had come first as a pipe organ student; later, as an instructor in pipe organ. In 1956 he succeeded William Volkel as official organist. In 1971 Dr. Remick appointed him as his assistant for education. Throughout Dr. Remick's years at Chautauqua, Bob Woodside became increasingly used in a variety of assignments. He returned to his post as official organist and became choir director. In 1976 he became Vice President for Program.

But he did not make application for the presidency, much as he may have longed to occupy this position of ultimate trust at Chautauqua. Why he did not actively seek the presidency is not apparent. He met more than once with the committee to talk about the position of the presidency in an effort to add to the members' understanding of their goals. Perhaps no one as much as he could fully appreciate the enormity of the committee's responsibility to find the best possible person to lead Chautauqua into the future. Perhaps he felt that his skill had been demonstrated sufficiently to be the equivalent of a formal application.

Chairman Miller at one point in the 1977 season

'Classy, brassy, elegant'—Ethel Merman "doing what comes naturally" in song to thunderous applause in the Amphitheater July 14, 1977.

urged Chautauquans to be patient about the presidential search, to refrain from applying pressure on the committee or circulating rumors about the presidential choice. But the impression grew that the committee was looking for a president outside the Chautauqua family.

Quite apart from the question of the presidency, the Chautauqua season and the Institution's fiscal matters were proceeding along an expected course. The Golf Club House would be completed before the season ended. The phrase, Chautauqua Festival '77 was being used in publicity. Better Homes and Gardens and the Allegheny Airlines Magazine carried articles on Chautauqua and a sizable, pre-season advertisement had appeared in the New York Times Travel Section. The 20th National Jury Show had opened. The Sports Club had a new, youthful director, David Peckinpaugh, a lifelong Chautauquan. Michael J. Rodgers was profiled in The Daily as the new director of administrative services. The voters in the Utility District voted approval of water meter installation and Marian Stranburg was elected president of the Property Owners Association. The 33rd National Federation of Music Clubs Weekend was held and two new tennis courts were attracting more and more players. Margaret Mead was announced as a CLSC-sponsored lecturer and a grant-in-aid to help with the beginning of Amphitheater restoration was announced. Hurlbut Memorial Church reached 100 years of age as a Chautauqua congregation and the Bird, Tree and Garden Club planted a memorial tree for Dr. Hurlbut in Knox Park. The Charles Edison Fund erected a special plaque in Miller Park commemorating Lewis Miller's role at Chautauqua as co-founder and first president. Patricia Klingensmith was chosen as a property owners' Trustee. Joseph Neubauer was elected to the Chautauqua Foundation Board and $124,000 was distributed to the Institution by the Foundation. A co-ed softball league was organized and Ethel Merman sang in the Amphitheater. The Baptists celebrated the 50th anniversary of their Chautauqua headquarters and rededicated it. Nathalie Hinderas played with the Symphony. Roberta Peters returned. Sergiu Comissiona spent his second season as Chautauqua's Principal Conductor. Outstanding clergymen chaplained, including Bishops Spong and Armstrong.

Suddenly in the midst of the business-as-usual, comfortable atmosphere of the last week, news began to circulate that a candidate for the presidency had been selected. In the final issue of The Daily, Aug. 27, 1977, the rumor was confirmed. The Daily stated that the Board of Trustees would meet that afternoon for the purpose of electing the Institution's 14th president. It was expected, the article said, that the President would be introduced to Chautauquans following the Sunday morning worship service.

Indeed, that's the way Dr. Robert R. Hesse met his first Chautauqua audience from the Amphitheater platform.

Once again it was Richard Miller's duty as chairman of the Chautauqua Board of Trustees to make the official presentation of a new president to his fellow-Chautauquans. Perhaps recalling the unctious occasion on Aug. 1, 1971 when he had formally invested

the presidency in Dr. Remick, Mr. Miller on Aug. 28, 1977 specified that "our purpose here this morning is not ceremonial. It is informative."[4]

He began by saying: ". . . . it is with a very real sense of both excitement and enthusiasm that I confirm to you that the Board of Trustees has acted unanimously to elect Dr. Robert R. Hesse as the 14th President of the Institution . . . .

"As you are aware from our discussions with the Chautauqua community, the Search Committee under excellent leadership had not arrived at a definitive decision, but during the past weekend, they were deeply engaged in final discussions with candidates and among themselves, and by Sunday morning made their priority choice. I was advised by the committee Sunday afternoon."

"They were authorized to proceed with discussions with Dr. Hesse and it was my personal expectation, given how these matters many times go, that it would not be possible to make this choice known to the Chautauqua community. However, Dr. Hesse was considerably more prepared for this challenge than I had personally anticipated and he came very promptly to an affirmative conclusion at the middle of the week and it became clear to us that we did, indeed, have an opportunity to bring him to you in this fashion."

Then as he prepared to introduce Dr. Hesse to the audience, he made a brief explanation of Dr. Hesse's professional experience and personal background. Chautauquans learned that their new president was coming from the presidency of Medaille College, a small liberal arts institution in Buffalo.

"Dr. Hesse's entire vocational and educational background is in the field of music and education. He received his B. S. degree in music from Fredonia State College and a degree in higher education administration from Syracuse University, a Master's degree, and finally, his doctor's degree from SUNY at Buffalo," Mr. Miller said.

"Following his college career, Dr. Hesse was active in the field of music for approximately eight years as a teacher, performer and as a concert manager, for approximately two of those years serving as a violinist with the Seventh Army Orchestra and as its concert manager in Germany.

"In the early 1960s, however, his vocational interests turned to higher education and higher education administration and following receipt of his degrees, he began a tenure of approximately ten years with Fredonia State College. For the last four of those years, he served as executive assistant to the president under the appointment of Dr. Oscar Lanford who was then president of the university. When Dr. Lanford left Fredonia, Dr. Hesse served briefly as acting president before going to Washington, D. C. where he served as the editor of the The College and University Journal and as the editor of Techniques, both magazines that are published by the American College Public Relations Association.

"It was from this position that he was called to the presidency of Medaille College approximately three years ago. In the period of his tenure as president, Medaille has more than doubled its enrollment, has completely revamped its educational program and has

Robert V. Woodside

Dr. and Mrs. Hesse with Richard H. Miller receive the best wishes of Chautauquans following their introduction at the final Sunday morning worship service of the 1977 season.

reestablished a new image in the Buffalo community as a college providing leadership help to the municipality. Dr. Hesse has achieved that remarkable record while maintaining unusual economic stability in that college and it operates today with no debt. Other evidences of his leadership capability are outside the educational experience. Two of these are particularly important to his leadership at Chautauqua.

"In May, 1977, Dr. Hesse was elected chairman of the Consortium of Higher Education in Western New York, an association of approximately 19 colleges in the State of New York, both public and private, large and small, giving him high visibility and access to the educational system of New York State."

"Secondly, through a concept of his own creation and through his own spirit of leadership and his own guiding genius, the Buffalo community in the last several months, has seen the birth of the Committee for the Revitalization of Buffalo, a molding of every diverse group of leadership talent from the community, to address in new and creative ways the many-faceted problems of the Buffalo area. For a man who had just come into that community a few brief years prior to that, his leadership capability seems evident. Chautauqua is. indeed, fortunate to attract a man of this background and capability."

"The Chautauqua Idea in all its bearings is like a kaleidoscope which must be turned and turned and adjusted to the eye, to see all its beauties and the departments must be observed closely to learn what they are."

About Chautauqua
Emily Raymond

Dr. Hesse stepped to the podium and acknowledged the warm reception of the audience and the words of introduction by Mr. Miller.

His remarks are quoted from The Daily as reported June 24, 1978: "Thank you very much, and thank you, Mr. Miller, for the opportunity to share this historic platform with you, with Dr. Loew and Rev. Harvey,[5] on this final day of Chautauqua's 104th season. As a former resident of Chautauqua County, I am keenly aware of the rich heritage of this distinguished institution. Today with so many of our nation's basic foundations shaken, and threatened in recent years, it is important, indeed, significant, to note that what was started here more than a century ago by Lewis Miller and John Heyl Vincent still represents the best of human and spiritual values.

"As we work together in the challenging days ahead, I ask for the help, the support and the prayers of all Chautauquans so that each of us can have a part in preserving this great institution for the continuing benefit, enjoyment and inspiration of generations still unborn. My wife, Barbara, and I are indeed mindful of the immense responsibilities you have asked us to assume and we are deeply conscious that Chautauqua is worthy of the very best from all of us.

"We are humbled. We are honored to be invited to participate with you in Chautauqua's future. Thank you."

At the conclusion of the service, Dr. and Mrs. Hesse were greeted informally at the rear of the Amphitheater after which they returned to Buffalo where much hard work lay ahead of them as they began immediately the transition process.

As previously planned the traditional closing of the season was performed by Howard G. Gibbs, a vice-chairman of the Board's executive committee and chairman of the Board's Program Committee.

Dr. Hesse was to continue his duties at Medaille College until January 1, spending weekends and occasional days at Chautauqua during the fall. He said he would spend his first year as an avowed listener and learner. If he were to lead, he said, it was important to know where Chautauqua and Chautauquans wanted to go.

So he made a conscious effort to learn the history, the sense of mission and the traditions of the past that he might better understand the present and be able to design a framework on which to mount the future.

He talked to many people both at Chautauqua and throughout the country. He watched and participated in the administrative structure as plans for the 1978 season were shaped. He accepted speaking invitations through which he promoted the season's program. He gave much thought to the total dimensions of Chautauqua.

Dr. Hesse's first summer was a pleasant introduction to the density of program, schools and people. By the end of August, however, he was ready to shed his quiet, contemplative preparation and don the full armor of leadership. It was toward the end of the season and in the fall of 1978, a year after he had accepted the presidency, that he took hold of the position firmly and said, in effect, to his fellow-Chautauquans, "Follow! We are going to move forward boldly!"

1977 PROGRAM FIGURES

Musicians
John Rose
Bill Crofut
Kenneth Cooper
Garry Graffman
Frances Gulli
Richard Morris
Martin Berinbaum
The Cleveland Orchestra Chorus
Soloists
Frances Yeend
Carolyn Stanford
Joseph Shore
David Evans
Michael Fardink
Ivan Davis
Millard Taylor
Maria Louisa Faini
Albert Markov
Catherine Christiansen
Charlene Chadwick
Brass Quintet
Charles A. Lewis, Jr.
Rolf Smedvig
David Ohanian
Norman Bolter
Samuel Pilafian
Ozan Marsh
Rebecca Root
Thomas Dumm
Chaim Zemach
Inez Hassman
Shigeo Neriki
Natalie Hinderas
Anthony and Joseph Paratore
Chet Atkins
Ethel Merman
Bach Aria Group
William Scheide
Samuel Baron
Robert Bloom
Norman Farrow
Lorna Haywood
Lois Marshall
Seth McCoy
Charles Treger
Laszlo Varga
Yehudi Wyner
Laurel Eldredge
Frank Pullano
Eugene Moye
Mary Louise Vetrano
Lauren David Gayle
Count Basie and His Orchestra
Roberta Peters
Marilyn Mason
Laszlo Varga
The School of Choral Studies Chorus
Abraham Kaplan, Director

The Manhattan Savoyards
Company
Doc Severinsen
Now Generation Brass
Today's Children
Phoenix Boys Choir
Dr. Harvey K. Smith, Director
Warren Covington and his
Orchestra
The Pied Pipers
Margaret Whiting
Bobby Goldsboro
U.S. Army Field Band and
Soldiers Chorus
Freddy Fender
Preservation Hall Jazz Band
Celeste Holm
Wesley Addy
Woody Herman and The Young
Thundering Herd
David Mitchell
Opera Apprentice Artists
Christine Flasch
Kathy Terrell
Mary Lee Farris
Allan Kays
Harold McAulliffe
Tom Poole
George Massey
Rodney Miller
Glenn Yarbrough and his
Limelighters' Reunion and
The Kingston Trio
New Black Eagle Jazz Band
Barbershop Quartets, Chorus
The Modifications, The
Vagabonds, The Canadian
Heritage, The Amherst
Friends of Harmony

Conductors
Sergiu Comissiona, Musical
Director
Doc Severinsen
Warren Covington
Robert Page
Major Samuel J. Fricano
Carl Topilow
Robert Irving
Jorge Mester
Walter Hendl
Henry Aaron
Evan Whallon
Rainer Miedel
Eric Knight

Other Programs in the Amphitheater
The Claude Kipnis Mime
Theatre
Covenant Players
Pops Photo Concert
Donald Sultner-Welles
The Amazing Kreskin
Underseas Classic Film
Stanton Waterman
Florida Film, Richard Kern
Switzerland Today,
Willis Butler

Platform Lecturers
Dr. Ralph Buultjens
Dr. H. Mark Roelofs
Dr. John H. Finley, Jr.
John Ciardi
Dr. Sydney E. Ahlstrom
Dr. Theodore A. Gill
Edward Weeks
Future Week
Dr. Brian O'Leary
Dr. Margaret Mead
Barbara Marx Hubbard
Dr. Carl H. Madden
Dr. George T. L. Land
Dr. Peter Vajk
August T. Jaccaci, Jr.
Jay Baldwin
Kathleen Whitacre
Congressman Ned Pattison
Paul Duke
Seymour Hersh
Les Whitten
Education Week
Dr. Stephen K. Bailey
Algernon Black
Jacqueline Grennan Wexler
Gregory Schneiders
Dr. Margaret N. Maxey

Five Education Week Institutes
had additional sessions which
involved approximately 20
professional educators Dr. Allen
Schmieder, U.S. Office of
Education, coordinator

Chaplains
Dr. David Poling
Bishop James Armstrong
Dr. James D. Glasse
The Rt. Rev. John S. Spong
Dr. Elizabeth Achtemeier
Dr. Browne Barr
Dr. Peter J. Gomes
Dr. Harold R. Albert
Dr. Charles A. Trentham
The Rev. Kenneth D. Harvey

Religion Department Lecturers
Dr. Solomon S. Bernards
Dr. Gabriel Fachre
Dr. Lewis Seymour Mudge
Dr. Carnegie Samuel Calian
Dr. James Wall
Dr. William H. Lazareth
Dr. Gregory G. Baum
Dr. Andrew A. Sorensen
Dr. James Scherer

Operas
Leonard Treash, General Director

The Tales of Hoffman
Evan Whallon, Conductor
Leonard Treash, Director
The Barber of Seville
Evan Whallon, Conductor
Whitfield Lloyd, Director

Albert Herring
Wolfgang Schanzer, Conductor
Leonard Treash, Director
Hello Dolly
Evan Whallon, Conductor
Leonard Treash, Director
Tosca
Evan Whallon, Conductor
Leonard Treash, Director
Rigoletto
Wolfgang Schanzer, Conductor
Whitfield Lloyd, Director
Tannhauser
Evan Whallon, Conductor
Leonard Treash, Director

Dance
Royal Danish Ballet
Suzanne Farrell
Peter Martins
Pittsburgh Ballet Theatre

Theater
The Cleveland Play House
Summer Theatre

A Moon for the Misbegotten
Man and Superman
Ladyhouse Blues
The Yellow Jacket
*Are You Now or Have You Ever
Been?*
The Hollow Crown
Table Manners (Part I of
The Norman Conquests)
Living Together (Part II of
The Norman Conquests)

Music School Festival Orchestra
Nathan Gottschalk, Conductor

Soloists
James Jacobson
Robert Portney
Carol Archer
Ethelyn Enos
Mark Robbins
Masa Omura
Victor Lerner
Carol Borgmann
Lori Seffren
Karen Brown
Lana Lum
David Hardy
Scott McFadden
Stephen Tieszen
Jeanette Mrowitz

David Hardy, Sigma Alpha Iota
Winner

CAA
Tom Hinson, Juror for the Chau-
tauqua Art Association's National
Exhibition of American Art

Yo-Yo Ma rehearses in the Amphitheater; Eve Queler,
guest conductor of the Chautauqua Symphony Orchestra.

3

Listening Year

FROM THE RECORDS alone, the season of 1978 can be characterized as "upbeat." There was a spontaneous anticipation of a new president's influence on everything Chautauquan.

The opening editorial in The Daily pointed out that Dr. Hesse's first summer coincided with several important anniversaries. It was the 50th year for both the Chautauqua Opera Association and the Chautauqua Symphony Orchestra, and it was the Centennial for the Chautauqua Literary and Scientific Circle. On such occasions Chautauquans are prone to search for new meanings of tested principles and Dr. Hesse's objectivity would be welcomed. The editorial called for a climate in which the new president "could find freedom for productivity and bring to pass a new period of brilliant success for Chautauqua."[1]

Dr. Hesse spoke to members of the Chautauqua Women's Club on the first Monday of the season on the topic, "Looking to the Future." Quoting Dr. Vincent that Chautauqua is an instrument for tomorrow, he said frankly that he felt he had been selected to serve as an instrument of responsible change and he raised questions which he thought should be addressed:

"What kind of place should Chautauqua be for your children, for their children and for future generations of children? What should remain the same? What should be different? How can we bring together the CLSC, the opera, the lecture series, the symphony orchestra, our religious programs and our special events? Can we strengthen them by bringing them together? Should we be extending our program via television and national public radio? How can we use our facilities for more than nine weeks?. . . ." Rather than drift into the future, we must SHAPE it, he affirmed.[2]

The second week of the season illustrated one of the possibilities Dr. Hesse had mentioned, that of bringing together separate parts of the overall program for a stronger impact. In this case, it was the Institution's morning lecture series and the CLSC. The lecture theme, "Children and the Family," had been related to a CLSC book selection, "All Our Children" by Kenneth Kenniston and members of the Carnegie Council on Children.

Appearing on the Amphitheater Platform that week were Edward B. Marks, associate director of the International Year of the Child Secretariat, United Nations, Dr. Gordon J. Kopf, U.S.A. chairperson for the Inter-

national Year of the Child, American Committee for UNICEF, and members of the Carnegie Council on Children.

Included in the tightly-packed CLSC schedule were: 4 p.m. seminars Monday through Wednesday, conducted by Kenneth Wooden on "The Neglected Children in Our Society"[3]; an international book fair with a concentration of children's books (approximately 300 titles) each afternoon at Alumni Hall; a display of children's art from around the world on loan from UNICEF; and appearances and performances by Mr. McFeely and the Purple Panda from Mr. Roger's Neighborhood, arranged as a gift to Chautauqua's children.

At the regular Thursday afternoon Round Table, after giving the morning lecture, Dr. Laura Nader reviewed "All Our Children," and at the Friday Sidewalk Session Katherine P. Messenger who had lectured on child health in the morning, completed the week's discussions. Both Dr. Nader and Ms. Messenger had been part of the Carnegie Council's research and staff team.

This concerted programming coupled with the fact that CLSC members were reading the Carnegie Council book, made the week an in-depth learning experience for many Chautauquans. While Assembly and CLSC programs had been coordinated by Dr. Vincent in the early days, such concentration in one week had not been attempted for some time. It confirmed the logic that the coordination of program elements within the Institution could be expanded to great advantage.

The CLSC celebrated its centennial with intensified programming throughout the season. "Most favorite lecturer" John Ciardi conducted a CLSC mini-course on Dante's "Divine Comedy." Dr. Margaret Mead gave the Recognition Day Address and also reviewed her book, "Letters from the Field" at a Thursday Round Table.[4] A Baccalaureate Sunday Vesper Service was held in Founder's Glen with members of the Vincent family as special guests.[5] A plaque honoring Dr. John Heyl Vincent as founder of the CLSC was dedicated during the service which was led by Dr. Ralph W. Loew, head of the Religion Department. Dr. Carl S. Winters who had formerly served the CLSC as director and president of the Alumni Association was one of the speakers. Dr. Charles R. Kniker from the State University of Iowa, who has written extensively about the history of the CLSC, gave a profile of Dr. Vincent whom he called an "educational evangelist." Dr. Hesse spoke on the central educational thrust of the CLSC and said that we need to review and challenge its potential for the future so that it will not trade permanently its former position as innovator, leader, forerunner to one of traditionalist, follower, emulator. "I am convinced that there are exciting avenues to explore and there are many Chautauquans and others eager to serve as contemporary pioneers." Among other writers who appeared at CLSC Round tables in 1978 were James A. McPherson, winner of the year's Pulitzer Prize for Fiction, and Helga Sandburg, daughter of the revered Carl Sandburg.

There were many "extras," most of which originated with members under the inspiration provided by CLSC Director Nately Ronsheim. A Centennial Banner was designed by Darwin Marshall and constructed by Charlotte Crittenden, assisted by Virginia Cushman. It hung all summer in the Amphitheater. A tile mosaic of the Banner design was installed by the Class of '78 in the floor of the Hall of Philosophy. A Class Banner was designed and painted with oil on velvet by Chautauqua's Resident Artist Maritza Morgan, with Caran Redington, class president, completing the Banner's embroidery, mounting and finishing. The graduating class numbered 177 members, who had voted to call themselves the Margaret Mead Class and to choose for a motto "Each as Part of the Whole," a phrase from Mead's book, "World Enough."

The CLSC Alumni Association held a Country Fair on the lawn of Alumni Hall and during the summer members presented programs of mini-book reviews. Centennial mementoes included a souvenir booklet containing the history of the CLSC, Centennial CLSC pins in pewter and attractive book bags. Over the Brick Walk near the Veranda a large street sign proclaimed the 100th anniversary of the "Oldest Book Club in America."

Director Ronsheim had written in The Chautauquan before the season: "It is apparent that CLSC does have

a distinctive and challenging role to play. The adult learner is being discovered by higher education and a great emphasis is being put on lifelong learning."

Then she added that the future well-being of the CLSC will depend on its willingness to present facets of important issues in society as well as to function on "the cutting edge of new ideas." Her perceptions seemed to be in step with the questing, questioning new President.

There was also an encouraging impression in 1978 that the physical aspects of Chautauqua were well cared-for. The new sewerage treatment plant was 90 per cent completed and was expected to begin operation in August. An open house was held August 12th. Water meter installation which had become necessary because of the new treatment plant was on schedule. Michael J. Rodgers, executive director of administrative services, reported that the west part of the Amphitheater had been totally redone structurally. "We replaced old timber beams and joists with steel, strengthened columns and rebuilt the west end, replacing the wood with steel. We have also done some perimeter work," he said.

He also reported that the Library had been painted inside and out and the Colonnade was being painted. The post office and the Wensley had new roofs and the Wensley would be getting new siding in the fall. The first floor of the Summer Schools Dormitory had been remodeled and the roof of Norton Hall had been fixed.

Eleven lots that the Institution owned were put up for sale through sealed biddings. The Police Department had been reorganized with Alan J. Akin as Chief.

Reports by the scientists who had been conducting Lake Studies were received with interest by Chautauquans who know how important the lake's well-being is to their own. Some promise was held for solutions to lake problems and water quality was pronounced good.

Robert Osburn, chairman of the Trustees' Buildings and Grounds Committee, reported to Property Owners and to all Chautauquans on the matter of a

John Ciardi conducted a mini-series on Dante's "Divine Comedy," under the sponsorship of the CLSC, Nately Ronsheim, Director.

Margaret Mead, for whom the CLSC Class of 1978 was named, gave the Recognition Day Address to an attentive audience.

garbage collection study, and the problems of maintaining the historic buildings which are the glory of Chautauqua.

While it was not generally publicized, another step forward had been taken by the Trustees in meeting these preservation needs. At its meeting May 13, the Board voted to undertake a capital funds feasability study. The recommendation for the study had come from Chautauqua's Development Council. Consequently, on June 26, the New York firm of Brakely, John Price Jones, Inc. began the study. Fund-raising objectives, an analysis of buildings and Grounds requirements and policy questions were seriously examined by the Board following the firm's first report on Aug. 5. From the firm's representatives who had conducted confidential interviews with informed

people close to the Institution and the community, the trustees learned the consensus concerning a capital funds campaign and received guidance on whether or not the Institution should mount such a campaign, at what level, how it might be operated and how the funds might be sought. The Board was to wait until the Annual meeting in November to make a decision.

Richard H. Miller who had served as chairman of the Board for eight years submitted his resignation as chairman at the May Board meeting. He reviewed his reasons for resigning: his length of service, the demands of other responsibilities and his feeling that with a new president in office, the time was appropriate for a change in chairmanship. He expressed his willingness to continue as a board member, as a member of the Development Council and as President of

On Old First Night, Richard H. Miller, left, was honored for his years as Chairman of the Board. His successor, Howard G. Gibbs, presented him with a Chautauqua Medallion and a citation which listed his extensive service. Vice President Brunskill leads the applause.

the Chautauqua Foundation. He gave July 29 as the effective date for his resignation, which would allow sufficient time in which to determine the procedure for selecting a new chairman in mid-term. In the meeting, Mrs. Carol Duhme expressed the Board's gratitude for Mr. Miller's leadership within the Board and spoke, as well, on behalf of the entire Institution community.

As a great-grandson of Lewis Miller and a senior partner in a distinguished Milwaukee law firm, he had both a strong family attachment to Institution goals, but also broad experience, especially in business and finance, to bring to their achievement.

When news of Mr. Miller's resignation was printed in The Daily (July 5, 1978), Dr. Hesse issued the following statement:

"His leadership has resulted in a renewed sense of mission and direction, and a measure of financial stability for Chautauqua Institution. He guided the Institution through a difficult period and it has prospered by virtue of his dedication, perseverance, foresight, and sheer hard work."

At a special meeting of the Board on July 29 then, Howard Gibbs was elected to be the new Chairman. Three evenings later on Old First Night Mr. Gibbs as his first official act, presented the Silver Chautauqua Medal to Richard H. Miller "for outstanding leadership in the highest Chautauqua tradition."

Mr. Gibbs had served a decade on the Board of Trustees when he became Chairman, and for two years previously had served as a vice-chairman. Since 1971 he had headed the program committee and was a member of the executive committee.

In his own professional life, Mr. Gibbs was associate national director of the Boys Club of America and in his various capacities with Boys Clubs, has had extensive experience in working with funding sources and with a national board of trustees, as well as having responsibility for the internal administration and operation of this national organization.

In accepting his new post Mr. Gibbs said that he was looking forward "to working closely with the Board and with the President, Dr. Robert R. Hesse, to build an agenda for the '80s." There was a definite commitment to unified action.

In the Chautauqua tradition, distinguished lecturers appeared on the Platform to discuss nine ambitious weekly themes: Quality of Life, Children and the Family, Values, Future Week, Men and Women in Transition, Science, Education, the Economy and International Relations. Stewart Udall, Erik Erikson, Barrie Grieff, Herbert Goldberg, Margaret Mead, Louis Rukeyser, Maureen Reagan and Carter Randall were only a few of those who spoke.

Gil Gallagher's series of articles on the history of Chautauqua Opera began in The Daily early in the season in anticipation of the observance of the 50th year of Chautauqua opera in its own opera house, Norton Hall.

In cooperation with the Institution, the Chautauqua Opera Guild under its president, Beverly Dame Esch,[6] led the plans for the celebration. Invitations were extended to former members of the Company to return for an Opera Gala on July 15. Under the baton of Evan Whallon, the apprentices of the 1978 Company performed with the Chautauqua Symphony Orchestra at that evening's concert. Afterward a reception was held at the Golf Club for invited guests and members of the Opera Guild. The next day Mrs. Francesca Rappole was host in her historic lakeside home[7] at a brunch for the returning performers who continued their leisurely reminiscences. The Chautauquan Daily also participated in the weekend by publishing an opera supplement in the regular Saturday issue which served as a souvenir of the anniversary.

Another high point of that Opera anniversary year, was the lecture-operalogue of Baroness Maria von Trapp. In order to accommodate the expected large audience, the Institution had made Norton Hall available to the Guild for this event which was held the afternoon before the first performance of "Sound of Music." Membership in the Opera Guild climbed throughout the summer as the Guild focused on the opera heritage at Chautauqua.

The Institution's entire musical program had its usual variety, built around the Chautauqua Symphony Orchestra's three concerts per week for approximately seven weeks, or twenty-one concerts in all. Sergiu Comissiona returned as Principal Conductor for eight concerts in his third Chautauqua season. There were a succession of soloists with the Symphony, including among others: Larry Adler who played the harmonica, Gary Graffman, Natalie Hinderas and Chet Atkins. The Cleveland Orchestra Chorus sang. Peter Martins and Kay Mazzo danced. Yo-Yo Ma appeared with the orchestra which was conducted that night by Eve Queler. There was the Annapolis Brass Quintet and the New Arts Trio, not to mention popular stars such as Victor Borge and Chuck Mangione. Returning to the Amphitheater were Roberta Peters, Dave Brubeck (this time with his sons), Ferrante and Teicher, the U.S. Army Field Band and Soldier's Chorus, the National Band of New Zealand and the Maori Dancers. Mitch Miller and the Buffalo Philharmonic appeared the last week of the season. That week was also designated as a Residential Week for Older Adults.

The taping of Chautauqua Symphony concerts to be edited for thirteen concerts for broadcast over WQED-FM Pittsburgh, and WQLN-FM Erie, was announced by Dr. Hesse as an extension of Chautauqua beyond the gates and beyond the season. The funds that made possible these broadcasts came from the A.W. Mellon Educational and Charitable Trust of Pittsburgh and from an individual donor who preferred to remain anonymous.

The recording of the Chautauqua Amphitheater concerts was an appropriate sidelight of the Orchestra's 50th season. Its founding under the aegis of Albert Stoessel in 1929 was celebrated in still another historical Daily supplement and a reception which honored orchestra members was held at the Golf Club following the last concert. Friends of the Symphony with Mrs. Samuel Shelburne as chairman, were hosts. There was a good feeling about Chautauqua music as the season of 1978 ended.

The report of the President to the Board of Trustees came before the end of the fiscal year and its vigorous tone presaged the months ahead. His August statements had the effect of leapfrogging to November, for

the new President could not wait for the Annual Meeting when reports were usually analyzed. He had undergone an intensive learning experience and he had come out of it confident that he knew where and how Chautauqua should proceed along the lines suggested to him by the Search Committee. He was no longer awed by the judgments of those who had been here "a few years longer." He had studied Chautauqua and Chautauquans; he had surfaced ideas and he had faced problems. He was convinced that there was no time to waste and that he must speak with directness, first of all, to his Board of Trustees.

He complimented them first for their own constancy to duty. He noted important steps that the Board had taken within the year. They had voted to undertake a Capital Funds Feasibility Study. They had shown a growing awareness of the need for extra funds to maintain and restore Institution buildings, 90 per cent of which were over 50 years old and some, much older. The urging to raise capital funds was becoming a certainty. The Buildings and Grounds Committee under the chairmanship of Robert Osburn had wisely prepared an assessment of Chautauqua's physical plant. A resurgence of the Board's committee structure also encouraged Dr. Hesse to believe in the Board's serious commitment. He welcomed the opportunity to be associated with a "working Board," he said.

If Chautauquans could have heard him quote the Program Committee's deliberations, they might not have been so shocked the next spring by questions that Dr. Hesse asked publicly. These questions concerning the "basic fabric" of the Institution were first raised within the Program Committee: Should we continue to have a symphony orchestra and if so, should it be ours? Should we have a theatre program? If so, should it be the Cleveland Play House? How long should the season last? What should pre- and post-seasons be like? How can we generate more support for what we do and what we are?

Gil Gallagher, who wrote the story of Chautauqua Opera for the 50th year celebration, is shown (left) at the Anniversary Gala with President Hesse.

Facing page: The Chautauqua Symphony Orchestra marks its 50th year at a concert conducted by Sergiu Comissiona. Dr. Hesse is shown as he made appropriate historical and congratulatory remarks.

W. Thomas Smith was appointed vice president for operations at the annual meeting in November. He had been previously named manager of the Athenaeum Hotel.

The Education, Youth and Recreation Committee also raised similar basic questions about what Chautauqua was trying to do in its educational offerings and it indicated that the programs in all areas of this segment could be improved.

The major impressions had come to Dr. Hesse during his "listening" year and he was anxious to share them with the Board. They were: Chautauqua was enjoying a state of "less than excellence;" and Chautauqua lacked coordination. Thus, improving quality, identifying goals and coordinating efforts to achieve those goals were to be the thrust of the President's leadership in the months ahead.

To achieve these purposes, Dr. Hesse addressed the Board-President relationship and most specifically, his own functions.

In his view the President is the Chief Executive Officer and responsible *alone* for providing the Board with data on operational matters, budget personnel, development, programming, education, public relations, security and maintenance. He helps trustees define policies and can recommend policy alternatives. He implements Board policy through an administrative structure. He is the Institution's final executive authority and with him rests the delegated power of appointment and its implication.

Then Dr. Hesse approached a matter which apparently was a source of deep disquietude for him: President-staff relations. He reported that there were some lines of authority that were continuing to function independently oblivious to the fact that there was new, *elected* leadership. In addition, various directors of activities or department heads reported administratively to staff members who had neither the expertise, time, nor interest to give counsel, much less supervision. The allegiance of workers to someone other than the President was understandably frustrating. The President's inability to receive needed information when requested from officers and workers had become baffling, if not unacceptable. He pointed out that it had become apparent that among some workers, loyalty to certain Board members seemed to supersede loyalty to the President. This was strong, confrontive language he was using to the Board before asking for its understanding as he would move ahead to make administrative changes in personnel. He knew, of course, that changes might not be popular, but long-term goals necessitated short-term disappointments. Substantial risks must sometimes be taken to cope with the possibility of success.

He stated that he wished to engage by October 1, two excellent people, Marie O'Connor and W. Thomas Smith.

Miss O'Connor had been serving as an assistant to Dr. Hesse since May. He wished her to continue. She had served four years at Erie Community College (Buffalo), first as a part-time English instructor and later as an assistant to the president and director of community relations. She had also taught at the SUNY College at Buffalo and at Canisius College. Her bachelor's degree had been earned at the latter school; her master's degree, from the former. She was also pursuing a doctoral degree in Higher Education. He had become acquainted with Ms. O'Connor when they represented their colleges (Dr. Hesse, Medaille College) on the Public Relations Council of the Western New York Consortium of Higher Education, and there he had firsthand knowledge of her ability.

Mr. Smith had already been made manager of the Athenaeum Hotel. As a year-round staff member, he would also be in charge of the Book Store, the dormitories, food service and store rentals. Mr. Smith had carried a heavy and varied responsibility at SUNY College at Fredonia. During sixteen years, he had supervised dormitories which housed 2600 students, the food service operation, the book store, campus minibuses and the College Lodge. He had been involved with the updating of the Fredonia campus by the architectural firm of I.M. Pei and Partners. He previously owned and operated Winston's Lodge in Vermont and had served nine years as co-director of food services at SUNY Albany.

Dr. Hesse implied that since he was responsible for the coordination of the season's program, he was studying the program functions as they were then centered in the Vice President's office.

The Board approved his request to make the new manager of the Athenaeum Hotel a part of the year-round administrative staff and to continue Miss O'Connor as administrative assistant to the President. They could not have been surprised tn learn shortly after the season ended that Vice President Woodside had left the Institution's employ at the President's request. The President needed a unified force working with him and one that supported fully his vision of the future. When news of Mr. Woodside's departure from the official family began to circulate among Chautauquans, there was questioning and some anger among longtime friends of Mr. Woodside who failed to realize that new executives usually bring in people who are congenial to their work habits and long-range plans.

THE CHAUTAUQUA CHALLENGE

to be a national center for the identification and development of the best in human values through a program of continuing education which:

encourages the identification and exploration of the value dimensions in the important religious, social and political issues of our times;

stimulates the provocative, thoughtful involvement of individuals and families in creative response to such issues on a high level of competence and commitment;

promotes excellence and creativity in the appreciation, performance and teaching of the arts; to be a community in which religious faith is perceived, interpreted and experienced as central to the understanding and expression of our social and cultural values, and which, while open to us all, is distinctly founded upon and expressive of the convictions of the Christian tradition.

to be a resource for the enriched understanding of the opportunities and obligations of community, family, and personal life by fostering the sharing of varied cultural, educational, religious and recreational experience in an atmosphere of participation by persons of all ages and backgrounds.

The Chautauqua Challenge was adopted by the Board of Trustees in 1976.

But there was a sadness involved with the situation that was never erased, even though it came to be understood.

When the Annual Meeting of the Board of Trustees was convened in November, there was a sizable agenda to be dealt with in the two-day Board session.

First, the trustees needed to take action on the Capital Campaign Feasibility Study. Robert Pierpont and John Riley of Brakely, John Price Jones Inc., gave brief reports of the Study. Mr. Riley who had conducted interviews with a cross-section of Chautauquans during the summer stated that it was his firm's conclusion that Chautauqua could and should launch a capital fund-raising operation. He recommended that Chautauqua launch a campaign rather than initiate a program within the Development Department. He pointed out that Chautauqua's tax-exempt status offers potential external donors an incentive to give. Furthermore, Chautauqua's constituents understand the need for physical plant renovation, the value of endowments and the necessity for new, significant programs. Mr. Riley recommended that a precise cost-estimate for the items needed should be made; that a Case Statement outlining the Institution's long-range capital and programmatic goals be created and that a strong national program chairman be appointed.

A question and answer period followed. The Board considered many aspects of a capital funds campaign. At length a motion to develop a national campaign for capital funds was made by Dr. McElree, seconded by Mr. Bargar and passed unanimously by the members present. A second motion to conduct a separate capital funds campaign and a separate annual fund was passed with one dissenting vote. A third recommendation was unanimously approved by motion, that the capital fund be conducted in phases, such that the first phase might be a three-year effort with donors able to designate payments up to a five-year one-month period and that the amount to be raised and announced be determined at a future date, pending further research.

The concept of staffing for the Capital Funds Campaign was approved, subject to further information. After authorizing the executive committee and staff to proceed on certain items, a motion was passed stating that the capital fund be financed outside the regular budget.

The second day's meeting began with the auditors' report, certifying that the Institution had an excess of $25,000 in operating revenues over expenses. Thus, the Gebbie Challenge had been met.

Dr. Hesse in presenting the budget for 1979, indicated that it represented some change in direction and an attempt to respond to requests made by Chautauquans and Board Committees. New insights from new staff members were contained in the budget, he said, but lack of familiarity with budget planning procedures at Chautauqua had been a problem. New federal policies such as wage increases are apparent in the budget and further reviews of salaries paid to seasonal employees need to be made, he said. After a considerable discussion the budget was adopted, as amended. The motion to amend the budget denied the programming of a mid-season special in the Amphitheater with a proposed extra fee beyond the regular gate ticket.

The idea had been suggested as a means of raising additional program income.

New ticket price proposals were used in determining projected income for the 1979 season. Proposed season gate tickets reflected a 9.4 per cent increase. The tariffs were approved with authority given to the Executive Committee to adjust them for either budget purposes or for compliance with guidelines.

One of the serious sidelights of the discussion on an extra fee for mid-season entertainment, perhaps with a super-star, was an examination of the whole concept of Chautauqua programming. The question was asked: Are we diluting the program with the presentation of performers for fundraising purposes? Should we adhere to programmatic expressions of the Chautauqua ideal? The belief was emphasized that the Amphitheater should always be available to persons on the Grounds with gate tickets. *The consensus was that program focus should be on cultural programming rather than on mass entertainment.*

The report of the Program Committee was especially interesting in view of the fact that programming is crucial to the philosophical basis of Chautauqua as well as to its viability in the Market Place.

Mrs. Reading, chairman, stated that the primary goal of the Program Committee was to upgrade the quality of programming across the board. For this accomplishment, it seemed best to turn to experts. She reminded the Board that the Presidential Search Committee had already recommended that panels to review programming be appointed by the President. The Program Committee was suggesting that two panels of consultants be appointed first, since every area could not be addressed simultaneously: one for opera and one for religion.

In addition, she suggested that questionnaires be distributed to all trustees and to selected Chautauquans who are based in various regions of the country to help the President's office become aware of talent that might be ideal for a Chautauqua audience.

She said that the committee endorsed the idea of engaging an intern assistant for Dr. Loew, and that this intern in addition to assisting Dr. Loew with pastoral duties, could also demonstrate some sensitivity to the spiritual interests and needs of the youth on the Grounds. The Program Committee also endorsed a scholarship program for young clerics who have been away from academic experiences because of their pastoral or missionary duties and would profit from the opportunity for residency and participation at Chautauqua.

In the matter of ticketing, the Program Committee favored the showing of gate tickets at the entrances to the Amphitheater for evening programs.

The Program Committee also recommended that the cost of Symphony Guarantor tickets for two people be raised from $25.00 to $50.00 and that the name of this contribution be changed to Symphony Patrons.

The quality of programming at Norton Hall came under discussion, including the reach for high moral standards as well as high artistic standards. Mrs. Reading referred the Board members to the Chautauqua Challenge which gives a broad framework within which to expand our intellectual and emotional horizons, as well as spiritual and humanistic horizons. There is danger in trying to specify what is moral and immoral, she continued, within general programming goals. The Program Committee feels comfortable in saying that Chautauqua will meet the highest possible standards.

The Education Committee Report recommended that a new position be funded within the budget: that of a Director of Education, Youth and Recreation. Educational and recreational programs sponsored on the Grounds would be coordinated within that position.

At the moment, the funds to develop a New Educational Model are not available, but the committee will continue to explore such a concept.

The change of philosophy that would guide the activities of the College Club was discussed. Henceforth, recreation, sports and programming should be under the Director of Education, Youth and Recreation. Religious programs would be under Dr. Loew. This division of responsibility would replace the use of Coalition for Christian Outreach at the College Club.

The Committee also recommended a review of faculty salaries and the facilities used by the Theatre School.

The chairman also reported good income generated through the tennis courts.

The Buildings and Grounds Committee Report was extensive. Robert Osburn, chairman, reported that two non-trustee members had been added to the Buildings and Grounds Committee: Charles Heinz, an urban planning consultant, and Howard Chadwick, a retired Jamestown businessman. Both are now full-year Chautauqua residents.

He indicated that the Committee was attempting to comply with certain requirements for planning for the handicapped, which had been stipulated by the National Endowment for the Arts, a potential funding agency. The timetable for filing a needs statement describing how facilities and programs can be made available to the handicapped and transitional plans for architectural modification was explained.

A revision of the map of the south end of the Grounds was presented. It includes a configuration of a new avenue with an old Chautauqua street name, Bryant Avenue, which extends to the sewerage treatment plant. The new map was made "official" by action if the Board.

With regard to parking, gate and traffic control, Mr. Osburn reported that the Property Owners endorsed the committee's recommendations for taking a "tough stance." Space outside the Grounds will be found for parking and budget allocations will be needed for lot construction.

A four-part parking proposal was made by the Committee, to reduce automobile traffic on the Grounds to the absolute minimum; get all cars currently parked on Institution lots and streets into parking areas outside the Grounds; provide adequate and easy access to the Grounds from "outside" parking areas; provide easy-to-use and frequent public transportation to major program and accommodation areas. Mr. Osburn added that there is no way to prohibit property owners from parking in their own property, but their driving on the Grounds can be controlled, he said.

The Board approved the Committee's proposal which specified that budgeting for project implementation should become the responsibility of the Administration.

The Board also endorsed the idea of drilling for gas on Institution property, "if the program is well-conceived and executed."

Toward the end of the meeting Mr. Miller moved that the Institution proceed as needed in finding the means by which a Capital Campaign can be funded. The motion was seconded by Mr. Rittman and unanimously approved.

Personnel policies were amended to provide for mandatory retirement at age seventy, instead of age sixty-five.

Chairman Gibbs stated that appointment of non-Trustees to various committees of the Board must be first approved through him and that membership on task forces be developed by terms and not continued ad infinitum.

In other business, Mrs. Reading was elected vice-chairman of the Board. Philip J. Brunskill was re-appointed as Vice President for Development and Public Affairs; W. Thomas Smith was appointed Vice President for Operations; Marshall D. Nelson was reappointed Secretary-Treasurer. Philip Zimmer who had been brought in earlier in the year as Director of Communications, was to continue in this position.

Mr. Zimmer, before coming to Chautauqua had been Director of News Services at SUNY, College at Brockport. Previously Zimmer had been Assistant for Community Relations at SUNY, College at Fredonia. His work at Fredonia was well-known to Dr. Hesse, good reason for the new President to make Zimmer his first senior staff appointment. A native of Jamestown, Zimmer was a graduate of the College at Fredonia with a Master's degree in journalism from Penn State. Immediately following graduation from college, he had worked as a reporter for the Jamestown Post-Journal.

With the appointment of Mr. Smith as manager of the Athenaeum Hotel and the expansion of his duties to include all of the Institution's operations, two valued employees left Chautauqua. James R. Bussey, a former Chautauqua hotel owner, who had been persuaded by the Hotel Corporation to become manager of the Athenaeum, had indicated before the 1978 season that he wished to retire. Michael J. Rodgers who had been in charge of the Institution's administrative services, resigned to open his own private engineering firm.

The new team was now in place and looking forward to the 1979 season, the beginning of the new President's dreams for renaissance.

Phil Zimmer, Director of Communications

1978 PROGRAM FIGURES

Musicians
Victor Borge
Anita Darian
Rod MacWherter
Eunice Mobley
Ronald Rogers
Richard Start
Steven DeGroote
Aaron Rosand
Annapolis Brass Quintet
 David Cran
 Robert Suggs
 Arthur LaBar
 Martin Hughes
 Robert Osten
Larry Adler
David Arnold
New Brubeck Quartet
 Dave Brubeck
 Darius Brubeck
 Chris Brubeck
 Dan Brubeck
U.S. Army Field Band and
 Soldier's Chorus
Frances Veri
Michael Jamanis
Angelo Bello
Bonia Boyd
Maria Luisa Faini
Cheryl Bond
Ruth Cahn
Frederick Swann
The New Arts Trio
 Rebecca Pennys
 Piotr Janowski
 Steven Doane
Richard Hayman
Jerome Rose
Jan Curtis
Matthew Dooley
Fred Buda
Richard Johnson
Kenneth Wenzel
Henry Wiktorowicz
Ferrante and Teicher
Harvard Glee Club
 Dr. F. John Adams, Conductor
 Gregory Smith, Assistant Conductor
Yo-Yo Ma
Daniel Waite
Kathleen Battle
Peter Zazofsky
Daniel Gorgoglione
Stan Kenton, The Thad Jones and
 Mel Lewis Orchestra
New York State Summer School of
 the Arts, School of Choral Studies,
 Abraham Kaplan, Director
Angel and Celin Romero

National Band of New Zealand
 and the Maori Dancers
Susan Starr
Eugene Fodor
Mitch Miller with the Buffalo
 Philharmonic
David Golub
John Alexander
William Walker
Donald Hassard
Manhattan Savoyards
Johnny Rodriquez
Chuck Mangione
Billy Eckstine
Earl (Father) Hines
The Lettermen
 Tony Butala
 Gary Pike
 Donny Pike
Cleveland Orchestra Chorus
 Robert Page, Conductor
Robert V. Woodside
Claude Frank
David Hardy
Michael Fardink
Barbershop Harmony Concert
 Southerntiersmen Chorus,
 Entertainment Committee
 Quartet, Metric Maid Quar-
 tet, Nova Chords Quartet

Conductors
Sergiu Comissiona,
 Principal Conductor
Andrew Schenck
Robert Irving
Walter Hendl
Rainer Miedel
Newton Wayland
Harvey Biskin
Patrick Flynn
Eve Queler
David Gilbert
David Loebel
Mitch Miller

Other Programs in the Amphitheater

Film Lectures
Israel and the Sinai
 William Stockdale
Charming Vienna
 Andre de la Varre, Jr.
The Spell of Ireland
 Bill Madsen

Platform Lecturers
Stewart Udall
Alec Poinsett
Dr. Leon Martel
Michael Sandlofer
Edward B. Marks
Dr. Max Kaplan
Clifton Daniel
Dr. Gordon J. Klopf
John P. Demos
Katherine P. Messenger
Louis Rukeyser

William Rusher
Dr. Albert Hibbs
Ashley Montagu
Elizabeth Yates
Dr. William Pierce Lytle
Dr. Joseph Duffer
Dr. Robert Gordis
Dr. Jerry L. Fletcher
Dr. Margaret Mead
Dr. Erik H. Erikson
Dr. Edgar D. Mitchell
Audry Rowe-Colom
Dr. Herb Goldberg
Dr. Zelle Andrews
Maureen Reagan
Dr. Samuel B. Gould
Dr. Alfred L. Moye
Dr. James Hall
George W. Bonham
Ambassador Ivor Richards
Robert Evans
Ronald A. F. Alvarez
Jacqueline T. Sunderland
Ted Koppel
Dr. Anthony Campolo
Dr. William Vogel
Dr. Laura Nader
B. Carter Randall
Lucian Warren
Milton Jacques
Dr. Jean Houston

Chaplains
Dr. Robert C. Holland
Dr. Fred B. Craddock
The Rev. Arthur H. Kolsti
The Rev. Christopher
 Fitzsimmons Allison
Dr. John C. Brokhoff and the
 Rev. Barbara Brokhoff
The Rev. Andrew B. McLellen
The Rev. John W. Vannorsdall
Dr. James A. Forbes, Jr.
Dr. David R. Darnell
Father William McNamara

Religion Department Lecturers
Dr. Mary Catherine Bateson
Rabbi Lewis C. Littman
Dr. Paul E. Irion
Dr. Ralph Edward Peterson
Dr. Granger E. Westberg
Dr. Faith E. Burgess
Robert Samples
Mark Sheldon
Dr. Calvin G. Seerveld

Operas
Leonard Treash, General Director

Madame Butterfly
 Wolfgang Schanzer, Conductor
 Whitfield Lloyd, Director
The Marriage of Fiagro
 Evan Whallon, Conductor
 Leonard Treash, Director

The Sound of Music
 Evan Whallon, Conductor
 Leonard Treash, Director
La Traviata
 Wolfgang Schanzer, Conductor
 Whitfield Lloyd, Director
Eugene Onegin
 Evan Whallon, Conductor
 Leonard Treash, Director
Faust
 Evan Whallon, Conductor
 Leonard Treash, Director

Dance
Massenkoff Russian Festival
 Nickolai Massenkoff
Kay Mazzo, New York City Ballet
Peter Martins, New York City Ballet
The Jose Limon Dance Co.
The American Ballet Repertory
 Company of the American Ballet
 Theater

Theater
The Cleveland Play House
Summer Theatre

Knock Knock
The Prague Spring
The Romantics
Round and Round the Garden
Great Expectations
The Learned Ladies
The Little Foxes
The Club

Music School Festival Orchestra
Nathan Gottschalk, Conductor

Soloists
Marc Raubenheimer
Dance students
Concerto Concert
 Jen Chang
 Ruth Ann Harmon
 Ralph Padgug
 David Cohen
 Joyce Caryn Goldsmith
 Mi Hyon Kim
 Lauren Schaller
 Sandy M. Consiglio
 Grier Taylor
 Jean Galton
 Susan Benkin
 Patricia Cochrane
Betsy Sturdevant
Nicholas Kehayas

Catherine Smith, Sigma Alpha Iota
 Winner

Chautauqua Youth Orchestra
Brent S. Wissick, Conductor
One Concert

CAA
Patterson Sims, Juror for the
 Chautauqua Art Association's
 National Exhibition of American
 Art

Chautauquans enjoy the diversity that is available.

4

New Strategies; Alarms Sounded

THERE WAS EXCITEMENT among Chautauquans as program announcements were received for the summer of 1979. Dr. Hesse had approached the work of program-building with a spirit of intellectual adventure. Since records of past procedures and contacts were lacking, new ways of selecting themes and talent were as much a necessity as a preference.

One new strategy he tried was speaking directly to lecturers and performers, not only exploring the possibility of their coming to Chautauqua, but piquing their curiosities about what was happening in this venerable, but lively institution in southwestern New York State. Dr. Hesse found through these conversations that he was not only making commitments for 1979, but sometimes for the year beyond. His enthusiasm for his task grew, even though there were difficulties. Budget limitations were an important factor and lack of recognition of Chautauqua's Platform by some of the country's foremost lecturers was a disappointment.

In an interview with The Daily as the season began, Dr. Hesse said that answers on 1978 questionnaires had indicated a desire among Chautauquans for better programs.

"Therefore, our goal is to keep improving the program . . . I am comfortable with it (this year's program) because it is balanced."

In speaking about program balance Dr. Hesse was echoing the sentiments of past programmers at Chautauqua. Perhaps he didn't realize how clear an expression of continuity, his 1979 achievement was.

"But," he added, "change is inevitable. Chautauqua isn't a museum. It is a community that is alive and vital."

As it happened, there were enough changes that summer to engender fear of indiscriminate change in the future and as the weeks succeeded one another, strong feelings developed.

The need to use Chautauqua facilities for more than nine weeks a year to generate more income for the Institution, led Dr. Hesse to think of extending the season from Memorial Day to Columbus Day, "but not with the intensity of the nine-week season." The idea of scheduling top entertainers for pre-season weekends and perhaps post-season seemed an acceptable way to earn money for the Institution whose program expenses were growing and were only partially met by Gate receipts.

Consistent with his aim to have "nothing but the best" for Chautauqua, Dr. Hesse engaged the highly respected and well-loved Pearl Bailey for Saturday evening, May 26, as the first pre-season Amphitheater event. Her husband, the outstanding drummer Louis Bellson also performed that night. The Hotel Athenaeum had been readied for early opening with the assumption that Chautauqua COULD start early. Unfortunately for the experiment, the temperature in the Amphitheater at concert time was cold enough for football blankets. Attendance was disappointing. But Miss Bailey gave a superb performance. She ended her concert very touchingly sitting on the edge of the stage, singing "Let there be peace on earth. . . .and let it begin with me."

Two more concerts fared better. On June 9, Rosemary Clooney, Rose Marie, Helen O'Connor and Margaret Whiting, billed as The Four Girls Four, drew a bigger audience presumably because of better weather conditions. On June 16, another headliner, Ben Vereen, captivated a comfortably-filled Amphitheater as he sang, danced and ran up and down the aisles. Peter Nero was scheduled for the final pre-season artist the night before the season was to open, but once again the weather was cold and the concert was actually moved to Norton Hall.

The lecturers and performers announced for the regular nine-week program however, indicated that the new Hesse "broom" was sweeping toward excellence.

There were outstanding speakers scheduled: Arthur Schlesinger, Jr., Leon Jaworski, Elizabeth Drew and John Stoessinger during National Affairs Week. Future Week brought Dr. Gregory Bateson and his daughter, Dr. Mary Catherine Bateson. Revitalization Week (a new weekly theme, but an old Chautauqua concept) was distinguished by the presence and unction of Buckminster Fuller and a more familiar figure at Chautauqua, Dr. Barrie S. Greiff.

Dr. Hesse's avowed intention to improve the quality of the musical programs was also noticeable in the array of soloists with the Chautauqua Symphony orchestra and the guest conductors which he had engaged. Sergiu Comissiona while no longer music director, conducted five concerts. An interesting innovation was made before the Chautauqua Symphony Orchestra arrived. The Syracuse Symphony Pops Orchestra with Calvin Custer conducting performed June 28 and the following night, the full Syracuse

Symphony Orchestra under its conductor, Christopher Keene, presented a concert with Lili Kraus as piano soloist. The third evening Eileen Farrell sang with the Syracuse Symphony, Custer conducting again.

The wholehearted reception of the program by all-season Chautauquans was diverted unfortunately by fear of what was in store for the Chautauqua Symphony Orchestra. Even the appearance of the Syracuse Symphony Orchestra was interpreted by some to be a threat to "our own orchestra."

One of the reasons for some of these misgivings came from an attempt by Dr. Hesse to lead Chautauquans into an open examination of all the options that might be open in today's socio-arts-education environment. Dr. Hesse had suggested in some of his pre-season appearances before Chautauquans that Chautauqua must assess what it wants and determine what is appropriate. It must decide what it can afford and what it can "market." He set forth Chautauqua's goals: To pursue excellence and to reenter the sanctums of national prominence. Such a course might indicate, he said, that the Institution should exercise its prerogative to reorganize the Chautauqua Symphony Orchestra. The intention to do so, under the existing contract, would have to be communicated to the Musicians Union with whom the negotiations are carried on by December, 1979.

Dr. Hesse didn't realize that his attempt at honest discussion would be troublesome to his beginning presidency and even disruptive within the community. His boldness in facing change for the sake of the future development of Chautauqua was not easily matched even by those who sensed his vision.

Most of the fear of what might happen to the orchestra became articulated with the summer arrival of the members of the Symphony. Rumors from benign to violent began to circulate. Personal loyalties were put under pressure; sides were eventually drawn. Two position papers, prepared as a guide to the thinking of the Program Committee during the winter, only exploratory in nature, were made available by "someone" to members of the Orchestra Committee. The term—pursuit of excellence—was offensive to orchestra members because it implied a present lack of excellence. Members didn't believe that the administration was sincere in wanting to improve the quality of the orchestra's performance or in wanting to give better wages and more rehearsal time. Suggestions for reorganization made the members feel insecure about their continued service at Chautauqua.

The situation might not have deteriorated as it did had it not been for other changes that were occurring. Most of them were connected to regulations which had been recommended by the Buildings and Grounds Committee and approved by the Board or through the Operations Department. Some were the outgrowth of the Utility District's enlarging role after the construction of the sewerage treatment plant. These regulatory changes involving water meters and garbage collection bags should not have been blamed on the President, but by some Chautauquans, they were.

The new vice president for operations, W. Thomas Smith, described changes he had initiated for the administration as an attempt to preserve Chautauqua's "essence." One of the most popular changes took place in the fall of 1978 when it was decided that the Book Store should remain open again throughout the year. Mr. Smith, under whose department the Book Store functioned, made an effort to recapture the "old Chautauqua Book Store" atmosphere and some winter residents volunteered to help. In late winter a new manager, Jack Finefrock, added another "down-home" touch of coffee-pot sociability, combined with his own sophistication in the realm of books.

By the start of the 1979 season, Mr. Smith had also restored the old charm and atmosphere to the Traction Station, better known these days as the Main Gate Building. He set up a guest relations office and a Book Store sub-station there. He invited the Heritage Committee to assemble a Mini-Museum display and he relocated the Farmers' Market under roof at the far end of the building, arranging for it to be open six days a week. The Play and Opera Ticket Office still occupied space at the Main Gate, but the Information windows were arranged to open BOTH ways. "We want the Main Gate to be a friendly place," he said.

When he talked about new restrictions on the use of automobiles, on the Grounds, he said, "Here again, we are getting into the 'essence' of Chautauqua where its quiet is one of its greatest charms. We want to maintain that quiet, our clean air, and safety for those who walk on our streets, our older adults and children. We hope Chautauquans will use our free bus service instead of driving everywhere they want to go." He announced the opening of a new South Gate and the request that residential drivers on either side of Vincent Avenue use either the North or South Gate, leaving the Main Gate for new arrivals. His idea to reduce automobile driving on North and South Lake Drives would allow those lake front streets to become promenade areas again. "Chautauqua is a walking community," he observed.[1]

Then he explained his interest in Bestor Plaza. "I have wanted to restore Bestor Plaza to its real place in Chautauqua life. For that reason the fountain has been repaired and the Plaza will be lighted at night so that people can see where they are walking." Flowers had been planted and pots of greenery had been set on the street in front of the Colonnade where people used to park and double-park in profusion. Eliminating the clutter of parking in front of the Colonnade made it possible for the Institution's main administrative building to be seen and appreciated, and it seemed to open up the Plaza, as well.

The latest development in the relationship between the Institution and the Chautauqua Utility District was the transfer of the filtration plant to the Utility District, but these rather significant functional changes were gradually being understood by the community and accepted. It was small requirements, such as using a certain kind of garbage bag, that whipped up resentment.

Another almost extraneous situation developed over the future of the Chautauqua Diner. It became a public issue before the parties directly involved knew what what happening.

In an attempt to make the entrance to Chautauqua as attractive as possible, a suggestion was entertained by the administration to remove the Chautauqua Diner from its accustomed site. For this reason an extension of the lease with the Diner owner-operator had not been signed and the future of his business and his investment seemed to be in jeopardy. Loyal patrons began signing petitions for the Diner's continuance on its "historic" spot and many of the patrons openly criticized the administration's attitude which they interpreted as a lack of sensitivity to people's needs both— the proprietor's and the customer's.

The matter was diffused early in the season by a Daily article in which Dr. Hesse and Jim Jackson, the owner, expressed mutual confidence in a satisfactory solution.[2] Unfortunately the orchestra trauma did not as easily disappear.

In the meantime, the Board had been going forward with positive plans. The executive committee, meeting in March, had agreed that the firm of Will, Folsum and Smith would be named as fund-raising Counsel for the Institution. A priorities proposal for the Capital Campaign was drafted and organized according to categories, including: improvements, necessities, endowment, enrichment, income generation etc. An interim Campaign Cabinet had been formed to function as an informal discussion and reaction group in considering materials and programs to be prepared for the campaign. The basis for the Capital Funds Campaign appeared to be taking firm shape. The initial stages were proceeding according to plan, but with wise caution and attention to detail. Robert Dodge was serving as the resident fund-raising Counsel.

By the time the Board met again late in June, Miriam Reading had been appointed the National Chairman of the Capital Campaign. She reported that the trustee solicitations would begin during the summer, but that outside solicitation would not begin until after the Gebbie Challenge had been met. The Case Statement was being prepared, but it is not a public statement, she specified. It is nonetheless a statement of the purpose of Chautauqua, the history of Chautauqua and the goals of Chautauqua.

She announced the names of those who would make up the Campaign Cabinet: John T. Bailey, Edward P. Boyle, Philip J. Brunskill, Mrs. Marcia Connolly, George L. Follansbee, Sr., Howard G. Gibbs, Robert R. Hesse, Robert C. Holland, James C. Levinson, Frank E. McElree, Richard H. Miller and Robert B. Osburn.

Other encouraging news was that preliminary written approval had been received from the National Endowment for the Humanities. For every $150,000 raised toward lectureships, Chautauqua would receive $50,000. Mr. Brunskill also reported that an application in the National Historic Trust was approved for $50,000, and that an application for a 1979 grant for financial help with roofing and electrical work on the Amphitheater, a $751,500 application, had also been made. A pre-application to the Appalachian Regional Commission had been approved.

The President told the Board that the Institution had agreed to purchase from Welch's all the equipment in the Pavillion and that the Hotel Corporation would be in charge of operating it. He also announced some staff changes: Alexander McMahon would now be

The Chautauquan Daily

News of a Famous American Center of Culture

Saturday, August 25, 1979

Guest of the editor
Together we share heritage,
potential, responsibility

by Miriam Reading

How can Chautauqua think, at this juncture, with this economic climate, of trying to raise capital and endowment funds?

The answer is clear: because the alternative - seeing our buildings reach a point beyond repair, seeing our programs gradually diminish in quality, seeing Chautauqua's history and tradition of leadership on a national level erode into only a sense of past grandeur - is simply intolerable.

Chautauqua III

The Chautauqua idea of the enrichment of man's soul, mind, and body is transcendent. The Chautauqua spirit, that special love, vitality, and commitment that motivates those touched by the idea, is powerful. The challenge that will *always* face Chautauqua, how to utilize these strengths for the greater glory of God, and the greater good of society, lies squarely ahead. Thus, we have chosen the threefold base, Chautauqua III, as the symbol of our campaign and our goal.

We must restore and preserve the buildings; we must maintain and enhance the program; and we must plan creatively and positively for sharing what we learn and experience with others.

Hope Chautauquans will lend support

These things are going to require a great deal of money - but - if we do not act now, the fiscal need will increase geometrically with inflation and additional decay of our vital structures. Professional fund-raising counsel has been retained to help us get the Campaign launched. Already, a cadre of able, dedicated Chautauquans have been approached to act in leadership positions and include: Edward P. Boyle, Marcia H. Connolly, George L. Follansbee Sr., Howard G. Gibbs, Robert R. Hesse, Robert C. Holland, James C. Levinson, Frank E. McElree Jr., Richard H. Miller, and Robert N. Osburn.

It would be my hope that many more Chautauquans will lend their support in a similar fashion. This Campaign must become the rallying point around which we work together to build the future for Chautauqua we all want. The idea - the spirit - the challenge: together we share the heritage, the potential, and the responsibility.

working as Program Associate with Ms. O'Connor who is aiding in program planning in addition to her other duties; Sherry Bailey would replace Mr. McMahon as Administrative Assistant to Mr. Brunskill; Kevin Byrne had become Coordinator of Planning and Facilities; Richard Redington would assume responsibility for coordinating summer programs for youth and recreation. An interview process for a director of education and youth was not yet completed, Dr. Hesse reported.

The Board authorized the President to sign the oil and gas lease with Envirogas, Inc. on acreage owned by the Institution, known as the Whallon Farm and the Golf Course.

The Program Committee announced to the Board that the Chautauqua Art Association had elected not to hold a Bestor Plaza Show because of the proliferation of art festivals in the vicinity and because of the difficulty in finding sufficient volunteer help.

While some Chautauquans chose to worry and fret in this "paradise beside the lake," there were hundreds who came in and out of the Grounds and happily enjoyed the outstanding program. There was the accustomed density of activities on different levels, big and little occasions which combine to give the unique

Jack Danzinger is honored for his many active years with the Chautauqua Symphony Orchestra. Mrs. Harry A. Logan and Mr. and Mrs. Harry A. Logan, Jr., name a violin scholarship for Mr. Danzinger and host a party to make the announcement.

Chautauqua experience, and there were new people doing familiar things.

Doris Eicher became the first woman to be named official organist. Edward Polochick became the new choir director. (He was also the current associate conductor of the Baltimore Choral Arts Society and in the fall would join the staff of the Baltimore Symphony Orchestra and Peabody Institute.) Peter Perrett, an Exxon-Arts Endowment conductor with the Buffalo Philharmonic Orchestra, was named assistant conductor of the Chautauqua Symphony Orchestra. He conducted the orchestra on Saturday, July 31, and was available if needed during the season. A new Association for those who rent property was formed.

On Old First Night Dr. E. Dorothy Dann Bullock, beloved and efficient president of the Chautauqua Women's Club, was recognized by the Institution for her extended, high quality service to Chautauqua. Dr. Bullock had announced her intention to retire at the end of the summer. As the season ended, Dr. Hesse appointed Mrs. Mary Frances Bestor Cram, a former club president and now an Institution trustee, to serve as interim Women's Club president. The Chautauqua Volunteer Fire Department also received a special plaque of recognition on Old First Night.

Buckminster Fuller was given the Chautauqua Salute on his birthday which happened to occur while he was on the Grounds. Claudia Bonn became the new head of the Children's School. The Ohio Ballet was in residence for a week and the 22nd Chautauqua Exhibition of American Art, a national jury show, drew over one thousand entries from forty-nine states.

Ozan Marsh, head of the piano department in the School of Music, received an invitation to go to Russia the following December for the 75th anniversary of Dmitri Kabalevsky, dean of contemporary Russian composers. Jack Ossofsky, executive director of the National Council on Aging, came during the last week of the season for the Residential week for Older Adults. Four successful 55-Plus weekends were reported by Dr. Helen M. Overs who had developed the Program Center for Older Adults at Chautauqua

following the Centennial. These weekends as well as a mini-arts festival which was held on the Grounds in cooperation with the Chautauqua County Association for the Arts, had been held between the 1978 and 1979 seasons. The Program Center for Older Adults represents a portion of the planning to extend the Chautauqua experience throughout the year.

The CLSC Library in Alumni Hall was dedicated to the memory of a former CLSC-Alumni Association staff-member and Chautauquan, Winifred Kemp. Nately Ronsheim planned another active CLSC program year with two seminars: one with Tad Mosel, author of a CLSC book selection, "Leading Lady," the life and theatre of Katherine Cornell; and the other with John Ciardi on the topic, "How Does a Poem? Poetic Method."

A former president of Chautauqua, Judge W. Walter Braham, died July 13, 1979 in his home city of New Castle, Pa. He had been a prominent member of the Chautauqua community for approximately fifty-five years, a trustee and vice-president before becoming president.

A heart-warming reception was given Aug. 20 in the Athenaeum Hotel honoring Jack Danziger for his sixty years of combined membership in the Chautauqua Symphony Orchestra and in the New York Symphony Orchestra when it played at Chautauqua in the 1920s. The hosts, Mr. and Mrs. Harry A. Logan, Jr., and Mrs. Helen Temple Logan, also announced that evening their gift of a full scholarship for violin for the 1980 season which would be known as the Danziger Violin Scholarship. Mr. Danziger had received a Centennial Medal in 1974 for his years of association with Chautauqua and the orchestra.

The fiftieth anniversary of the Chautauqua Women's Club House dedication was marked by the presentation of the plaque designating its place on the National Register of Historic Places. C. Dudley Brown, a member of the National Trust and a past president of the Victorian Society in America, spoke at the Women's Club meeting on "Historic Sites," and dedicated the plaque at the Club House. This dedication was coordinated with another at the Hall of Missions, which had also received a plaque from the Department of Interior, specifying its inclusion on the National Register of Historic Places. The Hall of Missions had been built in 1924 and because of its connection with the Religion Department and with the prior use of the site by CLSC classes, it was amply qualified as a structure associated with historic events.

"Gil's Story"—Chautauqua Opera 1928-1978—was published by the Chautauqua Opera Guild. On July 13 a Meet the Author party was held in the Patio and Garden of the Lewis Miller Cottage through the graciousness of the present owner of the Cottage, Nancy Arnn. The book was a collection of Gil Gallagher's columns on Chautauqua Opera which had appeared in The Chautauquan Daily in 1978. It was edited by The Daily editor who was also a member of the Chautauqua Opera Guild Board. Publication costs were provided by David and Martha Carnahan, Mrs. Bartlett Richards and Mrs. Betty O. Wood, so that all sales would benefit the Chautauqua Opera Guild.

Dr. Oscar E. Remick, former president, addressed

a YMCA Seminar at the first of the season on a subject relevant to Chautauqua, "The Philosophy of the Arts in Our Society."

One season-long celebration revolved around the 50th year of the Cleveland Play House Summer Theatre. In a special anniversary issue of The Chautauquan Daily, it was recalled how Frederic McConnell, director of the Cleveland Play House, happened to be in Maple Springs in the summer of 1929 and came to Chautauqua to see what was going on. He found a new Norton Hall and approached Dr. Bestor on the opportunity to introduce the Cleveland Play House to Chautauqua. The idea was warmly received and the very next year a regular drama season was present in Norton Hall.

In connection with the anniversary year, Margaret Hamilton, well-known movie and television actress who began her career at the Cleveland Play House, returned to Chautauqua to recreate the role of Miss Prim in "The Importance of Being Earnest." Miss Hamilton also performed in a second 1979 production, "Night Must Fall." It was fortunate that the Play House in its Chautauqua anniversary summer could bring all nine plays of its previous Cleveland season, for they were all outstanding examples of theatrical literature. There was some anxiety within the Institution that some of the plays, although they had been either hits or prizewinners, might face audience resistance. But Chautauquans apparently relished the entire bill and proved their own sophistication. The overall attendance reached a high 65 per cent of capacity. The history of the taste for drama at Chautauqua was traced in a special Daily issue, showing that monologues and readings had been included in early Chautauqua programs along with Bible dramatizations and pageants. Outside groups had also come in to present plays and for a couple of years, Chautauqua had its own Drama Company whose productions were given in Higgins Hall. Lucille Ball played at Chautauqua with the Jamestown Players in June, 1930[3], three weeks before the Cleveland Play House opened its first summer season.

Another fortunate aspect of the Play House's 1979 season was its expanded Theater School which had been given new quarters in the first floor of the Laundry Building and the rear portion of the old Power House, two buildings that sit side by side with usable outside space between them. The faculty, comprised of actors and directors from the Cleveland Play House, offered a unique cross-section of theatrical experience to students who received instruction in Movement, Voice, Improvisation, Stage Combat and Scene Work.

The 100th anniversary of the invention of the Edison light bulb was also observed in a variety of ways during the summer. The latest biography of the famous inventor, "Streak of Luck," by Robert Conot, was a CLSC book selection and the author appeared at a Round Table lecture. Another Edison researcher, Dr. Allen Stahl, presented a slide lecture on "The Incandescent Lamp—Edison's Chase and Discoveries." The Charles Edison Fund had contributed an Edison invention exhibit which was on display all summer at several different locations. Two separate Edison issues of The Daily, one each in July and August, gave information about the work of Edison, his relationships at Chautauqua and the current efforts to preserve and catalogue all of the existing Edision memorabilia.

Chautauqua's attention to the anniversary was concentrated on the weekend of July 21-July 23 when all of the members of the executive board of the Charles Edison Fund were present on the Grounds for the Fund's summer meeting. In this visit they were acknowledging the strong ties that exist between the Edison family and Chautauqua. Mrs. Edison, the daughter of Chautauqua's founder, Lewis Miller, restored the Lewis Miller Cottage after she acquired it in 1922 and served on Chautauqua's Board of Trustees, part of the time as vice-chairman. When the 50th anniversary of the incandescent light was celebrated in 1929 at Chautauqua, the 100th birthday of Lewis Miller was also celebrated and Mrs. Edison took a leading role.

When the Miller Cottage was designated as a national historic landmark in 1966, Charles Edison, son of the inventor, received the historic plaque on behalf of the family and made the principal address. At his death in 1970, The Charles Edison Fund was set up for the support of philanthropic research, education and preservation. The Board of the Fund has shown interest in supporting lectureships, scholarships and preservation at Chautauqua. The Fund has aided the Lewis Miller Lectures, provided funds for the auditions of students, brought the Mina Miller Edison Papers and some of the other Miller Family Papers to the Historical Collection. The Fund has been instrumental in establishing the Heritage Room in Smith Memorial Library, as well as maintaining the Miller Bell Tower, the Bells and the area between the Bell Tower and the Miller Cottage. In 1977 they erected a marker in Miller Park to commemorate Lewis Miller's contributions to Chautauqua and to point out to passerby the significance of that area.

At a dinner in the Athenaeum Hotel on Saturday evening, July 22, the Institution honored The Charles Edison Fund and its Board Members. It was a sentimental occasion for it contained also the celebration of the 92nd birthday of Margaret Miller Newman, granddaughter of Lewis Miller. Mr. Gibbs, as chairman of the Chautauqua Board of Trustees and host of the evening, spoke about the place of Thomas Alva Edison in the history of the world, but he added: "We are somewhat parochial and view him as part of the Chautauqua family." He expressed the Institution's pride in the fact that the Miller and Edison names were linked in the marriage of Mina Miller Edison and Thomas Edison and for the commitment of other members of the Miller family to Chautauqua.

Then Mr. Gibbs introduced Dr. Hesse who took the occasion to speak of the 150th anniversary of Lewis Miller's birth which would be observed the next Monday. His words were a statement of his own commitment to Chautauqua:

"For those of us to whom the care and current stewardship for Chautauqua is entrusted, I say that we take our responsibilities very seriously. Down through the generations, there have been literally thousands of unselfish, dedicated persons who have loved and cared for Chautauqua to bring it to this moment of history where it thrives and flourishes, enriching the lives of so many persons of diverse backgrounds and persons of all ages.

"It is a great personal privilege for me to serve as President of Chautauqua on this historic occasion and I pledge to serve. . .the great ideals of Chautauqua as first they were envisioned by our founders."

Toward the end of the program Mr. Gibbs announced that the Institution wanted to present to The Charles Edison Fund a personal and lasting tribute to symbolize the long and enduring relationship between the Miller and Edison names and Chautauqua Institution. To Mr. Paul Christiansen, president of The Charles Edison Fund, he presented an article about the Lewis Miller Cottage which had been etched in metal and mounted on oak for hanging in the offices of The Fund in East Orange, New Jersey.[4]

Mr. Christiansen accepted the plaque and emphasized the accomplishments of Charles Edison whose achievements had been outstanding and whose gifts continue to enrich mankind.

Richard H. Miller gave the invocation.

There were many high moments throughout the season which fulfilled the compelling need of Chautauquans to return time after time to the place where they have experienced new awarenesses or reawakened aspirations.

One of Chautauqua's great strengths, the deeply-rooted loyalties of its people, kept the "orchestra question" simmering all summer. Many Chautauquans who might be called perennial had become friendly with the individual members of the orchestra and sprang to their defense when a call for general improvement was expressed by the administration. Furthermore, Chautauquans' pride in their own Symphony and Opera Company was strong. Although they recognized that major symphonies were now requiring full-year service and some of their former favorites could not participate in Chautauqua, they could not see

that new attention to quality programming and performance was needed. They recognized the difficulties of mounting a symphony season "in the woods," but they asked, "Who could do better under these circumstances?"

In 1976 Sergiu Comissiona had been selected as music director and principal conductor of the orchestra. But Maestro Comissiona soon became too busy for extra responsibilities at Chautauqua, reduced his conducting here and could not give the Institution the help it needed or expected from him in coordinating its entire musical program. When Dr. Hesse began arranging the season of 1979, he and the Maestro agreed that the latter would conduct five concerts and that would be the extent of his responsibilities.

Dr. Hesse, then, in effect, became the musical director of the orchestra, choosing the conductors and the programs. The very fact that he undertook this part of the programming himself, offended some members of the orchestra who resented his implied criticism of the orchestra's quality. They put little confidence in his music degree or in his performance experience.

Preparations for negotiations were understandably handicapped. The orchestra through its own spokesmen prepared a statement which they distributed to private homes on the Ground when the Daily Editor chose not to print it. In an attempt to allay fears, describe the Institution's motives and rationale, The Daily did publish a Board of Trustees' view of the future of the Orchestra and the objectives to be pursued. Dr. Hesse explained Chautauqua's pursuit of excellence in a guest editorial and Chairman Gibbs was interviewed concerning elements of the Institution's ways of functioning. Honest examination and cooperation were requested.

Mr. Gibbs had set up the machinery of public forums when he was chairman of the Program Committee. He had always believed it was helpful for leadership to hear the ideas of the rank and file Chautauquans. So he arranged a public forum specifically for a discussion of the orchestra question.

In introductory remarks. Mr. Gibbs explained that he had chosen to call the day's topic "The Chautauqua of the Future," not "The Future of Chautauqua" which might imply that there might not be a future. He expressed great regard for Chautauquans and their ideas and said that he did not believe the Board of Trustees should be a hidden enterprise. But he also said that misinformation, misinterpretation, rumors and distortions which had been circulated by Chautauquans had not been encouraging.

There was an amazing variety of comment by Chautauquans of different ages and experience, spoken into microphones so that everyone in the packed hall could hear. As the Open Forum closed, Mr. Gibbs said that was encouraging for Chautauqua's future to have "such a plethora of ideas." Even though the main thrust of the discussion was clarifying the issues of the orchestra study, there were other topics and statements given. "We are doing alot of things right at Chautauqua," one person pointed out. Both Dr. Hesse and the chairman of the Program Committee, Gertrude Shelburne, spoke in response to questions and remarks, and one Chautauquan expressed his reaction

The Institution honored The Charles Edison Fund and its Board members at a dinner at the Hotel Athenaeum. Following Dr. Hesse's remarks, Mr. Gibbs who was presiding, announced a gift to the Fund by the Institution. It was an article about the Lewis Miller Cottage which had been etched in metal and mounted on oak for hanging in the offices of The Fund in East Orange, N.J. (4) Mr. Christiansen, Fund president, accepted the gift and made a response.

rather adroitly: "I am very comforted by the forthright, measured, rational response of Dr. Hesse and his manner of addressing this extraordinarily complex and emotional situation. I am very comforted by the remarks of Mrs. Shelburne (about the large amount of time the Program Committee is spending on the question) whom I had not heard before . . . I think this is a perilous juncture in the history of Chautauqua and on the eve of a critical major fund-raising effort which must succeed to insure the Chautauqua of the Future, and I think you—we—should consider this complex question in a rational way to avoid further assault on what is the rather delicate fabric of Chautauqua."

Jason Weintraub, a member of the Orchestra Committee, also spoke from the orchestra members' viewpoint. He asked that there be more input from the orchestra, along with evaluations from outside experts. He said:

"We are proud of what we accomplish in one two-and-one-half-hour rehearsal. We put on performances and make no apologies . . . Part of the orchestra members' attraction to Chautauqua is the challenge that it represents . . ." He admitted that a big problem is the lack of direction or the lack of a musical director. He said that more rehearsal time is not needed except in unusual situations . . . "We know that the questions are complex, but our voice is heard less than it should be . . . As for the money, we are poorly paid, but we never thought we would be called to task on the matter of money. What we are not paid, we feel we are donating to Chautauqua," Mr. Weintraub concluded.

The Forum was reported in full in seven segments in The Chautauquan Daily between August 7 and 17th. Its publication had a beneficial effect within the community, serving to meet the criticisms of those who felt the administration had sinister motives in questioning the present modus operandi.

A second Open Forum on the program was chaired by the Program Committee Chairman Gertrude Shelburne. One of the recurring aspects of the Forum was the acknowledgment that many factors were interrelated at Chautauqua: costs, conditions of buildings, land use, lack of adequate housing, the need to attract more people to programs, selection of lecturers (including those for the Religion Department), selection of Amphitheater guests (soloists, conductors, entertainers), pre- and post-season events. Dr. Loew and Leonard Treash were present with Dr. Hesse to comment on remarks concerning their program areas.

Dent Williamson of the Orchestra questioned Dr. Hesse's projection of orchestra costs and said that it was different from his. The two men agreed that the figures would be examined in the meetings with the Orchestra Committee.

On one of his visits to the microphone, Dr. Hesse said: "Nothing is easy. We have a situation where we have a built-in contract with the orchestra and I'm not finding fault with that . . ." But then he went on to explain the complexity of the situation because of the number of professional contracts the Institution enters into in the production of opera, an orchestra season and the Schools Department, to name only a few. He referred to the Play House factor and the difficulties with sharing Norton Hall for rehearsals . . .

President Hesse and Board Chairman Gibbs prepare for the Open Forum which provided Chautauquans with the opportunity to discuss "the orchestra question."

"Before we can deal with these problems, with the opportunities, if you will, we have to unravel the contracts to give us a chance to talk about it so that we can see how we might solve them. That's why it is easier for you to listen to someone who says, 'Hesse wants to do away with the Symphony'. . . but that's not the truth. The truth is we're trying to improve all that is Chautauqua and that centers around the program and we have to surface the problems and then we have to deal with them one at a time . . ."

One man asked that the contract be extended, "but get a fine, prominent director."

Dr. Hesse admitted that the speaker had surfaced a question that had to be considered. "We have difficulty looking for a music director who probably doesn't exist, the one who would satisfy each and everyone of us. But we are looking for a very, very good music director."

Mr. Gibbs pointed out another fact that might have been overlooked, that a contract is negotiated with the union, not with the orchestra.

It is a curious, but cherished fact of Chautauqua life that its bounties are too great to be completely diverted by occasional disagreements about policy. The Forum ended on a positive note with the spontaneous statement by a 1979 "newcomer:"

"When you're here for the first time, it's great. I'm absolutely thrilled. Maybe you're doing some things wrong, but the attitude and the atmosphere superimposes itself on everything. I think we should do everything we can for the kids' program. If we don't have them, there will be no Chautauqua of the future. Boy! We're coming back next year."

Like it or not, Chautauquans had to rest their faith in the Board of Trustees who in the words of Mr. Gibbs "weigh carefully all suggestions before making a decision in any of these major areas where differences of opinion exist." The contract with the orchestra for the 1980 season was not in doubt. It was in place. It was the season of 1981 which was in question.

At the Annual Meeting which was convened November 9, 1979, the Trustees promptly decided the orchestra question according to the recommendations of the Program Committee which had been submitted for approval to the Executive Committee as early as Sept. 29, 1979.

The recommendations were:

To maintain, reorganize, and thereby improve the Chautauqua Symphony Orchestra;

To authorize the administration to engage a Music Director for the Chautauqua Symphony Orchestra and the Opera Orchestra, their members and their conductors; to engage, promote, re-seat and have authority in the termination process; and to act in a consulting capacity in all music matters for Chautauqua, effective 1981;

To attempt to achieve in 1981 a Chautauqua Symphony Orchestra of 84 members for 10 services per week, whose membership shall participate in symphony and opera performances and rehearsals as deemed appropriate by the Music Director, with all of the members assigned to the Chautauqua Symphony Orchestra and certain of the members also regularly assigned to the Opera Orchestra;

To maintain 24 presentations per season on an average schedule of three presentations per week by the Chautauqua Symphony Orchestra.

Dr. Hesse reported that he had begun preliminary discussions with the local musicians' union following the executive meeting September 29. In addition to the president of the local union, Dr. Hesse had also met with the vice-president of the national union in New York City. Dr. Hesse had also consulted twice with Howard Hanson who expressed his belief that the Institution needs a resident Music Director. Dr. Hesse also met with the Dean of Juilliard School of Music and with the executive director of the American Symphony Orchestra League concerning assistance in engaging a Music Director.

Thus, the union was informed before Dec. 15, 1979 that it was the intention of Chautauqua Institution to reorganize the Chautauqua Symphony Orchestra and to renegotiate a contract for the 1981 season. Further action was taken by the Board to authorize the chief executive to hire legal counsel to assist in negotiations with the orchestra and to determine whether he, the president, or the legal counsel would be the leading factor in negotiations.

The Buildings and Grounds Committee in its annual report stated that the Garbage Bag experiment had not been successful and that an arrangement with an outside contractor for garbage pick-up was being negotiated.

It was also reported that a contract for a terne steel roof for the Amphitheater had been accepted. The plan was that the roof would be completed by June 1, 1980. An electrical and lighting contract was expected to be let out, probably by January 1. A new roof was planned for Kellogg Hall and at Norton Hall the former method of relieving the roof of ice and snow was to be reinstituted. Four gas wells had been drilled and a fifth one was to be drilled near the 5th hole of the golf course. The fourth hole appeared to be definitely commercial, the chairman said. In connection with the Long-range Facilities Planning Paper, Mr. Osburn noted two critical needs at Chautauqua: to increase the base of constituency and to provide improved housing for a mix of people (families, young, old, all-season, for lesser periods).

In other business, Mr. Boyle was named Chairman of the Annual Fund Committee and as chairman, he reported that the Institution had met all of the conditions of the Gebbie Challenge for the fifth and final year. Thus, the Institution could claim the fifth and final $200,000 installment from the Gebbie Foundation. He expressed appreciation to the Gebbie Foundation and its directors for their creative assistance which had inspired Chautauquans to meet the challenge. He thanked all of the thousands of Chautauquans who had participated in the five-year effort. He thanked Dr. Frank E. McElree and Mr. Joseph Neubauer for their leadership through the Gebbie Challenge.

A new standing Committee on Religion was established and a proposed amendment to the bylaws was passed. The amendment provided for the election of Class A trustees at the last regular board meeting of the season. David Carnahan, a newly elected Class A trustee, was welcomed to the Board at this meeting. Howard E. Chadwick, who had been elected to the Board by the Property Owners in August, was not present, nor was George F. Follansbee, Sr., who had been named an honorary trustee by the Board in August.

The need to complete Bellinger Hall was pointed out by John W. McCredie, Jr., chairman of the Education Committee. He also introduced in some detail the plan for a new Educational Model—a plan to mold the wide spectrum of learning from museums, reading, the performing arts, travel, television, lectures, workshops and formal courses into a cohesive program of purposeful continuing education.

A great deal of Board discussion centered around the budget, finance, the Annual Fund and the Capital Funds Campaign. During the last week of the season, key Board members addressed their fellow-Chautauquans through The Daily concerning crucial needs for endowments and other gifts so that maintenance of high standards of excellence in program and facilities could be met. In the final issue Miriam Reading, National Campaign Chairman, affirmed that Chautauquans together share a heritage, a potential and a responsibility in the Chautauqua Idea, the Chautauqua Spirit and the Chautauqua Challenge. Those who listened to her message began to feel some of the excitement of the future.

In the President's Report, Dr. Hesse announced that five conductors, including Sergiu Comissiona, had already been booked for the 1980 season, along with two conductors for Pops Concerts. Confirmation of six soloists could be announced and they included Sherrill Milnes and Ruth Laredo. Nine weekly themes had been selected for the Platform and a few lecturers were already engaged. Among these were: Harry Chapin, Lorin Hollander and Dr. Michael DeBakey. Dr. Hesse was well into 1980 program-building. Forward excellence!

1979
PROGRAM FIGURES

Musicians
Jared Jacobsen
Phoenix Boy's Choir
  Dorothy Lincoln, Soprano
  Dr. Harvey K. Smith, Director
Syracuse Symphony Pops Orchestra
Syracuse Symphony Orchestra
Lili Kraus
Eileen Farrell
Eugene Istomin
Jeffrey Chappell
Frances Yeend
James Benner
Judith Somogi
Stephen and Frieda Manes
Gary Steigerwalt
Oberlin Baroque Ensemble
  Marilyn McDonald
  Robert Willoughby
  James Caldwell
  Catharina Meints
  Lisa Goode Crawford
Sergiu Luca
Mariana Niculescu
Benita Valente
Catherine Smith
Henry Rubin
Marian McPartland
Philharmonic Virtuosi of New York
  Richard Kapp, Founder, Director
Duke Ellington Orchestra
Mercer Ellington
Claude Monteaux
Ruth Laredo
George Shearing
New Arts Trio
  Rebecca Penneys
  Piotr Ianowski
  Steven Doane
Jim Cullum
Jimmy Dorsey Orchestra
Johnny Desmond
The Four Lads
Bob McGrath and His Children, Lily,
  Alison and Cathlin
Fred Waring and his Pennsylvanians
Josh Logan's Scrapbook
Melba Moore
Brian Gould
Janos Starker
Resident Company of the
  Chautauqua Opera Association
  Margaret Chalker
  Jean Howell
  Debra Borkovich
  Sharon Munden
  Christine Jaqua
  Neil Breeden
  Gary Harger

Ron Boudreaux
  Bruce Cain
  Stephen Smith
Chautauqua Chamber Music
  Players
Swingle Singers
Diahann Carroll
Carlos Montoya
New York Summer School of the
  Arts, School of Choral Studies,
  Abraham Kaplan, Director
Barbershop Quartets
  Boston Common Quartet,
  The Local Chord Company,
  The Love Notes Quartet,
  The Erie Commodores

Conductors
Sergiu Comissiona
Calvin Custer
Christopher Keene
Nathan Gottschalk
Walter Hendl
Ronald Ondrejka
Anshel Brusilow
Gerald Schwartz
Kazuyoshi Akiyama
Kenneth Schermerhorn
Evan Whallon
Harvey Biskin
Judith Somogi

Other Programs
in the Amphitheater
Jacques Brel Is Alive and Well
  and Living in Paris
  Elly Stone
  Margery Cohen
  Shawn Elliot
  Joseph Neal
  Eric Brau, Director
  Steve Helliker, Stage Manager
William Windon—*Thurber I*
The Amazing Kreskin
The Paul Gaulin Mime Co.
Mark Russell

Travel Films

Northern Italy, Philip Walker
Egypt, Doug Jones
Tigris Expedition, Norman Baker
Denmark, John W. Roberts

Platform Lecturers
Arthur M. Schlesinger, Jr.
Leon Jaworski
Elizabeth Drew
Dr. John Stoessinger
Dr. Benjamin Lichtenberg
Dr. Gregory Bateson
Dr. Buckminster Fuller
Dr. Barrie S. Grieff
Nancy Teeters
Dr. Lee Preston
Congressman Jack Kemp
Dr. Daniel Sisler
Robert Evans
Dr. Gerard O'Neill
Roger Caras

Dr. Virginia Johnson Masters
Dr. William Masters
Dr. Richard Restak
Albert Rosenfeld
Dr. Ruth Maklin
Dr. B. Bruce Dearing
Dr. Robert L. Dickman
Dr. David Klein
Dr. Marvin Kohl
Dr. John Barth
John Ciardi
Leslie Fiedler
Ken Kesey
Clive Barnes
Congressman William Clinger
Congressman Stanley N. Lundine
Jeffrey Siegel
Milton Ronsheim
Dr. Allen Whiting
Senator William Proxmire
Robert O'Donnell
Elizabeth Holzman
Leonard Treash
Richard Oberlin
Robert R. Hesse
Nicholas Roussakis
Frederick Wiseman
Edwin McArthur
Sergiu Comissiona

Chaplains
Dr. Gene E. Bartlett
Dr. Bryant M. Kirkland
The Rt. Rev. John S. Spong
Dr. John H. Tietjen
Dr. John Killinger
Dr. James D. Glasse
Dr. Ian Pitt-Watson
Dr. James Forbes, Jr.
Dr. Walter Burghardt, S. J.
Dr. Louis H. Evans

Religion Department
Lecturers
Dr. Hans Schwartz
Dr. Hagen Staack
Dr. Jack Spiro
Hedda Bluestone Sharapan
Dr. Martha Lentz Walker
Dr. C. Charles Backmann
Dr. Dean M. Kelley
Dr. Francis E. Ringer
Dr. Glenn R. Bucher
Dr. Millard Fuller
Dr. Robert J. Marchall

Operas
Leonard Treash, General Director

My Fair Lady
  Evan Whallon, Conductor
  Leonard Treash, Director
Lucia di Lammermoor
  Richard Woitach, Conductor
  Whitfield Lloyd, Director
Falstaff
  Evan Whallon, Conductor

  Leonard Treash, Director
Abduction from Seraglio
  Richard Woitach, Conductor
  Whitfield Lloyd, Director
Ariadne auf Naxos
  Evan Whallon, Conductor
  Leonard Treash, Director
Die Fledermaus
  Evan Whallon, Conductor
  Leonard Treash, Director

Dance
Ohio Ballet
  Mischa Semanitzky,
  David Fisher,
  Conductors
Jose Greco and Nana Lorca

Theater
The Cleveland Play House
Summer Theatre
50th anniversary year at Chautauqua

Something's Afoot
The Importance of Being Earnest
Night Must Fall
The Shadow Box
Gemini
Equus
Threads
The Odyssey
The Last of the Marx Brothers' Writers

Music School
Festival Orchestra
Nathan Gottschalk, Conductor

Soloists
Ralph Padgug
Donna Amato
Rena M. Caulfield.
Barbara Kemper
Shellie Bransford
Cedra Kuehn
George Morales
Mark Johnson
Annette Hult
Richard Sherman
Arlene Jones
Karen Peolini
Chautauqua Dance Department
  Statia Sublette, Director

Richard Sherman, Sigma Alpha
  Iota Winner

Chautauqua Preparatory
Division
Concert Band
  Cecil S. Adams, Jr., Director;
  Russ Bova, Assistant Director

CAA
William C. Landwehr, Juror for the
  Chautauqua Art Association's
  National Exhibition of American
  Art

The Children's School and the Hall of Education are close
neighbors at Chautauqua.

5

Second Century Campaign Launched

AFTER an active program-building winter and spring, Dr. Hesse set the tone of the 1980 season with a statement in the opening Daily that he hoped Chautauquans would *really enjoy* themselves this summer. He, himself, seemed to be looking forward to the season.

He expressed pride in the 1980 program. "We haven't just filled up the program slots," he said. "We have searched to find the best quality of artist and performer within the bounds of our fiscal responsibility.

"I and my staff have gone to New York to meet directly with agents and artists, partly to make them more aware of Chautauqua. We want those who have never been here to realize what Chautauqua is and that they should want to come here. They should want us as much as we want them. Chautauqua is all-encompassing. We are more than a festival. I keep telling them that Chautauqua is the best kept secret in America!" His voice was spirited.

"I think this approach is making a difference," he continued more seriously. "There are many in the arts community who are convinced that our long-term goals are believable.

"It is of particular significance that Chautauqua, prodded by the Gebbie Challenge, has put its financial house in order so that it is in a position to shape its future. Chautauquans have done that and now we face a future of great promise."

However, even at the start of what he hoped would be a relaxing summer for vacationing Chautauquans, he warned: "We will still be confronting complex questions which could not be addressed in previous years. We will find differences of opinion, but that is to be expected when issues are complex. But we can reconcile our differences and discuss them in good faith, freely, without animosity toward each other."

As early as January Dr. Hesse had started to coordinate public relations tactics with program development. Not wanting to tell all the good news too early, he scheduled four issues of The Chautauquan between February and April, planning to step up anticipation of the season as he gradually announced program "names."

He climaxed this strategy by holding a press conference in New York City in April where he could speak directly with media representatives.

Other marketing strategies were coordinated with program development. The new Chautauqua Symphony Orchestra (CSO) schedule of *Thursday* and Saturday concerts with Friday night "specials" was the basis for Institution promotion of Chautauqua Weekends in connection with specific hotels in the area. Selection of artists and variety of programming were carefully calculated to attract weekend patrons in large numbers.

Early-week programming, on the other hand, included the traditional CSO Tuesday evening concerts and Monday evening concerts by the Music School Festival Orchestra, which would replace the film lectures of previous years. A different concept of non-musical, dramatic programs had been planned for Wednesday evenings with artists such as William Windom and Joan Fontaine.

Dr. Hesse could also report that Station WWXI, Rochester, N.Y., had prepared introductory and interpretative material to accompany the taped Chautauqua Symphony Orchestra concerts of the year before, and Chautauqua's colorful film, "The Chautauqua Experience," was being shown at the Winter Olympics in Lake Placid.

By early March season ticket sales were already ahead of 1979 and at the May Board meeting, Dr. Hesse proudly pointed to the engagement of these additional artists: Emanuel Ax, Ruth Laredo, John Browning and Jean-Pierre Rampel.

Certainly the season began joyfully and dramatically enough with two outstanding black Americans appearing within the first twenty-four hours. Ella Fitzgerald performed Saturday night with the opening Daily proclaiming: "Welcome back, Ella!"

Then at the first Sunday morning worship service, Dr. Jesse L. Jackson served as chaplain. Dr. Jackson, true to his role as civil rights activist and Baptist minister, spoke fearlessly on behalf of the needs of people in troubled conditions and pleaded for immediate action.

In a combined press conference and dialogue following the service, Dr. Jackson spoke informally, but more specifically on the issues of minorities, political action, education and Americans' misconception of the world.

To the question, "Why don't you run for the Presidency?", he replied spontaneously, "I'm available and I'm capable."[1] He referred to the number of Presidents who had visited Chautauqua and said with quasi-seriousness that Chautauqua might be a good place from which to launch his campaign. It was a sign of the times that security for Dr. Jackson while he was on the Grounds was of some concern.

Also on the first Sunday two separate conferences were convened. They were the first annual Chautauqua Dental Congress and The Archeology and The Bible Seminars, the latter sponsored by The Biblical Archeological Review Magazine. Conferences held on the Grounds within and beyond the season were being interpreted as undeniable evidence of Chautauqua's growing usefulness as a meeting-site for small groups. Later in the summer students in Clinical Pastoral Education from the Erie County Medical Center in Buffalo, spent a week on the Grounds, attending lectures and intermingling with Chautauquans.

On the evening before Miss Fitzgerald's concert, the 23rd Annual Exhibition of American Art, a national, juried show, opened with a reception honoring the artists. Over $4,000 in prizes were awarded. Almost one thousand entries had been received from forty-eight states and from that number, eighty-two paintings by seventy-three artists had been selected for hanging. Jane Livingston, a consulting panelist for the National Endowment for the Arts, was the juror. The show was scheduled to hang for three weeks in the Chautauqua Art Association Galleries on Wythe Avenue.

Those who arrived early for the season noticed immediately the improvements on the Grounds. The administration estimated that approximately $1 million had been expended by private property owners while Chautauqua Institution had spent almost the same amount, a great deal of it through the first receipts from the Capital Fund Campaign.

Kellogg Hall, one of the most venerable of Chautauqua's historic structures, was sitting squarely on top of a new foundation.[2] Its third floor had been gutted, rebuilt and rewired so that it could be safely used again as a dormitory. The varied wood exterior, one of Kellogg's significant architectural characteristics, had been painted white with a surprising touch of raspberry appearing on the ornamentation near the front roof line, a color which conformed to an early postcard view of the building. This massive edifice was originally erected in 1889 on a portion of the public square known now as Bestor Plaza, opposite Vincent Avenue. It was moved to its present site in 1905.

Atop the Amphitheater, a light-colored steel roof glistened in the sunshine (all 1.3 acres of it). It could hardly be missed while nearer the ground, new drains and gutters looked promising for the rainy periods which were bound to come. New lighting and sound equipment had been installed. A new booth for sound and light control had been "cut into" the ceiling so that the old floor-level booth could be carted away. New catwalks had been constructed above the ceiling. During the last few days and nights before the season the large expanse of the ceiling was painted by men working precariously from large slings high above the benches.

Logan Dormitory, Sherwood Hall and Golfview[3] had also received new roofs. Jewett House had been repainted in earth tones that were appropriate to its 1886 period. A Capital Campaign gift had provided for complete interior renovation of the Hall of Missions.

Interior improvements at Norton Hall could not be seen by the casual observer, but were nonetheless extremely valuable. They included a new electrical system, new stage machinery, new stage lighting, a fire curtain, new star dressing rooms and a new door cut into the rear of the stage area to facilitate the moving of scenery.

The placing of a new fence from the Main Gate to the South Gate allowed for one hundred and seventy-nine more parking spaces in the South Parking Lot with access to the Lot only from the South Gate. Dangerous outside parking along the highway was eliminated.

A new retaining wall had been installed at the South End Tennis Courts while the North End Tennis Courts had been resurfaced. During the late winter and spring, maple trees on the Grounds had been tapped and some of the more than two hundred gallons of maple syrup derived from the effort was on sale at the Book Store.

Yellow benches appeared at major bus stops throughout the Grounds while approximately $17,000 was spent on Massey Organ repairs and maintenance.

It was reassuring to Chautauquans to see that the administration had been serious in its intention to restore historic structures.

"Some people don't realize," Vice President Smith said, "that within the core of the Grounds we have a concentration of Victorian and other compatible styles that make Chautauqua a treasury of late 19th and early 20th century architecture."

Mr. Smith, who also manages the Athenaeum Hotel, was looking forward to the hotel's 100th anniversary in 1981 and was already making some preparation. The lobby floor had been refinished so that its natural color was apparent once more and the main desk area had been restored to its original condition. The hotel's goldleaf sign on the glass over the front door had been freshly repainted.

More mundane operational changes were made. Among them, Miller Avenue became one-way *down* and Ames Avenue, one-way *up,* to facilitate traffic. Garbage collections were being made by the Westfield Disposal Co. at a cost of $30.00 per household for the season. Two 35-passenger and two 40-passenger buses were attempting to provide adequate free bus service to encourage Chautauquans to refrain from driving to and fro on the Grounds.

While the Board's long-range facilities planning was not yet understood by Chautauquans, such planning was going forward. In a report to the Board in May, the Buildings and Grounds Chairman discussed the matter in as much detail as possible.

The objectives were consistent with all of the other activities that had been initiated to take the Institution into the future. They were: (a) To increase the population base to its former level of up to seven thousand people on the Grounds and ultimately up to eighty-five hundred people;[4] (b) to plan housing for younger families; (c) to encourage hotels, rooming houses and apartment dwellings to update their facilities; (d) to provide modern accommodations for families who visit Chautauqua for short periods of time; (e) to provide efficient transportation; (f) to provide housing for students; and (g) to grow a self-contained service community for essential services.

Chairman Osburn distributed to the Board members a Project Plan for Housing Expansion which explained a development proposal for the Elm Lane Development Site in the North End of the Grounds.

After full discussion the Project Plan was accepted unanimously.

In the proposal for development of the north end, however, one of the "complex issues" of which Dr. Hesse had spoken, could be spotted. As soon as property owners in that section of the Grounds learned of the Plan, some of them began expressing their opposition to increasing the density of population in that area. They were fearful, when not downright hostile, over the possibility that the atmosphere of the north end and their property values would be adversely affected. But balanced against these risks was Chautauqua's need to increase its constituency, an acknowledged factor in the Institution's future progress.

At the end of May there was also welcome news for the Education Department. It was then that Dr. Hesse announced the appointment of Richard R. Redington as the new Director of Education, Youth and Recreation. This was an enlargement of responsibilities on a year-round basis for a young man who had coordinated youth activities and recreation during the 1979 season and had served as a Boys' Club Counselor for two years before that. His appointment boded well for the department since a new level of professional supervision would be functioning in the allied areas of education and recreation for both youth and adults.

For a period of a year Dr. Hesse had conducted a search for a professional educator who could grasp the traditions of the Chautauqua System of Education while implementing them in today's environment.

Mr. Redington came from the Albuquerque Academy in Albuquerque, N.M. He had extensive credentials; a solid liberal arts background, experience as a teacher of English, a soccer coach, a counselor of high school seniors with a thorough knowledge of younger children's educational requirements. He had carried a focus on mathematics throughout his own schooling and had an avocational interest in music. When he was interviewed, Mr. Redington called himself a "generalist" in educational philosophy and experience. He expressed the belief that this might be the best possible preparation for his work at Chautauqua.

The new director had an expansive program to evaluate as he took charge at the beginning of a new season. Over two hundred courses were being offered and a total of $68,000 in scholarships was to be administered.

Another 1980 educational development was plainly visible to those who studied their program books. This was an integrated program theme, The Elizabethan Era, which was to run like a colorful thread through the summer schedule. It could be followed with more or less informality by individual Chautauquans as a source of compounded enrichment on a number of levels. It was planned and executed by Marie O'Connor, program director, herself an educator and a generalist in operatic, dramatic and orchestral resources. It

was a first step toward the implementation of a proposed Educational Model based on the diversity of learning opportunities at Chautauqua.

Another educational program at Chautauqua, the Chautauqua Literary and Scientific Circle, was also carrying out a stimulating season.

The CLSC book selections included two books on separate aspects of science. The first, *Disturbing the Universe* by Freeman Dyson provided the average layman with a view of the world as a scientist sees it. The second, which was really the "extra book" of the year, was *Energy Future,* the report of the energy project of the Harvard Business School. *Close to Home* by Pulitzer Prizewinner Ellen Goodman and *For Instance* by John Ciardi provided good quality essays and poetry, respectively, both "keepable" books in the CLSC tradition.

Richard R. Redington

In addition, problems of feeding the world were addressed at the first Round table with Dr. Anne Hollingshead as the lecturer. Extra Round Tables and Sidewalk Session appearances by Amphitheater lecturers added immeasurably to the total impact of the lecture program. The multiple use of lectures illustrated once again the Educational Model concept that was being developed by Ms. O'Connor, as she worked closely with the President on activating Chautauqua's educational potential. While Chautauquans easily recognize the interaction of different parts of the Chautauqua experience within themselves, Ms. O'Connor through her doctoral research, was later to articulate in depth the philosophical basis for this process, the study of self-actualization, and the methods to be employed in the future to make this ideal obtainable. Her Chautauqua program work kept step with her scholarly studies to the benefit of both.

The publication of *The Celebrity Cookbook for the Elegant Eighties,* sponsored by the CLSC and edited by its director, Nately Ronsheim, also added excitement to the summer. It was a cookbook which featured favorite recipes by distinguished program guests and personalities and in this way offered another view of Chautauqua history.

The idea for a cookbook connected with Chautauqua celebrities was born in the President's office, and when it was suggested to Mrs. Ronsheim that this project would be an appropriate one for CLSC, she promptly accepted it and went to work. She corresponded with hundreds of artists, entertainers and lecturers who had appeared at Chautauqua and collected recipes from two hundred who responded. She enlisted the help of Chautauqua's own artist, Maritza Morgan who illustrated the cookbook which was designed and produced by Chautauquan John B. Clark while another Chautauquan, Jackie Briggs, contributed the book's decorative calligraphy. The all-volunteer effort reaped an ample harvest for the CLSC, as the book proved popular.

Another important appointment was made by Dr. Hesse as the season began. Dr. Margaret Hasebroock was named president of the Chautauqua Women's Club. Dr. Hasebroock had had a distinguished career in education, music and political life. Among her many prestigious posts had been the presidency of the

General Federation of Women's Clubs. Mrs. Hasebroock's appointment came too near the start of the season for her to assume full leadership in 1980. Therefore, Mrs. Cram who had been serving as interim president and who had arranged the 1980 program continued to direct the program and share other responsibilities with Dr. Hasebroock.

Mrs. Cram, daughter of a beloved former president of Chautauqua and an educator in her own right, called on her wide professional contacts to assemble a club program of outstanding substance and interest. She also called on her brothers, Dr. Arthur E. Bestor, Jr., and Dr. Charles Bestor, two distinguished "sons of Chautauqua," who had not lectured at Chautauqua in many years. Chautauquans enjoyed renewing their friendships with the Doctors Bestor who remained on the Grounds for several weeks.

Mrs. Francesca Rappole continued as president of the Bird, Tree and Garden Club whose weekly Tuesday afternoon meetings and programs, open to the public for a small fee, provide another significant resource for Chautauquans. Nationally known and regionally important lecturers on nature, conservation and beautification appeared in 1980 at meetings held in the club's home, Smith-Wilkes Hall. Social occasions and money-making benefits were held on the Grace Newbury Terrace and the House Tour of eleven interesting Chautauqua homes brought visitors from as far away as Buffalo, Rochester and Erie while attracting a large local audience. Included on the tour was the President's home where punch was served, and a pleasant social time was enjoyed.

The Bird, Tree and Garden Club is more than seventy years old and has made a steady contribution to the community. It regularly cares for certain gardens. It takes responsibility for arranging the large vases of flowers on the Amphitheater Platform. It promotes home and garden improvement and provides nature education. It has been active in the care and feeding of Chautauqua's trees.

The Second Century Campaign, meanwhile, one of the most important factors in the immediate future of Chautauqua, was proceeding according to plan.

The goals of the Campaign were set forth in a special Daily supplement so that Chautauquans could have in their hands the outline of anticipated accomplishments. The goals represented the opportunity to preserve and restore Chautauqua's buildings, provide reasonable amenities for Chautauqua visitors and a solid base for program support for the future.

Progress in contributions was being recorded. By the end of January, approximately $1,339,000 had been pledged by trustees and former trustees. Area campaigns were being set up and teams were eventually to begin work in Buffalo, Cleveland, Erie, New York City, Northwest Pennsylvania and Florida. Buffalo was the first to report gifts totaling $20,000 by late spring.

A matching grant from the National Endowment for the Humanities was received early in 1980, whereby the N. E. H. would match with one dollar every three dollars of new endowment money which the Institution might obtain for lectureships.

A gift of $30,000 for Amphitheater roof restoration had been awarded by the Historic Conservation Recreation Service under the National Historic Trust. Later in the year this grant was frozen by President Carter as was a $200,000 Appalachian Regional Commission Grant, but both were eventually received.

In early March, Mrs. Reading, chairman, announced that almost $650,000 had been donated to the Campaign by "unofficial members of the Chautauqua family." By March 31, pledges totaling $2,207,596 had been received.

Within another month a $1 million grant for Amphitheater restoration had been promised by the Gebbie Foundation and a pledge of $450,000, by the Carnahan-Jackson Foundation. Soon the rank and file Chautauquan would be coming to a full awareness that the Capital Campaign was, indeed, a fact, that its seemingly tremendous goals were reachable and that steady progress was being made.

A Master Memorial Project was being developed for the Campaign whereby those who would give $1,000 would be represented in a Brick Walk or Wall near the Amphitheater. Each brick would be marked to honor a person or family of the donor's choosing, or to serve as a memorial. The idea was well-received in Buffalo where it was first offered.

Another far-reaching project of the Campaign was "The Chautauqua Auction," set for August 11. Gifts to the Auction were solicited through the winter publications by Dorothy Hill, chairman, who had worked through the winter and spring to set up committees and procedures. The Auction would benefit the campaign and more specifically, the Amphitheater restoration. It was hoped that it would be viewed as a "fun program" for Chautauquans—a Flea Market Deluxe with a fast-talking auctioneer,[5] a white elephant sale, a silent auction, even a barbecue dinner!

Almost all Chautauquans participated one way or another, as it turned out, and over $22,000 was contributed to the Campaign. The Auction and other accompaniments to the Campaign proved that the effort was far from stodgy. For example, Dr. and Mrs. Karl A. Menninger had graciously accepted the honorary chairmanship and a prestigious Honorary Committee was announced.

The Campaign was perceived as "a new standard for giving to Chautauqua." Proof of this lay in the announcement that $1,306,000 had already been pledged to the restoration of the Amphitheater and total gifts and pledges had reached $4 million.

Another tool that was being prepared about this time by one of the Institution's staff-members, Alexander McMahan, was an economic impact statement which showed the Institution's effect on the area business community. The impact study would no doubt encourage local giving to both the Capital Campaign and the Annual Fund, but also strengthen the appeals to national sources of giving.

One of the delicate balances that had to be maintained was the relationship between the Capital Campaign and the Annual Fund. The simultaneous factor in both efforts was later to make their successes seem truly miraculous.

Meeting the 1980 Annual Fund goal of $790,000

was absolutely essential if the operating budget was to be met. It was apparent that an annual fund would always be necessary. In contrast, the Capital Campaign was a once-in-a-lifetime opportunity. In 1980, Annual Fund donors increased in number even as the Capital Campaign was receiving support.

One of the most heartening boosts to the Campaign was announced Aug. 11, 1980, the day of The Chautauqua Auction: a matching grant from the Kresge Foundation for $125,000 for Amphitheater restoration. The gift was "conditioned upon the Institution's raising from other sources by June 15, 1981, the balance of the funds needed to complete the $1.8 million project," said Wiliam H. Baldwin, chairman of the Board of the Kresge Foundation. Dr. Hesse pointed out the significance of a major national foundation's recognizing the worthiness of Chautauqua's need to restore the Amphitheater, the heart of its program center.

Further encouragement came from the notification by Senator Javits' office that the Institution's Challenge Grant Request to the National Endowment of the Arts had been favorably received, although no final numbers were indicated. All in all, the Board could be pleased that it had taken bold action in initiating the Campaign that would "save Chautauqua" for the future. This time the circumstances, though critical, were a bit happier than the 1930s when that phrase— Save Chautauqua—was so poignantly used.

The diversity of Chautauqua was delivering a delightful summer in 1980. In addition to the structured advantages of schools and program, there were community happenings and friendly relationships which gave warmth and color to the season.

Jerry and Joyce Maggs were new owners of the Glen Park Cafeteria, one of the oldest resturants on the Grounds. They promised to continue the Whittemore tradition. During the summer the Utility District held another affirmative vote on a proposed bond issue so that further improvements to the secondary sewerage treatment plant could be made.[6] Nine lots were put up for sale under the Board's scheduled plan of increasing housing and six were sold.

A Chautauqua Opera Poster in art nouveau style was an accoutrement to the Opera Company's productions.

The "traditional look" of Chautauqua was noted in new townhouses that had been built on Ames Avenue and in new private single dwellings. An example was the new year-round home of Geoff Follansbee near the Hall of Christ.

A lifelong Chautauquan, Scott Lawson, and his architectural firm, Lawson, Knapp and Pulver, were later to receive professional awards for their Ames Avenue townhouse designs. Lawson also designed the Follansbee home.

The restoration of The Keystone whose main sections date from 1885, proved to be a morale-booster for the entire community. Mr. and Mrs. Ambrose Cram had purchased the old hotel and rooming house and undertook its rehabilitation as a statement of belief in Chautauqua. The restoration was planned and executed by Mr. Cram.

Mignon Dunn returned to play Carmen, a role in

which she had made her Chautauqua debut in 1957. Paul J. Christiansen conducted his annual choral workshop and the University of Alabama students completed a summer's graduate credit course on The Chautauqua Movement with a week's field trip to the Grounds. The Chautauqua Foundation held its annual meeting and announced assets of $3,154,000, an increase of $214,000 during the year. Net income distributed to Chautauqua Institution was $158,330, but President Richard H. Miller pointed out that the Foundation had also paid $47,400 to Development expense during the past year.

Charles H. Heinz was elected as an Institution trustee, effective November, 1980, to succeed Donald F. Pembridge whose second term on the Board would be completed then. Howard G. Gibbs was continued as Chairman of the Board with John D. Hamilton and Miriam Reading as vice-chairpersons. The Property Owners reelected Robert Osburn to another term as a Property Owners' Trustee.

Dr. Helen M. Overs was honored at Old First Night for her extensive service to Chautauqua. A former head of the Chautauqua Summer Schools, she was specifically commended for her volunteer work since the Centennial year in connection with Chautauqua's Center for Older Adults. In developing this program, she has shown how Chautauqua facilities can be used year-round for the benefit of an ever-widening group of those who desire lifelong learning.

The music of a revered Chautauquan, Dr. Howard Hanson, was presented at a Sacred Song Service in August with the composer present. The Chautauqua Dance Department presented the premiere of a ballet choreographed by Statia Sublette to the music of Hanson's "Forest Play."[7] The Regional Choir performed Mozart's "Requiem," carrying on another tradition, valuable because it reaches out into neighboring communities to offer singers there opportunities to extend their choral experience and to participate in music at Chautauqua. Alumni Hall received its own bronze plaque in recognition of its listing on the U.S. Register of Historic Places.

Miriam Reading, National Campaign Chairman, and Howard G. Gibbs, Board Chairman, are shown as they plan for the ambitious Second Century Campaign.

The sound of trumpets following the Morning Worship Service on August 9th heralded the ceremony of rededication at the Hall of Missions. Dr. Hesse in his official remarks stated that the renovation, restoration and rededication of the Hall of Missions confirms the fact that Man's relationship with his God, has always been and continues to be central in the Chautauqua experience. He added that it is significant that the Hall of Missions is the *first* facility to be fully funded and completed in the Capital Campaign to restore all of Chautauqua.

Dr. Warren Hickman gave the CLSC Recognition Day address. Dr. Michael J. DeBakey drew a large Amphitheater audience as he spoke about heart disease and heart surgery. Harry Chapin performed both as a folk singer and as a person with a compelling concern over world hunger. The Department of Religion presented as chaplain, the Rev. June Nillson who works with the Metropolitan Milwaukee Lutheran Campus Ministry. The Chautauqua String Quartet gave its customary concerts in Norton Hall under the direction of Millard Taylor, the orchestra's concertmaster. In 1980 Andrew Galos, violin, Thomas Dunn, violist, and Chaim Zemach, cellist, were the other members of the quartet.

The Kingston Trio, one of the first contemporary singing groups to make it big at Chautauqua, returned after an absence of twenty-two years. Another outstanding musical personality, Sarah Vaughan, added distinction to the program. The climax of the concert season was reached in the performance of Sherrill Milnes of the Metropolitan Opera.

There were reliable records to prove that the program was pleasing a growing audience. At the Public Forum, Dr. Hesse said that season ticket sales were up to 1319 compared with 954 in 1979. Day and shorter term tickets for periods from one or two weeks, were also up and attendance at evening programs had advanced by twenty per cent.

Fortunately, the rank and file Chautauquan was not worrying about the intricacies of orchestra management, for example, one of those "complex issues" which Dr. Hesse no doubt had in mind when he spoke of the matters that needed to be resolved without animosity. Since it had been decided by the Board in November that negotiations for a new contract would be pursued immediately, many Chautauquans relaxed in the knowledge that their own Symphony would be continuing.

But some orchestra members were still fearful of the outcome and distrustful of the administration. Their worried comments served to stir up some doubt and suspicion. Others who had other complaints found it easy to be drawn into the swell of dissatisfaction, much of it directed toward the President. Some took the opportunity to find fault with Dr. Hesse by criticizing his assistant for program who was more visible on the 1980 Platform where she frequently made introductions. The petulance of disagreement turned to maliciousness in some quarters, far below the basic idealism that would normally be expected from the community. While the need for improving quality was acknowledged by all, the issue of whose judgment should be followed was splintering the inner core of the constituency. Doubt of Dr. Hesse and his staff seemed to be invading even the ranks of the Board of Trustees, despite all the good news from the season.

Even before becoming President, Dr. Hesse had told the Board that in his opinion Chautauqua Opera productions should be better if they were to be worth doing at all. In recalling this outburst of candor, Dr. Hesse later smiled ruefully and said that he had expected it would eliminate him as a candidate. But since it didn't, President Hesse gradually sought to improve the opera segment of the Institution.

His own views of Chautauqua Opera were reinforced by representatives of the National Endowment for the Arts and the New York State Council for the Arts, both

The Hall of Missions receives a bronze marker, designating its place on the National Historic Register. Participating in the ceremony are: Dr. Ralph W. Loew, left, President Hesse, Gwen Read of the Hall of Missions staff who presided, C. Dudley Brown, consultant to the National Trust for Historic Preservation, Mrs. Ambrose Cram and Howard G. Gibbs. Mrs. Cram gave historic anecdotes concerning the Hall of Missions. Mr. Brown and Mrs. Read unveiled the plaque. Mr. Brown also officiated in a similar ceremony at the Chautauqua Women's Club House.

of whom indicated in their statements that consistently better quality would be prerequisites for increased funding.[8] The program office thus insisted on direct involvement with opera and star selection.

By mid-summer in 1980 Mr. Treash, sensing the need for change, decided to resign as general director of Chautauqua Opera, thus terminating fifteen years as head of one of the proudest of Chautauqua's pioneering efforts. His resignation was accepted with regret by the President and a statement of appreciation of Mr. Treash's extended service coming from the Board, was printed in The Daily. Mr. Treash's interest in young singers was noted and he was commended for his development of the Opera Apprentice Program and his educational, academic approach to opera. It was announced that the Apprentice program would not only be continued, but broadened. But it was also assumed that other new directions for Chautauqua Opera lay ahead.

As far as Symphony negotiations were concerned, progress was admittedly slow. Dr. Hesse had reported at the January, 1980 Executive Board meeting that he had met with members of the Local Jamestown Musicians' Union three times. He had reviewed with the Union the concept of a ten-service week. He said that the Union had requested a twelve to fourteen per cent salary increase over the current scale for the next three-year contract. Dr. Hesse also reported on his search for a music director. He hoped to have an announcement on that position before the coming season.[9]

By March nothing substantially new had evolved from negotiations. The basic issues were the salary increase, dismissal procedures and weekly services. Dr. Hesse expressed concern over the fact that the new music director, whoever he might be, would not have input in the development of the orchestra contract. The interviewing process for the music director position was continuing.

When April arrived, the interaction between the calibre of music director who might be attracted to Chautauqua and the orchestra contract seemed more clearly defined to Dr. Hesse, the Institution's chief negotiator. Ample rehearsal time was one of the factors that a music director would consider of great importance, Dr. Hesse emphasized. It had also become apparent that two contracts needed to be negotiated with the Local Union: one for Symphony services and one for Opera services. The reasons had to do with the overriding goal of enhancing the quality of performances which require, among other things, additional rehearsal services. In a single contract situation, the only way to improve quality without demanding a highly atypical work load was to reduce the number of weekly concerts from three to two.

After extended discussion, the Executive Committee moved to instruct the Program Committee to consider the number of desired concerts in the 1981 season with appropriate rehearsals, taking into consideration the requirements of the Opera Orchestra for performances and rehearsals.

The Program Committee subsequently met and prepared a resolution which the full Board promptly approved at the May 10th Board meeting. The committee recommended that the CSO perform no fewer than twenty-one concerts in the Amphitheater within a fifty-one-day season; that it have increased rehearsal times scheduled at the discretion of the music director; and that its membership be extended to eighty musicians.

It was also recommended that a separate orchestra of thirty-four musicians be engaged to perform four opera productions within six weeks with increased rehearsal opportunities. In the matter of salaries, it was recommended that a larger financial commitment within the service framework be approved. The potential for budget impact was believed to be $124,000.

During this presentation to the Board, Dr. Hesse reminded the trustees that "if the quality of the orchestra is improved, grants from the NYSCA and N.E.A, may be more available and that approval by these two funding agencies might be expected to attract other donors to the Institution. Mr. Rittman mentioned that the Opera Orchestra would also be called the Chautauqua Symphony Orchestra. Mrs. Cram pointed out that the orchestra's repertoire would be increased by virtue of the added rehearsal times.

With still no progress made in orchestra negotiations by August, 1980, however, the Board moved that Dr. Hesse be authorized to use a labor attorney and a group of trustees to assist in the negotiations.

Another element was introduced into the whole orchestra situation in August when the entire membership of the orchestra signed a formal request that Kazuyoshi Akiyama be engaged as the Music Director of the Chautauqua Symphony Orchestra. Members of the orchestra, furthermore, asked their fellow-Chautauquans to sign petitions supporting this request. Maestro Akiyama who was guest conducting at Chautauqua at the time was assumed to be willing to listen to a call for a permanent position.

The search for a Music Director had started by asking for recommendations from all of the orchestra members, from members of the Board of Trustees, other Chautauquans and some consultants. Some potential nominees recommended themselves. There were approximately thirty nominees, many of whom were eliminated quickly for one reason or another: "too busy," "not interested," and so forth. The list was first shortened to fourteen, then to ten and finally to six who came to the Grounds to have a firsthand glimpse. In the end there were only three who remained plausible candidates.

While Dr. Hesse had hoped to announce his selection earlier and could not do so, he told the Board that he would make the decision by early September.

But these were really internal matters that did not occupy the minds and hearts of most Chautauquans who still believed that all would be well with their favorite place. This trust was supported by news in the final issue of The Daily which included the announcement of major program enrichment gifts through the Capital Campaign: a $250,000 endowment for a major lectureship; a $200,000 addition to the Department of Religion Fund for the enrichment of that department; a $50,000 lectureship in the Department of Religion; and an endowment gift of $250,000 established for continuing maintenance of the Hall of Christ. Innovative scholarships for young families and for elderly persons had also been made available through gifts to the Foundation. As the season closed, $4,236,000 could be reported as the Second Century Campaign total. Chautauqua's future certainly appeared to be bright!

During Foreign Affairs Week which was the last week of the season, an unusual dilemma developed in the Amphitheater following the lecture of Ambassador Mohsin Ahmed Alaini, Permanent Representative of the Yemen Arab Republic Mission to the United Nations. Booing from the audience began interfering with the lecturer's responses during the customary question and answer period. Dr. Hesse spoke out against such a display and reminded the audience that the Amphitheater Platform is by tradition a place where all should be able to speak freely. The crisis abated, but it was the most ominous outward threat to free speech at Chautauqua within present memory.

True to his promise, Dr. Hesse announced in September that he had selected Varujan Kojian to be Music Director of the Chautauqua Symphony Orchestra. In addition to being Music Director of the Utah Symphony, Kojian had just completed several years as principal guest conductor with the Royal Swedish Opera in Stockholm. He had previously served as concertmaster and assistant conductor of the Los Angeles Philharmonic under Zubin Mehta and assistant and associate conductor of the Seattle Symphony, as well.

Born in Beirut, Lebanon of Armenian parents, he had begun the study of violin at the age of eight. He very soon became noticed for his ability, so much so that the President of Lebanon arranged for him to study in Paris at government expense. He graduated with first prize honors at his Paris Conservatory when he was thirteen and came to the United States to continue his studies.

He enrolled with Ivan Galamian at the Curtis Insti-

tute and also studied with Jascha Heifitz. At 19, he became the concertmaster in Los Angeles. So highly thought of was he that Zubin Mehta encouraged his young assistant to go to Vienna to study conducting under his own teacher, Hans Swarowsky.

At last Chautauqua had a Music Director who would be in charge of this most vital part of the Institution's program. But it was not Akiyama. How would the orchestra react?

During the December Board meetings, Mr. Ray Anderson who had been engaged as the Institution's labor attorney, reported at length the lack of progress in the union negotiations. He stated that he felt Dr. Hesse had been following correct procedure in his negotiations.

After extenseive discussion, the Board named three trustees to work with the President in negotiations with the union. They were: Howard G. Gibbs, Richard H. Miller and Robert O. Wilder.

Periodic references to Board committees have already called attention to the fact that the Chautauqua Board of Trustees is a working Board. Both Dr. Hesse and Board Chairman Gibbs believe in the committee system and were willing to take the time to make it an effective instrument. In this connection, therefore, it is relevant to show how two other Board committees were thinking creatively concerning the future of their areas.

Dr. Holland, chairman of the Religion Committee, said that a program of continuing education for the clergy was being proposed and that the committee wished to coordinate it with the overall educational program through Mr. Redington and Dr. Hesse. The committee also supported the idea of combining the 10:45 Amphitheater lectures during Religion Week with the continuing education program.

The committee also requested that it be given

The Franklin (Pa.) Silver Cornet Band, the oldest band of its kind in the country, returned to give the final Sunday afternoon concert of the season. The Band had performed on Bestor Plaza on Stamp Day in 1974.

responsibility for the improvement and upkeep of Palestine Park, and made other suggestions of a more routine nature. The report was attached to the minutes and later discussions between the administration and the committee were promised.

The Education Committee report was much longer and gave a comprehensive view of the type of educational activity that seems appropriate for Chautauqua Institution at this particular time.

Examining the report, one picks up the idea that "the blend" at Chautauqua is what makes it unique. Chautauqua, itself, is "a blend" of education, religion, art and recreation for the benefit of a blend of age groups. But the committee asserted that it is impractical to consider any facet of the educational program outside the vacation/recreation framework: "Keeping this in mind, the stated purpose of education at Chautauqua is to involve all ages of all generations of the Chautauqua family in the continuing education of the educated."

After dealing with the probable philosophical and directional goals of Chautauquans, the report dealt with the role of the Summer Schools, the School of Fine and Performing Arts and the School of Special Studies. Here again, the needs of varying levels of individual study goals were delineated as the committee laid out the structure of the total educational opportunities.

In the report the School of Fine and Performing Arts was newly designated to include four divisions of instruction formerly thought of as separate schools: Dance, Fine and Applied Arts, Music and Theater.

All four divisions would share the goals of attracting a few professionally oriented students of advanced skills; a larger group of serious students of intermediate skills; and many hobbyists and vacationers at beginning levels and above; and all categories would operate irrespective of age.

A new unity between the Art Center and the Chautauqua Art Association Gallery was recommended with the Gallery Director a participant in the Division of Fine and Applied Arts.

The Program Committee had brought forward in late August a prospectus for Chautauqua Opera. Since the resignation of Mr. Treash, the Committee had gradually reached a consensus that policy should be enunciated before a new director was engaged.

It was stated that the purposes of Chautauqua Opera should be:

1. To present high quality artistic productions in an effort to promote opera as an integral part of the Chautauqua experience;

2. To cultivate a following for fine opera as an art form;

3. To create an environment where young singers mingle with, perform with and develop under the tutelage of established professionals who offer their services in the continuation of a structured apprentice program designed specifically to prepare young talents for serious professional careers;

4. To complement the program thrusts or thematic concepts mounted by the Institution each season;

5. To revive chamber operas that can be presented very well on a small stage and in so doing, to create a

Varujan Kojian was announced in September, 1980, as the new Music Director of the Chautauqua Symphony Orchestra.

repertory unique to Chautauqua and a regional Company;

6. To introduce new American works to the repertoire.

As far as the educational values of Chautauqua Opera were concerned, it was urged that the apprentice program be strengthened to provide vocalists with classes in movement, acting and diction, apart from vocal coaching. It was also suggested that further production vehicles for apprentice artists be found, beyond their regularly scheduled opera productions.

Funding should be solicited from Federal and State agencies, from private foundations and from individual donors in an effort to minimize or eradicate operational deficits.

The Board voted to present no less than four operas in 1981 and no fewer than six plays by the Cleveland Play House.

In an update from the Buildings and Grounds Committee, the 1981 work on the Amphitheater and Norton Hall, Logan Dormitory and the Golf Clubhouse was projected. It was reported that all five gas wells had proven to be good producers with the one on the golf course, the best producer. Average royalty payments had been running approximately $900.00 per month. Lack of demand by National Fuel Gas Distributing Co., however, was expected.

The administration and the Program Committee received unanimous commendation by the Board for the season of 1980.

Consideration of the 1981 budget, however, occupied the attention of Board members at the annual meeting in December. Dr. Hesse reported that the budget for the coming year represented an overall increase of six per cent over last year's actuals. Earned income had increased so that it could be expected to provide for seventy-two per cent of the budget while gift income would supply the remaining twenty-eight per cent. However, Dr. Hesse pointed out that the

Gebbie Challenge Grant of $200,000 would be lost due to the completion of that Challenge program, that the $50,000 Wendt Grant would not be available and that the unrestricted category of the annual gifts had been reduced from $625,000 to $570,000.

When the Board examined the budget, there were many questions, but foremost was that of the projected increase in the Play House budget. Dr. Hesse reported that the Play House would perform in 1981 seven productions, one of which would be a musical. The projected total cost of the Play House for 1981 was $209,250; projected annual income, $122,000; and gift subsidy necessary, $87,250. Dr. Hesse told the Board that it would be impossible to obtain another play house at Chautauqua for the same cost. However, the steadily increasing costs of the Play House became a focus for discussion.

At length, the Board passed a motion that the Cleveland Play House be eliminated from the 1981 budget, subject to legal review, and that the Board thoroughly explore the potential of a solid drama program at Chautauqua and implement those potentials.

When overall approval of the budget was finally voted on, it was moved that the Board accept the expenditure side of the budget with the intention of modification of both the expenditure and the income side for the elimination of the Cleveland Play House and that the administration reevaluate its gifts and grants income projections to a number they consider to be totally realistic for appropriate, achievable fund raising goals and that the resulting budget be submitted to the Executive Committee for final endorsement and subsequent action.

Thus was created another "complex issue" for the administration, one that would demand immediate attention and finesse with an ultimate solution to follow who could tell when. The disruption of theatre at Chautauqua would no doubt result in another outcry over changes in the status quo.

At the Annual Meeting, Dr. Hesse also presented his report to the Board. He analyzed four main areas of concentration: programmatic excellence, financial security, physical facilities and national visibility. He also raised some philosophical questions concerning how best to take Chautauqua into the future, a conundrum that has continued to perplex Chautauqua leaders.

Evening programs in the Amphitheater, he said, are at their highest level in many years. The tremendous array of talent, increased attendance, audience response and gate revenues all point to the success that has been achieved. He predicted that the orchestra would again reassert itself into the front ranks of music-making with a resident music director and increased rehearsal time. He noted the higher level of conductors and soloists during 1980. The lecture programs had registered increased audience size and response. The Religion Department lectures had continued to grow in quality, stature and audience size. The Opera Company had made some strides in reaching the degree of excellence that is sought, he said, pointing out that opera is a very expensive program for Chautauqua and will require considerable attention to bring it to the level to which the Institution aspires. He admitted that the Play House was a disappointment. "We have no control; it is expensive; it plays to only a forty-two per cent capacity; and since it is presented in an inappropriate facility, it forces us to share a facility which remains unacceptable. This is a major issue which must be addressed. It may have been put off for fifty years, but the time has come to resolve one of our most pressing problems," he said. His report gave the impression that progress toward programmatic excellence was on target. Now what was needed was a successful conclusion to the Union negotiations for the symphony orchestra and an answer to the future of theatre at Chautauqua.

The necessity to move forward in the area of financial security must be acknowledged, he declared. While the mix between earned income and gift income has changed radically and has proven that the administration has managed the Institution's endeavors in a business-like way, the need to match need with gift income has not been met, he said.

"Chautauqua is still at a crossroads in terms of its future," Dr. Hesse continued. "It can only be as good as its program. It can only raise funds in keeping with its performance and aspirations, and it can only earn income in relation to its ability to manage its affairs in a business-like manner."

In physical facilities, Chautauqua had made more progress in 1980 toward restoring and rebuilding Chautauqua than it had made in many years. It will still require a massive effort and years to complete, the president said, but our reward will be in the satisfaction of knowing that we have literally saved Chautauqua. "We have not tried to change it," he affirmed. "We have tried to preserve it . . ., a treasure worth saving and it falls on this generation to do so."

In the area of national visibility, "we have started very slowly through painstaking efforts to become involved at the national level . . . More of the people in places of influence are beginning to learn of Chautauqua and to once again take us seriously. . ."

Then he addressed himself to the problems that concern direction, priorities and goals. He asked for a definition of what the Board really wanted and expected from an Institution President. He confessed that he was unsure of their confidence, that he was being destroyed by rumor and gossip and that he was dismayed by the way disruptions were occupying his time and energy when there was so much positive improvement to be achieved. He asked the Board members to reassess their role vis-a-vis staff and/or President and that they focus on the most important functions of their stewardship toward shaping Chautauqua's future and dealing with policy rather than management. "We desperately need your valuable assistance on major policy questions," he urged.

At the end of the discussions which followed Dr. Hesse's report, the Board reaffirmed the established goals that Dr. Hesse had outlined for the coming year. There remained much to be done and in renewing Dr. Hesse's appointment as president, the Board was in effect giving him a mandate to press forward and to exert his powers of leadership with confidence. The unity of will and purpose that would be vital in the months ahead seemed to have been forged.

1980 PROGRAM FIGURES

Musicians
Spyro Gyra Band
Ella Fitzgerald
Maynard Ferguson
Preservation Hall Jazz Band
Mel Torme
John Browning
U. S. Army Field Band and
    Soldier's Chorus
Composers String Quartet
Eugene Moye
Elmar Oliverira
Victor Borge
Lorin Hollander
Boehm Quintette
Christopher Rex (NFMC Winner)
Kingston Trio
Buffalo Guitar Quartet
Millard Taylor
Jean-Pierre Bonnefoux
Sarah Vaughan
Lotte Goslar Pantomime Circus
NYSSA Choral Concert
Richard Sherman
Emanuel Ax
Pinchas and Eugenia Zukerman
Robert Merrill
Louise Russell
Kenmore West Senior High School
    Concert Band
Ellwood City Area Civic Chorale
Jimmy Dorsey Orchestra
Veri and Jamanis
Bert Lucarelli
Ruth Laredo
Ferrante & Teicher
Harry Chapin
Andrew Tunis (Aldredge Comp.
    Winner)

Jean-Pierre Rampal
Peter Nero
Sherrill Milnes
Dottie West
The Lettermen
Jane Olivor
Dionne Warwick
Tony Bennett
Rita Coolidge
Booker T. Jones
Barbershoppers:
    Chorus of the Genesee
    Four-For-The-Show
    Crazy Rhythms Quartet
        (Sweet Adelines)
    Blue Grass Student Union Quartet
Helen Reddy
Jeff Tyzik's 13 Piece Big Band

Conductors
Sergiu Comissiona
Henry Mancini
Kurt Klippstatter
Semyon Bychkov
Gunther Schuller
Edward Polochick
Peter Perret
Jorge Mester
Walter Hendl
Robert Irving
Kazuyoshi Akiyama

Other Programs in the Amphitheater
Joan Fontaine: *America*
Jose Ferrer: *My Favorite Shakespeare*
William Windom: *Thurber II*
Mercedes McCambridge: *Dramatic
    Readings*
David Fendrick: *Albert Einstein*
An Evening With Graham Kerr
Phyllis Newman: *The Madwoman of
    Central Park West*

Platform Lecturers
Congressman Anthony Moffett
Congressman Thomas J. Downey
Congressman James Jeffords
Congressman George Miller
Jeff Greenfield
Mary Evans-Johnson

Robert Brustein
Jean-Pierre Bonnefoux
Lorin Hollander
Robert Evans
Jack Nessel
Eli Evans
Barry Jagoda
Nancy Dickerson
Julian Bond
Bruce T. Mazlish
Dr. L. Pearce Williams
Kevin Tierney
Fereydown Hoveyda
Dr. John Stoessinger
Joseph Sugarman
Kenneth Robinson
Daniel Yergin
Michael DeBakey, M. D.
Joel Elkes, M.D.
William Regleson, M.D.
Albert Rosenfeld
John Edmond
Edward Lindaman
Elizabeth Dodson Gray
Harland Cleveland
Harvey Cox
Harry Chapin
Doris Kearns Goodwin
Robert Donovan
Richard Valeriani
Joan Fontaine
James Roosevelt
Joseph Nye, Jr.
Andrew A. Mulligan
Amb. A. D. Jim Blankson
Amb. Moshin Ahmed Alaini
Chia-Ching Fan
Diane Kirkpatrick

Chaplains
Dr. Jesse Jackson
Dr. Ernest T. Campbell
The Rev. June Nilssen
Dr. John Guest
Dr. J. Ellsworth Kalas
Dr. John T. Conner
The Rev. Walter Burghardt, S.J.
Dr. James A. Forbes
Dr. Lloyd John Ogilvie
Col. Ernest A. Miller

*Additional Speakers at
Morning Devotionals*
Dr. John Peters
Dr. Harold K. Babb
Dr. Robert Cleveland Holland
Dr. Maurice Phillips
Dr. Robert Hewett

Religion Department Lecturers
Dr. Mary Catherine Bateson
Dr. Joseph Sittler
Dr. Richard S. Gilbert
Dr. Robert Gordis
Dr. Carney Gavin
Dr. John Swomley
Dr. Carnegie Samuel Calian
Dr. Russell Chandran
Dr. Reuel L. Howe

Operas
Leonard Treash, General Director

Fiddler on the Roof
    Evan Whallon, Conductor
    Dallas Johann, Stage Director
La Cenerentola
    Evan Whallon, Conductor
    Whitfield-Lloyd, Stage Director
Carmen
    Kurt Klippstatter, Conductor
    Leonard Treash, Director
Taming of the Shrew
    Nicholas Flagello, Conductor
    Robert J. Murray, Stage Director
The Magic Flute
    Evan Whallon, Conductor
    Leonard Treash, Director

Dance
Merrill Ashley and Sean Lavery
    New York City Ballet Principals
Yoko Ichino, American Ballet
    Theater Principal, and Helgi
    Tomasson, New York City Ballet
    Principal

Theater
The Cleveland Play House
Summer Theatre

A History of the American Film
Custer
Wuthering Heights
A Midsummer Night's Dream
Catsplay
Present Laughter
Wings
Da

Music School Festival Orchestra
Nathan Gottschalk, Conductor

Soloists
Arlene Jones
Lisa Emenhiser
Sheila Reinhold
Chautauqua School of Dance
Concerto Concert:
    Tamara Goldstein
    Heather M. Hurley
    Katherine Diener
    Dan F. Via
    Kevin Fardink
    Anne Cholakian
    Robert West
    Robert Amchin
    Maureen Strenge
    Renee Fleming
    Martha deVries
    Herbert Perry
    Natalie Dalschaert

Natalie Dalshaert—Sigma Alpha Iota
    Winner

CAA
Jane Livingston, Juror for the Chau-
    tauqua Art Association's National
    Exhibition of American Art

Mignon Dunn and John Alexander appear in "Carmen."

The Chautauqua String Quartet has performed
informally sometimes to the delight of many.

6

'Nothing Succeeds Like Success'

WITHIN the first few weeks of 1981 the successful completion of negotiations between the Musicians Union and the Institution resulted in agreements for a new three-year contract for the Chautauqua Symphony Orchestra. This accomplishment laid the basis for the next year's planning, removed the uncertainty over orchestra costs and represented a boost in morale for everyone.

Dr. Hesse acknowledged the contributions of the trustees' committee whose members had been added to the Institution's negotiating team.[1] "Without their help, the negotiations could not have been successfully completed," he said.

Mr. Miller, on the other hand, acknowledged the valuable service of the President's Assistant, Ms. O'Connor, who had assembled the facts and figures necessary for the entire settlement process.

Since the resolution of the contract dilemma had been sincerely desired by both parties, there was plenty of gratification and relief for everyone.

Major points covered by the new agreement centered around three areas: The musicians' work load, the tenure procedures and the rate of compensation.

According to the agreement, the annual range of services for the orchestra lay between fifty-two and fifty-six for the next three years, not counting opera services. Between twenty and twenty-four concerts per year were possible within that range. The contract would call for no less that twenty-six services for opera. The settlement gave both the Institution and the orchestra flexibility and along with flexibility came a change from a three-day week to a five-day week.

An evaluation committee, comprised of five members of the orchestra, was set up to decide questions of tenure. The Music Director would have the decisions over who would be reviewed for dismissal. Each of the five committee members would have five votes, by secret ballot, and seventeen votes out of a possible twenty-five would signify retention. However, an unretained player might choose to come back for one additional year and go through the appeal process or he might accept severance pay beginning at fifty per cent of his salary.

Monetary compensation was figured on an increase of approximately fifteen per cent the first year, eleven per cent in each of the second and third years.

Soon to follow was other welcome news that Cynthia Auerbach had been named Artistic Director of the Chautauqua Opera Company. Since the Chautauqua Opera Company and the orchestra had been organized in the same year, both have shared central program positions. To have their details of operation and key personnel determined for the new year gave Dr. Hesse at last a strong position for overall planning. After three years of intermediate moves and the restructuring of ultimate goals, he could now proceed to the unified effectiveness he had envisioned.

Miss Auerbach, a stage director with the New York City Opera, had had wide experience in regional opera throughout the United States. She has staged opera for the Kansas City Opera, Asolo Opera, Aspen Opera, Lansing Opera, Rochester Opera, Opera South and San Jose Opera.

She had also served as theory professor, choral conductor and assistant director of the Preparatory Division of the Manhattan School of Music.

She had earned acclaim in 1980 at New York City Opera for a new production of "The Pearl Fishers," and had already established a reputation for innovative restagings and revivals with that company.

Two other appointments, both included in the 1981 budget, implemented the recommendations of the Education Committee concerning the Arts programs:[2] Rob Erdle as Coordinator of the Division of Fine and Applied Arts, and Millie Giles as Director of the Chautauqua Art Association Gallery. Mr. Erdle would plan core experiences for serious full-term students as well as correlate the offerings of all the studios. In addition, he was to help with curriculum and teacher selection. Among other related changes was the shifting of some courses from the Arts Division to the Special Studies School where the courses would seem more accessible to vacationing Chautauquans. A closer working relationship between the Arts Quad and the Art Gallery was viewed as a strengthening of the total arts program. Ms. Giles was to share faculty status at the Arts Quadrangle.

Early in the year also, Marshall Nelson resigned as Institution Secretary-Treasurer and Chief Financial Officer. Joseph C. Johnson of Jamestown was appointed to succeed him. Mr. Johnson came to Chautauqua from the position of finance director of the City of Jamestown where he had served for seven years. Before that he had been business manager of that city's Board of Utilities. He had earned a bachelor's degree in economics from the University of Michigan before serving seven years with the U. S. Navy's Supply Corps.

As the Executive Committee studied the financial reports in January, it was noted that the Annual Fund had one hundred more donors in mid-January, 1981 than it had had the year before. The goal for the Annual Fund had not been set but the committee had been requesting a twenty per cent increase in the level of giving for the President's Club.

Concerning improvements, it was reported that an architect would be submitting plans for the backstage area of the Amphitheater and the restrooms. Work was expected to begin on that project by September, 1981. Also, a committee was being formed to plan for the needs of the handicapped.

Mr. Osburn also reported that the Fire Department had made the following request: that three paths of stable runways to the lake be constructed along the lake shore so that in case of a major fire, water could be promptly taken from the lake.

The Executive Committee moved to set aside property at the requested locations and enter into a dialogue with the Chautauqua Utility District regarding the cost. In a related matter of fire safety, the Committee chose not to exercise the Institution's prerogative to do its own fire inspection.

Planning for other imperative fire safety changes was placed in the hands of the Buildings and Grounds Committee and the Task Force appointed by Dr. Hesse. The anticipated cost for these changes was set at $84,500.

Concerning the North End Development, Mr. Osburn reported that no bids had been received. The Buildings and Grounds Committee, however, was recommending that the same basic plan be kept and made ready for another appropriate bidding time.

Mr. Osburn explained another area for possible development on the south side of Elm Lane where there are at least five to six lots that could be sold without having to build major roads. The Executive Committee instructed the Buildings and Grounds Committee to move forward with the sale of lots on the south side of Elm Lane subject to the approval of the full Board of Trustees.

The functioning patterns of the Main Gate were discussed at length. Sales terminals had been ordered from IBM which would almost totally automate ticket procedures at the Main Gate.[3] It was recommended by the Buildings and Grounds Committee that the present property owner pass be replaced by a guest pass which would be free and good for a maximum of five hours, but not beyond 11:00 p.m. on the day of issue. A guest who stays beyond the expiration hour is subject to pay the full day's rate. It would be expected that a property owner would arrange beforehand for guest passes, but guests arriving on short notice could obtain guest passes by asking the hospitality staff to call the Chautauqua host and arrange for the passes. Renters and short-term visitors can also use this plan for their guests. It was also recommended that the Sunday Gate Pass should not include overnight privileges and be valid only until 10:00 p.m. The Committee recommended that a person with previous Chautauqua experience be selected as manager of the Main Gate.

The need for a central housing reservation authority was agreed upon along with the formation of a task force to investigate the possibility of providing such a service to persons seeking vacation housing.

Mr. Miller reported that Mr. Logan had made a gift to the Chautauqua Foundation in the amount of $250,000 to establish an endowment fund for the performing arts, the net effect of which would be to provide to the Institution's program budget in the performing arts, beginning in the 1982 season with approximately $30,000 of productivity for that specific purpose. Mr. Miller said that productivity will be approximately twice as great as normal so that really the gift has a much higher capital value to Chautauqua in terms of the Institution's Endowment Fund.

The Winter Chautauquans meanwhile contained among its other announcements the news of a $250,000 challenge grant in federal funds from the National Endowment for the Arts. The terms of the grant required Chautauqua to raise three times the NEA amount in new gifts from other donors over a three-year period. When successfully completed, another $1 million would be added to the endowment of programs in the performing arts.

"Only eighty-four grants were awarded from two hundred and ninety-eight applications," Dr. Hesse said in his statement of appreciation. "This grant pays great tribute to the quality of our cultural program and offers us an unparalleled opportunity to improve the quality of Chautauqua's full spectrum in the performing arts."

The NEA grant was the second large matching grant which Chautauqua had received during the past year after having satisfied a challenge grant from the National Endowment for the Humanities in 1980. The Gebbie Challenge Grant, of course, had been successfully completed in 1979, setting the stage for the Second Century Campaign.

A surge of gifts in December had lifted the Capital Campaign to receipts or pledges of $4,764,408.

Scholarships totaling more than $60,000 were announced by the Chautauqua Summer Schools as an indication that educational opportunities for students in music, art and the dance were on the rise. Audition schedules were announced for twelve major cities. Taped auditions were also acceptable for the Music School Festival Orchestra, for the Aldredge Piano Scholarship, the Mu Phi Epsilon Memorial Foundation Scholarship and the National Federation of Music Clubs Scholarships. Auditions for remaining scholarships would be held immediately before the season, Schools Director Redington said.

Several scholarships for families having at least two children between the ages of two and high school age were given by Mr. and Mrs. David Carnahan and the Joseph H. and Florence A. Roblee Foundation. These scholarships expressed a sensitivity to the needs of families who might otherwise be unable to find the resources for a complete week at Chautauqua.

Dr. Nathan Gottschalk was continuing for the third year to direct the Summer School's Music Division, but it would be Dr. Gottschalk's ninth year as conductor of the Music School Festival Orchestra.

Other aspects of the Music School included Blanche

Altschuler's pre-concert lecture series, her classes in informed listening and her course in Music for Teachers of Young Children.

The Vivaldi Chamber Orchestra for Chautauqua Vacationers offered a unique opportunity for amateur, professional or student instrumentalists who want performing experience while enjoying the other advantages of Chautauqua. Those playing stringed instruments, flute, oboe, bassoon or keyboard were eligible for this group. The workshop, available for one, two, three or four works, was directed by Stephen Covella.

The phrase "Chautauqua Has It All" had become a watchword for Chautauqua. Not only did this claim appear on publications and advertisements, but it was taken seriously as a focus by the administration. Word was received in the spring of 1981 that the colorful Advance Program Sheet for 1980 had received first place honors in national judging by the prestigious International Society of Performing Arts Administrators, Inc. Dr. Hesse credited the design concept and publication content to Phil Zimmer, Chautauqua's Director of Communications.

But part of the "all" actually came up missing in 1981, the Cleveland Play House Summer Theatre. This elimination by the Board shocked oldtimers when they saw the announcement in the March issue of The Chautauquan. So much worry had been spent over the orchestra situation that the intricacies of the Play House dilemma had been generally overlooked. Chautauquans didn't realize how steadily the Board had been struggling with this problem.

After the December Board meeting when a provisional removal of the Cleveland Play House item from the 1981 budget was enacted subject to final approval of the budget by the Executive Committee, Dr. Hesse had approached Richard Oberlin, director of the Cleveland Play House, for further explanation of alternative proposals. Mr. Oberlin, in turn, presented a revised proposal which he described as a "bare-bones" austerity budget.

The cost of providing the play productions and Theatre School staff was $115,500.00, considerably below the original projection. However, the financial shortfall in the operating area in 1980 and the severe inflationary spiral were still sources of anxiety for Board members who were continuing to take their fiscal responsibilities very seriously. On top of that were the other concerns; for example, the difficulties in sharing the use of Norton Hall, all of which led some to believe that other ways to have drama at Chautauqua could be found.[4]

Therefore, at the January Executive Committee meeting, when Mr. Oberlin's counter proposal was put to a vote for approval, the measure was lost, although admittedly, it was a close tally.

Another motion stating that the Board's original intention not to have a contract with the Play House be reaffirmed, "but the exploration of solid drama at Chautauqua be immediately pursued," was withdrawn after discussion. It was pointed out that if the Executive Committee or the Board tells the administration that it *has* to do something this summer, the administration will be blamed for the entire Play House situ-

ation when the Trustees should take the responsibility for making the decision regarding the Cleveland Play House. Dr. Hesse said at the end of the discussion that he would try to schedule some isolated events in Norton Hall around the Opera schedule.

In The Chautauquan announcement, Dr. Hesse emphasized the Board's sense of responsibility in making policy decisions which would ensure the financial integrity as well as the future of the Institution. He also expressed his regret over the loss of the seven-week Theatre School in addition to the more obvious loss of theatre productions. It will "adversely affect the program and educational diversity in which we take such pride," he said. "Chautauqua has been privileged to have the Cleveland Play House in residence for the past fifty-one seasons. We are grateful for the objectives it met, both in providing a wider program format and for helping to make its audiences more sensitive to global problems and to human emotional needs."

More discussion about drama at Chautauqua was to occupy the full Board in May. The Program Committee through its chairman, Mrs. Cram, reported two possible courses of action: to find an outside group much like the Cleveland Play House; or to form a Chautauqua Company for play production similar to the way it presents opera with its own apprentice plan along with its theater school. Money was needed to explore all of these possibilities, it was added. Although no choices were made, it was agreed that of necessity there would be no drama at Chautauqua until 1982. At the May meeting, the Board approved a resolution of appreciation which would be prepared and sent to the Cleveland Play House, citing the Play House's association with Chautauqua for the past fifty-one years.

The effect of inflation on arts organizations across the country was being acknowledged in national news articles. There was a climate of fear for the future of the arts even in the face of a greater demand. Chautauqua was not alone in its worries over matching quality to budget.

Early in the winter of 1981, Nately Ronsheim, CLSC director, announced that a series of programs on Shakespeare under CLSC sponsorship would provide some outlet for those Chautauquans interested in drama and literature, "Celebrating Shakespeare at Chautauqua," scheduled for July 20-25, would include lectures, seminars, workshops and a travel exhibit from the Folger Shakespeare Library in Washington. Dr. Samuel Schoenbaum, one of the world's eminent Shakespeare scholars, had been engaged as a lecturer. Dr. A. Fred Sochatoff, of Carnegie Mellon University, was to conduct a series of seminars on "King Lear," "The Tempest," and "An Introduction to Shakespeare and His Writing."

In conjunction with the Chautauqua Summer School, the CLSC was also offering three mini-courses: Creative Writing by Pulitzer Prizewinner James A. McPherson; Language as an Art by John Ciardi; and Trade-Offs, The Executive Family, taught by Psychiatrist Barrie S. Greiff. (This latter mini-course was cancelled in August, shortly before it was to take place.)

Other program announcements began to appear:

The operas for 1981; Dr. William Sloane Coffin, Jr., to preach the first sermon of the season; lecturers whose names caught attention—Alger Hiss and John Henry Falk, both of whom would be speaking on the McCarthy Era.

Cleo Laine and James Galway, whose album "Sometimes When We Touch" went gold before it was released, were announced as the season's opening artists. The first week was to offer a variety of blue grass, Mark Russell, Canadian Brass and folksinger Judy Collins. Chautauqua was "sounding" excellence!

As the budget continued to be studied in March, the Annual Fund goal was set at $800,000. The Institution's meager cash flow was improving as season tickets were offered for sale. A schedule of discounts on early purchase of gate tickets with or without opera subscriptions, which was circulated in the March Chautauquan, had brought in over two hundred orders for season gate tickets and over five hundred for opera tickets. Part of the cash flow problems during the first of the year had resulted from the postponement of the Annual Meeting from November to December with the consequence of delayed decisions on prices. Improved techniques for the financial operation of the Institution, recommended by the new treasurer, were showing up in March. The idea that the fiscal year should coincide with the calendar year was reaffirmed. The necessity to add a controller to the Treasurer's personnel was agreed upon. The cost effectiveness of the 1981 budget continued to be studied.

Also, the rigorous solicitation of gifts for the Capital Campaign was urged on Trustees and other solicitors. The Buildings and Grounds Committee and the Institution's Operations Department faced grave, immediate needs while the amount expended on the Amphitheater continued to demand a large share of the funds. The goal of $8.5 million had finally been set as the amount needed for the highest priority projects to be funded by the Capital Campaign.

One encouragement to Dr. Hesse's efforts to extend Chautauqua beyond the gates and beyond the season was the report that thirteen tapes of Chautauqua lectures were on stations around the country and orders for three hundred and four cassettes had been received. Sunday morning services were to be aired by delayed broadcasts by six radio stations in the east.

This goal of widening Chautauqua's influence received another boost with the announcement of a grant from the Claude Worthington Benedum Foundation of Pittsburgh, Pa. The grant was specified for audience development and new multimedia efforts aimed at making Chautauqua's diverse programs available to more people throughout the nation. The grant would support efforts to attract more people to Chautauqua through group tours, specialized marketing and promotion; and to reach a broader audience through radio, television and video-cassettes.

The potential of this new educational thrust was exciting for all Chautauquans, but especially for Dr. Hesse who had been building into his plans this very element of widespread distribution of enrichment. Dr. Hesse called the grant for audience development "a breakthrough of historic proportions" and those familiar with Chautauqua's past saw in the possibilities

ahead an avalanche of creativity similar to that which followed Chautauqua's founding.

In the winter of 1981 Chautauqua lost one of its valuable resources and treasured Chautauquans, Dr. Howard Hanson. Dr. Hanson had participated at Chautauqua throughout his professional life, giving bountifully of his counsel, artistry and presence at Chautauqua. His music had soared through many years of the Institution's programming, and sometimes under his own baton. His students filled Chautauqua's halls and studios. He had served as an advisor to the Chautauqua School of Music. Chautauquans were proud to claim him as one of their own, proud to know that he wrote music in their midst, proud to see him sitting in the Amphitheater for concerts, lectures and Sunday morning worship services. Public memorial tributes to Dr. Hanson were planned for the opening night of the Chautauqua Symphony Orchestra July 4th and for a Sacred Song Service August 2nd.

The plans to conduct two accredited continuing education courses for the clergy during the summer of 1981 were announced by Dr. Ralph W. Loew in the March Chautauquan. This educational outreach for the clergy was a renewal of a tradition dating from 1881 when the Chautauqua School of Theology was established.

Another announcement by Mr. Redington pointed up a new cooperative arrangement between the Chautauqua Central School and the Institution. The Chautauqua Central School Board had agreed to allow the Institution to use the parking lots at the high school and the elementary school on nights when Amphitheater programs attract very large crowds. The Institution would supervise the parking and protection of the school's property and share the revenues with the School.

A second major joint effort lay in the use of the Turner Elementary School as a home for the Youth Division of the Institution's Music School for a period of four weeks in the middle of the season. Since the County Music Teachers Association has been involved with the development of this program and many students from the area commute to the sessions, the values of the program to the schools of the region are well-served by the arrangement. This particular youth program had been changed from a two-day-a-week schedule for seven weeks to a three-day-a-week program for four weeks. Strain upon Chautauqua's rehearsal spaces was thereby increased and the use of the elementary school was crucial in solving the dilemma. Mr. Redington noted that school administrators have in the past played important roles in Chautauqua's community and institutional life. He commended Robert Dimicco, the present Chief School Officer, and Mr. Dimicco's staff for helping to facilitate the summer's plans.

At the May meeting of the Board of Trustees, reports were quite encouraging. The Institution had received money from the NEA Grant. As of May 9th, one thousand, three hundred and ten nine-week gate tickets had been sold, compared with eight hundred and sixty-eight the year before. Opera subscriptions were up by thirty-five per cent. A task force had been formed to coordinate all fund-raising activities.

Mrs. Reading reported that in Capital Campaign giving, there was an even split between money given for endowment and for general restoration and preservation. She also pointed out that there was not nearly enough in the general restoration fund for all of the things that needed to be done. But the immediate need, she said, was gifts that would help meet the Kresge Challenge Grant or the sum of $245,823. Mr. Brunskill added that there were foundation and individual proposals pending that could possibly result in gifts usable for the Kresge challenge, but contributions in actual dollars were sorely needed.

Two changes in Colonnade personnel were noted. Ms. Marie O'Connor who had served as Dr. Hesse's assistant for program had left fulltime service in March although she continued to work on program matters from a distance. By June 1 she would have completed her three-year commitment to assist Dr. Hesse as he launched a dramatic improvement in Chautauqua's program and educational offerings. She planned to return to her doctoral program in higher education which she had interrupted by coming to Chautauqua.[5] Also in March, Bob Dodge, vice president of the American City Bureau, completed his resident participation in the Second Century Campaign.

Other changes in personnel were announced. Phillip Carey would be replacing Ed Polochick as Choir Director. Edward Keating, a Chautauquan of many years, had been hired as Main Gate Manager. Norman Lindell would be in charge of the maintenance crew and Kent Akin had begun work as the new Controller. Darlene Benson and Jean Church who had begun working with Ms. O'Connor were to continue in the program office. More shocking to Chautauquans was the news that Richard Miller had expressed his intention to resign from the Board of Trustees.

Dr. Hesse reported his satisfaction with the publications which Director of Communications Phil Zimmer had prepared, and also with the articles about Chautauqua which would be appearing in national magazines. An article by Al Rosenfeld giving his own interpretation of Chautauqua's unique ambience was to appear in the Smithsonian Magazine. U. S. News and World Report planned to send a writer during the season to give a three-page spread on Chautauqua in the August issue. Gourmet Magazine had indicated that it would feature the Chautauqua Celebrity Cookbook. A complete tabloid section on Chautauqua was being prepared by the Jamestown Post-Journal. Other newspapers were planning interviews and articles of various kinds. The Communications Office was commended for its part in stimulating this kind of coverage.

Dr. Hickman, speaking for the Education Committee, reported that Mr. Nassif, Mr. Redington and he were working on a statement of objectives for the Boys and Girls Clubs and for the Youth Center. The former College Club at the Point was envisioned as a Youth Center that could serve all youth through a well-organized, many-leveled program. With this change in concept came the opportunity to open up Seaver Gym, which had long been the home of the High School Club, to regular use for basketball and volleyball, both activities to be scheduled through the Sports Club.

This represented just one Chautauqua example of the interaction of different ages in sharing recreational facilities. It was viewed as a positive and beneficial policy and an extension of an already existing rapport among all ages at Chautauqua. The Sports Club was becoming at the same time more of a focal point for recreation. David Peckinpaugh, the manager, was a willing cohort in the effort to coordinate lake front recreation. He, himself, had initiated at the Sports Club women's exercise classes, badminton play, sailing and canoe instruction while continuing shuffleboard, lawn bowling, duplicate bridge and fellowship dinners. He had also promoted the Old First Night Marathon Run, a benefit event which was attracting more runners every year. The Yacht Club's sailing races three times a week continued to add beauty and interest to the lake front.

As Dr. Hesse discussed the upcoming season, he said that there would be a pre-season event in the Amphitheater June 20th. The Kingston Trio and the Association had been engaged for this first summer "special."

Also at the May Board meeting, Mr. Osburn summarized for the Board the improvements that would be completed before the season: provision for fire safety on all Institution buildings where people are living, including new fire escapes on Logan Dormitory and Kellogg Hall and fire alarms over all; a complete renovation of Logan Dormitory[6]; a new roof and new paint for the Oriental Bazaar (an Institution-owned building); the reconditioning of ten practice shacks in Piano Village;[7] a new roof on the grandstand at Sharpe Field, new gutters and downspouts at Smith-Wilkes Hall; new drainage at the South Tennis Courts; new street signs; a new seawall at University Beach; repair and repainting of the Colonnade Pillars; some limited road resurfacing; and improvement of the east parking lot. The restoration of Kellogg Hall was ninety-five per cent completed.

At the Amphitheater the following renovations were in progress: perimeter drainage, electrical work, new audio additions for the hard of hearing, new lighting, new risers and benches where needed and new orchestra chairs. Another improvement at the Amphitheater which was not directly connected with preservation was the enlargement of the platform. Extra space had been gained by removing the first few benches in the choir loft so that built-in storage cupboards could open onto the stage but extend backward under the choir loft. Pianos, the organ console, other instruments, music stands and even chairs could be placed into the cupboards. While the increased platform space was needed on concert nights for a larger orchestra, it provided day-to-day ease in setting up for various programs, a great advantage for the Amph crew.

The approach of the season was presaged by the return of property owners and the inevitable hurry to get repairs and refurbishing completed before 1981's three taps of the gavel.

The season began with a sense of resurgence. Dr. Hesse called it a renaissance. "Our direction has become focused," he said. "While a renaissance can be unsettling, we shall be persistent in our rebuilding efforts." His whole demeanor was one of confidence.

He reemphasized the priorities: to continue to improve the quality of every aspect of our programming elements; to restore, renovate and preserve our physical facilities; to increase our summer residential population; to add significantly to our endowment and to achieve national presence and visibility.

He pointed to the appointment of a new musical director for the orchestra, Varujan Kojian, as evidence of progress toward the achievement of program goals; to the selection of a new artistic director for the Opera Company, Cynthia Auerbach; to the interaction of all departments to realize national recognition; to the increase of endowments through the Chautauqua Foundation for the support of excellence in education and program. He acknowledged that much of the $2 million increase in holdings by the Chautauqua Foundation had come through the success of the Second Century Campaign. Dr. Hesse announced a new total for the Campaign—$5.5 million. Through some of these gifts, significant progress had been made on preservation of treasured buildings. Through a grant from the Benedum Foundation, "we have been able to make our programs more attractive to people." He added, "We hope to establish Chautauqua as a well-recognized year-round conference site and a purveyor of year-round learning possibilities." The prospect of opening twelve lots on Elm Lane in 1981 also was mentioned as an encouragement for it would offer the possibility for more families to commit themselves to long-term participation at Chautauqua.

There was confidence "in the air" as organizations began their meetings, as the season's major program was mounted and new improvements caught the community's eye. The Amphitheater was taking on more glory each year through restoration, and this in itself was affecting the spirits of Chautauquans since the Amphitheater is the heart of Chautauqua's program.

There was other excitement generated by the announcement that the value of scholarships had increased to over $77,000. During the first week of the season the Dental Congress convened for the second year. The popular entertainment programs attracted a wide audience from the immediate area. The Institution designed the nights of the first week as salutes to their neighbor communities. On the evening of Jamestown Day, the performer was Mark Russell, who was a former resident of Jamestown, as well as a nationally-known personality. He admitted that the present beauty of the Amphitheater had robbed him of a source of jokes about the face of "the venerable lady." First week attendance totals were up 20 per cent over 1980.

The Fourth of July weekend brought extra people to the Grounds and the first symphony concert on Independence Day evening packed the Amphitheater. It was Kojian's first appearance and this in itself was a drawing card. The prospect of hearing the orchestra 21 times during the coming seven weeks gave Chautauquans a feeling of affluence, a Daily editorial said, while the Music Editor Maritza Morgan pointed out the contribution this particular orchestra has made historically. Forty to fifty years ago when the native artistic potential was not fully realized in America, the Chautauqua Symphony demonstrated such an aware-

ness "in a melting pot sort of way." Orchestra members have continued to be multi-racial in personal derivation and also multi-state in winter assignments. Coming from a cross-section of professional musical life, their experience is blended in what becomes a richly American statement. In addition, they play to a distinctly varied popular audience.

For this first concert a distinctly American flavor was produced through the programming of Samuel Barber's "Medea," Howard Hanson's Symphony No. 6, Aaron Copeland's "El Salon Mexico" and Sousa's Marches. The effect of the latter was dramatized through a spectacular use of laser lights which slashed through dry-ice-induced clouds while stick men marched across a movie screen above the stage. It was if not anticlamatic, at least a strong contrast when resident Chautauquans finished the evening on the lake front, watching the quietly-produced red ring of flares which appear regularly at 10 o'clock around the lake on the Fourth of July. Fireworks in Mayville and Midway are sometimes visible in Chautauqua at the close of Independence Day, reminiscent of the time when the Chautauqua Assembly itself featured cascading pyrotechnics along the shore and from platforms or boats on the lake.

The second week of the season continued the upbeat vibrations of the first. The Amphitheater lectures were devoted to science and brought Dr. Edward Teller of Manhatttan Project fame on the first day. The National Federation of Music Clubs had extended its annual Chautauqua meeting to a full week.

A Property Owners Association survey revealed that 30 per cent of Chautauqua property owners had held their properties for 30 years or more, and that 75 per cent spend the whole season on the Grounds. Furthermore, 63 per cent of property owners viewed the orchestra as the main program attraction and most felt that a housing shortage, especially of apartments, was limiting Chautauqua attendance.

The Tennis Association was holding its closed singles tournament. Vandalism was visible when a kiosk was turned over into a flower bed in front of the post office. Other mischief had been reported earlier when obscenities had been burned into the bowling green and painted on some public buildings. It was acknowledged as a concern to the community and was not "overlooked" in The Daily, proving that the Institution's newspaper could print truthful unpleasant news. At a public forum, Richard Rodes re-expressed his contention that Chicano Americans, American Indians and liberated blacks should be part of the Chautauqua scene. "We need them more than they need us," he affirmed and was roundly applauded. "The Student Prince" opened the opera season. A writer from the Chronicle of Higher Education was quoted as saying that she could tell from the books in the Book Store that Chautauquans were more intellectually-oriented than she had supposed.

The Chautauqua Art Associations's 24th annual National Exhibition of American Art "exceeded regional dimensions," Anthony Bannon of the Buffalo Evening News said in a guest review in The Daily. Eighty-two works by 76 artists hung in the galleries for three weeks, coming down on July 13th. They had been selected from 2,535 entrants and not one of the prizewinning artists claimed New York origins. "It suggests the level of sophistication the Galleries have reached," Bannon wrote.

A significant public issue was supported actively in early July by the Institution, the Chautauqua Utility District and a county group of concerned citizens. A strong stand was taken at the county government level against the operation of an industrial waste treatment plant at the Dinsbier Landfill three and one-half miles from Mayville toward Sherman. The importance of safeguarding the quality of Chautauqua Lake waters and the vacationland future of the area was argued before the County Legislature. During the discussion the Institution's role within the county was articulated. Property-owning Chautauquans at the time were paying an estimated $700,000 in annual taxes (Town, County and School District) and the activities of the Institution and its constituents impinge upon the county's economy by an estimated $35 million each year. The dependence of the Institution on the lake for its drinking water was pointed out as a crucial element in its opposition to the proposed use of the landfill. There was great relief when the Legislators voted the measure down.

Expected and unexpected events took place as the days went by. The Chautauqua String quartet opened its 54th summer series. At the time no one knew that it would be its last performing season for a while. Miss Louisa Knox, revered as the oldest living Chautauquan, whose birthday was almost identical with the Institution's, was interviewed by The Daily.

Dr. Hesse hosted 140 major donors to the Annual Fund at a President's Dinner in the Athenaeum Hotel. Among his other statements in his State of the Institution address was this: proof of the potential for Chautauqua's multiple programming policy is evident in the previous Friday's statistics (July 10th). On that evening 4,586 had attended the Burl Ives' concert while 1,367 were enjoying the opera and the Cinema was filled to capacity.

The Women's Club Flea Market, held behind the Colonnade, had been a resounding success. Twenty-two students were enrolled under the King's Daughters and Sons Scholarship Program. Patricia McBride and Bart Cook brought ballet to the Amphitheater. Tony and Jackie Joy's new solar home was completed on Crescent Drive.

The 50th anniversary of Dr. Loew's ordination was celebrated and the child care class graduated a group of potential babysitters. The Rev. John Guest returned as chaplain of the week. The Freeman sisters, Ruth and Betty, played for the Women's Club. Kitty Carlisle Hart, chairman of the New York State Council on the Arts, visited Chautauqua and enjoyed the opera, "Tales of Hoffmann."

On Old First Night George L. Follansbee, Sr., received a special citation for his distinguished service to the Institution for many years. In making the presentation, Chairman Gibbs said, "We honor a Chautauquan who perhaps more than any other may carry the honor and nickname of 'Mr. Chautauqua.' You have had a love affair with Chautauqua all your life and Chautauqua has had a love affair with you. We honor you for what you think, what you feel, what you express; we honor you for being Shorty Follansbee."

Shorty made a heartfelt reply. "I can never repay Chautauqua for what she has meant to me and my family. I hope that in years to come your families' sixth and seventh generations can enjoy Chautauqua too the way ours has. This world needs a Chautauqua—and it's up to you all to see that there always is one."

A variety of performers appeared in the Amphitheater, from Karl Haas to Melissa Manchester, from Lorin Hollander to Lynn Harrell, from the Regional Choir to Herman Bauman. Chuck Mangione drew over eight thousand.

The community was saddened during the season when two Chautauquans who had served in extraordinary ways were suddenly taken by death. Joseph Neubauer had served the Institution as a trustee, had chaired the Annual Fund, was active in the Development Council and was a member of the Chautauqua Foundation Board when he died suddenly on August 7, 1981. Robert V. Woodside, former Institution Vice President and organist, who had taught in the summer school for many years and had begun his Chautauqua Experience as a young student, also was stricken as he was playing the organ at Hurlbut Church during a memorial service for Miss Alice Madge Ward. Former President Dr. Oscar E. Remick came to the Grounds to speak at Mr. Woodside's memorial service in the Hall of Philosophy.

The year 1981 was distinguished by its anniversaries. The congregation of the Hurlbut Memorial Church had been observing the 50th anniversary of its building all year and would continue to do so in the fall.

Smith Memorial Library was also 50 years old. It was given by Mrs. A. M. Smith Wilkes in memory of her parents, Mr. and Mrs. Henry Sumner Smith. The handsome library has Neo-Georgian lines and is constructed of red brick with white wooden trim. Its location opposite the Colonnade gives it prominence. Equally prominent is its place in the lives of Chautauquans who are inveterate readers and students. This anniversary was formally observed on Library Day, under the auspices of the Friends of the Library.

Because the CLSC Building and Museum were razed to make way for Smith Library, the Chautauqua Book Store with headquarters in the CLSC Building was moved to the basement of the Post Office Building. Therefore, the Book Store celebrated its 50 years in that location.

Also, the main Chautauqua headquarters of the United Church of Christ reached its golden jubilee in 1981. It had been built by the Congregational Association on the site of that denomination's first building, but since the merger with the Reform Churches, the present location bears the new denominational name.

By far the biggest anniversary celebration in 1981, however, was the Hotel Athenaeum's centennial which was highlighted during the weekend of July 21-26. The miracle of survival and continuing service by this all-wooden structure, the oldest public building still in use at Chautauqua, had been tacitly acknowledged, but the "Grand Dame's" 100th birthday was cause for general jubilation.

Vice President W. Thomas Smith who also serves as manager of the Athenaeum had planned the summer's observance. Approximately $70,000 had been spent for structural repairs and other refurbishing to prepare for the season. Mr. Smith, who is a preservationist by personal inclination, and thus, well aware of the historic values represented by the hotel made some improvements at the hotel that were appropriate to the building's spirit.

The hotel's centennial weekend began with a gala anniversary dinner served to hotel and invited guests on the evening of July 24. This date coincidentally was the 152nd birthday of Lewis Miller, the man who had initiated the building of the hotel and who had secured other private investors to join him in the project. The dinner menu was elegant. The bountiful buffet tables were set in the drawing room and guests then proceeded to their regular tables in the dining room where they were later served a selection of desserts, one of the most unusual of which was a puff paste swan full of rich cream pudding.

The next evening the hotel gala continued with a dancing party. Miss Peters, herself, appeared briefly in the drawing room and the atmosphere was joyous and happy. Scores of Chautauquans joined hotel guests for cookies and punch and a peek at the dancers, even if they themselves didn't get a chance to waltz.

On Sunday evening the Lake Erie Players turned the hotel drawing room into a theatre following the Sacred Song Service, bringing the weekend observance to a close.

While the hotel's age and condition was a marvel to Chautauquans, it was becoming an intensifying problem to the Hotel Corporation and the Institution. At the August 8th Board meeting, steps were taken to deal with the major decisions which had to be faced. Dr. Hesse read to the trustees from the minutes of the hotel board's last meeting where it was recorded that further structural repair would be needed and he presented an engineer's study which stated that it would take from one to one and a half million dollars to extend the life of the hotel for another 25 to 50 years.

Dr. Hesse discussed the importance of the hotel to the overall life of the Institution. He indicated that the scope of the problems made necessary a greater participation by the Institution's Board of Trustees. It was thus recommended that the Board of Directors of the Hotel Corporation be restructured, initially by replacing three non-trustee members (namely, Mrs. Arnn, Mr. Peirce and Mr. Trimble) with at least two trustee members. Dr. Hesse and Mr. Gibbs recommended that these two trustee members be Gertrude Shelburne and Robert Osburn. Since the Institution holds all the shares of voting stock in the Hotel Corporation, the Institution President, Dr. Hesse, and the Chairman of its Board of Trustees, Mr. Gibbs, are by virtue of their offices, authorized to vote the shares for the election of Board of Directions of the Hotel Corporation. No action had been taken on the election of Hotel Corporation directors at the Corporation's Annual Meeting pending the report of the Hotel Corporation's situation to the Institution Trustees. The Trustees' recommendations were requested. Following discussion, the Board of Trustees unanimously passed a motion which authorized Howard Gibbs and Dr. Hesse to vote the shares of the Hotel Corporation for the election of the following as directors of the Hotel Corporation: Gertrude Shelburne, Robert Osburn, Richard H. Miller, Howard G. Gibbs and Dr. Robert R. Hesse. The Board also passed a motion expressing their thanks to the retiring members of the Hotel Corporation Board.

In addition, the Board requested that the new hotel board report to the Trustees its recommendations on specific matters: the organizational structure of the Hotel Corporation, the question of whether or not the hotel should have a full time manager, the identification of immediate and long range needs and the development of plans for addressing those needs.

Dr. Hesse reported that the Board of Directors of the Hotel Corporation had approved a resolution drawn by Attorney Samuel Price that the principal amount of the first mortgate bonds held by Chautauqua Institution, which matured on August 1, 1981, be extended to August 1, 1986, as mutually agreed upon between the officers of the Hotel Corporation and the officers of the Chautauqua Institution, with interest at the rate of 12 per cent per annum, payable semi-annually. The Hotel Board had also recommended that the Institution retain the Hotel site, restore it and upgrade it. The Institution Board followed this recommendation by passing a motion which stated that the Chautauqua Institution Board of Trustees view the Hotel as something to be preserved. Another matter which had a relation to the Hotel was the gift of $10,000 to the Institution for a memorial garden in memory of Mrs. Kim Haker and her father and mother. The hope of the donors was that the garden might be located between the Presbyterian House and the Athenaeum. Dr. Hesse stated that there might be a possibility that long-range plans might require the use of that lot for upgrading the Hotel. Also, the Hotel, he said, is not the proper vehicle to receive such a gift or maintain such a garden.

The matter of the location of the memorial garden was tabled for further study, following which the Board voted to extend to the family appreciation of the gift and to promise a resolution of the request as soon as back-up material could be obtained from legal counsel.

It was also voted to add the 12 lots on the south side of Elm Lane to the official map of the Institution. Another motion approved the Buildings and Grounds Committee's intention to seek bids for the development of the North side of Elm Lane during the fall months. This development calls for town houses or/and condominiums.

The proposed razing of part of the Spencer Hotel following the season and the offering of those lots for sale caused some anxiety among Board members concerning what type of building might be out there. The possibility of establishing an architectural review board was discussed.

In a report by Mrs. Cram concerning the status of drama at Chautauqua, the Board learned that a musical theater consultant had visited Chautauqua and was preparing a statement concerning the possibility of Chautauqua's conducting its own theatre school, using Normal Hall for dramatic presentations to small audiences and otherwise pursuing drama productions at Chautauqua. Budget prospectives would also be prepared. Dr. Hesse added that he was in communication with the National Youth Theatre of Great Britain and was recommended that the Institution explore the offers of this group, as well.

Mrs. Cram stated that the Lake Erie Repertory Theater which would be presenting three performances in Norton Hall at the end of the Opera Season had no expectations for a permanent connection and had come simply to provide drama this season.

In an updating of Annual Fund figures, Mr. Brunskill reported that the Fund was $150,000 ahead of its receipts of a year ago at this date.

The nominating committee reported its efforts to identify those Chautauquans who might be named to special committees, special boards or as non-board members of Board Committees. Robert Wilder, chairman, also said that the committee was exploring ways to engage the interest, skills and wisdom of former Board members.

At the August 29th Board meeting, the trustees followed a succession of recommendations by this committee. It moved to formalize a group of former Board members which would convene at least once a year to provide a continuing dialogue with an important leadership group at Chautauqua. This group would be called "The Chautauqua Council."[8]

It moved and passed unanimously the recommendation to elect Mrs. Helen Temple Logan as an Honorary Trustee. Appreciation of her ardent interest and generous support of Chautauqua as an expression of her love for this special place was included in the motion.

It also recommended and approved that Howard Gibbs, Dr. Warren Hickman, Arthur Holden, Jr., and Harry Logan, Jr., be elected for additional terms of four years, commencing October 1, 1981. James A. Zurn, administrative vice president of Zurn Industries, Erie, Pa., and a Chautauqua property owner, was elected to one full-term on the Board. Dr. Paul Irion was elected to fill the unexpired term of Richard H. Miller. A professor at Lancaster Seminary in Lancaster, Pa., Dr. Irion, also a Chautauqua property owner, was already serving as a member of the Board's Religion Committee.

In connection with these elections a resolution of appreciation was voted to Patricia Dietly for her dedicated service over the past eight years of active Trusteeship.

Concerning financial matters, Dr. Hesse reported that day and evening single ticket income would no doubt reach $511,000 which was $100,000 over budget. He discussed the decline in term ticket sales of the last three weeks of the season. Lateness of the season, the air controllers' strike, weather and program were suggested as possible reasons for the decline. He summarized the remainder of the report and concluded that while total income would reach $100,000 over budget, expenditures were also running from $70,000 to $100,000 over budget so that the budget would be balanced if the Annual Fund goal is reached.

The change in the Institution's fiscal year was voted with the following change in the By-Laws Article X, Section 1: "There will be a short fiscal year for the Corporation from October 1, 1981 to December 31, 1981. Thereafter, the fiscal year of the Corporation shall be January 1 to December 31."

Dates for the next season, June 26—August 29, as presented by the President were approved by the Board.

Miriam Reading reported that the total now in Capital Fund pledges has reached $5,740,600. She pointed out that more than the original $8.5 million is needed to cover rising costs of projects, both future and those now in progress. A great deal of the work being done is repair and restoration work that should have been done in a routine maintenance program over the years, she said.

The Open Houses which had been held at newly restored buildings had drawn large numbers. The necessity to extend open house at the Amphitheater for two days reflected both the general interest in the structural work, and the extra time needed for visits to the new control booth.

At the August 29th Board meeting the new Annual Fund Director, Walter Heid, was introduced. Heid had come from the Cleveland Ballet where he had been assistant development director for the past three years. Before that he had been orchestra manager and administrative assistant for that organization. Heid had formerly been an apprentice with the Chautauqua Opera Company also.

A point of Annual Fund procedure was noted by Howard Gibbs, that only paid pledges can be counted. On that basis $206,000 is still needed to meet the 1981 goal. Counting present pledges, however, only $118,951 is needed. There was general encouragement over the prospect of reaching the $800,000 goal by September 30th.

Further committee reports included recommendations by the Education Committee over Library functions and service. It approved the continued 12-month service, the centralization of tapes and lecture reprints in the library with sales and distribution continuing at the Book Store. It proposed the development of the Chautauqua archives as a national source and the coordination through Mr. Redington's office of space reorganization and utilization at the library. The Committee approved the use of the library for winter community activities, programs and meetings.

The Program Committee asked the Board's approval of immediate investigation of the feasibility of using Normal Hall for drama so that such programming could be scheduled there in 1982. The possibility that a theatre consultant or architect might be needed by the administration in renovating Normal Hall was included in the Committee's report. The Board approved the recommendation.

Dr. Holland, chairman of the Religion Committee, reported that there are ten religious organizations who own 21 properties on the Grounds. All but one will pay license fees in 1982, he said. The one exception has a special clause written into its original deed.

Dr. Holland asked the Board's approval in principal of a young clergy seminar for the 1982 program. It will provide an opportunity to bring to Chautauqua young clergymen who will profit both personally and professionally from participation in the Chautauqua Experience. The Board gave its approval.

Dr. Holland reported that increased attendance at the afternoon lectures of the Religion Department was in part due to the topics which had provided equal interest to both Jews and Christians.

Improvement of the weekday music of the Motet Choir under Phillip Carey's direction was noted by Dr. Holland, along with the importance of this year's Sacred Song Services. In particular, Dr. Holland commended the Messiah "Sing In" which Mr. Carey had arranged for the Song Service which was a memorial to Dr. Hanson.

The Buildings and Grounds Committee presented a printed report to the trustees which revised the estimate of the total costs of the backstage work at the Amphitheater. The contract would not be put out for bid before mid-September. The original estimate of the backstage work was $380,000. The possibility of an increase in that amount might come from the need to raise the height of the walk bridge for truck delivery backstage and also the need to alleviate surface water run-off problems, such as flooding in the kitchen of the Hotel Athenaeum. The installation of heat and smoke detectors in the super structure of the backstage area and wired to the security officer was another "extra" as was additional storage required under the choir loft area. Landscaping around the Amphitheater had to be decided upon soon. The impact of this meant an additional $400,000 not currently covered by Amphitheater pledges. If that amount is taken from the General Restoration Fund, the amount available to other projects, such as Normal Hall, would be lowered, Mr. Osburn said. More details of all this and the possibility of an architectural review board were promised at the November Board meeting.

The season ended on a high note of accomplishment, and the general sense that Chautauqua was on its way to a brigher-than-ever future.

At the September Executive Committee meeting, the last remaining title-holding under a lease was redeemed by its owner according to the arrangements initiated during the Institution's receivership.

A dilemma concerning the status of Amphitheater restorations arose in September when the backstage area started caving in and the National Trust in Albany instructed the Institution NOT to proceed with current plans since they did not meet approval. The NHT was requiring changes in window, columns, structure and other matters which Chautauqua was attempting to meet, "but time is pressing," Vice President Smith said. He hoped to have these changes approved "within the next two weeks" so that the work could go out to bid immediately. The project demands dispatch, he emphasized, since the work must be completed by June, 1982. Not only that, the building, itself, is falling and in order to commit Gebbie funding, Chautauqua must go ahead. Smith explained that the Institution is trying to keep within the spirit of NHT guidelines but the risk of having to pay back the $80,000 already received from NHT is one that must be taken if approval of plans is not received.

Another temporary problem loomed in the three-month fiscal year that had just been enacted. The problem was one of expenses versus income in that three-month period. The consensus was that active solicitation of funds be undertaken before December 31st for both the Annual Fund and the Capital Campaign from potential major donors who will be affected by the new tax laws.

Exploratory discussions over proposed ticket prices for next year suggested that for each season ticket purchased, the price would remain at the 1981 level with later purchase requiring a higher price. Because of what amounts to a 15-month year (the short three-month fiscal year before the start of a new fiscal year), service fees would have to increase by 25 per cent, but it must be emphasized that this is not a raise, only the total cost of five quarters. Garbage service would no doubt increase by eight to nine per cent, it was estimated. Income from license fees will go down because of the changes from rooms to apartments at both the Spencer and the Cary. There was some expectation that increased ticket prices would be necessary to compensate for the increase in expenses, rather than put an additional strain on the Annual Fund. Dr. Hesse said that the administration thinks the major increase in income will come from endowment.

The loss of the opera tour to Rochester was due to lack of sales, Dr. Hesse reported. It had been expected that the tour would break even at the $30,000 cost level, but only $12,000 was actually received. One of the factors was that the apprentice cast was used instead of the stars. Furtunately, New York State Council on the Arts funding was increased to make up some of this shortfall.

Dr. Hesse reported that Chautauqua Symphony Orchestra broadcasts are now being heard over 64 stations. There is no income from this, but valuable publicity, he said. Chautauqua had applied for funding for this project, and the New York State Council on the Arts will fund WXXI's expenses for taping; however, it will give nothing for the musicians. So specific funding for part of the expense for this should be looked for elsewhere, Dr. Hesse said.

He also disclosed that the Ben Vereen Show which was mounted on September 5th drew an audience of only 2,900 because of weather, and was not a financial success for the Institution.

At the next Executive Committee meeting, budgets for 1982 were reviewed. Concerning opera, Dr. Hesse said that costs can be reduced and quality of production improved if *only* four operas are undertaken. Originally four operas plus a musical, had been planned. Four hundred season tickets for four operas have already been sold, he said, with the understanding that ticket-holders could have the same seats for an additional musical production if it were offered.

Jack Finnefrock, manager of the Book Store, was congratulated for making the Book Store a viable operation.

A motion was passed that the administration should present a balanced budget with a modest surplus. So it was "back to the drawing board" for department heads.

As the Annual Meeting convened, Chairman Gibbs welcomed the new trustees, Paul Irion and James

Zurn. Mr. Raymond Haines of Seidman & Seidman made the annual audit report. In reviewing the balance sheet, Mr. Haines commented that the Institution was in a good cash position and that the financial position was very solid. He also reviewed and explained the operating statement.

Then came the presentation of the current update of the budget for the coming year. Dr. Hesse reported that the Institution's earned income ratio to gift income remains "almost unreasonably high" at a 72 to 28 per cent ratio.[9] An increase of gate tickets has been projected at a 9.1 per cent average. Last year (1981) more season tickets were sold than ever before, in recent memory at least, 1,412. An increase in sales is not anticipated, Dr. Hesse said, but an increase in income is expected. This latest pricing of gate tickets reflected a slight change from previous estimates.

A chart showing the distribution of estimated income from the various departments was studied by the Board. The low expense of the Development Office for the amount of income generated was pointed out. It was then that Dr. Hesse announced the resignation of Mr. Brunskill and Mr. Brunskill addressed the Board.

Philip J. Brunskill was named Vice President for Development at Chautauqua in the summer of 1975. He was elected Vice President and Secretary of the Chautauqua Foundation the same year. He came from Albion College where he had been serving as Executive Director of Public Affairs and head of the college's fund raising program. During his tenure at Chautauqua, Annual Fund giving had reached new heights; the Gebbie Challenge was completed and the Second Century Campaign was launched. Mr. Brunskill had accepted a position at Baldwin-Wallace College.

Concerning the Annual Fund goal of $900,000, Mr. Brunskill explained that in prior years church collections and scholarship monies had been listed in restricted totals, this year the figures will be listed separately so that donors will be able to differentiate between these two areas and the unrestricted Annual Fund.

Before the first session of the Annual Meeting adjourned, Mrs. Cram, Program Committee Chairman, reported that the committee believes that drama is an integral part of the concept of Chautauqua and recommends presenting the highest type of dramatic production that is possible to obtain. At the next day's

meeting, Mrs. Cram gave more details of the Committee's projections concerning drama. The Committee recommended that eventually the Institution should produce drama rather than present it, but for 1982, presentation is necessary and recommended. Negotiations with touring drama groups are going forward, along with consultation with architects for possible drama production in the future. The Program Committee recommends that funds be built into the budget so that a high level drama school can be operated at Chautauqua by 1983. The Trustees agreed without a formal motion that this was a proper approach.

Among the questions which emerged from the discussion of the annual audit report concerned the yield which the Institution is realizing from its endowment. Trustees who are also Foundation Board members, as well as Foundation Vice President Brunskill, addressed the question, explaining the Foundation's investment procedures, noting that the payout rate for unrestricted funds is 5½ per cent and for restricted funds, six per cent. However, actual earnings and growth performance of Foundation assets are greater, Mr. Brunskill said. Mr. Gibbs pointed out that the Chautauqua Foundation is a separate entity and there is no reason why the Trustees' discussion could not be passed along to the Foundation Board. Mr. Hamilton suggested that the President of the Foundation might make a presentation to the Institution's Board of Trustees annually. Subsequently, a motion was passed that the results of the handling of the endowment become a part of the annual report issued to the Trustees and that at least one direct report be made each year to the Board of Trustees by the Foundation.

The reelection of Board officers and the Institution President was conducted, with the secretary instructed to cast a unanimous ballot. Dr. Hesse then presented his own staff nominations which were approved.

The latest financial figures of the Capital Campaign were distributed to the Board and explained by the Campaign Treasurer, Ambrose Cram.

Standing Committee reports followed.

Dr. Holland reported for the Religion Committee that the two-week pilot project of Continuing Education for Clergy would be expanded to four weeks next year, if present plans materialize. He also spoke of enriching the quality of Sunday Evening Song Services, the possibility of commissioning a Chautauqua Anthem and implementing the proposal for young clergy scholarships.

Mr. Boyle, speaking for the Annual Fund Committee, gave the totals of the 1981 drive: $812,000 cash and $57,000 in outstanding pledges. He reminded the Board that the 1982 goal had been set at $900,000. Mr. Brunskill then added possible strategies for meeting the $900,000 goal.

Robert Osburn, chairman of the Buildings and Grounds Committee, reported that the L. H. Ludgwig Co. of Falconer had the lowest bid for the work on the backstage area of the Amphitheater. The plans call for the porch area to be closed in before winter so that the total job can be completed by May 15, 1982. Osburn added that there is the possibility of having some overruns because of unknown elements that might appear.

Philip J. Brunskill, Vice President for Development, 1975-1980

Osburn reported that two lots have been sold in the North End development. There are to be two new streets. The Committee had recommended that these streets be named Gebbie and Hazlett Drives to honor the Gebbie Foundation and former Institution President Samuel M. Hazlett.

Architectural review procedures are still being worked on by the Committee, the Chairman said. He distributed a committee memorandum on the subject. He added that the property north of Elm Lane would be available for bid and would be brought to the Board of Trustees for approval.

In the President's formal report to the Trustees, he asked that they keep their eyes focused on the goals that have been set and use those as a measurement of the year's accomplishments. "We are committed, department by department, to continued and relentless pursuit of those goals."

He turned to a consideration of the Chautauqua Symphony Orchestra. "This orchestra has or can have a glorious future. The contract is in place. The needed changes have been made. The new Music Director is extremely demanding and while at least a few of the orchestra members may plan to continue to resist his leadership, in the long run he will succeed for the benefit of us all. He demands preciseness of playing; he insists on discipline; and he brings a quality of excellence no one has been able to command since Walter Hendl stepped down. The quality of soloists and guest conductors will continue to improve." He mentioned certain artists with whom he was negotiating for the 1982 program.

"The Opera Company has shown a tremendous improvement and I predict that this coming year's productions will be some of the finest ever produced at Chautauqua."

"In terms of our financial resources, we must and will balance the budget. It is essential that we do so and return to absolute financial integrity. It means that we must achieve our Annual Fund goal of $900,000. It means that we must secure other operating gifts and grants income from other sources of no less than $493,000. We must successfully conclude our Capital and Endowment Campaign with gifts of at least $2.8 million.

He turned to the restoration of Chautauqua's public historic buildings, one of the goals by which the year's accomplishments and future accomplishments were to be measured. After recalling all that had been done, he declared, "We must complete the Amphitheater restoration, and begin on Norton and Normal Hall restoration. We must address the problem of the restoration of the Athenaeum Hotel—NOW! We require an upgrading of our facilities to continue to attract the clientele on whom we must depend. We must search for new ways to improve housing on the Grounds. We must continue to develop lot sales. We must continue the overall improvement of the Grounds. We must continue to improve computer, ticket and Main Gate operations."

Speaking of national visibility, Dr. Hesse said that new articles that have been proposed or commissioned by national magazines would build on the wide recognition we had received in print journalism during 1981.

"But more than that can be done, and must be done," he said. We hope to expand the use of Chautauqua Symphony Orchestra concert tapes, lectures and Sunday services on radio, he said.

The improvement of the professional schools is anticipated and from this there will come to Chautauqua the very best students from across the land. We anticipate making a *national* appeal for students, he said. We are hoping that the Music Festival Orchestra will be able to appear in concert in Lincoln Center in 1982. We are excited about the prospects of the Chautauqua Youth Orchestra. Our Art Center Program is beginning to serve more talented young students. In Dance Education this year, we will recruit a number of high quality dancers with increased scholarship support to produce stronger programs in the Amphitheater. Better dance teaching facilities are crucial to our efforts to raise the quality of this popular program."

"And later will come a fine drama school. We are working toward that. We hope to engage the best faculty we can find and provide scholarship funds for the best students."

"We have not even yet begun to tap our potential," Dr. Hesse continued with enthusiasm. "The future excitement of Chautauqua lies in combining our quality resources with our education component, and the new technology with our efforts at outreach.

"The proposal of a Chautauqua Fellows Program seeks to unite the educational and programmatic functions of the Institution for a wider audience. An endowed fellowship could bring an established scholar, a leading thinker, to our platform. He might help us plan a week of lectures and lead us to speakers; he could deliver his own keynote summer lecture, perhaps teach a seminar, write an original article for publication, help lead a weekend seminar between seasons and suggest follow-up topics for the next summer's program. What a wealth of possibilities the Fellows Program opens to us!"

He mentioned the increasing audio cassette sales in lecture series units with study guides and bibliographies. He enlarged upon the idea of a new educational model in which the many aspects of the Chautauqua offerings might be brought together for focused learning supported by the technological helps of video tapes in addition to audio cassettes. He held out the dream of presenting Chautauqua on television or cable programs.

Then he approached the means of accomplishing these dreams for Chautauqua. "An atmosphere of trust is necessary. A mutual belief in the future. In essence, a coming together.

"Since 1975 we have raised $14 million, so unbelievable things can be done. If we all pull together, there is nothing to keep us from restoring Chautauqua to the ideal envisioned by its founders."

On this high point of unity and pride in what had been accomplished, the Board voted a statement of thanks to Mr. Brunskill for his years of service to the Institution and another motion expressing appreciation to the Chairman of the Board of Trustees, Howard G. Gibbs, for his tireless efforts and exemplary leadership during the past years.

1981
PROGRAM FIGURES

Musicians
Franklin Silver Cornet Band
Cleo Laine
James Galway
Glenn Miller Orchestra with Jimmy
    Henderson
Canadian Brass
Bill Monroe
Doc Watson
Judy Collins
New Arts Trio
    Rebecca Pennys, Piotr Janowski,
    Steven Doane
Jonathan Mack (NFMC Winner)
Burl Ives
Andre Watts
Ransom Wilson
The Four Freshmen
Gustavo Romero
Swingle Sisters
Hermann Baumann
Fred Waring Show
Roberta Peters

Natalie Dalschaert
Lorin Hollander
Lynn Harrell
Melissa Manchester
Leslie Browne
Cambridge Buskers
Garrick Ohlsson
Guy Lombardo Orchestra,
    The Royal Canadians
    Directed by Teddy Phillips
Glenn Dicterow
Judith Blegen
Chuck Mangione
Carlos Montoya
Pete Fountain
Woody Herman
Gerry Mulligan
John Aleaxander
Clancy Brothers
U. S. Army Band
Andre-Michel Schub (Van Cliburn
    Competition Winner)
Richard Alston (Aldredge Winner)
Veri & Jamanis
Porter Wagoner
Ben Vereen
The Kingston Trio
The Association
Barbershop Harmony
    Conewango Clippers
    Musictime Quartet
    Mystical Touch (Sweet Adeline
    Quartet)
    Grandma's Boys

The Lutheran House on Clark Avenue (the Brick Walk)

Conductors
Varujan Kojian, Music Director
John Mauceri
Walter Hendl
Carmine Coppola
David Zinman

Other Programs
in the Amphitheater
Harry Blackstone, Magician
Mark Russell, Political Satirist
Jerry Rockwood, Dramatist
Carol Teiter, Dramatist
Jennifer Dunegan, Dramatist
Richard Brown, Classic Films
Jack Anderson, Political Columnist

Platform Lecturers
David Schoenbrun
Richard Reeves
Dr. Edward Teller
Dr. Elizabeth Loftus
Dr. Heinz Pagels
Dr. Robert Murray, Jr.
Al Rosenfeld
Douglas Casey
Irwin Lerner
Dr. Lester Thurow
Dr. Philip Wernette
Alger Hiss
John Henry Faulk
Dr. Schoenbaum
Lorin Hollander
Dr. Karl Haas
Michael Brown
Dr. George Sheehan
Dr. William Rea
Joseph Raposo
Barbara Bannon
Albert Gottesman
Seymour Malamed
Michael Rudell
Richard Brown
Bob Evans
Romen Basu
Mrs. Basil Basu
Bruce Laingen

Chaplains
Dr. William Sloane Coffin
Bishop Roy C. Nichols
Dr. Richard M. Cromie
Dr. John Guest
Dr. Bruce Larson
Dr. Murdo E. MacDonald
Dr. Hugh George Anderson
Dr. Henry Sawatzky
Dr. Howard M. Fish
Dr. Bruce W. Thielemann

Additional Speakers at
Morning Devotionals
Father Conrad Harkins, O.F.M.
The Rev. Mathias Doyle
Father Joachim A. Giermek, O.F.M

Religion Department
Lecturers
Dr. Charles V. Bergstrom
Dr. John M. Swomley, Jr.

Dr. Donald Evans
Rabbi Israel Mowshowitz
Dr. A. Emerson Johnson III
Karl A. Schneider
Dr. Katherine Doob Sakenfeld
Dr. Robert McAfee Brown
Dr. Jean Koenig
Dr. Margery Brown
Dr. Cedric Smith

Opera
Cynthia Auerbach, Artistic Director

The Student Prince
    Andrew Meltzer, Conductor
    Dorothy Frank Danner, Director
La Boheme
    Varujan Kojian, Conductor
    Cynthia Auerbach, Director
Rigoletto
    Varujan Kojian, Conductor
    David Hicks, Director
The Tales of Hoffman
    Varujan Kojian, Conductor
    Cynthia Auerbach, Director

Dance
Amanda McKerrow and Simon Daw,
    Ballet
Patricia McBride and Bart Cook,
    Ballet
Crownsnest, Dance Ensemble

Theater
Lake Erie Repertory Theatre
Plays in Norton Hall following
the close of the opera season:
Fantasticks
Dames at Sea
Sleuth

Music School
Festival Orchestra
Nathan Gottschalk, Conductor

Soloists
The New Arts Trio
Flutist Katherine Diener
Artists and Students of the
    Chautauqua Dance Department
Nina Kennedy
Cedric Leake
Peter Minkler
Amy Mugavero
Eugene Perry
Patricia Marie Shands
Sue Ann Phillips
Beth Sussman
Glenn Visgitus
Lee Wilkins
Evan Wilson

Eugene Perry, Nina Kennedy share
    Sigma Alpha Iota Award

CAA
Nancy Hoffman, Juror for the Chau-
    tauqua Art Association's National
    Exhibition of American Art

The Arts and Crafts Quadrangle, designed by Henry Turner
Bailey, brilliant teacher, lecturer and developer of this department
at Chautauqua, has a sweeping view of the lake and shoreline.

7

Renaissance of Buildings and Spirit

THERE WAS reason to hope in 1982 that Chautauqua was settling into a steady climb toward its goals without interruption or detour. An aura of success seemed to encircle the Institution now that many momentous decisions had been reached. Dr. Hesse, himself, was showing a sense of belonging and permanence although his presidential appointment continued to be made at the pleasure of the Board of Trustees for only one year at a time.

At mid-point in January, 291 season gate passes and 691 opera subscriptions had already been sold. The new calendar-fiscal year was in place.

After Dr. Hesse reported to the committee the progress of negotiations for proposed television cable programs from Chautauqua, he received authorization to proceed subject to the approval of the attorneys.

Some "housekeeping" proposals by the Building and Grounds Committee were approved (by the executive committee): a building code amendment would require a property owner at the time of the granting of a building permit, to agree to replace damaged roads or right-of-ways, (presumably this would apply to major construction projects); and the creation of an architectural review committee to make decisions on multi-family dwellings, in view of the imminent construction of condominiums or dwellings of more than three units per building. This latter proposal would require Board action in May.

The winter issue of The Chautauquan brought the first program news for 1982. Pianist Alicia de Lorrocha, flutist James Galway and composer/pianist Marvin Hamlisch had been engaged to appear with the Chautauqua Symphony Orchestra. Dr. Robert Schuller, popular television minister, would preach August 22nd. Other chaplain and four continuing education seminars for ministers were announced.

News of Mr. Brunskill's resignation was announced in The Chautauquan with Dr. Hesse noting that during Mr. Brunskill's six and one-half years with Chautauqua, $14 million had been raised due in large measure to his efforts. Mr. Brunskill was to become vice president for institutional advancement at Baldwin-Wallace College in Berea, Ohio.

Another resignation was announced by Dr. Hesse, that of Alfreda Irwin as Editor of The Daily. Although it had not been generally known, Mrs. Irwin had told Dr. Hesse before the 1981 season that she thought it should be her last and that she now wanted to devote her serious attention to Chautauqua history. When Dr. Hesse did accept Mrs. Irwin's decision after the season, he appointed her Editor Emeritus of The Daily and historian-in-residence for the Institution. He then selected Jane T. Mead, lifelong Chautauquan and a member of a distinguished newspaper family in Westfield, to succeed Mrs. Irwin. Mrs. Mead was familiar with the Chautauqua newspaper operation since the firm owned by Mr. and Mrs. Mead had been printing The Daily since 1963. She had most recently been working as customer service director of the Westfield Republican and editor of the Chautauqua County Summer Calendar. She holds a bachelor's degree in English from Cornell University, has taught pre-kindergarten and is an ordained elder in the Presbyterian Church. She and her husband with their four children enjoy a family home at Chautauqua. With this change, Mrs. Irwin completed 24 years with The Chautauquan Daily, 16 years as editor.

News of another major CLSC event was announced by Director Ronsheim, the 100th anniversary of the first CLSC graduation. For this 1982 celebration-year books by Isaac Bashevis Singer, Edward L. Weeks and Dr. Frederick Franck had been selected and all three authors were expected at Chautauqua.

Meanwhile the Summer School faculty in music and dance were auditioning in 21 cities across the nation, seeking the most talented students. Available scholarships had risen 30 per cent to reach a value of $100,000. A $9,500 scholarship grant had been received from the Martha Holden Jennings Foundation in Cleveland to be used for Ohio residents who wish to study at Chautauqua. This was the second year in which the Jennings Foundation had offered this specific support of the Institution's scholarship program.

Dr. Nathan Gottschalk was to continue as Director of the Music School and as Conductor of the Music School's Chautauqua Festival Orchestra.

A new Youth Orchestra was to be formed under the direction of Anthony Milograno who had conducted a four-week Youth Orchestra program in 1981. This year the Youth Orchestra program would be increased from four weeks to a full season, seven-week project for advanced high school students. Anthony Milograno, who conducts the Youth Orchestra, is also a member of the first violin section of the Chautauqua Symphony Orchestra.

The Dance Department under Statia Z. Sublette planned to create a new company of 20 advanced ballet dancers who would perform as the Chautauqua Dance Festival Company. The Dance Department was to continue ballet instruction on Levels I, II and III, as well as its classes in aerobic dancing, modern, jazz and character dance. A dance medicine seminar was announced along with eight Saturday dance workshops. As it turned out, the Dance Festival Company was given the restored Normal Hall as its studio.

Letters of inquiry and actual applications to art, dance and music courses rose substantially during the spring. While Chautauqua emphasizes quality rather than quantity, the growing interest was encouraging.

March and April 55-Plus Weekends were announced along with Nature Study excursions led by Robert Sundell, one as far away as Trinidad; both were evidence of Chautauqua's educational potential beyond the season.

In February Annual Fund Reports showed additional cash and pledges received for a total of $218,488.

Dr. A. Wesley Rowland was appointed by Dr. Hesse in February to be Chautauqua's Second Century Campaign consultant. Dr. Rowland would temporarily fulfill Mr. Brunskill's former duties as Vice President for Development. Dr. Rowland had most recently served as professor of Higher Education at the State University of New York at Buffalo, and prior to that had held the position of vice president for University Relations there for ten years. He has also served as executive director of its foundation. Rebecca Robbins who had worked with the Second Century Campaign as a research assistant since its first summer became associate director of the Campaign.

The Buildings and Grounds Committee reported that only one proposal had been received for the development of Phase #1 of the property north of Elm Lane. (February 12th had been set as the date for the proposals to be reviewed.)

The lone proposal was made by Chautauqua Enterprises, Inc., of which Charles Heinz is principal owner. Mr. Heinz and his attorney, George L. Follansbee, Jr., are also both members of the Buildings and Grounds Committee and members of the Board of Trustees of Chautauqua Institution. When the proposal was reviewed by the committee, the two new members abstained from voting on the question, but the proposal was approved and recommended by the other members of the committee.

Mr. Heinz appeared before the Executive Committee and explained the "time-sharing" concept involved with his multi-unit buildings. The first ten units of the proposed 30-unit complex were to be ready by the fall of 1982 with 10 more planned for the next year and ten more in 1984. The Institution would receive purchase money for the land and six per cent from each unit purchased. A model apartment was already planned for construction in April on Lot #1805 which had been previously purchased by Chautauqua Enterprises. The architectural design was presented by members of the Lawson, Knapp and Pulver firm of Rochester.

The Executive Committee voted to bring the proposal to the Board of Trustees for final consideration. Some concerns were identified.

It was felt that letters should be sent to residents of the North End who would be directly affected by this development; that problems of traffic and public transportation should be addressed; that approval of Mr. Heinz' temporary office on Wiley Avenue should specify that such use of that site should, indeed, be considered temporary.

The consensus of the discussion was that short-term housing of a nature competitive with other resorts should become available at Chautauqua; that new housing is needed to insure the sale of more residential and gate tickets and more participation in Chautauqua activities; and that this particular project, apparently well-thought-out, had been organized by responsible people who have a solid understanding of Chautauqua.

A review of the architect's sketch of landscaping plans for the perimeter of the Amphitheater was studied. The administration was subsequently authorized to let bids and sell contracts for the development of the park behind the Amphitheater (in front of the Methodist House). The backstage work at the Amphitheater was progressing.

Mr. Osburn brought up the question of Institution lots which could be sold, identifying an area on Judson Avenue which would be suitable for a multi-family dwelling. The Executive Committee approved the sale of the Judson Avenue lots.

Mr. Johnson reported that the Chautauqua-Cattaraugus Library System of which Smith Library is a member, has asked that the Institution consider a proposal for outreach services. If approved by the state, the program would give the Institution an opportunity to apply for a grant to improve facilities for the handicapped at Smith Library. Approval was voted.

Dr. Hesse made additional reports: 625 season gate tickets and 777 opera subscriptions had now been sold.

A new monthly reporting system had been instituted by the Treasurer. This was presented so that department heads and the Executive Committee could be fully informed of the Institution's and the departments' financial situation from month to month. The Second Century Campiagn report indicated that total gifts and commitments stood at $5,963,846.48 while payments had reached $4,610,921.75.

Happy news was soon to come from the TRW Bearings Division of Jamestown. That company had chosen to allocate a gift of $20,000 to the *Chautauqua Fellows* Program. The *Chautauqua Fellows* project which is in the planning stages, will bring internationally prominent people to the Grounds as program participants, as liaisons among academic and professional circles and as a source of new funding. As part of the Second Century Campaign the program tied to the Institution's future growth and national outreach.

In conjunction with the development of the North End for single dwellings, two new Chautauqua streets were to be constructed. One, Hazlett Avenue, was to be named for a former Institution president, Dr. Samuel Hazlett, who led the drive to save Chautauqua in the 1930's. The other, Gebbie Drive, would honor the foundation which had played such a strategic role in Chautauqua's renaissance. Plans called for the sale of 10 more lots in this area, two already having been sold.

The death of Helen Heinz Sample, an honorary trustee of the Institution and well-known figure at Chautauqua, occurred in February and was noted in the March Chautauquan. Her service to the Institution was acknowledged with sincere affection and respect.

In March it was learned that live theatre would, indeed, return to Norton Hall the last two weeks of the 1982 season. Not only would The Acting Company be performing at Chautauqua then, but its founder, John Houseman, had been engaged to give 10:45 morning lectures in the Amphitheater August 16 and 17. This announcement was an encouragement to those Chautauquans who especially enjoy theatre and had mourned the Institution's separation from the Cleveland Playhouse. The Acting Company had been formed in 1972 by Mr. Houseman when he was head of the Theatre Center at the Juilliard School. In 1980 this Company became the touring arm of the Kennedy Center in Washington, D. C.

The names of more entertainers, artists and lecturers were released by the Institution as season ticket sales soared to 1,304 and opera subscriptions reached within 60 of the 1,000-subscription goal.

In financial matters, Dr. Hesse told the Executive Committee that the National Endowment for the Arts had awarded the Institution $19,800 over what had been budgeted and that the 1982 Annual Fund now had $232,152 in cash and pledges.

The Board of Directors of the Hotel Corporation had passed a resolution which was presented to the Institution's Executive Committee for approval. It contained a statement of objectives for the renovation of the Athenaeum Hotel, using a partnership structure to include private investors. Among the objectives was authorization for preliminary application to the Chautauqua County Industrial Development Agency for financing of the debt portion of the project costs.

A suggestion had been made that the Haker-Kimball Garden be located to the rear and side of the Amphitheater to complement the Amphitheater's total beautification plans. Members of Mrs. Haker's family received the suggestion positively, so that Mr. Smith was authorized to engage a landscape architect to proceed with the planning.

At the May Board meeting, Dr. Rowland met the full Board of Trustees for the first time and a Capital Campaign Report was distributed. Commitments for the Campaign had now exceeded the $6 million mark. In analyzing strategies for the completion of the Campaign, Mrs. Reading, Chairman, commented that property owner non-donors represent a large portion of untapped resources. The high percentage of non-donors do not reflect refusal to contribute, she said, but rather that many have not yet been solicited. She urged trustees to make the calls they had agreed to make. She set the goal that each trustee should solicit 10 property owners during the summer. She also reminded the trustees that the remainder of the National Endowment for the Arts Challenge Grant must be raised by June, 1983.

Dr. Rowland sketched the ongoing status of the Campaign and Dr. Hesse's schedule of appearances with Chautauqua "Societies" which were being coordinated in each city with visits to corporate and foundation executives. Dr. Hesse had been in Pittsburgh April 27-29. He had spoken to Chautauquans of northwest Pennsylvania at a dinner meeting in Reno, Pennsylvania May 7. He was to spend several days in Buffalo May 25-27 and in Erie, Pennsylvania, June 1-4. Fall meetings were already being set up in Jamestown, New York City, Cleveland and Northeast Ohio as well as the nearby Dunkirk/Fredonia area. Earlier Dr. Hesse had visited Florida.

Dr. Hesse reported to the Board on Chautauqua's "Renaissance."

"The massive effort is paying off," he said. "Priorities are being met. Gate tickets are on target as projected, and with season opera subscriptions at 962. the goal of 1,000 will be met for the first time. The all-time high for subscriptions for the Cleveland Playhouse was 206, and there have been 215 already sold for The Acting Company's short season. He predicted that the Institution would meet its income projections, but that he had instituted a 2 per cent savings for each area in expenditures as a "safety net" to protect from over-expanding.

George Shearing was a frequent visitor during the early and mid-'70s. This view of his Jazz Workshop at Chautauqua in 1972 calls attention to the educational workshop pattern indigenous to Chautauqua.

He then turned to the restoration and renovation of physical facilities. He asked Mr. Smith under whose supervision these improvements are made, to make a building-by-building report.

Mr. Smith began his detailed report by saying that the Amphitheater work would be completed by the beginning of the season. "The Hall of Christ will be cleaned, the stains removed, the building siliconed and the trim painted," he continued.

"The Hall of Philosophy is having major rehabilitation. The mosaics are being repaired and cleaned. The seats are being painted in the original color. The oak beams and stenciling are being renewed." He predicted that returning Chautauquans would be thrilled to see the gold Greek design reappear on the beams under the roof. The removal of overgrown trees and shrubbery is allowing the Hall to be seen as it once was years ago. New cement walks and improved rest rooms have been part of the project, he said. He reminded the trustees that the year before the roof had been repaired and the concrete portions of the building had been carefully sandblasted and repainted a soft white, believed to have been the original color. "The building is going to be maintained," Mr. Smith promised, "and a new sound system will be installed for use this season." All this had been made possible through a generous gift to the Second Century Campaign.

Mr. Smith then called attention to Normal Hall which, if work had not been started this year, might have been totally lost as a building. The Institution staff had performed much of the needed restoration of Normal Hall as well as of other buildings at a great savings to the Institution, he added parenthetically. Normal Hall dates from 1885 when it was built by the Chautauqua Normal Alumni Association. It originally included a second floor. It has many exterior architectural features which will become noticeable, he predicted, when it is repainted in contrasting shades of gold with beige. Essential repairs to foundation piers, porches and steps, reinforcement of interior arches and the installation of new hardwood flooring have prepared this old hall for use in 1982, he said.

Norton Hall will be painted on the outside and the doors will be refinished, he continued. A touch of magenta added to the white exterior paint will give Norton a new look. A deeper magenta tone in the back walls and ceiling of the entrance-way will be even more striking and will pick up the color of the original glass light fixtures which are still in use.

The Arts quadrangle renovation is proceeding well, he noted, as he reminded the Board that the trustees of the Helen Temple Logan Trust have provided the funds for this restoration. Decaying portions of the piers have been replaced and repaired. New roofing has been installed. Lentals have been repaired or replaced and the entire exterior has been stained and painted. A new drainage system had been installed which necessitated taking up the brick walks and then rebuilding them. "We used as many of the old bricks as we could," he said. Interior work will be done later and this, too, has been provided by the gift from the Logan Trust.

Other improvements were under way. Smith-Wilkes Hall was being painted and drainage, walkways and lighting were being repaired, he said. Storm drainage for Phase 1 on Elm Lane had been completed and underground utilities work had been started.

As he completed his report on the buildings, he spoke of another aspect of the Operations Department, gate tickets. He said that every early-purchase gate ticket had been prepared, laminated and filed for pickup at the Main Gate. He, thus, anticipated fewer problems for season ticketholders at the Gate this year.

A slight change of relationship between the Institution and the Chautauqua Foundation was explained to the trustees by Dr. Hesse. Because of changes in the Internal Revenue Code, in order to put the Foundation in a position where it can operate as a total part of the Institution from a donor point of view, an arrangement has been made for an interrelationship between Institution trustees and Foundation directors. The President of the Institution is an ex-officio member of the Foundation Board. Now three positions on the Foundation Board must be held by Institution trustees. The trustees must take a leadership role, Dr. Hesse stated, in defining the Institution's needs and in communicating them to the Foundation. An attempt to shape mutually agreed-upon directions will thus be facilitated.

Mr. Redington, director of education, youth and recreation, told the trustees that while many familiar instructors would be returning, there were to be a few changes. "Mary Peck will replace Claudia Bonn as the director of the Children's School, and Paul Sire will replace James Achuff in ceramics," he said. Flat contracts now prevail in all the schools, except the special studies and private instruction. All faculty members, except those mentioned, will be moved from commission-style contracts to flat contracts. This change gives the Institution a better 'lead' on expenses and relieves the pressure on faculty members to recruit for their classes." He also reported that the Logan Family had made an annual appointment of the Helen T. Logan Chair in Painting and Drawing. It would be filled in 1982 in an honorary capacity by Revington Arthur, he said.

Dr. Hesse said that the Institution is trying to produce a drama program for the 1983 season and is also trying to mount a drama school. The effort requires the cooperation of the Education and Program Committees. A new proposal has been received for study. It surveys the possibility of the Institution's joining with the Acting Company to obtain what is needed both in theater program and theater education.

At the May Board meeting, the North End Development was taken up with the full Board. Charles Heinz, the major stockholder in Chautauqua Enterprises, Inc., which had submitted the proposal for 30 units of time-sharing housing on the northwest side of Elm Lane, was present to answer questions. George L. Follansbee, Jr., a director of the firm and the attorney for Chautauqua Enterprises, was also.present.

William Foley, an attorney for seven North End property owners opposed to the development, attended the discussions as well, and stated the reasons for his clients' opposition.

After thorough deliberation, the Board accepted the

The Main Gate Building offers many services now.

proposal of Chautauqua Enterprises, Inc., for a parcel of land consisting of approximately 2.9 acres on the north side of Elm Lane.[1]

The Architects' drawings and the literature concerning the time-sharing units were on display in the Colonnade as approval for the plan was sought from rank and file Chautauquans. At a public meeting of Chautauquans in Hurlbut Church before the season began when Dr. Hesse was updating the residents on programs and restoration of facilities, an opportunity was given the developer to present his plan, including the financials. Community support for the development was actively addressed.

There was general community approval and amazement at the way improvements were taking place throughout the Grounds. However, Chautauquans, as they were forced to detour around the mud of the Amphitheater's perimeter, couldn't believe that the landscaping and brick work at the Amphitheater would be completed in time for the dedication July 4, not to mention the opening of the season. Dr. Hesse, himself, frequently walked through the Grounds on pre-season evenings to see what progress had been made day by day. He was feeling the pressures, too, for he had spoken widely in the spring to many groups and had promised confidently that all the projects would be ready by June 26th.

In May, Dr. Hesse released news to the media that the internationally famous heart surgeon, Dr. Christian Bernard, would lecture at Chautauqua in July and the well-known author, Alex Haley, in August.

Dr. Hesse also announced that an unrestricted gift of $45,000 had been received from Zurn Industries, Inc. of Erie, Pennsylvania, making an immense impact on the Second Century Campaign and the Institution overall.

The Oral History Project which had been part of the Centennial observance in 1974 was being reinitiated, Dr. Hesse said. The newly-appointed historian would conduct interviews during the summer with various Chautauquans. Their lifelong experiences in connection with Chautauqua would be added to those already preserved in the Chautauqua Historical Collection.

Interested Chautauquans and historians will have access to the valuable information contained on the tapes.

But Dr. Hesse had his mind on future planning, as well as the season just ahead. He had suggested to the Board in May that the course for the next three to five years should be charted now: the ongoing needs of the physical plant, financial forecasting and planning, program development, educational outreach and coordination, national and international markets.

As the season started, "the excitement that is Chautauqua now" was plainly evident.[2] The Amphitheater actually was finished and it sat beautifully surrounded on the Clark Avenue side by a park area of grass, small trees and other stretches of brick walkways. Gone were the old parking places of many years and the muddy flats in front of the Methodist House. The blocked concrete and brick "floors" inside the Amphitheater fence were artistic as well as practical. The Haker-Kimball Patio proved to be an inviting place for Chautauquans to sit and rest. The new fence, itself, with its brick posts and iron pickets turned out to be acceptable even by those who regularly stand outside during programs to enjoy their friends as much as the program.

Headliners were in abundance that first weekend: Neil Sedaka in the Amph that first Saturday night; returned Iranian Hostage Moorhead Kennedy at the preaching service as the season opened; Phil Donahue on Sunday afternoon with a SRO audience. The CAA had already opened it 25th annual National Exhibition of American art. Seventy-one works were chosen from almost 2,500 entries to hang at the Wythe Avenue Galleries for three weeks.

The Lecture Platform's National Affairs Week, which seems to have established itself as a regular first-week feature, started with Richard Valeriani. The House of Representatives' Chaplain, Dr. James Ford, conducted the 9:30 a.m. Devotional Hour all week. The Dental Congress convened for its sessions. Nobel Prizewinning author Isaac Bashevis opened the CLSC Round Table Series and Presidential Counselor Edwin B. Meese lectured on "An Era of Change."

Evening Amphitheater programs the first week saluted different areas of the county each night, so there were good crowds even before the arrival of the Chautauqua Symphony Orchestra.

In its opening concert July 3rd, the Chautauqua Symphony Orchestra honored Igor Stravinsky. Varujan Kojian, music director and conductor, was on the podium, beginning his second year with the CSO.

The Fourth of July at Chautauqua is usually a quiet holiday, although it is fair to say that its deeper meanings are always remembered and have been "programmed" in various ways. (Who can forget the deep basso voice of Julius Huehn when he gave annual readings of the Declaration of Independence during the '50s? Or the Independence Day addresses by Governor Nelson Rockfeller, or Senator Barry Goldwater in the '60s?)

In 1982, Independence Day fell on Sunday. After a stirring morning sermon by Dr. Thielmann, campus chaplain of Grove City College, the Army Field Band and Soldier's Chorus attracted 6,000 to its Amphitheater concert in the afternoon. No more rousing a patriotic observance could have been scheduled for "whole-souled" Chautauquans. But an added ceremony held more than matching significance, the rededication of the Amphitheater. This unusual structure, so central to Chautauqua's total educational impact, had been completely restored from funds given through the Second Century Campaign. Before the ceremony the Institution held a luncheon in the Athenaeum for those who had contributed specifically toward the Amphitheater preservation project.

President Hesse and Chairman Gibbs officiated at the rededication, which preceded the main part of the concert. Dr. Hesse spoke historically of the 89-year-old program center. Quoting from the 1893 Assembly Herald, he made whimsical comparisons between the construction process in 1893 and the reconstruction process in 1982. In neither year did Chautauquans believe the work would be finished in time for the season. He praised the vision of the early Chautauquans as well as the modern Board of Trustees whose members had made the bold decision to enter upon the Capital Campaign through which the restoration had become possible.

Mr. Gibbs said: "In essence, this Amphitheater is a place for repose, reflection, renewal; a place to learn, to question and to share; a place where history is made."

The audience was moved by the heightened sense of history as the bronze plaque marking the achievement was unveiled on the platform so that all could see. Later it would be permanently installed near the Amphitheater entrance closest to Bestor Plaza.

The season was full of highlights connected with the culminating effect of the Second Century Campaign. Special dedication ceremonies commemorated the renaming of two Chautauqua locations on the Grounds, in honor of designated campaign gifts.

Members of the T. James and Hazel C. Clarke Trust met at 1:30 p. m. Friday, August 13, 1982, in the Colonnade to christen the lobby "the Clarke Lobby" in memory of T. James and Hazel C. Clarke of Jamestown.

At 12:30 p. m. Sunday, August 22, 1982, the family

and friends of the late Frederick and Margaret Heinz of Pittsburgh, met at the public bathing beach on South Lake Drive where this area was formally designated as Heinz Beach in recognition of the family's long-standing attachment to Chautauqua. The Heinz family whose homes have been part of the lake front at the south end of the Grounds for many years, found this an appropriate memorial for their loved ones. It had been planned originally by Margaret Heinz in memory of her husband, Frederick, but became a memorial for both after Mrs. Heinz death in late 1981.

Second Century Campaign Tours of renovated buildings were conducted by volunteers on Saturday mornings during the season. Included in the tours were the Hall of Philosophy, the Amphitheater, Kellogg Hall, Normal Hall, Norton Hall and the Arts and Crafts Quadrangle.

The Brick Project continued as Chautauquans chose to honor or memorialize friends and family members through gifts of $1,000 or more. Inscribed bricks were to enclose the newly renovated grandstands at the Amphitheater. The installation of bricks was delayed when the Institution rejected as unsatisfactory the first delivery of bricks.

An accelerated schedule of receptions for artists, added to the enjoyment of the season, and Dr. Hesse hosted a number of luncheons so that lecturers could meet the families represented in the endowed lectureships.

It was a summer of rejoicing over the progress of the Institution's retooling for the Second Century and it was a time for frequent "Thank you's."

As usual, the events of each day were important to differing segments of the community.

The Chautauqua Craft Alliance set up a colorful weekend show along the edge of Bestor Plaza, attracting Fourth of July tourists as well as Chautauquans.

Mrs. J. Roy Cooper was announced as the new president of International Order of King's Daughters and Sons. Mrs. Cooper, from New Brunswick, Canada, is the Order's first Chautauqua scholarship holder to become its international president.

The first Open Forum tackled the question of fewer eating places and the proliferation of condos and apartments. Emerging answers: people often prefer to go off the Grounds for dining; present number of eating places seems adequate; people nowadays prefer apartments to rooms in rooming houses; times have changed even at Chautauqua; private baths are expected with hotel rooms; the Institution is not building condominiums, but encouraging increased residential population.

A limited edition of a poster commemorating the 100th anniversary of the first Recognition Day went on sale. Created by Maritza Morgan, the poster shows a Victorian family out for a stroll by the Hall of Philosophy. A pictorial history of the first CLSC graduation was arranged in Smith Library by Margaret Wade.

The Northeastern Region of the National Federation of Music Clubs convened with national officers in attendance.

Young Chautauquans at an informal forum on the Athenaeum porch had a chance to talk about abortion and sex education with Dr. Jack Lippes and Dr. Gene

Outka, Chautauqua lecturers during the season's second week. Ashley Montagu returned, this time with a directive to "die young—as late as possible." He sat for his Amphitheater lecture on the "Science of Growing Young," but had no difficulty in holding his audience. Montagu first lectured at Chautauqua in 1953.

The new choral director, Philip Aley, began his duties. A long-time Chautauquan, he had sung in the Chautauqua Choir in previous years. He said he hoped "to provide fine, worshipful music."

Prince Henry College with Chautauquan John S. Rogers as chairman, conducted summer classes at Chautauqua for 40 international young women students. Also, the college's three-masted schooner returned to the lake and was offered for part-time use to the Boys and Girls Clubs. Prince Henry College and Mr. Rogers were instrumental in arranging for the appearance of Economists Dr. Leopold Kohr and Kirkpatrick Sale on the lecture platform during the third week of the season.

In a Daily interview, new trustee James Zurn raised questions of "how to go." "Does Chautauqua want to think in numbers or maximizing the offerings?" he asked. "Our strength lies in our history, but educational and cultural aspects need to be brought into today's focus."

Rededication of the Presbyterian House was held on Sunday afternoon, July 18. Tours followed the service in which Dr. Loew and Dr. Hesse participated. The main part of the house was built in 1890.

English Bell Tower Scholars Kay Smith and Peter Warren arrived for study.

Franklin Delano Roosevelt, Jr. spoke in the Amphitheater in celebration of the 100th birthday of his father, who was himself a four-time speaker in the Amphitheater.

New Trustee Paul Irion suggested the potential for discussion groups at Chautauqua. "Modest think-tanks" he called them and suggested that they could accelerate the Chautauqua enrichment process. Dr.

and Mrs. Richard Antemann celebrated the centennial of their Chautauqua home, new to them in 1982 and newly restored. The couple arranged a concert in Smith-Wilkes Hall July 24th to commemorate 1982 century homes. Five other houses in addition to the Antemann's qualified for recognition. Open house at the Antemann's home near Smith-Wilkes followed the concert.

The Annual Fund effort under the chairmanship of Ed Boyle proceeded in tandem with the Second Century Campaign. Chautauquans continue to provide for Chautauqua's strength and future growth. The Second Century Campaign total in July was listed at $6,156,000.

Special studies in the Summer School offered vacation study in more than 125 courses. The range was broad and extended from computers to gourmet cooking. Scholarships reached over the projected $100,000 for the Summer Schools.

Dr. Hesse sent greetings to Pacific Grove, California, a community that has 103-year-old connections with the Chautauqua Movement. He also sent the Institution's Historian to the Monteagle Sunday School Assembly in Tennessee as a speaker for that Assembly's Centennial program.

Firemen's Day was celebrated July 31 with a parade, rides on a fire truck, fun with fire-smothering foam and an abundance of food for sale. The occasion gives Chautauquans an opportunity each year to say "Thank you" to a valued volunteer service organization.

Gustavo Romero, an Epstein Scholarship holder under the Boys Club of America, appeared in recital in the Amphitheater. For some years now Chautauqua has had the opportunity to hear outstanding young musicians whose talent has been encouraged by the Boys Club and Epstein Scholarship Program. Several have gained international prominence. Mr. Gibbs, chairman of the Chautauqua Board of Trustees, directs this Young Artists Program in connection with his work as Associate National Director of the Boys Club of America.

Kellogg Hall was one of the first buildings to be preserved in the effort to save Chautauqua's architectural treasures.

An earlier view of Kellogg Hall

Bernice Group was elected president of the Friends of the Library. John Neville qualified for the Lightning North Americana at a race hosted by the Lakewood Yacht Club and would thereby sail in the North American championships on Lake Erie in August.

Old First Night was anticipated, said Dr. Hesse, because we have "the whole Chautauqua renaissance to celebrate...celebration of Chautauqua for its being, its people and its ideals." The Old First Nightingales offered a new singing telegram service to Chautauquans as a benefit for the Annual Fund. The Nightingales were a group of fifteen choir members under the direction of Carl Badger. The Sports Club's Old First Night Run raised $1,000 as many Chautauquans of all ages participated, some of them walking!

At the annual OFN program, the presence of Dr. Karl A. Menninger and Mrs. Nina Terrill Wensley was acknowledged by Chairman Gibbs. Mrs. Wensley was attending her 66th consecutive Old First Night.

Dr. and Mrs. Carl S. Winters received official recognition for their many gifts of service to the Institution. It was the first time that a couple had been honored in this way. A citation detailing their contributions to Chautauqua's official, programmatic and community life was read by Mr. Gibbs.

Dr. Hesse announced that the Chautauqua Festival Orchestra would perform in Corning, in Guelph, Canada and play in Avery Fisher Hall on Sunday evening, August 15.

The Keystone State won the competition for having the most citizens present and the Annual Fund reached $611,463 by evening's end.

The next day was the 101st Recognition Day for the CLSC. One hundred years of reading had been completed. One member of the 1982 graduating class had had a great-grandmother in the very first class. "It's fun to be part of a tradition," Director Ronsheim said. CLSC Alumni are by and large extremely loyal, numbering approximately 57,000. The 1982 class president, "Cappy" Patch, and Bonnie Bryer, the designer of the class banner, were the first graduates to pass through the Golden Gate.

The Old First Night Community Gift gets an assist from David Carnahan, left, Shorty Follansbee (with the laundry basket) and Chairman Gibbs.

"La Traviata" had a matinee performance August 7th. That evening the Chautauqua Dance Festival Dance Company appeared with Ballet Partners Starr Danias and Gregory King and the Chautauqua Symphony Orchestra. Sue Reis won the Chautauqua Women's Golf Association's Margaret B. Jones Memorial Handicap Tournament. Jane Newton was season champion for the eighth time. John Ciardi opened Literature Week which was also highlighted by Dr. and Mrs. Robert McAfee Brown, lecturers for the Department of Religion.

The National WCTU President, Mrs. Kermit S. Edgar, was in Chautauqua for the 101st WCTU Day. Dr. Menninger agreed to speak to an admiring Chautauqua audience in an unscheduled lecture on a provocative topic: "Wrong Dealing with Wrong-doers; Crime, Punishment and the Bomb."

The 16th annual American-Scandinavian Day was observed and Chautauqua architecture was written about in the New York Times. Doris Goodrich Jones entertained the Children's School with a puppet show and the identity and source of the Egyptian Statue that had been found at the Main Gate in 1978, was finally established. Approximately 3500 Chautauquans signed a petition asking the President to ban further production of nuclear arms.

The delicate question of financing the Athenaeum Hotel restoration had to be faced by the Board during the summer board meetings. The extent of the project and therefore, its cost, had been entrusted to Vice President Smith and Architect Robert Gaede. Mr. Gaede believed that the project could be divided over a two-year period with no interruption of service. The search for funding had been led by Treasurer Johnson and the Institution's attorney, Mr. Price.

Mr. Price explained to the Board that certain legal requirements had discouraged efforts to form a syndication of private investors on a tax shelter arrangement and that, therefore, the Institution had approached the Chautauqua County Industrial Development Agency. That agency had agreed to sponsor the project. In this process, the Hotel Company would have to convey the property to the Agency which would then issue tax free revenue bonds. This concept was agreed to by the Board of Directors of the Hotel Company. In exploring the marketing process it was determined that in order to market the bonds, the Institution must be willing to guarantee them. The Board of Directors of the Hotel Company passed a resolution asking the Institution's Board of Trustees to consider guaranteeing these bonds.

The Institution's Trustees, therefore, after due consideration, approved by motion the concept of the importance of the hotel to the Institution, and the concept of the guarantee by the Institution of the payment of principal and interest on bonds having a face value of two million dollars proposed to be issued by the Chautauqua County Industrial Development Agency, the bonds to be secured by a mortgage on the hotel property. However, before final approval was to be given, the Board needed to satisfy itself that such action would be in the best interests of the Institution from every standpoint. For this purpose, a feasibility study was requested, along with financial projections, a description of the specific physical aspects of the project and reasonably accurate cost estimates. Also, legal Counsel was instructed to prepare an opinion on the Institution's legal authority to make a guarantee of the bonds and to determine that no adverse tax consequences would be experienced by the Institution. In addition, a committee from the Board was appointed to study and report on the possible effects on the Institution from any of the intricacies of the proposed financing. Messrs Anderson, Bargar, Wilder and Zurn were appointed to that committee.

Dr. Hesse reported to the Board that an "upbeat" spirit seemed to be permeating the season in regard to buildings, Grounds, orchestra and opera. He thought the Board should take pride in this perception of well-being. He also reported that a committee from the Property Owners Association were seeking some form of self-government to obtain funding from the County and/or some sort of school tax reform. He also informed the Board that because of the economy, Exxon had not been able to accept the Institution's proposal for funding of the cable television programming.

Another intriguing topic was discussed: what to do about "Ralph," an Egyptian statue which had been found by Mr. Smith when he first started to reactivate the entire Main Gate Building. A student on the Grounds who had been researching the statue had given it a code name, "Ralph." It now seemed an accepted fact that the statue was one that had been "lost" for fifty years. It had been a gift to the Chautauqua Museum by the Egyptian Exploration Fund and formerly occupied a prominent place in Newton Hall. When the Hall was razed to make way for Smith Memorial Library, it is presumed that the statue was left at the Main Gate.

The proposed sale of the Glen Park to Tony Joy Associates for the development of condominiums and town houses in the Glen Park area was explained. The Institution owns one of the adjacent lots that would be needed for the project. The Board agreed to the sale of the lot on North Terrace to Tony Joy Associates.

Some discussions on lakefront use were held. Due to the proliferation of small sailboats and density of buoys, the aesthetics of the shoreline is being adversely affected. It was agreed that some resolution of the dilemma needs to be found.

A further exploration of Chautauqua's aim of national visibility was presented to the Board by Dr. Hickman, chairman of the Education, Youth and Recreation Committee, who suggested that such organizations as the Library and the CLSC might achieve national presence by coordination and cooperation through the taping and marketing of study cassettes and other outreach programs. The Committee recommended that a study be made of outreach activities and the possibility that added staff would be required to meet those needs.

Dr. Holland reported extremely good response to the Continuing Education Program for Clergy. He said that there is a high level of interest in the Religion Committee in the possibility of Chautauqua's becoming a satellite of a theological seminary so that educa-

tional programs during the summer could lead to the professional Doctor of Ministry degree, but he added that housing might present a problem for such a program.

Figures for the year were released by the Chautauqua Foundation, Inc., when it held its annual meeting at Chautauqua on August 20th. The total assets were listed at: $5,111,177 with the notation that gifts, bequests and endowments in 1982 represented a gain of $454,977 for the Foundation. The amount payable to Chautauqua Institution in annual support according to its regular, specified formula, totaled $146,789. The additional sum of $69,858 had been expended in support of the Institution's Development and Second Century Campaign expenses.

Richard L. Bechtolt was elected to the Foundation Board to fill the vacancy caused by the death of Joseph A. Neubauer. Richard H. Miller was reelected president and treasurer of the Foundation; Robert S. Bargar was elected vice president; Rebecca Irwin Robbins was elected secretary and assistant treasurer; and Samuel P. Price, assistant secretary and assistant treasurer. Lewis W. Morgan, John S. Rogers and Mr. Bargar were reelected as directors. The Board's membership includes in addition to the ones mentioned: Howard G. Gibbs, Mrs. Dan W. Cook, Mr. David H. Carnahan, Mr. George L. Cornell, Mr. J. Donald Patton, Dr. Robert R. Hesse, Mrs. Nancy Miller Arnn.

At the second Board meeting in August, the trustees accepted the proposal of the Program Committee concerning the engagement of The Acting Company for the full season of 1983. In The Acting Company's proposal, both the educational and performance needs of the Institution would be met. The Education Committee concurred with the Program Committee's recommendation.

Three new trustees were elected to four-year terms: Malcolm Anderson, Marilyn (Mrs. James) Levinson and Paul Branch. Reelected were Paul Irion, Mary Frances Cram and Robert Holland.

Expressions of appreciation were voted to the retiring trustees who had each served eight years and had performed extraordinary leadership. Gertrude Shelburne had chaired the program committee during a difficult transition period. Her leadership was firm and courageous and her experience in the arts made her unusually knowledgeable. Robert Bargar's wide knowledge of Chautauqua County and his business experience had made him especially effective in fund raising and other Institution matters. William C. Rittman brought the perspective of a lifelong Chautauquan, as well as experience as a lawyer and top-level executive. He had served faithfully on committees and had served as secretary of the executive committee.

Annual Fund receipts were reported as $690,000. Miriam Reading expressed a real sense of urgency about the lack of major gifts to complete the work which had been begun under the Second Century Campaign by December, 1982. She reminded trustees to make their solicitation calls.

A request from the Chautauqua Hotel and Inn Association for permission to serve wine with dinner at some of the larger hotels was discussed and referred to the appropriate committee.

Trustee Geof Follansbee reported that from efforts to obtain a traffic light on Route 394 at the Main Gate entrance he had learned from the New York State Department of Transportation that since the high volume of traffic at that point is only for a nine-week period of time, the cost of the installation of a traffic light for that period would have to be borne by the Institution. Estimated cost would be $25,000. The Board passed a resolution authorizing the staff in conjunction with the Buildings and Grounds Committee to take necessary steps to obtain the installation of the traffic signal. The density of traffic at the Main Gate area and the necessity for several thousands of persons to walk across the highway from the parking areas were noted in the resolution.

Further discussions were made August 28th relative to the financing of the Athenaeum restoration rehabilitation.

Miles Lasser presented the results of the requested feasibility study. He stated that while a comparable hotel could scarcely be found since both the Institution and the hotel are unique, an attempt was made to compare the hotel with other resort hotels and the Athenaeum compares very favorably.

Robert Wilder, reporting for the ad hoc committee, said that the committee felt an arrangement should be made which would be short of a total guarantee, but that since the Board would not be meeting again until November, a decision should be made now authorizing the power to negotiate and act on behalf of the Board in the best interests of the Institution.

The legal opinion of Counsel had been sent to Board members before the August 28th meeting and, therefore, on the basis of all three reports, Mr. Price submitted a resolution for the consideration of the Board.

The resolution reaffirmed the Board's belief that the Athenaeum Hotel is a major factor in the proper implementation of the Institution's purposes and authority to provide for recreation, health and comfort on the Grounds and that, therefore, its proposed renovation and preservation is called for. It specified that the proposed financing by the conveyance of the hotel property to the Chautauqua County Industrial Development Agency and the issuance by that agency of bonds in an amount not to exceed $2 million will be in the best interests of the Institution and will materially contribute to the fulfillment of its overall objectives including its capital improvement campaign. It stated that the Board had received satisfactory reports of a feasibility study and financial projections, a preliminary description of the physical aspects of the project and reasonably accurate cost estimated. It had also received Counsel's opinion that the Institution has legal authority to make such a guarantee and that no adverse tax consequences would be experienced by the Institution. The Board must also realize that lenders in the commercial marketplace may be unwilling to undertake financing arrangements with the Chautauqua Hotel Company, Inc. or the CCIDA without obtaining the consent of the Institution to the subordination of the existing mortgage securing company bonds held by the Institution in the face amount of $50,000. Also, the Institution must undertake to stand behind the obligations of the Company in the event that the cash flow of the hotel operations should at any time prove insufficient to fully amortize the debt service.

The resolution included the Board's agreement and consent to actions taken and approved by the Hotel Company. It included authorization to the President of the Institution and the Chairman of the Board to vote the shares of the Company in order to accomplish the intent of the Company resolutions. The appropriate officers of the Institution were authorized and directed to take such action as they may deem necessary and in the best interests of the Institution in order to carry out the intention of the resolutions.

These resolutions were discussed at length and then adopted by the Board of Trustees.

Further action was taken on the sale of lots owned by the Institution. Mr. Osburn reported that only one of the ten single-unit lots on the North End of the Grounds had been sold. He requested approval to put the remaining lots on the market over the winter, selling first the four lots on Elm Lane and then next summer rebidding the entire package. The board voted approval of the sale of the remaining lots (Lots 1801-1812) on a first-come, first-serve basis under terms and conditions which the officers of the Institution deem appropriate, and for amounts not less than the minimum bid price already established.

Concerning the lot on Judson Avenue which the Board had approved to be put out to bid, Mr. Osburn reported that there had been many complaints from neighbors, stating that it was their understanding when they bought their properties that this land would remain a park. The neighbors have been contacted and told that the Institution still intends to sell the land. At the time bids were to be received, there were no bids but two letters of interest for a future time. The Committee recommended resetting the bid date to late June since it was promised to the neighbors that they would be notified before action was taken and contact during the winter is difficult. The Board passed a motion setting the new bid date for next June.

As the meeting closed, Mr. Gibbs expressed enthusiastic appreciation and gratitude to the Administrative Staff on behalf of the Board for a most successful season. Dr. Hesse extended his appreciation to the staff for a very successful season, although it had been a difficult and demanding one, and one of the most exhausting, he said. He called attention to the dates for next season, June 25 to August 28 and added that full statistics would be ready for the November meeting. He could say that gate ticket sales had increased in 1982 and attendance at lectures and concerts had naturally followed suit.

Two personnel changes emerged in the fall. Statia Sublette, director of dance at Chautauqua since 1962 decided to retire and her resignation was accepted with regret. Dr. Ralph Loew had informed Dr. Hesse that he would continue to head the Religion Department in 1983, but would like to retire from that position at the end of the 1983 season. This prior notice would allow the Institution ample time in which to choose a successor. Dr. Hesse expressed regret over the prospect of Dr. Loew's retirement and immediately proposed that the Institution begin planning appropriate recognition of Dr. Loew's service to Chautauqua. Dr. Loew had offered to help in the search for his successor.

The Second Century Campaign reached the $6.4 million mark in October. Two generous gifts had been given toward the renovation of Norton Hall by Mr. and Mrs. C. D. Norton and Mrs. Bartlett Richards.

In October, the Annual Fund still needed $150,000 to reach its $900,000 goal. Since operating expenses are met by the Annual Fund, Dr. Hesse stressed the importance of the completion of this drive.

Other personnel changes were shared with the Executive Committee in October. Rob Erdle had resigned as head of the Art Department and was assisting in the search for his replacement. Marlena Malas had been engaged in the Voice Department of the School of Music where she would succeed Charlene Chadwick. Miss Chadwick had been associated with the Voice Department for 25 years.

Dr. Hesse told the Executive Committee that projected total income seemed likely to exceed final expenses which seemed to be staying within budgeted figures. Of course, the success of the Annual Fund was factored into this encouraging expectation.

The possibility of charging for property owner guest passes was discussed along with the question of charging gate fees on Sundays. Mr. Smith reported that over 8,000 property owner guest passes had been issued during the summer of 1982.

It was reported that more work was being done at the Amphitheater. Roofed gate entrances were being constructed according to the original plans for Amphitheater restoration. The architects for the Amphitheater restoration, Lawson, Knapp and Pulver, Architects, had received an award for that design in the fall of 1982. Dr. Hesse presented the award to John Hamilton to be hung in the Gebbie Foundation office since the Gebbie Foundation played a major role in the renovation of the Amphitheater. Other work was continuing at Lincoln Dormitory, Sherwood Studio, the Arts Quadrangle and Norton Hall. Painting of practice shacks and the Summer School Dormitory was also being completed.

An ad hoc committee had been appointed to consider Dr. Hesse's contract requests and during this committee's meeting, there was a discussion of evaluation reports of members of the senior staff. The President had routinely made evaluation reports of senior staff members in connection with recommendations for salary increases. Heretofore, the Chairman of the Board gave the evaluation of the President directly to the President on a one-to-one basis. It had been suggested that the practice should be changed, either by using a special committee or the Board as a whole. It was decided to appoint a committee composed of the Board Chairman and the Chairman of the Board's standing committees to function as evaluators of the President's performance in office. It was also recommended that the President, himself, make a personal assessment of his performance.

At the Annual Meeting recommendations for salary increases for senior staff were presented and approved. A recommended salary increase for the President was approved. A vote of confidence in the President was recommended for the success with which he had furthered and carried out the objectives of Chautauqua. It was voted to reaffirm the more-than-satisfactory assessment reported by the Evaluation Committee. (There was some indication that the President's own evaluation report had been similar to the committee's. Some less-than-satisfactory viewpoints were frankly addressed during the process.) It was also voted to approve a request by the President for a three-month leave of absence for self-renewal. Dr. Hesse had suggested that such a sabbatical every five years would be good Institutional policy no matter who was president. A vote of confidence in the Chairman of the Board was also voted for the manner in which he had conducted his office. The question of establishing a New York office for the president was left as open for study as was the possibility of extending a contract to the president for more than one year.

Mrs. Reading requested that receipts from potential donors be allowed to be included in the Second Century Campaign statistics even though they would not be in hand before the December 31, 1982 deadline. She said great efforts were being made to bring the campaign to a successful conclusion. The total figure had risen to nearly $7.1 million with only $1.4 million to be raised.

The proposed opening of a new parking area beyond the west lot was reported. The new lot construction would include paths for walking from the new lot through the west lot and across Route 394. Every attempt was being made to accommodate overflow crowds outside the Gates, especially since overflow crowds had become so frequent due to the popularity of Amphitheater programming.

The first phase of the North Shore Development has been closed with the Institution receiving the amount specified for that phase before the end of the year.

The restructuring of the golf course rates was explained. It is expected that more pre- and post-season players can be accommodated, with condominium use anticipated for off-season weeks, especially when the North Shore Development is fully realized and because the new bridge across Chautauqua Lake facilitates access from other parts of the county.

Elections were held, as follows: Howard G. Gibbs, chairman; John D. Hamilton, vice-chairman; Miriam Reading, vice-chairman; Robert B. Osburn, vice-chairman; Robert R. Hesse, president.

For committee chairmen and Executive Committee members: Robert O. Wilder, Nominating Committee; Mary Frances Cram, Program Committee; Robert B. Osburn, Buildings and Grounds Committee; Robert C. Holland, Religion Committee; Warren L. Hickman, Education, Youth and Recreation Committee; members-at-large, Executive Committee: Miriam Reading, Harry A. Logan and Paul E. Irion.

Ad-Hoc Personnel Committee: Malcolm Anderson, chairman, Paul M. Branch, David H. Carnahan, Mary Frances Cram, Arthur S. Holden, Jr. and James A. Zurn.

Other officers: W. Thomas Smith, vice president for operations; Joseph C. Johnson, secretary and treasurer; Carol M. White, assistant secretary.

The President's formal report usually is the climax of the Board's Annual Meeting and the 1982 report was no exception. It was future-oriented as Dr. Hesse declared. . . "we have every reason to believe based on the previous five years, ten years and indeed, 109 years, that this very special place has the capacity and capability to prosper."

He spoke first of the program as the heart of Chautauqua. "The key to the program is its diversity which begins to define the Chautauqua Experience." It is "a rich mixture that runs the gamut from a 13th century play to today's country-rock star; from the nuclear freeze advocates to Army Generals; from ministers to rabbis; from Blitzstein's 'Regina' to a Paganini concerto."

Reporting on theatre, he said that good theatre had been returned to Chautauqua and figures have proved that a strong market for live theatre exists.

The Opera Company has presented us with a particular set of opportunities, direction, balance, sound, acting and the ensemble of Chautauqua Opera has improved dramatically, he continued. He said he was working toward a higher degree of financial discipline and accountability for the opera. The fact that overall opera attendance has declined over the past several years even though subscriptions continue to rise, has determined the strategy of producing quality opera at manageable subsidy levels; that strategy is to offer a limited number of productions with a maximum number of performances playing to a maximum number of people at popular prices.

He praised the guest conductors and soloists with the orchestra and affirmed that Varujan Kojian was not afraid of choosing "the best." Orchestra concert attendance has increased by 15 per cent, he said.

An average of 6,000 or a full house attended most of the Amphitheater specials. New programs in the Religion Department, (the Youth Program, Continuing Education Seminars and the Youth Clergy Seminars), hold promise for the future while the traditional services and programs of this department continue on a high level. "We will honor Ralph Loew who has decided to retire at the end of the 1983 season. We will honor his contribution to Chautauqua. When we search for his successor, we will reexamine our objectives and give direction to this department for the '80s," Dr. Hesse said.

He continued by noting the tremendous strides that had been taken in teaching and learning. Numbers of students and numbers of course enrollments have increased in 1982, especially in the category of Special Studies. Intentional reductions of enrollments in music and dance were accompanied by student-quality increase. Concerts by the School of Music's two orchestras, voice and piano students recitals and displays of student art and dance skills rounded out the excitement that the Schools bring to Chautauqua and Chautauquans.

The busy schedule of the CLSC, the Program Center for Older Adults and the development of audio cassettes with study guides all support the basic adult education goals of the Institution.

Outdoor and indoor recreation on multi-age levels also enriched the summer for many Chautauquans.

The coordination of recreational opportunities has improved the benefits experienced by individual Chautauquans.

Improved marketing and promotional techniques have contributed to the success of the season which was marked by a climb in gate revenue to $1.75 million, a 14 per cent increase over 1981. Cost-free publicity through articles and features in diverse, high-profile national publications have carried the Chautauqua story throughout the country to a widely-varied accumulation of readers. This national outreach and visibility is just beginning and is part of its long-range goals.

Surveying the improvements that have been made by the Second Century Campaign, he summarized: we have been addressing the problems of the past and present and now we are setting the stage for the opportunities of the future. He completed his report by outlining some of those priorities.

As the holiday season approached, Dr. Hesse was spending considerable time on the Second Century Campaign and the 1982 Annual Fund. There still was needed $1,112,627 to meet the Second Century Campaign goal and $86,000 for the Annual Fund goal.

One of the encouragements received in December was news that the Gladys Brooks Foundation of New York City had awarded a $96,200 grant to the Second Century Campaign for the preservation of Smith Memorial Library. The commitment would enable Chautauqua to repair and insulate the library roof, install storm windows and a fire security system, rewire the building, modernize the restrooms and provide carpeting.

Another gift for $50,000 to the Second Century Campaign was received from Envirogas, Inc. of Hamburg and Mayville, New York. The gift would serve as a memorial to the late Willard F. Clarey, Sr.

Dr. Hesse also could report progress on some personnel matters. Jean-Pierre Bonnefoux who had performed frequently at Chautauqua would now become Artistic Director of the Dance School at Chautauqua. Jean-Pierre Bonnefoux had begun his dance career with George Balanchine at the New York City Ballet as principal dancer and partner of Patricia McBride. During the past four years Jean-Pierre has worked as a company director and as a choreographer for organizations such as the New York City Opera and the Metropolitan Opera Companies.

The full-season residence of Theater School at Chautauqua holds great promise, Dr. Hesse said as he explained that two directors would share management roles for The Acting Company Theater School at Chautauqua. Margot Harley has been named executive director; Michael Kahn, artistic director.

Dr. Hesse also reaffirmed that Dr. Nathan Gottschalk would direct the Music School in 1983 and conduct the Chautauqua Festival Orchestra.

Other good news was that Bellinger Hall had been booked solid by various groups who were planning ski weekends and that a sleigh rally was planned for January 30.

"As the new year rings in," Dr. Hesse wrote Chautauquans, "please keep Chautauqua and the hope of a bright future in your thoughts and prayers."

1982 PROGRAM FIGURES

Musicians
Neil Sedaka
1,000 Years of Jazz
The Letterman
The Rovers
Don McLean
Roberta Flack
U. S. Army Field Band
Gary Lakes
Paul Romero
Jerome Hines
Victor Borge
Nathaniel Rosen
Susan Dunn (D'Angelo comp. winner)
Kalichstein-Laredo-Robinson Trio
Carol Lawrence
Opera Apprentice Artists
Pat Boone
Marvin Hamlisch
Gustavo Romero
James Galway

Franklin Delano Roosevelt, Jr. resumes the Roosevelt tradition of speaking at Chautauqua.

Ferrante & Teicher
Shirley Verrett
Widespread Jazz Orchestra
Shlomo Mintz
Juice Newton/Tom Paxton
Chan-Hee Kim (Aldredge comp. winner)
Figgy Dugg
Misha & Cipa Dichter
The Glenn Miller Orchestra
Doc Severinsen
Livingston Taylor/Tom Chapin
June Anderson
Marian McPartland/Teddy Wilson
Frankie Laine & Teresa Brewer
Ruggiero Ricci
The Goldsmith-Hurlong Duo
The McLain Family Band
Mary Travers
Dukes of Dixieland
The 5th Dimension
Lynn Anderson
Bobby Goldsboro
Barbershop Harmony
    Chorus of the Erie Canal
    Nickel City Harmony Quartet
    Blue Grass Student Union Quartet
    Sigh-Tations
    Buffalo Guitar Quartet

Conductors
Varujan Kojian, Music Director
Walter Hendl
Stanislaw Skrowaczewski
Jonathan McPhee
John DeMain
Philippe Entremont
Lawrence Smith
Maxim Shostakovitch
Newton Wayland

Other Programs in the Amphitheater
Owen S. Rackleff
    Escoffier: King of Chefs
The Amazing Kreskin
Jerry Jarrett
    An Evening with Tevye
Phil Donahue

Platform Lecturers
Richard Valeriani
Edward Regan
Marvin Cetron
Edwin Meese III
General William C. Westmoreland
Dr. Chirstian Barnard
Dr. Jack Lippes
Dr. Estlle Ramey
Al Rosenfeld
Dr. Ashley Montagu
B. Carter Randall
Leopold Kohr
Kirkpatrick Sale
Thomas Haggai
Jody Powell

Sarah McClendon
Helen Thomas
Laurence Barrett
Franklin D. Roosevelt, Jr.
Dr. William Brown
Buster Crabbe
Dr. Theron Randolph
Dr. Joel Elkes
Dr. Lendon Smith
The Rev. Ralph Abernathy
Harold Krents
Jack Ossoffsky
Cleveland Amory
Sonia Johnson
John Ciardi
Bette Bao Lord
John Gardner
Belva Plain
Alex Haley
John Houseman
Edward Vilella
Dr. Karl Haas
Bernard Kalb
John P. Wallach
Major General John Kirk Singlaub
Dr. John Stoessinger
Ambassador Richard Townsend Davies

Chaplains
Moorhead Kennedy (Sunday only)
The Rev. James Ford
Dr. Bruce Thielemann
Bishop Lesslie Newbigin
The Rev. Angus MacQueen
Bishop John S. Spong
The Rev. Yvonne Delk
The Rev. George Williamson
Dr. Fred Craddock
Dr. Robert H. Schuller (Sunday only)
The Rev. William N. Jackson

Additional Speakers at Morning Devotionals
The Rev. Charles Ransom
The Rev. William N. Jackson

Religion Department Lecturers
The Rev. Robert Benne
Dr. Bene Outka
Dr. Carnegie Samuel Calian
Dr. James M. Wall
Rabbi Alexander Schindler
Rabbi Israel Mowshowitz
Dr. Leonard Sweet
Dr. Robert McAfee Brown
Sydney Thomson Brown
Dr. Edmund Pellegrino
The Rev. Harold Wilke
Mrs. Charlotte Shedd
Dr. William Rusch
Dr. Paul McCleary

Operas
Cynthia Auerbach, Artistic Director

South Pacific
    Mark D. Flint, Conductor
    Dorothy Frank Danner, Director
The Barber of Seville
    John DeMain, Conductor
    Cynthia Auerbach, Director
Regina
    John DeMain, Conductor
    Cynthia Auerbach, Director
La Traviata
    Varujan Kojian, Conductor
    Cynthia Auerbach, Director

Dance
Patricia McBride and Bart Cook, Ballet
Starr Danias and Gregory King, Ballet
Edward Villella and Dancers, Lectures/Demonstration

Theater
The Acting Company
John Houseman, Producing Artistic Director

The Country Wife
Twelfth Night
Tartuffe

Music School Festival Orchestra
Nathan Gottschalk, Conductor

Soloists
Charlene Chadwick
    Joseph Donohue, Narrator
Nadia Salerno-Sonnenberg
Nina Kennedy
Eugene Perry
Ballet Students from Chautauqua Dance Festival Company, Statia Sublette, Director
Concerto Competition
    Russell Stern
    Coryn Lerner
    Jeffrey Rathbun
    Janet Harmon
    Mary Floriano
    Luanne Berk
    Evan Wilson
    Marie-Michele Sorel
    Kirby Nunez
    Luis Baer
    Da-Hong Seetoo
    Hyoung Joon Chang

Da-Hong Seetoo, Sigma Alpha Iota Winner

CAA
Jack Beal and Sondra Freckelton, Jurors for the Chautauqua Art Association's National Exhibition of American Art

The completion of the Bellinger Hall Dormitory Complex by the Gebbie Foundation in memory of Mrs. Geraldine Gebbie Bellinger is a gift of immeasurable and long-enduring benefit to students and others who will be using the multifaceted facilities for many years to come. Mrs. Bellinger during her lifetime was deeply interested in youth and students. This view of the inner court is a slightly different one, accenting the livable, pleasant spirit of the extensive six-unit complex

8

New Directions in Rhythm with the Past

"The beginning of each new year is a time when we pause to reflect upon our many blessings," Dr. Hesse said in his January, 1983 Special Report to Chautauquans. Among the blessings he had to declare was the continuing progress of the Second Century Campaign which had passed the $8 million mark. "We are hopeful that the entire Second Century Campaign will be concluded successfully by June 30th," he said.[1]

"A great blessing was recorded in the successful completion of the Annual Fund Drive," he continued. "The Institution wrapped up its 1982 campaign for operating expenses with a total of $903,440, signifying the largest amount of money raised in one year for this purpose in Chautauqua's history." He congratulated Ed Boyle, the Annual Fund chairman, and all the many friends who had helped meet this vital goal.

He made other announcements that he obviously classified as good news.

He had appointed a new Women's Club President, Mrs. Rex Stowers Clements. Mrs. Clements had been active in the field of religion and education throughout her career.

Dr. Hesse also named Robert Gilson to fill the vacancy of Art Center Coordinator. Mr. Gilson had taught photography at Chautauqua for the past two summers.

Concerning the CSO concerts for the 1983 season, Dr. Hesse reported that Varujan Kojian, Music Director, would conduct five concerts during July and three in August. Soloists who would be appearing with Mr. Kojian in July included Carol Wincenc, flute, Phyllis Diller at a Pops concert and Lynn Harrell, cello. The National Federation of Music Clubs Competition winner would also be scheduled. Other soloists who had been suggested were violinists Uck Kim, Jaime Laredo and Pianist Byron Janis.

He also announced several guest conductors, Philippe Entremont, Walter Hendl and Newton Wayland.

He completed his Special Report by inviting Chautauquans to return for the "I Love New York" Winter Festival planned for January 30th. Snow has finally arrived, he reported.

By the time the Board's Executive Committee had met in February, some of the leftover duties for staff and committees had been completed. Along with the Capital budget which had been referred back to the Buildings and Grounds Committee, there was one small item that held some general interest. This was the purchase of pagers for Fire Department members to eliminate the need for fire sirens except for actual fires. Ninety-five per cent of fire department calls at Chautauqua are for medical emergencies and the interruption of programs for these frequent, but private situations has often been deplored, especially during symphony concerts. To maintain the fire department's excellent service, but avoid the unnecessary use of fire sirens, the expenditure for pagers, which would be shared evenly by the Institution and the Fire Department, seemed a wise investment.

Already in February the sale of season gate tickets had exceeded the figures of the second month of 1982 and inquiries about Summer School courses were showing a tremendous increase, especially when they were compared with the 1981 figures. Dr. Hesse distributed to the members of the Executive Committee the new designs of Schools brochures which had been strategically keyed to the levels of current interest.

Also at the February meeting the sale of the Egyptian statue was authorized. This statue which had been discovered in a crate at the Main Gate four-plus years before had been definitely identified as a gift to the Chautauqua Assembly in 1887 by the Egyptian Exploration Fund. The Institution was thus free to dispose of it as it chose.

Miriam Reading shared an update of Second Century Campaign progress and discussed how current goals as well as future plans might be fulfilled. She also pointed out that fund raising strategy in the future should be different than before the Capital Campaign, all of which was related to the Institution's total development program.

A list of physical improvement priorities and cost estimates, as determined by the Staff and by the Buildings Committee was presented for discussion and approval. Some of the monies for the projects had already been received, and Mr. Logan commented that the $62,000 for the Arts and Crafts Quadrangle had been committed (through the Helen Temple Logan Trust).

Dr. Hesse observed that as the Capital Campaign winds down, a plan should be developed for continued fund raising.

Concerning the report of the 1982 Annual Fund, Chairman Ed Boyle asked for guidance on the Symphony Patron program and the church collections which are no longer considered as part of the Annual Fund. After discussion, the Committee moved that the Symphony Patron program be changed to an endowment program specifically for the Symphony and that those funds be applied to the NEA Challenge Grant match. Thus, the Symphony Patron program would be definitely removed from the Annual Fund for giving purposes. A gift of $150.00 would provide two reserved seats; $75.00, one reserved seat. The church collections, on the other hand, were moved back into the Annual Fund. The Annual Fund goal for 1983 was set at $970,000.

Mr. Osburn distributed a short form of Institution Rules and Regulations which had been drawn at the request of the Liaison Committee of the Property Owners Association.

Progress on financing and the renovation and restoration of the Athenaeum Hotel was reported in some detail.

The treasurer, Mr. Johnson, said that although the final audit had not been received, preliminary results show that 1982 had been a very favorable year for the Hotel. He said that after dealing with many banks, it was decided on January 28 to accept the offer of Lincoln First Bank of Rochester to underwrite the sale of the bonds on a "best effort" basis with another investment banking company in Rochester and with backup from Bankers Trust of New York. The sale of bonds was opened on February 6, he said, and the entire issue was sold by 3:00 p. m. that day. He anticipated a closing date of March 10.

Another important matter was broached before this meeting of the Executive Committee was concluded. It had to do with the proposal of a new organization chart for the Board of Trustees. The idea had started with the Nominating Committee during the summer of 1982. Dr. Hickman, as a current member of that committee, reported on a meeting of an extended group of that committee. He said that this group felt that there was a need for a Finance Committee within the Board for the purpose of long-range planning; and that there was need for more coordination among Board committees before bringing plans to the Board, especially in overlapping areas. The Executive Committee discussed at some length the new chart which delineated the new suggestions. One of the questions that surfaced was the advisability of having a Chairman of the Board separate from a Chairman of the Executive Committee. Present problems of communication, extra work-loads and the need to draw further on the abilities available within the Board were frankly addressed by members of the Executive Committee. After the discussion, it was agreed that Mr. Gibbs, Dr. Hesse and Mr. Price would study the entire reorganization chart and proposed changes in the By-Laws and present their recommendation to the Executive Committee in March.

Following through on this, Mr. Price had mailed to the trustees before the next meeting the recommendations concerning the plan.

The advisability of having a separate Chairman of the Executive Committee seemed to have wide acceptance and led to the question of how such a chairman would be elected. The Executive Committee finally passed a motion (in March) that the Chairman of the Executive Committee be elected by the full Board with names of candidates to be submitted to the Nominating Committee by any/all Board members who will then submit to the full Board the names of candidates who are willing to stand for election.

Then it was voted that Mr. Price would draft the proposal for the restructuring of the Executive Committee as well as the changes in the By-Laws. These would be mailed to the members of the Board prior to action scheduled for the May 14 Board Meeting. If the changes are approved, a special meeting of the Board would be set for June 25 for the sole purpose of electing a Chairman of the Executive Committee.

It was determined that there would be only one full Board meeting during the season, on August 27.

Dr. Hesse then made a lengthy report.

He and Mr. Johnson explained the financial statement. The good positive cash flow was due, in part, Dr. Hesse said to the early deadline for discounted ticket sales. Total season tickets sold to date were 1,145.

He reported that Sotheby's in New York would handle the sale of the Egyptian statue by auction sometime in June.

Dr. Hesse reminded the Committee of his efforts to achieve television from Chautauqua. "The possibility of cable television is an exciting one," he said, "both for the orchestra and the Institution." He remained hopeful that funding would be found. (As it turned out, this was one dream Dr. Hesse was unable to fulfill for Chautauqua.)

The orchestra's complaints concerning the acoustics of McKnight Hall where extra rehearsals are held were being studied, he said.

Long-range planning came back into consideration with Mr. Gibbs' suggesting that he and the President draw up some guidelines for future discussion. It seemed to be generally thought that standing committees would have plans for their corresponding areas. Dr. Hesse said that he had asked his staff to gather documentation to assist in long range Planning.

In April The Chautauquan announced exciting "big names" for the 1983 program:

Grammy Award Winner Melissa Manchester, who had spent some summers at Chautauqua when her father was a member of the Chautauqua Symphony; Roger Williams, "Mr. Piano;" Pete Seeger and Arlo Guthrie, "folk singers par excellence;" Pete Fountain, "king of Dixieland jazz;" Emmylou Harris, "the first lady of contemporary music;" Shields and Yarnell, internationally known mimes; and Rod McKuen, "poet, composer, performer."

Dinah Shore and Woody Herman, two of the nation's most popular performers, were to open the 110th season.

"Big names" were also to be associated with theatre at Chautauqua. Directing The Acting Company's production of "The Cradle Will Rock" (August 25-27) would be the company's own artistic director and co-founder, John Houseman.

It was also announced that the Acting Company would be selecting fourteen talented actors from the finalist competitions of the American College Theatre Festival (ACTF), regionally and nationally, for the formation of a touring company. These actors would further develop their skills at Chautauqua in the summer before beginning a 26-week tour as The American National Theatre and Academy Touring Company (ANTA).

The Religion Department, also seemed to have filled its regular program with noteworthy and respected names. Coretta Scott King was to bring the opening sermon following the offical "three taps of the gavel" by President Hesse.

The announcement of morning lecturers in April further stimulated early ticket sales and encouraged vacationers to decide on arrival times. Former Presidential candidate John Anderson would appear at Chautauqua during National Affairs Week, along with George Gallup, Jr., Robert Taft, Jr., and Eugene McCarthy. The Science Editor of The New York Times, Walter Sullivan, would be speaking during Science Week.

Great Moments in the Forefront Week would bring Carl Stokes, America's first black mayor.

CLSC book selections and authors' summer visits to Chautauqua were also announced in the April Chautauquan, providing still another dimension to the season's program. Book selections were: *A Sentimental Education* by Joyce Carol Oates; *The Human Cycle* by Colin M. Turnbull; *Blue Highways: A Journey Into America* by William Least Heat Moon; and *Chinabound: A Fifty Year Memoir,* by John King Fairbank.

It was also announced that Sergiu Comissiona, former Music Director of the CSO, would return for a single appearance as guest conductor in the concert with Bryon Janis.

A referral service under the supervision of Ed Keating, Main Gate Manager and year-round Operations employee, was facilitating accommodations' procedures. Old and new Chautauquans were discovering new ease in housing arrangements by calling a special Colonnade number.

Significant to the effort to upgrade housing at Chautauqua came the brief announcement that The Venus guest house, located at the corner of Miller Avenue and South Terrace Avenue would be razed for the proposed construction of a South Terrace condominium.

The Board of Trustees, meeting May 14, 1983, moved to adopt the changes in the By-Laws as recommended by the Executive Committee. An additional motion which recommended the procedure for election of the Executive Committee Chairman was also passed.

On covering the current financial picture, Dr. Hesse stated that the Institution was in a strong financial position. The Audit Report for the 1982 fiscal year which had been mailed to the Board was detailed by Mr. Johnson for the Board and the Audit Report was accepted.

A report of the tornado which had struck Chautauqua, Chautauqua Shores and other nearby areas was given by Mr. Smith. The Yacht Club storage building had been destroyed, he said, and the sewerage treatment plant had been severely damaged. Also, some trees had been uprooted; others were partially mutilated by the force of the wind. Other portions of the county suffered greater extremities, he said. Two women living outside Chautauqua had lost their lives in the quick devastation of the storm and some houses and barns were completely lost. He commended the outstanding service performed by the Chautauqua Police Department, the Sheriff's Patrol and the Chautauqua Volunteer Fire Department.

Dr. Hesse announced that he had appointed Mary-Therese Mennino as Program Coordinator. Ms. Mennino had just completed eight years with the Wolf Trap Foundation for the Performing Arts where as director of program she had produced among other events a three-day international jazz festival and a three-day Bach festival. She holds a degree in speech and drama from the Catholic University of America in Washington, D. C.

Mary-Therese Mennino

The Program Committee recommended that the upcoming renewal of the orchestra contract follow normal procedures used in handling all other union and non-union contracts and should be conducted exclusively by the President of the Institution and his administration. The Board approved the recommendation.

The question of more student housing was addressed by Mr. Osburn on behalf of the Buildings and Grounds Committee. The plan proposed by the Committee involved the sale of three Institution properties: the Ames Avenue Dormitory, the Arcade and the Pennsylvania Apartments with the expectation that the funds realized from the proposed sales would cover the cost of a new wing of Bellinger Hall. The original plans for the Bellinger Hall complex included additional dormitory wings but none of these had been built, and the need for them was becoming increasingly apparent.

Mr. Johnson read letters of disclosure from Mr. Heinz and Mr. Follansbee relating to the proposed purchase of the Arcade. The letters indicated that one of the parties interested in purchasing the Arcade had also indicated a desire to contract with Chautauqua Enterprises, Inc. to assist him in construction and marketing of the renovated residential units which would be created. He had also indicated that he had retained the law firm with which Mr. Follansbee is associated for advice and legal services should the Institution agree to sell the building to him. Mr. Heinz is president of Chautauqua Enterprises, Inc.

Mr. Osburn explained to the Board the general terms and conditions under which the Committee recommended the Institution invite proposals from developers for the renovation of the Arcade:

The property should be developed for multi-unit residential purposes;

All renovation and rehabilitation should conform in all respects to state and federal rules and guidelines with respect to certified historic structures;

It must be approved by the President of Chautauqua and the Buildings and Grounds Committee of the Board of Trustees;

The purchase price be fixed by the President on recommendation of the Buildings and Grounds Committee after reviewing an appraisal made by a qualified appraiser and such other data which seems relevant;

Invitation for proposals should be given reasonable circulation and advertisement.

Concerning the proposed sale of the Institution property known as 15 Ames Avenue, it was recommended that it be offered for sale on a cash basis to the highest bidder under a system of sealed bids in accordance to the procedures normally followed by the Institution with the right of the Institution to reject any or all bids.

This same procedure was recommended for the proposed sale of the Pennsylvania Apartments designated on the official map as Lots 712 and 713.

The Committee further resolved that the sale of these properties could generate sufficient funds to underwrite the cost of the new wing at Bellinger Hall and that construction should be completed in time for the 1984 season.

However, the Committee specified that no offer for the purchase and development of the Arcade nor 15 Ames Avenue be accepted unless the President is satisfied that adequate alternate provision for student housing will be assured for the 1984 season.

Another proposal which had been received by the Buildings and Grounds Committee was explained. A property owner had expressed interest in purchasing the lots at the corner of Ramble and Palestine Avenues for the purpose of building a sculpture garden. An endowment for the maintenance of the sculpture garden had been promised. The Buildings and Grounds Committee was recommending that the profit realized from the sale of this property could be used to buy

electric conveyances which would aid in the Institution's transportation network during the season.

The Board gave general approval and authorization for negotiations on this sale to proceed.

In another matter, the Board decided to lease vehicles and employ drivers during the season to transport the Institution's program guests to and from the Grounds.

Mrs. Reading appealed to Board members to cooperate in any way possible with solicitations and gifts for the Second Century Campaign in a real effort to complete the campaign successfully by June 30, 1983.

Mr. Boyle expressed his enthusiasm over the appointment of his new co-chairman, Richard Bechtolt, and reported on a recent meeting of the Annual Fund Committee. He reported that the Institution had just received an award of $3,300 from the National Opera Institute in Washington to be used for part of the cost of engaging young American singers here in the opera program. Mr. Heid, Annual Fund Director, noted that while the National Opera Institute is not a major award-making organization, the award to Chautauqua was the largest made to any opera company and was greatly valued by the Institution.

Dr. Holland reported that the search for a replacement for Dr. Loew had begun. Dr. Hesse had earlier named the members of that committee: Dr. Holland, Mrs. Patricia Dietly and Mr. Redington.

An upbeat tone pervaded the President's Special Report in early June. He announced that Patti Lupone of "Evita" fame would bring a real flavor of Broadway to the production of "The Cradle Will Rock" in the June productions. Also, the original Acting Company

This interior view of Newton Hall, Chautauqua's Museum, gives some idea of the Collections which were housed there.

cast which presented "Pericles" on Broadway would be performing that work in Norton Hall before the start of the opera season.

Dr. Hesse also announced the purchase of three People Movers, similar to those at Disney World. Electrically powered, they are silent and easily boarded. "These will be a fine addition to Chautauqua's transportation system," he observed.

In announcing the future sale of Institution-owned buildings which the Board had approved in May, he also said that the Institution had for sale nine building lots (90 x 60 feet, lake view and located within Chautauqua Institution).

Dr. Hesse also made a plea for funds that could qualify for the NEA Challenge Grant Match, desperately needed by June 30th. He reminded Chautauquans that Symphony Patron gifts would help match the Challenge. Nor did he forget the Annual Fund which provides 18% of the Institution's annual budget. He reported that Jack Nord, President of Union National, Inc., would serve as Jamestown Annual Fund Chairman. Mr. Nord has set the Jamestown goal at $188,000 for 1983. Dr. Hesse expressed gratitude for his meetings with Chautauquans in Erie and Buffalo. Such meetings of Chautauquans in their home communities for programs and fellowship have been a traditional source of strength to the Institution through the years.

Then he held out great promise for the surprises Chautauquans would enjoy when they returned: "the spectacular" Athenaeum, the restoration of the "lovely Smith Memorial Library" and "the revival of the very useful Arts and Crafts Quadrangle."

"You will have much to explore. We've been working very hard to make your summer a good one. Come and enjoy!" he concluded.

On June 25, 1983, the Board of Trustees met to elect a chairman of the executive committee and thus activate the recent organizational changes adopted in May. Four individual trustees had agreed to be candidates: Miriam Reading, David Carnahan, Warren Hickman and Robert Osburn.

After the second ballot, the tellers announced that Warren Hickman had received a majority of the votes cast and had thus been elected as Chairman of the Executive Committee.

After staff members, including the President of the Institution, returned to the meeting, a resolution concerning the NEA Challenge Grant was adopted, as follows: That gifts of unrestricted funds received by the Institution on or before June 30, 1983, be designated as restricted funds and added to the permanent endowment for the performing arts in such an amount and in such a manner as may be necessary to complete the conditions of the National Endowment for the Arts Challenge Grant to the Institution.[1]

The Board also passed a motion of commendation for the great efforts of the administration toward the renovation and restoration of the Athenaeum Hotel.

That meeting of the Board of Trustees was to be remembered as a significant milestone in the Institution's efforts, through its Board of Trustees, to chart the future course of Chautauqua.

1983 the Egyptian statue, Marenpthah, is ready for auction June 11 in New York City.

Meanwhile, the Egyptian statue Merenptah had been sold at a Sotheby Parke Bernet auction on June 11 for the astounding sum of $310,000. Dr. Hesse, who went to New York to be present at the sale, admitted it was exciting to see the final bid price. The buyer also was obligated to pay Sotheby's an extra 10 per cent of the purchase price, making the total cost of the statue $341,000. The Institution was also obligated to pay a 10 per cent fee to Sotheby's. The money from the sale of the statue was to be set aside by the Institution in a special fund. The squatting statue of Merenptah represented a glorious, but early period of expansion at Chautauqua when the School of Theology through its Department of Archeology was developing the Museum under the guidance of Dr. J. E. Kittredge. Dr. Kittredge served as the secretary of the Archeological Society at Chautauqua. Through his influence and that of Bishop Vincent, as well, the Egyptian Exploration Fund made a sizable gift to Chautauqua University. (The Fund also gave a similar gift to the Boston Museum of Fine Arts.) Dr. Kittredge had grand hopes for the Museum, that it would steadily expand so that in the field of Biblical archeology, it would rank someday in importance with the British Museum. While his dreams were not realized, the Museum artifacts, plaster casts, books, maps and other materials enriched the educational experience of many Chautauquan students and for a time added prestige to Chautauqua University. The Assembly Herald of August 15, 1888, announced the arrival of the Collection from the Egyptian Exploration Fund. It consisted of 456 articles including lamps, amphora, pottery of the Roman period, bronze figures of gods and goddesses, coins, scarebs, moulds, statuettes, mosaics, bronze lattice work and, grandest of all, a large squatting statue. "The inscriptions still legible on the statue are sufficient to inform the reader of hieroglyphlcs that this is a monument to a former priest of the goddess Vati, Menepthah by name (spelling different from the one now used) and that the passersby are asked to offer oblations in his honor. The articles were all taken from excavations made of cities in the land of Goshen." W. M. F. Petri, British archeologist, had been in charge of the expedition which yielded these treasures.

In the August 20, 1888 issue, a general article on the

The "grand staircase" adds new openness to the Athenaeum veranda.

Museum placed the dates of the excavations as 1883-1886. The statue had been placed in the center of the Museum in a place of prominence. It was said to have been carved out of solid granite and that it weighed 1,100 pounds.

The Assembly Herald article continued to catalogue all of the contents of the Museum.

The discovery of the statue at the Main Gate in 1978, sixty or more years after the Museum was dismantled and converted to other uses remains an intriguing mystery. There are elements of sadness in the loss of the glories of antiquity which the statue represents and in the loss of Chautauqua's own temporal hopes for a continuing archeological museum. But there is also wonder at the way Chautauqua's past sometimes reaches dramatically into the present.

The week before the 1983 season began the Institution invited groups of Chautauquans to the Athenaeum Hotel on successive evenings so that they might see firsthand the completed first phase of the hotel's rehabilitation. W. Thomas Smith, vice presi-

dent and hotel manager, who had worked closely with the architects and had served as general contractor and interior designer, enjoyed the delight and astonishment of Institution employees, other hotel owners and innkeepers, the generous supporters of the Institution and others who were invited for special tours of the building.

There was plenty of credit to go around. Dr. Hesse's leadership was responsible for the preparation of basic conditions which made the project possible and he was a participant on all levels as the tremendous undertaking went forward.

Joseph C. Johnson as the Institution's chief financial officer worked on the economics of the venture. The financing was indeed a building program itself. It took many months of planning, detailed work and cooperation with great numbers of people. Certain Board members of the Hotel Corporation and Chautauqua Institution were also closely involved with the development of the financing.

One of the major problems was timing. If the work was to be finished for the 1983 season, Mr. Smith could not wait until February to place orders for wallpaper, carpet and light fixtures. Fortunately, the 1982 hotel profits allowed the first basic work to be started in the fall. The eventual sale of the IDA-sponsored 12-year tax-exempt bonds, although it was as late as February, provided the happy ending for Mr. Smith's necessary early shopping by "credit card."

This was what he faced: The redecoration of all of the hotel bedrooms, but also the creation of new rooms. The space formerly occupied for public bathrooms upstairs could in some cases become guest rooms. Some small rooms could be arranged in suites or as adjoining rooms. Some rooms could be left large enough to accommodate families. Mr. Smith, as manager, could best plan what sizes of rooms were needed to satisfy the demands of his clientele. With the rearrangement of rooms also came the plan to include a private bath with every room. Mr. Smith revealed great ingenuity in handling the structural problems of some of the rooms so that he could provide comfortable, private quarters with modern conveniences while preserving the 19th century aura of the building.

The improvement of the guest rooms represented a tremendous accomplishment, for each of the 160 rooms were freshly painted and papered. Each now had its own bath, heating and air conditioning. Wallpaper had been coordinated with carpet shades. Approximately eighty different wallpapers were personally selected by Mr. Smith. Most are beautifully Victorian. The four corner rooms facing the lake were designed to be distinctly different: One ultra Victorian with dark maroon paper; one modern with white-flocked beige paper; one, almost Federal in its design; and one, summer Victorian with wicker furniture.

The new dining room wallpaper is a daintier version of the pink and red flowers that Chautauquans were used to. The wainscoting and columns had been freshly painted. The tops of the columns had been lifted from their places above the dropped ceiling and reattached at the lower ceiling line where they may be seen for the first time in many years. New china and new napkin rings were selected. The pink of the wallpaper with a touch of mulberry appears in the new china pattern while the Athenaeum seal in mulberry appears on the new napkin rings. Dining on the porch became possible when this end of the porch was redesigned to match the octagonal extrusion at the upper end.

The safety exits from the dining room lead adroitly to the new tables.

Of course, the exterior appearance of the hotel was the most striking change in 1983. Mr. Smith's choice of colors was a deliberate attempt to draw attention to the structure's achitectural details. The all-wood massiveness of the 1881 building is lightened by folk art, open-work scrolls on wooden brackets, carved bracket supports around the roof, narrow indentations on the long columns, and the restrained, but dressy window frames.

The main structure was painted what Mr. Smith chose to name Athenaeum parchment. It is similar to the hotel's original putty color. White paint glistens on the columns and window frames. Beige is used for contrast along the sawn art which skirts the deep foundation area, and on the corner posts. Mauve beige is streaked into the column indentations serving to emphasize their imposing height. A dark mulberry shade tops the porch railings, the main beams in the porches' ceilings and the three main double-door entrances. A light shade of green outlines the inner facings of the windows. The Annex has also been painted parchment with white trim.

But even more striking than the new colors of paint was the opening of the veranda on the lake side.

The long veranda had been famous for its unbroken lines of high-backed rocking chairs. Mr. Smith envisioned "a grand staircase" which would begin at the mid-point of the veranda and lead to the spacious Athenaeum lawns below. When it was built, it did, indeed, fulfill Mr. Smith's expectations. It added not only graceful beauty but an additional exit from the hotel, a desired safety measure in itself.

As it was designed, the first set of steps lead to a middle platform. There the steps divide, curving down on either side. Immediately in front of the staircase at ground level, a fountain and a reflecting pool add aesthetic grace. On either side of the middle platform large candelabra, lighted electrically, follow the style of the lights on either side of the double doors which lead from the hotel lobby to the veranda. A pleasant sense of openness has been achieved while the integrity of the hotel's architecture has not been diffused since the change is considered compatible to the period which the hotel represents.

In the present restoration, the steps leading from the veranda to Janes Avenue have been eliminated, and it is on this newly-created circular space that outside dining is made available.

In addition to these eye-catching changes, essential, practical improvements were made. New concrete flooring was laid in the kitchen areas and new equipment was purchased, including two new walk-in refrigerators, new convection ovens, new hoods over pastry ovens and much more.

The entire strengthening of the hotel's foundation was a significant part of the project. The beautifully handcut stones in some sections remain strong and are an example of the craftsmanship of another century, but in other sections, new beams, new concrete bases for support and concrete blocks were engineered into the structure.

The Lake Erie Concert Choir joined with the Chautauqua Choir at both services on the first Sunday of the season. Conforming to tradition, President Hesse officiated at the opening "of this place of distinction." "Bishop Vincent in 1903 spoke of Chautauqua as an idea. He said, 'A place may give birth to a thought or a thought may give distinction to a place.' He defined Chautauqua as 'simply that of completeness; it conceives that every human soul on the green globe has a right to all the light, the liberty, the culture, the character it can find opportunity and has desire to attain; that one's endowment is as well the measure of his duty as of his privilege, and that therefore everybody should be inspired, directed, and aided in the

The lobby also was redecorated. It has been restored structurally with new steel beams that don't show, but provide, "solid comfort" to patrons.

great work of self-improvement, on all sides of his nature, and all this for the enrichment of his own life, the good of his race, and the glory of his maker.' "

"I am proud to say that in 1983 Chautauqua holds true to his ideal, his dream, his promise. Chautauqua continues to follow its dream, built on a firm foundation, reaching out to extend itself to the limits of its resources to provide the experiences which enable each of us to grow. . ."

At the morning service, Coretta Scott King spoke boldly for "active nonviolent resistance to evil."

As the season began, "the same things" were happening, but as always at Chautauqua, they seemed new, for everyone was feeling the joy of the place. A Juror, but a different Juror, Phyllis Kind of the Phyllis Kind Galleries in Chicago and New York City, had selected 78 pieces out of 2,603 entries to hang in the annual National Exhibition of American Painting at the Chautauqua Art Association. The Women's Club was holding its first meeting under its new president, Mrs. Clements, who wasn't new after all. She had been an Athenaeum waitress when she was in school. The Tennis Association under Tennis Pro Jeff Miller, a life-long Chautauquan, had already started its season and was anticipating good play, tournaments, clinics and social events. The well-remembered Kenneth Close was showing films on India and Ceylon. The lively Opera Guild was bidding for new members. It had announced its first operalogue with Cynthia Auerbach, COA Artistic Director, as the first speaker, and

Dr. Hesse leaves the Colonnade to go to the Press Conference to announce with Mr. Gibbs, the successful completion of the Second Century Campaign.

an elegant buffet reception for members after the first production of "The Merry Widow."

In the meantime, "The Cradle Will Rock" opened in Norton Hall and National Affairs was the focus at the 10:45 hour. Strong winds welcomed the first races of the Chautauqua Yacht Club and the Softball League met for organization. The Bird, Tree and Garden Club heard about and saw slides of English Gardens, while Clubs and Schools signed up their contingents of participants.

One newsworthy event was an afternoon follow-up to the National Affairs Lecture: A Eugene McCarthy-Robert Taft Debate over Reaganomics. It was presented as a seminar with a Schools fee of three dollars. Other seminars to be coordinated with morning lecture topics were promised for later in the summer.

As John B. Anderson, independent presidential candidate in 1980, arrived as the last speaker for National Affairs Week, additional excitement became apparent. The Chautauqua grapevine began whispering the unbelievable news that the NEA Challenge Grant Match had been met and that Chautauqua could close out its Second Century Campaign immediately. Chautauqua had achieved its $8.5 Million goal!

At a press conference on the Athenaeum Hotel veranda the next morning, July 1, 1983, Dr. Hesse and Mr. Gibbs jointly made the announcement that after four years, the first national capital and endowment fund drive undertaken by Chautauqua had been successful. Mr. Gibbs gave special recognition to Mrs. Miriam Reading for the leadership she had provided as national chairman of the Second Century Campaign and for her continuing effectiveness as Vice Chairman of the Board of Trustees. A second acknowledgement was made to current, former and honorary trustees who together contributed $2.4 Million to the Campaign.

"The triumph was achieved also through great volunteer leadership and a great love for Chautauqua," Dr. Hesse observed, as he expressed his pride in the completed task. "This exciting achievement includes the attainment of our National Endowment for the Arts Challenge Grant Match."

On the Platform before Mr. Anderson could begin his lecture, Dr. Hesse and Mr. Gibbs once more announced to the Chautauqua audience the happy news that Chautauqua had not only completed its Second Century goal, but had fulfilled its NEA obligation. The $250,000 grant received from the NEA was Chautauqua's to keep and what's more, there had been three times that amount in matching funds given to Chautauqua by other donors.

Since the beginning of the campaign, Chautauqua had raised $4.2 Million for capital improvement and $4.3 Million for endowments.

"We are thrilled with our present success and will take a breather for a few days before we begin work again to make Chautauqua even finer than it is now," Dr. Hesse said.

It was unfortunate that Mrs. Reading was unable to be present for the announcement of the end of the campaign, but she was in touch with Chautauqua by telephone from her home in Milwaukee. Special recognition was later given to Miriam Reading for her exceptional leadership during the Second Century Campaign.

Interdisciplinary exchanges were available to Chautauqua Summer School students in 1983 as a major result of Director Redington's planning and negotiations with faculty members.

For example, opera apprentices could study stage combat under a member of the Theater School faculty; some voice students would benefit from a new opportunity requirement to be a part of the Opera Chorus; and theater students would be able to study stage movement from dance faculty members. Music School students for some time have been assigned to ensemble playing in addition to their individual instrumental studies.

The School of Dance under Jean-Pierre Bonnefoux was experiencing some new directions toward ballet, although modern dance was still included in the curriculum. The Chautauqua School of Dance was divided into two groups: The Dance Festival Company and the Advance Dancers. The Martha Graham technique was taught as well as ballet. Included in the faculty were: Andrei Kramarevsky, former principal dancer with the Bolshoi Ballet and now a faculty member with the School of American Ballet; Helgi Tomasson, principal dancer from the New York City Ballet; and Violette Verdy, former principal dancer with the New York City Ballet and newly named Director of the Boston Ballet.

Students from the School of Dance would appear three times in Amphitheater programs during the summer, once with the Chautauqua Festival Orchestra and twice with the Chautauqua Symphony Orchestra.

The Theater School this year was a new educational venture co-sponsored by the Institution and The Acting Company.

The School planned to focus on the individual development of about thirty actors and actresses who would be divided into two groups: the Professional Studio and the Summer Theater Workshop. The Professional Studio would be composed of students who had completed graduate programs in theater, while the Workshop would enroll undergraduate or graduate level students.

The Music School which traditionally is one of the most active at Chautauqua was strengthened by the six-week residency of the New Arts Trio. This Trio which had won the Naumburg Award for Chamber Music in 1980 was well-known to Chautauqua audiences. Also, Marlena Kleinman Malas of the Manhattan School of Music had been engaged as chairperson of the Voice Department. Voice students would not only have the experience gained from opera and other workshops, but also from singing at the Sacred Song Services and in solo recitals. Ozan Marsh returned as the head of the Piano Department and the Chautauqua Festival Orchestra continued to attract top college and graduate level musicians. The Chautauqua Youth Orchestra was designed to serve talented high schoolers from across the northeastern part of the country.

Twenty-five to thirty full-time college and graduate level art students were enrolled at the Art Center while

John Anderson, former Presidential candidate, and Howard G. Gibbs visit on the Athenaeum veranda.

an open enrollment of five hundred was expected during the summer for shorter periods of study.

Benefits to Chautauqua students are similar to those which all Chautauquans experience as they participate in the aesthetic enjoyment of all the arts and take advantage of formal and informal intellectual discussions which are widely available.

The joy of learning is the added mystique of a Chautauqua vacation where learning is a form of recreation. So the over-one-hundred special studies courses easily lure even short-term vacationers at Chautauqua. These courses are a modern expression of the original Chautauqua call for lifelong learning.

As the season began in earnest, the Symphony Orchestra reassembled for its 55th year. Most Chautauquans realize that they are fortunate to have at least twenty-one concerts during the season, but they probably never have a grasp of the orchestra cost-figures. Over $541,000 of the 1983 budget would go to pay direct artistic costs, including salaries of musicians, guest conductors, soloists and music rentals. Total cost would reach $731,000 with $190,000 going for administrative costs. At that, the overhead is well below the national average for symphony orchestras. No matter how the figures escalate, Chautauquans still view the orchestra as the centerpiece of the Amphitheater's overall program.

The Opera, too, is an expensive program that many Chautauquans have come to take for granted. (Institution costs for opera usually exceed $250,000.) Nonetheless, they appreciate the professional level of the productions and believe that the quality of opera is achieving new excellence all along. It is reportedly one of Director Auerbach's aims to have the opera world know that the Chautauqua Opera Company is a quality summer company whose productions are worthy of enthusiastic reception.

Dr. Bob Nickeson and Ken Hardy won nineteen games out of twenty in an early July round-robin tennis mixer to share the top honors. The Main Gate was proving to be a busy place with 24-hour service on ticket purchases, a window for prepaid ticket pick-up,

CHAUTAUQUA'S SECOND CENTURY CAMPAIGN

GROWTH OF ENDOWMENT AND THE PRESERVATION OF BUILDINGS

Chautauqua Institution gratefully acknowledges the following donors whose generosity during the Second Century Campaign, 1979-1983, insured the growth of endowment and the preservation of buildings

ACCOMPLISHMENTS

PRESERVING THE PAST; ASSURING THE FUTURE

Major Restoration Projects
The Amphitheater
The Hall of Missions
The Hall of Philosophy
Logan Dormitory
Kellogg Hall
Arts and Crafts Quadrangle
Smith Memorial Library
Norton Memorial Hall

The Chautauqua Foundation, Inc.
The Chautauqua Foundation, Inc., a separate legal entity which holds and manages Chautauqua's endowment funds, joined with the Institution in sponsoring the Second Century Campaign with an eye toward assuring Chautauqua's future by increasing endowment funds. Approximately $4 million was raised in gifts and pledges to the Foundation.

Named Endowments and Locations
While some Chautauquans created named endowments through their campaign gifts, others took opportunities offered to name specific Chautauqua locations in recognition of specifically sized gifts to general restoration purposes.

General Restoration Funds
Have Assisted in Work at:
The Children's School
The Beeson Youth Center
Piano Village
Brick Walk on Pratt Avenue
Gardens have been created.
Special lighting has been installed in Bestor Plaza and behind the Amphitheater.
Renovations and improvements have touched almost every segment of Chautauqua, from Palestine Park to the tennis courts.

Commemorative Brick Project
Donors of $1,000 or more to the campaign were invited to inscribe bricks to be placed in a wall enclosing the Amphitheater grandstand. It will be a focal point of interest for many years.

ADDITIONAL ENDOWMENT PROJECTS

Two unique endowments attracted support through the Campaign.

A scholarship for families at Chautauqua was endowed by the Joseph H. and Florence A. Roblee Foundation, St. Louis, Mo.

The TRW Bearings Division, Jamestown, N. Y., supported the Chautauqua Fellows Program, to bring experts to Chautauqua to lecture and lead discussions in their disciplines.

Appalachian Regional Commission
Mr. and Mrs. Robert S. Bargar
The Claude W. Benedum Foundation
Mr. and Mrs. Edward P. Boyle
The Boyle Family Charitable Trusts
The Gladys Brooks Foundation
Mrs. Robert D. Campbell
Mr. and Mrs. David H. Carnahan
The Carnahan-Jackson Foundation
Jack and Dorothy Clark
The T. James and Hazel C. Clarke Memorial Trust
Mr. and Mrs. George L. Cornell
Mr. and Mrs. Robert W. Cornell
The Jessie Smith Darrah Fund
Mrs. Joseph H. DeFrees
The Elizabeth Elser Doolittle Charitable Trusts
Envirogas, Inc.
The Gebbie Foundation
Margaret F. Gnade
Margaret W. Heinz
Mr. and Mrs. Arthur S. Holden, Jr.
The Kresge Foundation
Mr. and Mrs. Reginald A. Lenna
Helen Temple Logan
The Helen Temple Logan Charitable Trusts
Mr. and Mrs. Harry A. Logan, Jr.
Richard H. Miller
Ministrare, Inc.
Jane C. Morgan
Mr. and Mrs. Lewis W. Morgan
Dr. and Mrs. John W. McCredie
National Endowment for the Arts
National Endowment for the Humanities
National Historic Trust
Mrs. Joseph A. Neubauer
Mr. and Mrs. Christopher Norton
Charles E. Peirce
Margaret A. Penn
Miriam Reading
Mrs. Harold F. Reed and Family
Mr. and Mrs. Bartlett Richards
The Joseph H. & Florence A. Roblee Foundation
John S. Rogers
Helen Heinz Sample
Mr. and Mrs. H. Parker Sharp
Walter Shaw, Jr.
Mr. and Mrs. Ralph C. Sheldon, Jr.
Donald T. Snow, Jr.
Mr. and Mrs. Henry B. Suhr, Jr.
United States Steel Foundation
Welch Foods, Inc.
The Margaret L. Wendt Foundation
Mr. and Mrs. Robert O. Wilder
Mr. and Mrs. Jack A. Winter
Mr. and Mrs. Jack R. Winter
Mr. and Mrs. Michael Winter
Henry L. Wood
Betty Offutt Wood
Zurn Industries, Inc.

LOCATIONS
NAMED THROUGH GIFTS

Reid B. Babcox Memorial Garden, to be located near the Chautauqua Post Office; named by Mrs. Reid B. Babcox

The Henry Turner Bailey Studio, located in the Arts and Crafts Quandrangle; named by Mr. and Mrs. Theodore L. Bailey; Mr. and Mrs. James M. Bailey; Mr. and Mrs. John T. Bailey and Mr. and Mrs. Robert C. Gaede

Clarke Lobby, located in the Colonnade Building, first floor; and Clarke Vocal Studio, located in the Piano Village; named by the T. James and Hazel C. Clarke Foundation

The Willard F. Clarey, Sr. Children's Library, located in the basement of Smith Memorial Library; named by Envirogas, Inc.

Haker Memorial Garden, located at the southeast corner of the Amphitheater; named by Mr. and Mrs. C. Frayer Kimball, III with assistance from Mr. George L. Follansbee, Sr., Mr. Walter Kimball and Mrs. W. A. Morrison in memory of Mary Kimball Haker and Mr. and Mrs. Charles N. Kimball

Heinz Beach, located on the south end of the Chautauqua Grounds; named by Mrs. Frederick C. Heinz and her children

Amphitheater Handicapped Access Walk; named in memory of Mr. Charles Heinz and Mrs. Louise Heinz Lockhart

The Rebecca H. Lytle Classroom, located in the Children's School; named by Mr. and Mrs. Charles H. Lytle

McCredie Grandstand, located in the southwest corner of the Amphitheater; named by Dr. and Mrs. John W. McCredie, Jr. in memory of Dr. John and Elizabeth McCredie

The Munger-Aldredge Recital Room of Sherwood Studio; named in memory of Mrs. S. I. Munger and Mrs. George N. Aldredge by Mrs. Samuel A. Shelburne.

The Sara Elizabeth McCracken Peters Rustic Bridge behind the Amphitheater, named by Mr. and Mrs. Henry B. Suhr, Jr.

Mr. and Mrs. Harrison Strickler Vocal Studio, located in the Piano village; named by Mr. and Mrs. Robert K. Dietly

Thunder Bridge, located over the south ravine; named in honor of Mrs. Helen H. Sample

The Margaret L. Wendt Board Room, located in the Colonnade; in memory of Miss Margaret L. Wendt, by the Margaret L. Wendt Foundation, Buffalo, NY

AMPHITHEATER ALCOVE PLAQUES
HAVE BEEN PLACED BY THE FOLLOWING

Mr. and Mrs. Robert B. Osburn in tribute to Chautauqua

Robert C. Eckhardt *and* **Lynne E. Ballard** *in memory of Mary Campbell Eckhardt and Robert Hunt Eckhardt*

The Ellis L. Phillips Foundation in honor of Kathryn S. Phillips and the Chautauqua Spirit

The Jon B. Gerster Family

Mrs. Martha S. Gasche

Mr. and Mrs. James C. Levinson

Mr. and Mrs. George L. Cornell in honor of their south shore friends

An Anonymous Donor in honor of Dr. Helen M. Overs

SPECIAL PROJECT

The Claude W. Benedum Foundation of Pittsburgh, Pa., provided a special two-year grant of operating funds to initiate a comprehensive marketing program.

RESTRICTED
ENDOWMENTS

Established or substantially increased through gifts to the Second Century Campaign

Program Funds—Lectureships
Crawford N. and May Sellstrom Bargar Lectureship in Business and Economics
Selina W. and Walter Braham Lectureship (Increased)
Edwin P. Booth Memorial Lectureship (Increased)
Carnahan-Jackson Lectureship
Chautauqua Fellows Program
Reginald and Elizabeth Lenna Lectureship in Business and Economics
National Endowment for the Humanities Lectureship
Joseph A. Neubauer Lectureship
Harold F. Reed, Sr. Lectureship
Wilder Lectureship

Program Funds—Performing Arts
Boyle Fund for Performing Arts
Eleanor B. Franks Fund for Opera
Harry A. Logan, Jr. Fund for Performing Arts
National Endowment for the Arts Fund for Performing Arts
Ralph and Julia Sheldon Fund for Performing Arts

Religious Work
Department of Religion Fund for Program
Department of Religion Leadership Fund
Campbell Audio-Visual Fund for Equipment Benefiting Department of Religion Work
Campbell Department of Religion Fund
Carnahan-Jackson Religious Lectureship
Holden-Daney Fellowship for Continuing Education of Young Ministers
Numerous chaplaincy endowment additions

Scholarships
Frederick Percival Boynton Scholarship
Family Scholarship Fund
Marianne Elser Markham Fund
Ralph J. and Florence L. Miller Scholarship Fund
Sylvia Lucas Miller Fund
Rauch Scholarship
Roblee Scholarship for Families
Glenn G. Vance Music Scholarship Fund (Increased)
Numerous additions to existing scholarship endowments

Physical Maintenance Funds
Hall of Christ Fund
Fund for Maintenance of Thunder Bridge

Endowment Funds with Miscellaneous
or as yet Unspecified Focus
Caroline Barnum Fund
Nancy S. Coburn Fund
Cook Fund
Cornell Fund
Locke-Irwin Fund
Richard H. Miller Fund (Increased)
Mary Ellen Pindyck Fund (Increased)
Martha and Scott Reading Fund for Library Book Purchases
Jack A. and Muriel Winter Fund
Jack R. Winter Fund (Increased)
Michael Winter Fund (Increased)

There were many donors to the Second Century Campaign whose participation brought victory.

Special recognition was given the Governors of the Gladys Brooks Foundation who attended Library Day and observed the improvements that had been made through the Foundation's gift to the Second Century Campaign. Harmon Hawkins is shown as he spoke at the ceremonies. Vice President W. Thomas Smith is seated (left) with the Rev. Thomas C. LeClere and Chairman Gibbs.

the Hospitality Center and a Parking Office. Bob Jahrling, Sr. took both C-Scow races over the next weekend, after capturing the Fourth of July Series. Most of Chautauqua's Lightning Fleet was in Canada for the Lake Erie District Championships. Jim Neville, meanwhile, had qualified for the North American Championships with his sister, Cherie, and Doug Bargar, assisting. The Sports Club's seventh Walk-Run for Old First Night was set for July 30th. The Women's Golf Association was already under way with Julie Follansbee as chairman and Carol Lewis as co-chairman.

Normal Hall was finding splendid usefulness as a small theatre for the Professional Division of the Theater School. This hall which was built by and for the use of the Alumni of the Sunday School Normal Course has served many purposes during its almost-100 years. (Built in 1885)

The annual Library Day observance was held Saturday, July 16, and included special recognition of the restoration of Smith Memorial Library through a grant from the Gladys Brooks Foundation. Mr. and Mrs. James Daly and Mr. and Mrs. Harmon Hawkins were special guests. Mr. Daly and Mr. Hawkins are both governors of the Gladys Brooks Foundation. Through the grant of $96,200, a number of major improvements to the library had been made: Repair of the building's slate roof, its drainage system, a fire and safety system, lighting updating with some new fixtures, electrical improvements, shelving in the main reading room and storm windows. Rest room facilities had been modernized and carpet was to be laid in the main reading room, in the children's library and on the second floor. The Gladys Brooks Foundation was established to provide for the intellectual, moral and physical welfare of people through supporting non-profit libraries, educational institutions, hospitals and clinics. Smith

Memorial Library is a beautiful neo-Georgian building, built in 1931. Its location at the south end of Bestor Plaza makes it not only highly visible but easily accessible. Dr. William Chazenoff, professor of history at SUNY, Fredonia, was Library Day speaker. Richard R. Redington, direction of education, youth and recreation at Chautauqua, welcomed the Library Day audience and recognized those who had participated in the restoration process.

Library Day is arranged by the Friends of Smith Memorial Library.

Chautauquans welcomed the opportunity to enjoy a quintet of talented apprentices from the Chautauqua Opera Company when they performed at a Tuesday evening Symphony Orchestra concert conducted by Philippe Entremont. At about the same time, they were also welcoming back to Chautauqua a former apprentice, Barry Busse, who has become a fast-rising young American tenor, and was appearing in the COC's productions of "Manon Lescaut" and "Of Mice and Men;" and Herbert Perry, also a former COC apprentice, who would sing the role of Figaro in "The Marriage of Figaro." Perry had just signed a contract with the Metropolitan Opera Company.

Mrs. Howard Minor and her family marked the 100th anniversary of their Chautauqua home, Walter W. Heid, director of the Annual Fund, accepted a new position as General Manager of the Eastern Music Festival in Greensboro, N.C. The Chautauqua Women's Club Poetry Contest was being announced and the year's Bell Tower Scholars[2] from England were settling in.

Paul Neubauer appeared as soloist with the CSO under the auspices of the Harry Logan Fund for the Performing Arts. Neubauer appeared at age thirteen with the Los Angeles Symphony. Now at twenty, he has already graduated from Juilliard, has won a special performance prize at the Naumberg International Competition and other awards. He has performed in London, Toronto, and Yugoslavia. He has also studied under an Epstein scholarship from the Boy's Club of America Young Artists Program. Howard G. Gibbs, is administrator of the Epstein Fine Arts Fund.

By the end of July the restoration of the Arts and Crafts Quadrangle was completed and the generosity of the Helen Temple Logan Trust was officially recognized. This Quadrangle whose first section was ready for the 1909 season has been an inspirational center for artists for many years. Now it is almost like new again as the roof, the brick walk-ways, and the exterior paint have all been renewed and new equipment has also been provided. Mrs. Logan has studied painting with Revington Arthur and used the studios steadily during recent years. She knew the imperative needs of the Art Center and of her fellow-craftsmen there. Mrs. Logan's own personal gifts to the Institution have often been connected with student activities and needs. The improvements to the Arts and Crafts Quadrangle were given by the Helen Temple Logan Trust as a gift to the Second Century Campaign.

Carlisle Floyd, one of America's foremost composers, arrived in Chautauqua for the production of his opera, "Of Mice and Men." He had been invited by the Opera Guild to give the operalogue the afternoon before the opening performance. He had been in Chautauqua previously for 1959 productions of his opera, "Wuthering Heights."

Soon after, Dr. and Mrs. Karl A. Menninger arrived in time for the CSLC Recognition Day ceremonies. The 1983 Class had selected its motto from Dr. Menninger's book "Love Against Hate," and were honoring him on the occasion of his 90th birthday. The Class Motto: "Love—the Medicine for the World." Maritza Morgan had designed the class banner. Robert Ludwig had designed the banner's structure.

The Chautauqua Festival Ballet Company was delighting Chautauquans by their appearances, first with the Chautauqua Festival Orchestra and then with the Chautauqua Symphony Orchestra. Chautauquans were excited to see the high quality of "their own company," achieved through the genius of Jean-Pierre Bonnefoux. A guest critic spoke of the "polish and presence" of the new Company.

Old First Night announcements were designed to produce enthusiasm for the Annual Fund whose $970,000 goal had only reached a one-third mark. A history of the celebration of OFN as a money-raising effort is traced to 1905 when it was decided to offer Chautauquans the opportunity to make contributions to the permanent life of Chautauqua.

In starting the tradition, President of the Trustees W. H. Hickman remarked wryly that up to 1905 "Chautauqua people had taken a kind of pride in the fact that no one was asked to give at Chautauqua." But giving at Chautauqua has grown tremendously since that time.

At an early-August meeting in 1983, the Executive Committee of the Board of Trustees adopted a formal resolution concerning the proceeds from the sale of the Egyptian statue. The net proceeds of $271,000 were to be separately held and accounted for in a fund to be known as the "Capital Replacement Fund." Income from the fund was to be accumulated and was to remain as part of the fund. The fund was to be used for specific capital projects approved by the Board of Trustees or the Executive Committee of the Board of Trustees. The resolution also included instructions for investment by the Institution's President or Treasurer in United States government bills or notes, certificates of deposit, money market funds, or commercial paper with no less than an "A" rating, all with maturities of no more than one year.

A lengthy discussion of long-range planning ensued following the presentation by Trustees Osburn and Logan of a draft of a statement of intent for long-range planning. The statement was adopted as amended.

The importance and inevitability of change was noted in the statement with the belief that "strategic planning, planning for the future, is a necessity so that we will be able to manage change rather than have change manage us."

It was suggested that the determination of specific objectives to be achieved by each of Chautauqua's units be in accordance with the general statement of objectives which are stated in the Chautauqua Challenge of 1976.

The "principal forum for this process" will be the executive committee and standing committees. It is expected that it will be a continuous process.

At an earlier meeting of the Executive Committee, Mr. Gibbs announced some committee changes. David H. Carnahan would replace Warren Hickman as Chairman of the Education, Youth and Recreation Committee. James A. Zurn would be chairman of the newly-formed Finance Committee. Both men would become members of the Executive Committee by virtue of their new chairmanships. Edward P. Boyle, Paul Branch and Harry A. Logan, Jr. had been appointed members of the Finance Committee. These appointments would be approved by the full Board at a later date.

Chairman Gibbs presides at the recognition of the restoration of the Arts and Crafts Quadrangle, made possible by the Helen Temple Logan Trust. Mrs. Logan (shown here) was a painter and deeply concerned over the importance of this building.

There was some discussion of the Executive Committee, but the consensus was that no discernible change would be expected. It was agreed that communication with the Senior Staff on the part of the various committee chairmen should continue to be through Dr. Hesse or his secretary.

Dr. Hesse spoke of some of the concerns of the Foundation and the need for communication between the Foundation and the Institution. Dr. Hickman asked that Mr. Zurn and members of the administration meet with Foundation directors.

Chautauquans celebrated Firemen's Day as the height of the season was reached. The community never fails to support the seventy-seven active members of the Chautauqua Fire Department who work tirelessly in fire-fighting and rescue work. The quality of this department's equipment, expertise and devotion to duty is well beyond above-average levels. The parade and activities of the day are a reminder of this important safety force on the Grounds. Articles in The Daily profiled some of its members and called attention to other good works the department performs throughout the year within the area.

Harold Anderson and Julia Kirkland were winners of the Sports Club's OFN Run which had enough entrants to make $1,500 for the Annual Fund.

Meanwhile, the cake was being baked for Old First Night. It would weigh 400 pounds and serve 3,000 people.

When the night actually arrived, it had its own highlights. Most auspicious was the third Chautauqua Salute given to Dr. Karl A. Menninger in honor of his 90th birthday. Another heart-touching moment was the recognition of Dr. Ralph W. Loew, who was completing ten years as head of Chautauqua's Department of Religion. Howard Gibbs, chairman of the Board of Trustees, delivered the tribute to Dr. Loew and presented him with a special plaque.

Happily, over $25,000 was given in the Community gift and the Annual Fund total ran upward to $610,000.

In former years when Old First Night giving was connected only with that one Chautauqua birthday night, the total goal was expected to be reached if not that night, by the end of the season at the latest. Now with the 12-month Annual Fund, giving can begin anytime in the year and extend until December 31. "We are now well on our way to reaching our goal," Walter Heid said confidently after Old First Night.

Of course, on Old First Night there were the usual moments of nostalgia and teasing. The Boys and Girls Club came running down the aisles. The children from the Children's School enchanted everyone. There was "Gala Entertainment." This year The Acting Company, The Dance Festival Company and Opera Apprentices performed while the Chautauqua Youth Orchestra and the Chautauqua Festival Orchestra also took part. The evening ended with everyone on his feet for the singing of the Hallelujah Chorus and then cutting of the cake. A truly homey night!

At Chautauqua good experiences pile on top of one another. After Old First Night came Recognition Day!

The Recognition Day Parade started on time under sunny skies and moved along the Brick Walk briskly. Dr. and Mrs. Menninger joined the Parade and were given positions of honor in the Hall of Philosophy. Twenty-two graduates composed the class of 1983. Dr. Leslie Fiedler, Samuel L. Clemens Professor from SUNY, Buffalo, delivered the Commencement address at the regular 10:45 hour in the Amphitheater on the topic, "What is Literature?" Later in the day the CLSC welcomed members of the new class into the Alumni Association at a buffet dinner on the lawn of Alumni Hall. Alfreda L. Irwin spoke about her visits to other Chautauquas and Phil Zimmer spoke about his work as Director of Communications.

The CLSC Alumni President Dr. Campbell Putnam presided at the dinner.

It seemed appropriate that on this very traditional day at Chautauqua, The Daily should carry a short article on the death of a distinguished Chautauquan, the actor Raymond Massey. A nephew of Bishop Vincent, Mr. Massey frequently acknowledged the influence of Chautauqua during his early years. He once said that he saw his first play, "Macbeth," at Chautauqua in 1905.

The CLSC emphasis continued the next day as William Least Moon, author of "Blue Highways, a Journey into America" spoke at the regular Round Table. His book had been chosen as a CLSC book and promptly made its way onto the bestseller list. Mrs. Ronsheim and her CLSC readers were understandably proud.

As if this were not enough news for the day, former Principal Conductor of the CSO Sergiu Comissiona returned to conduct the evening concert, with Byron Janis as soloist. Comissiona reminded Chautauquans through The Daily that it was at Chautauqua that he conducted his first concert as an American citizen. He had recently returned from performing at the York Festival in England, the Sofia Festival in Bulgaria, Wolf Trap and Aspen.

The usual Friday "abundance" confronted Chautauquans the next day as Pete Seeger and Arlo Guthrie were scheduled to bring a program of folk music to the Amph while "Manon Lescault" was playing in Norton Hall. An unusual situation threatened when some peo-

Mary Frances Bestor Cram, right, while an Institution trustee has also been chairman of the Program Committee and later, the Religion Committee. She is shown here with Dr. and Mrs. Nathan Gottschalk. Dr. Gottschalk is the Conductor of the Music School Festival Orchestra and Director of the School of Music. Mrs. Cram's father was the beloved President Bestor.

ple in Jamestown opposed to the Seeger activism said they would picket the Institution Grounds, but nothing came of the dilemma.

However, a Peace Vigil Against Nuclear War was held following the concert in the Plaza. Nearly 2,000 participated by carrying lighted candles and marching through and around the Plaza, sometimes singing, but always peaceable in their demonstration of personal protest against nuclear war. The vigil was organized by leaders of a variety of denominations. There were older and younger people. Even one woman in a wheel chair sat with a lighted candle to give her testimony against nuclear war. Before midnight Pete Seeger joined the group and there was more singing before the final break-up of the Vigil at midnight. The Nuclear War protesters did meet opposing advocates from Citizens for Freedom through Strength who nonetheless affirmed that those who support people such as Seeger, are working to the detriment of the United States.

The United Church of Christ denomination observed the 100th anniversary of the first Congregational Church headquarters at Chautauqua. The first Congregational Church House was built on the site of the present UCC Center between Roberts and Clark Avenues beside the Amphitheater, but a tent was first used by the Congregationalists on the same site. Following the union of the Reformed Churches of America with the Congregational denomination, to form the United Church of Christ, the UCC operates not only the main center and chapel, but also the Mayflower on Bowman Avenue and the former Reformed Church House at the corner of Miller and Pratt Avenues.

The Open Forum traditionally tackles the community's housekeeping problems of a practical nature and furnishes an opportunity for a free exchange of views. This year Chairman Gibbs also explained to the audience the long-range, strategic planning function of the Board's Executive Committee under its own chairman, Dr. Warren L. Hickman. He reiterated that the Chautauqua Challenge remains the guide for Chautauqua planning.

A Victorian Chautauqua Collection featuring treasured pieces of Chautauqua furniture and household items on loan from present cottage owners opened at the Art Association Galleries. The Exhibit showed sample rooms in early Chautauqua homes, including intriguing children's furniture and toys, fine wooden desks, beds, washstands, and an abundance of wicker. Among the latter was the wicker chair which President Franklin Delano Roosevelt occupied as he received guests at a reception in the Bestor home.

A conference of Other Chautauquas was held on the Grounds August 16-19. Eleven people from the Monteagle Sunday School Assembly in Monteagle Tennessee and two from Ocean Park, Maine participated, while two people from Mt. Gretna Chautauqua came during July to see Chautauqua for themselves. Each Chautauqua group showed slides and told about their histories, as well as their current seasons. Mutual problems and operational practices were discussed. At the end, it was decided that a network of Chautauquas, a loose confederation, should be formed for purposes

of communication and mutual enrichment. "The similarity of our value systems and goals created instant rapport," Richard F. Burns of Ocean Park stated. It was he who coined the new organization's name, The Chautauqua Network. At one time, the Chautauqua Movement was represented in more than 250 independent Chautauquas nation-wide.

"Survival" was the topic for Dr. Karl A. Menninger at an extra lecture arranged by the Department of Religion. Dr. Menninger, a beloved Chautauquan, is almost always persuaded to appear as a lecturer during his vacation stay, even when he has not planned to do so. This year, he was preoccupied with the existence and world-wide threat of "the bomb."

Evan N. Wilson, violist, won first place in the Sigma Alpha Iota Competition.

The newly restored Arts Quadrangle was rededicated August 15th in simple ceremonies at the historic Arts Center site. Participating in the event were Chairman Gibbs, Second Century Campaign Chairman Reading and Dr. Hesse. Mrs. Helen Temple Logan was honored as the significance of the Arts Quadrangle to Chautauqua was emphasized. The restoration which had taken two years to complete had been made possible by a gift from the Helen Temple Logan Charitable Trusts through the Second Century Campaign. Mr. and Mrs. Harry A. Logan, Jr. accompanied Mrs. Logan to the rededication of the Arts Quadrangle.

At the President's Dinner, Dr. Hesse spoke with great inspiration to those who were present concerning the future of Chautauqua. In thanking his audience which was composed of those who had given significant financial support to the Second Century Campaign, he ticked off "Remember When" items which showed how far Chautauqua has come in most recent years. Programs have achieved the level of excellence that has frequently filled the Amphitheater. Building after building has been improved, sometimes "saved" from collapse. The Grounds have become more attractive as both private and public structures have been maintained. Improved housing and new housing are both increasing Chautauqua residency figures, he said.

Then he launched into his dreams for the future.

The late Helen Temple Logan, patroness of the arts at Chautauqua and donor of Logan Dormitory, is shown with Cynthia Auerbach, Artistic Director of the Chautauqua Opera Company, as they enjoyed a festive occasion at the Hotel Athenaeum.

"Can we not use this place in Chautauqua history as a launching pad for what Chautauqua can be in the year 2083?" he asked. "Do we feel that what we have is good enough? Or can we make it better?..."Tough issues lie ahead...Changes not for the sake of change but for the sake of betterment of Chautauqua..." Then he began to speak in global terms, building on the thought that Chautauqua can be an international center. He defined "the soul of this place which might be found in intellect and culture, the conscious and subconscious pursuits of man, all of the arts, embraced into the wholeness of human development." Contrasting Chautauqua with other well-known festivals and centers, he said we should be proud to share in this place where technology, science, the intellect, culture and the arts are treated with equal respect.

He urged the leaders of Chautauqua to whom he was speaking "to get on with the FUTURE."

At the same dinner a special recognition was extended to John D. Hamilton for his twenty-four years on the Board of Trustees, part of that time as a Vice Chairman of the Board and for the generous amounts and the quality of time and effort which he has given to the Institution.

His other accomplishments and the honors which have been heaped upon him by his fellow-citizens and contemporaries were also listed in the formal citation that was presented to him by Chairman Gibbs on behalf of the Institution.

Waterfront problems were being studied by the Buildings and Grounds Committee and that Committee's Chairman Bob Osburn explained some of the matters which were being examined: The proper docking of boats and payment of license fees is not being followed, resulting in inequities; bathing beach rules are not being observed; increasing boat trailer parking is becoming unsightly; transient boats should probably be licensed and docked in a particular area; inequities should be remedied among those who use private docks. Remedies and policies would be decided upon and announced in due time, Osburn said.

As the Board of Trustees met the final Saturday of the season, Dr. Hickman explained the Executive Committee's thoughts on planning procedures, asking the Board to reaffirm the statement on Planning which had been made at the Open Forum.

He further explained that the Committee believed the Chautauqua Challenge should be kept in mind at all times as the overall objective to be attained.

Those planning for the Institution have to assign priorities to Chautauqua activities, to its resources and to assure that these are used to achieve the objective of the Challenge, he said. There is need to review past priorities to determine whether they are still valid. Maybe some need to be shifted. There is need to look at such things as the overall coordinating of planning by the committee chairmen and the members-at-large of the Executive Committee, along with the cooperation of the Administration.

Examples of the kinds of things which have been talked about as needing to be checked and handled in planning are: Whether there is a desire to improve elements of the program; seek to retain current levels or perhaps cut back in some areas; increase the residen-

tial housing base or remain the same or continue a slow attrition in housing...; how to use each facility most effectively; cost effectiveness of such facilities as Norton Hall and Smith-Wilkes—plant utilization; what are the philosophical goals of the Development Program; what are the questions and issues the Executive Committee should consider in cross-committee cooperation; relations with the Chautauqua Foundation (the President of the Foundation has asked that members of the Executive Committee meet with the Foundation in September because of the long-range planning to be undertaken by the Foundation at the same time as this planning is under consideration by the Executive Committee); need to establish programs, budgets and other elements of the ongoing operation a year in advance. (Whether this goal can be met is unsure. The transition year would be very difficult because the Administration would have to be handling the programs and budgets for two years simultaneously, but Dr. Hesse had said that although it would be complicated, it could be done.) Dr. Hickman reiterated that the first item in planning is to establish priorities and the Committee wished the full Board to reaffirm the Planning Statement and the role of the Executive Committee.

The Board took that action, reaffirming both the Statement and the role of the Executive Committee as a strategic planning organization.

Dr. Hesse distributed the financial figures of the season and commented on them before giving a more detailed report. There was a significant decline in both opera and theater attendance. He gave an update on orchestra negotiations. He detailed the status of the searches for both a Vice President for Development and a Director of the Department of Religion. He said he had made no decisions concerning a sabbatical, a New York office or 1501 North Lake Drive.

Miriam Reading gave a report of the remaining areas of the Second Century Campaign. The Board passed a motion expressing its heartfelt thanks for the magnificent work she had done for the Second Century Campaign. She replied graciously, sharing the credit for reaching the goal with administration, staff, trustees and many more who had helped by giving.

Chairman Gibbs discussed the continuing need for funds for further work on buildings which have not yet had attention or whose rehabilitation is not yet complete. He referred again to the importance of the Executive Committee's long-range planning and the need of a close liaison between the Board of Trustees and the Board of the Foundation, especially in light of the large endowment which the Endowment now contains.

Mr. Heid was present at the meeting although he was soon to leave for his new position as Executive Director of the Eastern Music Festival in North Carolina. The Annual Fund was reported at $685,000.

David Carnahan, the new chairman of the Education, Youth and Recreation Committee, reported that the Committee was recommending that renovation of the Children's School should proceed.

Dr. Holland reported on increased attendance at Sunday morning worship services and Sacred Song Services. He said the appointment of Dr. Loew's successor was imminent. He also mentioned the various forms of recognition of Dr. Loew that were taking place. An Institution-sponsored luncheon honoring Dr. and Mrs. Loew was scheduled for the Athenaeum Hotel following the final morning worship service. The number of tickets were limited by the capacity of the parlor where the luncheon would be served and they had been completely sold almost as soon as they were offered, he said.

At the morning service, however, Dr. Loew perhaps experienced the most memorable tribute of his entire ministry. It was a Chautauqua salute asked for by Dr. Hesse, the President of Chautauqua. But it was, indeed, the largest Chautauqua Salute in recent memory, since the Amphitheater was filled to capacity and latecomers were standing several-deep around the edge of the benches. "The lilies bloomed," as Dr. Hurlbut was wont to say, and Dr. Loew knew he had won the hearts of Chautauquans.

Chairman Osburn of the Buildings and Grounds Committee informed the Board of an urgent need recently discovered at the Women's Club for immediate attention to the roof.

He explained the need for a reevaluation of the Security policy and said this would be ready for the November Board meeting.

He reminded the Board of the prior resolution for the sale of three Institution properties. The sale of 15 Ames Avenue was ready for completion. Only one bid was received on the Pennsylvania Apartments so the price was lowered and new bids will be opened September 1st. He explained the proposal for the purchase of the Arcade. After detailed discussions, a resolution was passed which approved the proposal and placed responsibility on the President of the Institution to work with the Buildings and Grounds Committee to negotiate a contract with the developer substantially in accord with the bid documents and the proposal that had been approved, in furtherance of the Institution's objective of permitting the rehabilitation, renovation and development of the Arcade Building for multi-unit residential purposes. It also gave the President authority to execute such documents as may be necessary or appropriate, and if necessary, call on the Executive Committee if a matter comes up that requires further approval.

A motion was made that the funds from the sale of these properties go to the construction of a wing at Bellinger Hall as soon as possible.

Another property matter already acted upon by the Board needed further refinement and agreement. Mr. Osburn spoke of the plan to develop multi-family dwellings on property of Judson Avenue. Owners of property in the neighborhood had expressed concern and opposition to buildings being erected on this side of Judson Avenue. Following a presentation by the property owners, and further study, the Buildings and Grounds Committee has now made the following recommendations:

Only the northeasterly approximately 60 feet of the premises will be available for sale and development. The purchase price will be $30,000.

Development of that parcel will be limited to a two-unit duplex type dwelling with on-site parking for two automobiles, the design and placement of the structure and parking spaces will be subject to approval by the Buildings and Grounds Committee.

The balance of the triangular piece will be dedicated as a park and so shown on the official map of the Institution with the understanding that the Chautauqua Foundation will receive from or on behalf of the neighboring property owners a fund of not less than $5,000 as an endowment fund for maintenance of the park. No parking will be permitted in the Park.

The recommendations were approved and adopted by the Board.

The Chairman of the new Finance Committee said that a draft of a mission statement for the Finance Committee had been developed and would be brought to the Executive Committee before presentation to the full Board.

A motion was passed to elect John D. Hamilton as an Honorary Trustee as he completed his active service on the Board. A resolution of appreciation was read by Mr. Wilder, chairman of the Nominating Committee for the three men leaving the Board, Mr. Hamilton, John T. Bailey and Howard E. Chadwick.

David H. Carnahan, Miriam Reading and Walter C. Shaw, Jr., were reelected to the Board. Two new members, Jack Rice and H. David Faust, were elected for first terms.

Dr. Holland presided at this luncheon in the hotel honoring Dr. and Mrs. Loew. The occasion was a happy time of friendly thanksgiving for ten years of service and warm personal regard for both "Ralph and Maxine." Because Dr. Norman Vincent Peale was serving as the morning chaplain, Dr. and Mrs. Peale were present for the luncheon, and Dr. Peale spoke during the short program. Good wishes and gifts were presented. The Institution had established an endowment fund in Dr. Loew's honor and gifts to this Fund were being received steadily, it was reported.[3] A personal gift of paintings for their Wahmeda home was also presented to the Loews from the Institution.

An astonishing development went from rumor to fact on October 11th when Dr. Hesse addressed a letter of resignation to the Chairman of the Board, Mr. Gibbs. "It is with mixed feelings that I inform you of my decision," his letter began. "I do so with a tremendous sense of accomplishment, some sense of relief, a sadness at parting and a firm belief in Chautauqua's future."

He spoke of the taxing burden of professional leadership and that it seemed a good time to take on new responsibilities. The programs have been strengthened. The Capital Campaign has been completed, he said. The buildings have been restored and a renewed vitality will propel the Institution confidently into the next century of service. The long-range planning effort will enable the Trustees to select a successor compatible with future needs and directions.

Soon after, he sent news of his resignation to his regular list of Chautauqua's strongest supporters to whom during his tenure he had sent frequent reports. He included the information that he was joining the Joffrey Ballet as Executive Director of its Foundation

Joseph C. Johnson, Vice President and Treasurer of Chautauqua Institution, served as the liaison between the senior staff and the Board of Trustees following Dr. Hesse's leaving, performing the duties of chief executive officer until a new President would be named. He is shown here at the right, presiding in the Amphitheater at the question and answer period which followed Jules Bergman's lecture, "Space Shuttles, Space Stations and Human Life."

and Managing Director of its Board of Directors.

He also updated for the benefit of his supporters and co-workers the Annual Fund figures and urged them to work for the successful completion of that effort. He reminded them that changes of leadership are part of a never-ending chain of events experienced by every institution and that "we have built not only for today, but for the future."

The Executive Committee was meeting a few days after members of the Board had received Dr. Hesse's official letter of resignation. Therefore, a discussion of interim organizational options ensued. At length a motion was passed that Joseph C. Johnson should be named Vice President for Finance and Treasurer; Richard R. Redington, Vice President of Education, Youth and Recreation; and when Dr. Hesse departs, Mr. Johnson will also serve as Staff Coordinator. No interim President would be named. Dr. Hesse was expected to remain as President until November 15, 1983.

Other reports and updates of committee projects were made at the October Executive Committee Meeting. The Finance Committee Mission Statement was read and approved for Board consideration.

Only a few days before the Annual Meeting, on November 3, 1983, the sudden death of Dr. Robert C. Holland occurred in Pittsburgh. As an active Trustee of Chautauqua Institution, he was serving as the Chairman of the Religious Life Committee at the time of his death. He had been pastor of the Shadyside Presbyterian Church in Pittsburgh for twelve years.

Before the first deliberation of the Board at its Annual Meeting, a Service of Remembrance and Thanksgiving for the Life of Robert C. Holland was conducted in the Hall of Christ with Dr. Irion presiding.

The first Committee to report at the Annual Meeting was the Nominating Committee. The following officers were subsequently elected:

Howard G. Gibbs, Chairman; Miriam Reading, Vice Chairman; Robert B. Osburn, Vice Chairman; Warren L. Hickman, Chairman, Executive Committee; Joseph C. Johnson, Vice President and Treasurer; W. Thomas

Smith, Vice President; Richard R. Redington, Vice President; Philip Zimmer, Secretary; and Carol M. White, Assistant Secretary.

To conform to the By-Laws (Article VII, Section 7), the Board is required to designate one of the Vice Presidents to serve as President in the absence of a President. A motion was passed appointing Mr. Johnson to serve in that capacity until a president is named.

Certain banking resolutions and authorizations were decided upon.

A change in the By-Laws was accepted and approved concerning the time when a Class B Trustee would take office in order to conform to the Charter of the Corporation: (4) ("A Class B Trustee elected by such members of the Corporation shall assume his office and duties as a Trustee on October 1 next following." A minor change was proposed for Article V, Board of Trustees, Section 7, Standing Committees; the second sentence of the last paragraph defining the duties of the Nominating Committee.[5] It is proposed the "One or more Vice Chairmen of the Board" be substituted for "Vice Chairman of the Board" to conform to Article VII, Officers, which provides for one or more additional Vice Chairmen.)

Chairman Gibbs then presented a list of proposed Trustee Committee Chairs:

Program, Mary Frances Cram; Buildings and Grounds, Robert B. Osburn; Religion, not appointed; Education, Youth and Recreation, David H. Carnahan; Development, Edward P. Boyle; and Finance, James A. Zurn. They, along with proposed At-Large members Harry A. Logan, Jr. and Paul C. Irion, plus the officers just elected would comprise the Executive Committee. A motion was passed approving the composition of the Executive Committee.

A motion was passed approving the Presidential Search Committee which had been selected by the Executive Committee. The Presidential Search Committee would be headed by Dr. Warren L. Hickman. Members would include: Richard Bechtolt, David H. Carnahan, George L. Follansbee, Jr., Dorothy Hill, Paul C. Irion, Kay Logan, Robert B. Osburn with Howard G. Gibbs as ex-officio and Patricia Klingensmith and Robert Laughlin as alternates.

The Presidential Search Process was discussed at length. A presidential job description was considered. At length, a motion was passed that the Search Committee present one candidate to the Board for consideration rather than attempting to have several candidates.

Later during an executive session, certain guidelines for the Search Committee were proposed, among which were: that the candidate must accept the Chautauqua Challenge and be responsive to the challenge as it relates to his own leadership; he must understand the complexity of the Chautauqua concept and the Chautauqua program; have managerial and decision-making skills and also human skills to provide leadership to both a complex and able group of staff members and a complex and able group of volunteers; that the Committee should move expeditiously in hopes that the new President may be presented to the Chautauqua community during the 1984 season.

Mr. Miller, as President of the Chautauqua Foundation, addressed the Board, giving an update of the financial status of the Foundation, which he stated had more than doubled during Dr. Hesse's presidency. He gave illustrations of Foundation assistance to the Institution. He raised many questions and concerns to be considered in the development of long-range plans.

Mr. Zurn presented the 1984 budget and noted that no increase in the Annual Fund had been projected. After detailed discussion and some explanation from Dr. Hesse concerning projected increases and cutbacks in individual areas, the budget was adopted.

Dr. Hesse gave a brief report and sketched the progress of the 1984 season's program, the status of the orchestra negotiations and other matters. He concluded his remarks with a few words of farewell.

Mrs. Reading commented on the status of the Second Century Campaign projects and payments were included in a two-page chart which she shared with the Board members and which was attached to the Minutes.

Dramatic news from the Gebbie Foundation was announced at a Board dinner on Friday evening by Mr. Hamilton, president of that Foundation. As a lasting memorial to Mrs. Geraldine G. Gebbie, the Gebbie Foundation has made it its wish and intent to complete over a period of time all five contemplated phases of Bellinger Hall dependent on the continuation of the high standards of administration and financial management presently demonstrated.

The details of the agreement concerning the commitment would be addressed, probably by Mr. Johnson with some members of the Gebbie Foundation Board.

Mr. Gibbs, on behalf of all of the Trustees, expressed great appreciation to the Gebbie Foundation for its continued confidence in the Institution and its continued support.

Later when the business meeting was resumed, Mr. Osburn of the Buildings and Grounds Committee told his fellow-trustees that with the gift of the new wing of Bellinger Hall assured for the coming year, the funds from the sale of the three Institution properties would be placed in a maintenance endowment fund for Bellinger Hall. He confided that this contingency had already been discussed with the Gebbie Foundation and had been included in the Gebbie Foundation's gift proposal.

Mr. Osburn also presented a plan for road repairs using Institution machinery and labor, to be done on a year-by-year plan according to need, and to be incorporated into the Institution's annual capital budget. The Board gave the plan its approval.

In Amendments to the Security Policy and Procedures, it was recommended that off-season security at the Main Gate, currently extending from 7:00 p. m. to 3:00 a. m., be changed to 6:00 p. m. to 6:00 a. m. and that the current portion of the service charge to property owners for security be increased by fifty per cent.

Mr. Osburn presented a resolution setting forth preliminary steps toward opening the area at the southwest corner of the Institution Grounds known as the Barracks area for future development. The resolution carried.

Then Mr. Osburn presented a plan for initial development of the Whallon Farm with a new nine-hole golf course. A motion was made and passed approving the concept of the plans authorizing the Buildings and Grounds Committee and the Finance Committee to research creative funding for this project, with a projected five to six-year payback of the initial investment, to be presented to the full Board for final approval.

Thus, with the achievement of his main goals, Dr. Hesse completed his services to Chautauqua. He left knowing that the Annual Fund was within $200,000 of its goal, and to top it off, the entire Bellinger Hall Complex was now to become a reality. He left with sincere hopes that Chautauqua would go FORWARD.

The members of the Board on their part, presented Dr. Hesse with a copy of a Resolution which had been adopted in which they cited his "tireless efforts, his capacity for innovative thinking and his commitment to the realization of the ideals of Chautauqua." They thanked him for "his dedication to Chautauqua's aims, the unstinting expenditure of his energy and ability." The Board's Resolution also cited his numerous accomplishments and concluded by wishing him well in all of his future endeavors.

He had said, "We have built for the future," and one of the proofs lay in the capable working staff he had assembled. The interim year of 1984 went smoothly with the officers closely allied as they prepared for the next season.

Chairman Gibbs sought to reassure Chautauquans that continuity would be maintained. He, himself, kept in close touch with Chautauqua and with Chautauquans. Between-season issues of The Chautauquan reached an ever-growing constituency.

The second phase of the Athenaeum restoration went forward according to plan. The Annual Fund was successful. By March, Mr. Johnson could tell the Executive Committee that the orchestra contract had been settled and by April, it had been signed. A $30,000 NEA Grant for Opera/Music Theatre had been received. Dr. Charles Hill, associate professor of health, physical education and recreation at Trenton State College, was appointed the new Director of the Boys and Girls Club. William H. Waite, freelance artist and owner of The Studio in Jamestown was named director of the CAA Galleries. Paul Kane of Buffalo had assumed the duties of Annual Fund Director. Richard Bechtolt was elected to the Board of Trustees to fill the unexpired term of Dr. Holland.

A new resolution was adopted, providing that the Egyptian statue proceeds be changed to a new fund called The Fund for the Future. The resolution also contained provisions for the investment and reinvestment of the Fund in short-term investment vehicles; for the income and principle to be used for self-liquidating projects over a period of not more than ten years.

Preliminary work in the development of the construction of nine more holes at the golf course on the Whallon Farm property was authorized with an expenditure of not more than $40,000 to come from The Fund for the Future.

The construction of the nine holes was estimated at

$287,900. If borrowed from The Fund of the Future, repayment of $35,000 per year would begin in 1986 and payment would be completed in 10 years. In November the Board had endorsed the concept of the Whallon Farm Development and Golf Course expansion. The residential development of the Whallon Farm also seems critical to the future growth and success of Chautauqua, since it would bring more people to Chautauqua. The Buildings and Grounds Committee also believes two other factors are important to the decision to move ahead. Stan Marshaus of the Chautauqua Golf Club can do much of the actual golf course work internally, and Tom Smith, as vice president for operations, has already proved that he has the necessary vision to lead a program from planning stage to completion.

In October, Dr. William N. Jackson, senior pastor of the Christ Presbyterian Church of Canton, Ohio, had become the successor to Dr. Loew after an extensive search which had begun soon after Dr. Loew announced his intention to retire.

The Rev. Mr. Jackson is a long-time Chautauquan, a property owner in nearby Chautauqua Shores. Keenly aware of the traditions and standards of Chautauqua's Department of Religion, he was a Chautauqua chaplain in 1982. He is a former minister of the Westminster Presbyterian Church and dean of the chapel at Westminster College.

Continuing its philisophy of outreach, the Institution agreed to participate in an upcoming experimental program with the YMCA of America in an Arts/Education roving ambassador format. Also, a marketing survey by a team from the University of Buffalo was recommended by the Executive Committee and set in place.

The building of condominiums progressed during the year on the site of the former Glen Park Cafeteria and on North Terrace and on the site of the former Venice on South Terrace. The interval ownership concept was reported to be proving popular at the North

Shore development. But single home dwelling construction and restoration of older homes also continued. Nonetheless there was an outcry from some Chautauquans during the 1984 season that Chautauqua's ambience was being tampered with by the development of modern-appearing homes in repetitive design.

The Annual Fund goal was set at $1,020,000, with co-existing goals of a 10 per cent increase in donor base and a 30 per cent increase in $1,000-plus donors.

"A successful Annual Fund is vital for the maintenance of program quality and exceptional educational offerings," Co-Chairman Edward P. Boyle said as the over-million figure was announced.

The season was opened by Chairman Gibbs who used the traditional three taps of the gavel to signify "Recollection of our Past; Reaffirmation of our Present; and Renewal of our Future." It was a thoughtful presentation and allowed Mr. Gibbs the opportunity to remind his fellow-Chautauquans of cherished values and the resiliency of Chautauqua during times of transition. 1984 was such a time.

Evening programs, lecture schedules, schools, clubs and the fellowship of Chautauquans themselves proceeded on a high level with The Chautauquan Daily functioning as another cohesive instrument to give the aura of no-real-change. The administration, the Board and Chautauquans-at-large agreed that Chautauqua was alive and well, but they also were expectant, expectant of the choice of a new leader.

That choice was made and announced Saturday, July 21, amid general anticipation and excitement. Dr. Daniel L. Bratton was announced as the 15th president of Chautauqua.

Dr. Bratton is an ordained Methodist minister who has carried out his vocation in institutions of higher education. He came to Chautauqua from Salina, Kansas, where for 10 years he had been president of Kansas Wesleyan College. Before that he served as vice-chancellor for student affairs at the University of Maryland, College Park, Maryland. Previously he was

Dr. William N. Jackson, Director of the Department of Religion.

In an informal gathering with delegates from Other Chautauquas, Dr. Bratton discusses points of mutual interest with Corinne Franklin, later elected President of the Monteagle (Tennessee) Sunday School Assembly, and Irwin Crais, a Board member from Monteagle.

Millard Taylor, as concertmaster of the Chautauqua Symphony Orchestra, has also been the leader of the Chautauqua String Quartet. He is shown third from the left with Emile Simonel viola, Chaim Zemach, cello and Andrew Galos, violin.

vice president for student affairs at Adelphi University, Garden City, New York.

The search committee agreed that his career and personal commitments match the integrating function of Chautauqua where religion, art, education and recreation are joined for the benefit of the whole person. Taking into consideration the historical importance of Chautauqua in the field of education and in the development of creativity through the arts, principal leadership at Chautauqua has great potential for a person with Dr. Bratton's qualifications and academic preparation. In addition to other specialized work experiences, Dr. Bratton has been involved with securing support for educational institutions from government, corporations and individuals and has served as an officer in independent college associations.

Dr. and Mrs. Bratton and their children were introduced to the Chautauqua community before the Morning Worship Service July 22. This was an informal, friendly introduction during which Dr. Bratton revealed that he had spent childhood summers at his grandmother's home in Westfield and was quite familiar with Chautauqua. The new President is a native of the New York City area. He graduated from Allegheny College, Meadville, Pennsylvania, the Divinity School of Drew University, Madison, New Jersey, and received both his master's and doctor's degrees from Columbia University.

Mrs. Bratton is a psychology teacher and counselor and has been working at Brown-Mackie College in Salina. The couple has six children, ages 11 to 18, three of whom came from Korea to be a part of the Bratton family.

The Brattons spent as much time as possible at Chautauqua during the remainder of the season, although the task of moving had to be dealt with.

The Daily recorded July 30th as Dr. Bratton's "first day on the job." Gradually, there appeared other reports in The Daily that Dr. Bratton had spoken here and there. He took an appropriate place on the program at the Bishop's Garden, for example, when a new plaque was dedicated to Dr. Vincent's memory. It was

the gift of the Bishop's granddaughter, Mrs. Elizabeth Vincent Foster, who was present for the ceremony. He presided at Old First Night and both he and Mrs. Bratton playfully decided the contest between the states.

In an interview, he said, "I loved Old First Night; I just had fun with all the elements of it. And the parade of the CLSC, the very traditional things that are also great fun for the community. I'm getting to know the personality of the place, that which makes it so unique."

He said he was listening and learning and not trying to "manage" mid-season. "What I want to do is be out there with people . . ."

Before the season closed a further glimpse of what lay ahead was given in a dialogue between the new President and the Chairman of the Board which appeared in The Daily.

Dr. Bratton described his reactions to experiencing firsthand the great variety of the Chautauqua program and the seriousness of debate that is possible on the Platform.

Howard Gibbs, on the other hand, stated that Dr. Bratton had become a part of Chautauqua life in an amazingly short time. He had already begun to influence Chautauqua, he said.

At the President's Dinner, Dr. Bratton spoke about the search for a development person and the importance of the development program. He referred to Dr. Vincent's book, *The Chautauqua Movement,* as containing many good guidelines. As he began his tenure at Chautauqua, Dr. Bratton began emphasizing the timeless quality of the Chautauqua Idea. Again and again he returned to the theme of the timelessness of the "unique Chautauqua mission."

Chautauquans noticed the natural confidence of Dr. Bratton. Perhaps this quality of his personality is fostered by his knowledge of history. His viewpoints, his sense of values and his sense of timing may have evolved from this concentrated study. It may also explain one part of an interesting written statement he made to the Search Committee: "As much as I believe in growth and change, and as hard as I will work for appropriate change and growth, the existing strengths of Chautauqua will always remain central to my presidency there."

Dr. Bratton soon indicated that he would allow the staff's team effort that had developed and worked so well during the interim year to continue. A team volunteer effort, led by Co-Chairmen Bechtolt and Boyle, PLUS Dr. Bratton, brought the Annual Fund to a successful conclusion. But the next year's Annual Fund was renamed The Chautauqua Fund. Its goal was lifted to $1.1 million, and "Enhancing an Historic American Resource" was a significant sub-heading added to The Chautauqua Fund name.

A Task Force was put into place to study short- and long-range planning for historic preservation. A Task Force to study the parameters of the development of the Whallon Farm land was recommended. The President's home at 1501 North Lake Drive was sold and a new summer residence for the President's family was planned on lots adjoining in the Open Campus below the Arts and Crafts Quadrangle. (The President and his family would reside in Jamestown between seasons.) Millard Taylor was engaged to assist in Chautauqua Symphony Orchestra programming for 1985 since a new music director had not yet been named. James Stubbs was named as the new personnel manager of the Orchestra. James Copeland was the new Property Owner Trustee taking office. Robert Osburn, a former Property Owners Trustee, was elected a Class A Trustee. Edward P. Boyle, Barbara DeFrees and George L. Follansbee, Jr. retired from the Board of Trustees. Two other new trustees were elected: Elizabeth Lenna of Lakewood and John Nord of Jamestown. Mrs. Lenna is a member of the advisory board of Marine Midland Bank, a director of Blackstone Corporation and a founding member and trustee of the Chautauqua Region Community Foundation. Mr. Nord has been active recently in

heading up the Jamestown Drive for the Chautauqua Annual Fund. He is president of Union-National, Inc., treasurer with the National Association of Furniture Manufacturers, and a member of the board of trustees of the Security Trust Bank. He is active in many community organizations.

Mr. Boyle and a former Institution trustee, Dr. Frank E. McElree, had been elected as directors of the Chautauqua Foundation. Richard H. Miller was re-elected as President.

Douglas E. Conroe of Maple Springs, former executive director of the Chautauqua Lake Association, was named as assistant to Vice President Smith, to work in the areas of municipal services.

In mid-March, 1985, the new Vice President for Development, Thomas M. Becker, began his duties at Chautauqua. Vice President Becker came from St. Mary's College in South Bend, Indiana where his efforts substantially increased levels of support. Russell McMahon had begun work earlier at Chautauqua as Director of The Chautauqua Fund. McMahon had worked in the college admissions office at Kansas Wesleyan College.

The first year at Chautauqua for Dr. Bratton saw much travel as he appeared in many parts of the country on behalf of the Institution and its program and development. He visited groups of Chautauquans in their winter communities. At length in April, he and Mrs. Bratton flew to Russia with Mr. and Mrs. John Wallach in connection with the Conference on U. S.-Soviet Relations which was being developed for the first week of the season. It did seem, indeed, that Dr. Bratton was assuring substantive programming for a free and probing Platform that should earn national attention. This was just one way, more visible than others, for the new president to build on existing Chautauqua strengths and to prove that he could be bold in this intention. There were many Chautauquans who were anticipating what was yet to come.

Dr. Bratton and John Wallach in Moscow, as preparations for the Chautauqua Conference were continuing.

ADDENDA

LOOKING BACK NOW, it is interesting to see how President Bratton set a historical perspective in 1984 and how progress has followed the agenda he laid out so early in his first year.

"Chautauqua is entering its 12th decade which may be one of the most significant in its long history," he pointed out in The Chautauquan... "The sobering aspect...is not that change is occurring, but that we must be wise enough to direct that change properly."

He noted the matters at hand:

The Whallon Farm land which the Institution owns beyond the gates; the land and building development inside the gates; the expansion of our development effort; and matching program dimensions with available resources to assure high quality.

"We want to come out of this decade with Chautauqua strengthened and improved and with its charm and ambience intact. The changes that will come will probably be more in structure—how we plan and deliver programs and services to Chautauquans—while strengthening the substance of the comprehensive Chautauqua Experience," Dr. Bratton affirmed.

He observed elsewhere in his remarks that there is more of an unrealized potential at Chautauqua than he had dreamed (possible) when he arrived. Indeed, this unrealized potential and the substantial reservoir of goodwill the 1984 marketing study revealed had obviously enheartened the new President. Dr. Bratton predicted that Chautauqua would nourish the positive reaction uncovered by the survey and would more precisely plan its program and promotion.

There had been an undercurrent of dissatisfaction among some Chautauquans over the rapid development of condominiums and the fear that a galloping entrepreneurism would change the historic ambience of the Grounds. The perception of a lack of control alarmed many although a limited architectural review process was in place and functioning. Fear that Chautauqua might lose its place on the National Register as an Historic District was whispered. This undercurrent came to the surface in August, 1984 when rumors spread about more property buy-outs for development purposes. In a grassroots effort, some Chautauquans asked other Chautauquans to sign petitions in support of Historic Preservation. Dr. Bratton met with representatives of this contingent and assured them that the Institution was, indeed, aware of the importance of this matter.

In line with that, a Task Force was set up to study Chautauqua's unique situation, its background of land use policies and to write new Architectural and Land Use Regulations for the Institution.

Trustee H. David Faust was named to chair the Task Force which was comprised of: Kenneth G. Fradin, George L. Follansbee, Jr., Doris Nicholson, Jeffrey Simpson, Samuel P. Price—legal counsel, and Dr. Bratton, W. Thomas Smith and Douglas Conroe from the staff.

The dilemma of land use had been recently complicated by the community's need for more and adequate housing. The Board had agreed that the Institution's future growth would depend on an expanding constituency and adequate facilities for serving people's day-to-day requirements in addition to providing a cultural program.

The demanding condition of aging structures continued to impinge on the problem. The Institution while not wanting to discourage new investment, has wanted to give some direction to private development of new construction or the recycling of old buildings; all this, to safeguard the Institution's historical significance as it is represented in its architecture. But admittedly, it had been difficult to know how to proceed.

At the May, 1985 meeting of the Board of Trustees, the Task Force submitted Interim Architectural and Land Use Regulations which if accepted by the Board would go into effect immediately with final approval to be given at the Annual meeting in November. A month later a book on "Styles of Historic Chautauqua Architecture," prepared by Jeffrey Simpson, a member of the Task Force, was presented to the Board. It gave visual examples and historical explanations of the main styles of architecture to be found at Chautauqua with guides for restoration and renovation plus a bibliography. By identifying the major elements in each style, Simpson made it easy for Chautauquans to understand their own homes and the public buildings. The book was a splendid tool for use with the Regulations and had the effect, also, of showing the need for the Regulations.

While no detailed account of these Regulations belongs here, it can be noted that the Task Force divided the Chautauqua Grounds into districts with specific recommendations for the land use in each district. In a general way, regulations dealt with the

Thomas M. Becker,
Vice President for
Development

Dr. Pavel Podlesny,
Director and Chief of
Department, U.S.A.
and Canada Studies
Institute, USSR
Academy of Sciences,
during discussions at
Chautauqua. Dr. Pod-
lesny made the Soviet
response to a keynote
address given by Dr.
Helmut Sonnenfeldt,
former senior member
of the National Security
Council of the United
States.

height, size, bulk, location, construction, repair, reconstruction, preservation and use of the structures; the
sizes of yards and open spaces; percentages of lots to
be occupied; and controls restricting the alteration of
buildings determined to be of historical significance.
An amazing amount of detail was included in the book
so that Chautauquans for years to come will be able to
find there the answers to questions about their houses.

The Regulations also created an Architectural and
Land Use Appeals Board to provide for consideration
of applications for special exceptions and variances.
This Board was to be appointed by the Chairman of
the Board of Trustees and approved by the Board.

The members of the Land Use Appeals Board were
appointed in time to serve during the summer of 1985
and made a number of decisions. The one which drew
the most public attention was that concerning the proposed demolition of the St. Elmo Hotel and the proposed construction of a new building which would be
five stories high in part, and would contain stores, condominiums and hotel accommodations. It had been
designed by Scott Lawson and had won some popular
favor. The site in question involved an entire block,
bounded by Pratt, Ames, Wythe and Vincent Avenues,
located across from Bestor Plaza.

The Land Use Appeals Board at the end of a seven
and one-half hour hearing approved demolition of the
St. Elmo, although final approval by the Institution
was to depend on the owners' providing financial
guarantees that a new building would indeed replace
the buildings now occupying that block. Variances on
height, width and setback were also granted. Permission was given for a restaurant and for shops.

Chairman Faust of the Task Force was also the
chairman of the Appeals Board. The other members
are: Robert Dietly, Jack Rice, Jeffrey Simpson and
Eleanor Franks. Although the vote was four to one for
demolition, concern was expressed that not enough
thought had been given by the owners to the feasibility of preserving the old building and fearing the
precedent that would be set by replacing valued old
buildings with new.

Previously, the Institution had put on hold the
approval of new building proposals in the center core
of the Grounds until a more defined policy of historic
preservation could be agreed upon.

However, plans had already been under way for the
Ramble Avenue Condominiums near the tennis courts
and a development of multiple housing in the Barracks
area at the South End of the Grounds. Both of these
took place according to their individual time tables.
Ramble Avenue housing was occupied in the summer
of 1985, but the Overlook Condominiums were not
ready until after the 1985 season.

Other building included the summer home for the
President and his family. Designed along traditional
lines and set in a part of the Grounds considered to be
"old Chautauqua," it almost appeared to have been
there "forever."

One single dwelling lot in the North End had been
sold and four new houses had been built on lots
already sold.

So real progress had been made on building and land
development within the gates. Best of all, the commu-

nity had the perception that the problem was at least
being fully addressed by the cooperative efforts of the
Board and the administration. Studies of a broader
consideration of the historic preservation program at
Chautauqua have since been undertaken with the possibility that an amendment to Chautauqua's State
Charter will be proposed for the purpose of the rules
and regulations governing historic preservation within
the Institution; and that there will be a response to the
suggestion that a Preservation Society should be
formed.

Another segment for possible multiple housing units
is being studied in a plot in the northwest corner of the
Grounds, south of Elm Lane, west of Hedding Avenue
and extending to the Chautauqua fence. Developing
this acreage (1.78 acres) would satisfy the need for
more housing without disturbing the historical significance and ambience of the older sections of the
Grounds.

"We will be working with the National Trust for
Historic Preservation," Dr. Bratton explained, "with
the New York Landmark Society and the Preservation
League of New York state to develop policies by which
the goals of preservation can become a part of the
thinking of Chautauqua while still encouraging new
development." He added that change is welcome, but
it must be guided within the context and goal of
preserving the historical nature and charm of The
Chautauqua Institution.

The land outside the Chautauqua gates, usually
referred to as the Whallon Farm, was another item
which Dr. Bratton had mentioned. Consequently, after
the successful completion of the Annual Fund and the
start of the new year, a Structure Task Force was
appointed to consider how to plan for the use of this
property, how to deal with tax issues that might be
involved and where the planning and management of
the Whallon Farm project would belong within the
Institution. The Task Force was comprised of Paul M.
Branch, Jack D. Rice, Robert B. Osburn, Richard H.
Miller, Samuel P. Price, George L. Follansbee, Jr., Dr.
Bratton, Vice Presidents Johnson and Smith. While
some previous assignments had been made to begin
the planning process for the Whallon Farm, these
efforts were deferred until more comprehensive planning could be undertaken by the Task Force.

About this same time, Dr. Bratton moved ahead in
another important area, by recommending that
Thomas M. Becker be elected Vice President for
Development. It had been four years since the Institution had filled this position. As Dr. Bratton had said
on a number of occasions, he was capable of dreaming
big dreams for Chautauqua, but before he would make
those dreams come true, he must make sure that
Chautauqua was indeed ready for the achievement of
both national and international leadership. A creative,
even bold, Development program was part of his plan.

Chautauqua's Development philosophy includes the
premise that the Institution is an organization which
deserves to be supported by national corporations and
foundations. Its program scope, its broad constituency,
its open Platform for the discussion of national and
global issues are reasons for such a premise.

Once Mr. Becker arrived and became acquainted

with Chautauqua, he began to build on this philosophy. He observed that to be competitive for corporate support, Chautauqua needed to enhance its national image. The U.S.-Soviet Relations Week, therefore, which was already being planned when Mr. Becker arrived, was exactly the sort of programming that proves Chautauqua's significance and might attract support. Not only was support obtained from the Mary Hillman Jennings Foundation and the Pepsi Cola Corporation toward the extra expenses of the U.S.-Soviet Week, but Mr. Becker moved ahead to arrange for the makings of a documentary of that week so that the unusually open Conference between Russians and Americans at Chautauqua could be shared later with the nation through public television. This effort took more Development dollars.

The Mary Hillman Jennings Foundation, again, and the Ralph C. Sheldon Foundation gave support to the documentary project, along with New York State Public Television Stations and private individuals.

In addition to the outside funding sources for the U.S.-Soviet Relations Week, certain lectures were provided by the Wilder Family Lectureship Endowment Fund of the Chautauqua Foundation, the Carolyn Roberts Barnum Fund and others. Endowments for lectures, chaplaincies and concerts have been contributing to the program budget for years, proceeding in tandem with Development efforts. With rising program costs, some endowments are not meeting the present demands, so there is a constant opportunity for Chautauquans to undergird the program through program endowment.

The quality of the program during the U.S.-Soviet Relations Week met the high expectations that had been raised. Much credit is due John Wallach, foreign editor of the Hearst Newspapers, who shaped the Conference and obtained Soviet participation. The Soviet and American delegations include government officials, academicians, scientists and artists. They spoke or performed on the Amphitheater stage, appeared in the smaller lecture halls, answered questions of rank and file Americans and one another, met with Chautauquans on social occasions and in general experienced the beauty of the natural setting and the "chemistry" of the mixture of people to be found at Chautauqua.

The Week was indeed a multi-level, serious/light-hearted shopping spree of ideas and emotions. There was a pleasant give-and-take almost any way one might be facing: between Platform speakers; between Platform and audience; among members of the audience or other informal groups. Chautauquans feel comfortable speaking freely or listening attentively during discussions.

There were many newcomers on the Grounds during that week, a fact that was beneficial to Chautauqua and the Week's success, but best of all, it was giving newcomers a chance to discover the Chautauqua Experience.

Meanwhile, Mr. Becker had contacted Glen Pearcy, an award-winning producer of documentaries, who agreed to come to Chautauqua to film the Conference and edit a program which would give both the flavor and some of the solid substance of the week's events.

Aired first February 3, 1986 over WNED, Buffalo, the documentary, "From Moscow to Chautauqua," has been seen over more than two hundred PBS Channels across the country.

Nancy Gay Bargar had joined the Development staff July 1 as director of major gifts. Miss Bargar was formerly director of marketing for IDBI Marketers, Inc. of New York City, sellers of industrial development bonds insurance. After she arrived, in addition to her other work, she assisted Mr. Becker with the documentary project.

The participation of the Soviets in the U.S.-Soviet Relations Week in June, 1985, was a foretaste of what may follow the signing of the new cultural and scientific accords by President Reagan and Soviet Secretary Mikhail Gorbachev. As the Chautauqua Week drew to a close, there were expansive, friendly promises that a similar get-together would be planned for a site in the Soviet Union. Now this exciting prospect seems to be about to come to pass in 1986 and another Chautauqua Week is being prophesied for 1988. Chautauqua is thus taking an active role in the important search for world understanding by the people of the United States and the Soviet Union.

Another great encouragement came to Dr. Bratton and Vice President Becker as the 1985 season was about to begin. It was news that the Carnahan-Jackson Foundation had made a $500,000 grant to Chautauqua for the improvement of educational and youth activities and for the endowment of educational programs.

Dr. Bratton spoke of the gift as releasing great energy and enthusiasm toward Chautauqua's commitment to young people. It was announced that approximately half the amount would be used to transform the Lodge into a three-studio dance teaching facility with some residential space retained and to provide a maintenance fund for the renovated 1912 structure. The new dance facility will, in turn, release space for youth activities and programming previously occupied by the dance studios. This will accomplish a major Foundation goal of the Carnahan-Jackson Foundation gift.

Paul Nitze, senior advisor to President Reagan on nuclear armament and arms control, who spoke in the Amphitheater on the final program day of Russian Week. Viktor Malkov made the response to Nitze's statements on USSR research in defensive and space weapons. Viktor Malkov is professor of history and member of the Academy of Sciences, USSR, a recipient of the Lenin Peace Prize.

Oleg M. Sokolov, Minister-Counselor and Charge d'Affaires, Soviet Embassy in Washington D.C., gave the response to the keynote address of the U.S.-Soviet Relations Conference.

David H. Carnahan, chairman of the Carnahan-Jackson Foundation, is shown in front of The Lodge which has been restored and enlarged as the new home of The School of Dance through the Foundation's substantial grant for improved educational and youth facilities and endowment of the educational program. This center section dates from 1912; new dance studios have been built in one of the original wings and in new additions at the rear. The brown shingle/white trim is a style followed in other Schools' structures at Chautauqua.

H. David Faust, the new Chairman of the Chautauqua Board of Trustees

One of the adjuncts of the Development program was created soon after Dr. Bratton's coming. It was a new Development Council to be formed by three representatives from the Board of Trustees and three from the Chautauqua Foundation. The Council was designed to strengthen the Development efforts of both parent groups and perform other specific joint duties. The Institution named its members: the Board Chairman, the Annual Fund Chairman and the Second Century Campaign Chairman with Dr. Bratton as ex-officio.

Somewhat later there came from the Council, among other matters, a focus on program endowment with a suggestion that program costs be more accurately ascertained so that endowments could be better matched to programs. This seemed to be in line with Dr. Bratton's fourth initial point made soon after his arrival: "Matching program dimensions with available resources to assure high quality."

Indeed, in this statement, he seemed to be combining two goals, budget management and quality of programming. He was actually suggesting a different approach to programming and program-enhancement, and he was also addressing another criterion he had raised in connection with Development: the efficient handling of Development Funds.

Increasing specific program endowments, as the Development Council indicated, is one of the answers for providing high quality programs which are often high-cost programs, as well. Dr. Bratton had been alert to outside program funding for specific programs. During 1965, for example, the Laurel Foundation of Pittsburgh gave support during Global Issues/Megatrends Week because of its interest in the subject matter that was being discussed on the Platform. This example also suggests that there is a potential for creativity even when cost-restrictions are present.

But working with Vice President Becker, Dr. Bratton enunciated a clarion call for increased *unrestricted* endowments which would allow for an expansive growth of quality and excellence beyond budgetary restraints.

In addition, looking objectively at the broad scope of the Institution's program and its history, the two leaders could point out that endowments for the performing arts are not only appropriate, but acutely needed. Chautauqua's pioneering role as a center for creativity in the arts, demands that the Institution maximize the investment of past years and reach new levels of achievement.

"We need to more than double the $9 million endowment of the Chautauqua Foundation so that we will have the resources beyond the budget for program-enhancement," Mr. Becker said. Recalling that the Gebbie Challenge had taught Chautauqua budget-balancing and the necessity for new giving levels, he said, "Now we must go further so that we can accomplish more quality-building in the program areas."

Dr. Bratton's appreciation of the potential at Chautauqua was extending beyond the preoccupation with dollars and cents, however. He had already secured the cooperation of a number of Chautauquans on specific projects, committees and task forces when a major, though not unexpected change in Board leadership took place.

At the annual election in August, Mr. Faust was named chairman of the Board of Trustees; James D. Copeland, vice chairman; and Dr. Paul E. Irion, chairman of the executive committee.

Several situations had dictated that there would be changes within the Board. Mr. Gibbs had indicated his desire to retire from the chairmanship which he had held since 1978. Dr. Hickman, chairman of the executive committee, had completed his terms of Board membership. He, too, had given extraordinary service, having been chairman of the Presidential Search Committee during the 1983-1984 year. Earlier it had been decided to function with only one vice chairman of the Board, and a new nomination was expected. Dr. Irion was already a member of the executive committee, and could easily move into that chairmanship.

Three new members were added to the Board: Thomas R. Bromeley, Kenneth G. Fradin and Andrea Stutz Zarou.

Mr. Bromeley is a prominent business leader in Bradford, Pa., and is active in a number of areas of interest. He has been enjoying Chautauqua for years. The Bromeley summer home is at Chautauqua Shores.

Mr. Fradin is retired from a Buffalo-based law practice. He has been a Chautauqua property owner since 1965 and was active in the Second Century Campaign. The Fradins are now living near Boston.

Mrs. Zarou and her husband, Dr. Donald Zarou, and their four children, live in their Chautauqua home which was originally the home of Mrs. Zarou's great-grandmother, the Rev. Emily Woodruff. Mrs. Zarou's first career is teaching, but she is now an ordained minister.

Mr. Gibbs, Harry A. Logan Jr., and James A. Zurn were reelected to serve additional terms on the Board.

Mr. Faust, who practices law in West Palm Beach, Florida, is a lifelong Chautauquan, although he modestly claims his more recent fifteen years at Chautauqua as his background for serving on the Board of Trustees. He began coming with his wife and family about 1967. Their Chautauqua home is located at 17 Ames Avenue. However, his parents, Drs. Harold and Amy Faust, brought him to Chautauqua as a child.

Mr. Faust has said that he sees the role of the Board of Trustees as one of setting policy and interpreting it to the community. As chairman, he will seek to do this, he said.

At the Annual Meeting in November, special recognition was given to Howard Gibbs for his years of outstanding service to the Institution. An impressive picture album had been prepared, containing highlights of momentous occasions during his chairmanship, documented by photographs and printed reports of his presentations on the Platform and elsewhere at Chautauqua.

The Trustees also voted to present a Chautauqua Medallion to Mr. Gibbs, signifying the value which the Institution places on his years of commitment and dedication. Later they established a scholarship fund in his honor.

Mr. Faust said that he entered his new responsibilities with the assurance that Howard would be assisting him and other members of the Board "as we move forward into another phase of Chautauqua's history."

As the new Chairman later discussed his views of the future in an interview, he called attention to the Planning Committee which had been formed with James Copeland as chairman. This committee will be looking beyond the day-to-day activities to long-range planning, and they will be coordinating the efforts of other Board committees that will continue to make plans in their respective areas, he said.

Dr. Bratton, for his part, said that he expects this committee to have on-going work, for "a long-range plan is an ever-changing document."

Serving with Mr. Copeland are: Howard Gibbs, Betty Lenna, Robert O. Wilder, Marcia Connelly, Myles Fox, Tim Goodell and Harold Thurston. Ken Rogers, who coordinated last year's marketing study, has been retained as a consultant.

As Dr. Bratton reported coming events to Chautauquans in the spring of '86, he communicated excitement over achievements, performers and the world of ideas and skills.

The Athenaeum would open June 21st and remain open through Labor Day! There would be a pre-season special in the Amph on June 21st with Dinah Shore appearing the next Saturday night before the official opening June 29th. Governor Cuomo would be addressing the Jamestown High School graduation June 27th at Chautauqua and had been invited to stay overnight and to meet Chautauquans the next day. The Colonnade portico and steps had been replaced, along with the handicapped access ramp. (The columns glisten with new white paint.)

The Chautauqua Conference on the American Family would explore the changing nature of family patterns and connections between the generations, while a focus on China would bring distinction to International Affairs Week.

The Conservatory Theater under the direction of Michael Kahn would be presenting two productions of Norton Hall and four in Normal Hall while the Chautauqua Symphony Orchestra would bring one satisfy-

ing concert after another (twenty-one in all) with an array of guest artists and conductors. "Daughter of the Regiment" would have its first Chautauqua performance since 1934 and Stravinsky's "The Rake's Progress" would be having a Chautauqua premiere during the opera season. And there was more...

Before the season began, Dr. Bratton was able to announce the dates of the anticipated Chautauqua Conference in the Soviet Union: September 15-19, 1986 with the arrival of the USA delegation and tourist group first in Leningrad with departure from Moscow September 23 (eleven days inclusive).

He explained: "On September 11, 1986 The Chautauqua Institution (in cooperation/partnership with The Eisenhower Institute) at the invitation of the Soviet government will take a group of 220 American citizens, officials and performers to the Soviet Union. The purpose of this meeting will be to engage in a Chautauqua-style meeting with Soviet citizens, officials and performers in an open forum with access to media and without prior censorship...

"I am pleased to announce the continuation of what was begun in June of 1985. To our knowledge this will be the first time American and Soviet Officials will debate in public in the Soviet Union in front of an audience comparable to the size of the one at Chautauqua."

After his survey of the weeks ahead, he introduced a new phrase about Chautauqua that sounded as though it could be a watchword for the future: the *"essentiality* of this place...to our country, to our culture and to those who have discovered it." It sounded Vincent-esque in its assessment of national importance and individual rewards. It raises an implied question concerning all those who have yet to find the Chautauqua Experience in the future, and how this may come about. It seems to say, as Vincent said one hundred years ago, "There must be more to follow."[4]

Michael Kahn, Director of the Conservatory Theater Company and Theater School

President Bratton in a reflective mood as he looks across the Plaza from his office window. The original part of the St. Elmo Hotel, known as the Park Cottage, may be seen through the window.

1983 PROGRAM FIGURES

Musicians
Dinah Shore
Woody Herman
U. S. Army Field Band and
   Soldiers' Chorus
Kris Kristofferson
Billy Swan
Roger Williams
Emmylou Harris
The Symphonic Chorus
Faye Robinson
Patricia Griffin
David Britton
James Morris
Ming Feng Hsin
Carol Wincenc
Harry Belafonte, guest
   Dianne Reeves
Jeffrey Campbell
Geraldine Fitzgerald
Lynn Harrell
Melissa Manchester
Skitch Henderson
Opera Apprentice Artists
Tom Paxton
Bob Gibson
Anne Hill
Young Uck Kim
John Davidson
Philippe Entremont
Paul Neubauer
Takako Nishizaki
Ray Charles
Byron Janis
Pete Seeger
Arlo Guthrie
New Arts Trio
Hyoung Joon Chang
Jaime Laredo
The Tommy Dorsey Orchestra
   Buddy Morrow, Conductor
Air Force Band of the East

Harvey Pittel
Robert Goulet
Bobby Vinton
Bach-Elgar Choir
Mary Shearer
Lili Chookasian
Jerold Norman
John Brandstetter
The Amherst Saxophone Quartet
Al Albert and The Original Four
   Aces, The Ink Spots and The Pied
   Pipers
Ramsey Lewis Trio
Larry Elgart and his "Hooked on
   Swing Orchestra"
Pete Fountain
Tennessee Ernie Ford
Barbershop Quartets, Chorus—
   The Harrington Brothers;
   Syncopation Corporation Quartet;
   Monroe Doctrine Quartet; Friends
   of Harmony Chorus

Conductors
Varujan Kojian
Sixten Ehrling
Philippe Entremont
Hugo Fiorato
Sergiu Comissiona
Walter Hendl
Skitch Henderson
Newton Wayland

Other Programs
in the Amphitheater
Shields and Yarnell (Mimes)
An Evening with Ginger Rogers
Heloise
Mummenschanz (Mime)
Rod McKuen, Poet and Performer
Clement Conger, *The White House
   and Its Collections*
Phyllis Diller, Narrator and
   Comedienne

Platform Lecturers
Senator Adlai Stevenson
George Gallup, Jr.
Senator Robert Taft, Jr.
Senator Eugene McCarthy
Former Senator John Anderson
Colonel James Irwin
Dr. Allan L. Goldstein

Dr. Henry Keimlich
Walter Sullivan
Dr. Jonas Salk
James McIntyre
J. Peter Grace
Norman Robertson, Sr.
Robert Farrell
Venita VanCaspel
Carl Stokes
Victor Herman
Eric Meyers
Ashby T. Harper
David Powers
Ernest Michel
Rocky Blier
Dorothy DeBolt
Ed Walker
Max Cleland
John Simon
Judith Crist
Leslie Fiedler
Harold Schonberg
Martin Bookspan
Kate Rand Lloyd
Dr. Bruno Bettelheim
Nicholas Goncharoff
Letty Cottin Pogrebin
Betty Griedan
The Hon. Daniel Terra
Brendan Gill
Paolo Soleri
Boris Goldovsky
John Houseman
Dr. Luigi Einaudi
John Wallach
Joseph Montville
Amb. Diego Asencio
Amb. Malcom Toon

Chaplains
Coretta Scott King (Sunday Only)
Father John Weimer
Dr. Morgan Roberts
Dr. Herbert O'Driscoll
Dr. Maxie Dunnan
Dr. Graham Hardy
Dr. Bruce Thielemann
The Rev. Jean Curtis
Dr. R. F. Smith
Dr. Oswald J. C. Hoffman
Dr. Norman Vincent Peale

Religion Department
Lecturers
Dr. Claire Randall
George Gallup, Jr.
Dr. Lester Smith
Dr. Merrill Kent Schumaker
Dr. Bruce Lockerbie
Dr. Martin Marty
Rabbi Irving Greenberg
Elie Wiesel (one day only)
Dr. Leonard Sweet
James Bruce Nelson
Dr. Bonnie Kittel
Dr. Ronald Sider

Operas
Cynthia Auerbach, Artistic Director

The Merry Widow

Varujan Kojian, Conductor
Dorothy Frank Danner, Director
Manon Lescaut
   John DeMain, Conductor
   Cynthia Auerbach, Director
The Marriage of Figaro
   Graziella Sciutti, Director
   George Manahan, Conductor
Of Mice and Men
   John DeMain, Conductor
   Cynthia Auerbach, Director

Dance
Chautauqua Dance Festival Company
   Jean-Pierre Bonnefoux, Director
   Patricia McBride, ballet soloist
   Sean Lavery and Bonita Borne,
   ballet soloists with the CDFC
   Both programs with CSO
Chautauqua Dance Festival Company
   appearing with Chautauqua
   Festival Orchestra
The Vanaver Caravan

Theater
The Acting Company
The Cradle Will Rock
   Broadway Company June 27, 28
Pericles
El Grande de Coca Cola
A Chamber Musical
The Tavern
Plays and Other Plays by Samuel
   Beckett
The Merry Wives of Windsor

Music School
Festival Orchestra
Nathan Gottschalk, Director

Soloists
Nadja Salerno-Sonnenberg
Charles Curtis
Da Hong Seetoo
New Arts Trio
   Pennys, Janowski, Doane
Thomas Dewey
Barbara Whelan
Mira Folusx
Michael Burritt
J. Thomas Goodheart
Anne Snow Duraski
Donna Zapola
Angela Steroos
Diane di Marco
Tamara Seymour
Amy Bromeley

Evan N. Wilson, Sigma Alpha Iota
   Winner

Chautauqua Youth Orchestra
Four concerts
Anthony Milograno, Director

CAA
Phyllis Kind, Juror for Chautauqua
   Art Association's National
   Exhibition of American Art

Rod McKuen singing, reciting, talking to appreciative audiences
at Chautauqua

1984 PROGRAM FIGURES

Musicians
Tony Bennett
Buddy Rich
Grand Old Music Show
  starring Minnie Pearl
Anna Maria Alberghetti
Gordon MacRae
Billy Taylor
Marian McPartland
Adam Makowicz
Exile, Cross-over Group
Sarah Reese
Lili Chookasin
David Allen Wehr
Dmitry Sitkovetsky
Nitty Gritty Dirt Band and Tom
  Rush
Roberta Peters
Chautauqua Opera Apprentices
Mozart on Fifth
  Richard Goldfarb, Ethan Silver-
  man, Daniel Kelley
Happy Together
  The Turtles
  The Association
  Gary Puckett and the Union Gap
  Spanky and Our Gang
Alicia de Larrocha
David Jolley
Elmar Oliveira
Bill Monroe and John Hartford
Eugenia Zukerman
Richard Stilwell
Kerry McCarthy
Michael Austin
Lou Rawls
Patrick Gregoire
The Western Wind Vocal Ensemble
Yo-Yo Ma
Chuck Mangione
Liang Lin
Glenn Miller Orchestra
Joseph Steiner
Yefim Bronfman
Sheena Easton
Mary Burgess
Carroll Freeman
Julian Patrick
Rochester Oratorio Society
Chautauqua Chamber Singers
The Clancy Brothers
Theodore Bikel
Ferrante and Teicher
The Modern Jazz Quartet
Roger Whittaker
New Arts Trio
U.S. Air Force Band of the East
U.S. Army Field Band and Chorus

Jazz Ensemble From Jamestown
  High School

Conductors
Varujan Kojian
John DeMain
Henry Mancini
Sixten Ehrling
Lukas Foss
Paul Schwartz
Erich Kunzel
Bruce Ferden
Semyon Bychkov
Maxim Shostakovitch
Victor Borge
Ernest Jones
Hugh Fiorato

**Other Programs
in the Amphitheater**
The No Elephant Circus
Vincent Dowling in an Evening of
  Poetry by Robert Service

Platform Lecturers
Dr. Leslie H. Gelb
Paul Duke
Senator George McGovern
Marva Collins
Dr. Henry Steel Commager
Jules Berman
Dr. Gilbert W. Kliman
William Cunningham
Dr. Maurice J. Mahoney
Victor Gilinsky
C. Fred Bergsten
Dr. Jan S. Prybla
Eliot Janeway
Jack Lavery
Conrad Teitell
Drew Middleton
Dr. John Stoessinger
Gen. Daniel O. Graham
Richard N. Perle
Dr. Helen Caldicott
Sarah Weddington
Stewart Udall
Elizabeth Holtzman
Barry Reed
James B. Stewart
Madeleine L'Engle
Hon. John Dyson (in afternoon
  at Smith-Wilkes Hall)
Jean Shepherd
Lionel Abel
I. F. Stone
Alfred Kazin
Suzanne Braun Levine
Dr. William J. Winslade
Max Singer
Tom Logsdon
Dr. George Gerbner
Frank Hodsoll
Elizabeth McCann
Dr. Christopher Lasch
Jacques D'Amboise

Attorney Donald Millinger
Alexander M. Haig, Jr.
Amb. Meir Rosenne
Dr. Dmitri Simes
Kathleen Troia
Congressman Daniel Glickman
John Wallach, Moderator
Amb. Sol M. Linowitz

Chaplains
Dr. Bruce Thielemann
Dr. William N. Jackson
Dr. Neal Fisher
Bishop James Malone
The Rev. Barbara Lundblad
Dr. Ernest Campbell
Dr. Clinton Marsh
Dr. James Ford
Dr. Milton Engbretson
Dr. Graham Hardy

*Additional speakers at
Morning Devotionals*
Louisa Kennedy
Jeanne Wandersleben
Moorhead Kennedy
Dr. Carnegie Samuel Calian
Dr. Michael Quicke

**Religion Department
Lecturers**
Dr. Monika Hellwig
Bishop James Malone
Mrs. Verna Barrett
Rabbi John Spitzer
Dr. Charles MacKenzie
Dr. Peter Macky
Moorhead Kennedy
Dr. Carnegie Samuel Calian
Dr. James Ford
Dr. Sidney Hormell
Dr. Peter Hawkins
Dr. Roger Barrett
Dr. John H. Westerhoff III

Operas
Cynthia Auerbach, Artistic
  Director

Gala/Die Fledermaus
  Evening included tribute to
  Leonard and Martha Treash,
  other former members of the
  Company, and in celebration
  of Norton Hall's renovation
  and fifty-six years of opera at
  Chautauqua in Norton Hall
  John DeMain, Conductor
  Cynthia Auerbach, Director
Don Giovanni
  John DeMain, Conductor
  Cynthia Auerbach, Director
Man of LaMancha
  Anton Coppola, Conductor
  Dorothy Danner, Director
Hansel & Gretel
  Varujan Kojian, Conductor

Albert Takazauchas, Director
Two one-act operas, *Gianni Schicci*
  and *A Little Night Music* were
  staged in Normal Hall, at the Boys
  and Girls club and the Children's
  School, as well as traveling to
  Mercyhurst College in Erie.

Dance
Chicago City Ballet
  Paul Mejha, Co-director
Chautauqua Dance Festival
  Company
  Jean-Pierre Bonnefoux, Artistic
  Director and Principal Teacher
  Three Ballet Programs
Martha Graham Technique Dance
  Students
  Jean-Pierre Bonnefoux, Artistic
  Director
American Ballet Comedy

Theater
The Acting Company

The Skin of Our Teeth
Pieces of Eight, one-act plays
A Chamber Musical

**Music School
Festival Orchestra**
Nathan Gottschalk, Conductor

Soloists
Randall Hodginson
Concerto Concert:
  Beth Neely
  Jeanie Miller
  John Falcone
  Chandler Cudlipp
  John Dunlop
  Carolyn Comfort
  Julie Trudeau
  Deborah Grim
  Stephen Redfield
  Eric Koonig
  Brenda Lang
  Saekyung Park
Chautauqua Dance Festival Company
  Jean-Pierre Bonnefoux, Artistic
  Director, Principal Teacher

Saeyung Park, Sigma Alpha Iota
  Winner

Chautauqua Youth Orchestra
Four concerts—Soloist:
  Mary Jane Austin

CAA
Randall Williams of the Metropolitan
  Museum of Art, Juror for the Chau-
  tauqua Art Association's National
  Exhibition of American Art

1985 PROGRAM FIGURES

Musicians
Sergio Mendes and Friends
The Paul Winter Consort
Tom Paxton
The Kingston Trio
Louisiana Repertory Jazz Ensemble
Roy Orbison
Bella Davidovich
Eugene Fodor
Ekaterina Sarantseva
Seldom Scene
Jodie Gelbogis
Chautauqua Opera Apprentices
The 1985 Members only *Happy Together* Tour featuring the Turtles, the Grass Roots, The Buckinghams and Gary Lewis and the Playboys
Joseph Silverstein
Chaim Zemach
Sergiu Luca
Joan Baez
Shari Lewis
Stormy Sachs
Paul Sportelli
The New Arts Trio
 Rebecca Pennys
 Piotr Janowski
 Steven Doane
Spiro Malas
Peter Duchin and the Peter Duchin Orchestra
Beth Scwartz Robinson
The Quiet Riot with Oscar Brand
Cheryl Parrish
The Everly Brothers
Barry Tuckwell
Gustavo Romero
Karen Huffstodt
Michael Austin
Cornelis Opthof
Chautauqua Symphony Chorus
Lee Spear
The Temptations
Marvin Hamlisch
Martha Schlamme
Lorin Hollander
Sergio Franchi and the Mantovanni Orchestra with Jerry Seinfeldt
Laszlo Varga
Quest with David Liebman and Richard Beirach
Hakan Hagegard
Larry Gatlin & the Gatlin Brothers
Smokey Robinson
The Canadian Brass
 Frederic Mills
 Ronald Romm
 Martin Hackelman
Eugene Watts
Charles Daellenbach
The Lettermen
The Captain and Teneille
Paul Whiteman's Historic Aeolian Hall Concert with Maurice Peress, Conductor; Ivan Davis and Dick Hyman, Pianists
Gordon Lightfoot

Conductors
Sergiu Comissiona
Jerzy Semkov
John DeMain
Louis Lane
Catherine Comet
Shari Lewis
Jahja Ling
Erich Kunzel
Charles Wuorinen
Harvey Biskin
Franz Allers
Kenneth Schermerhorn
Anton Coppola
Theo Alcantara
Hugo Fiorato
Kazuyoshi Akiyama

Other Programs in the Amphitheater
Soviet Poet Andrei Voznesensky
Soviet Poet Yevgeni Yevtushenko
First Lady, Theatreworks/USA (Chautauquan Bijou Clinger in role)
Evolution vs Scientific Creationism, a debate
 Kelly Segraves
 Dorothy Nelkin

Platform Lecturers
Mark Palmer
John Wallach
Geoffrey Kemp
Helmut W. Sonnenfeldt
Dr. S. Frederick Starr
Paul Nitze
Soviet Delegation
 Viktor Malkov
 Pavel Podlesny
 Tatiana Chervakhova
 Oleg Sokolov
 Andrei Parastaeyev
 Georgei Garanyan
 Yekaterina Sarantseva
Elsa A. Porter
Karen Horn
Robert W. Lundeen
Elliott L. Schlang
Rep. Barber B. Conable, Jr.
Gaylord Nelson
Alan Gussow
Dr. Robert F. Weaver
Patrick S. Osmer
Sherry Turkle
Susan Sontag
John Van Doren
Alan Roland and Steven Aaron
Paul Goldberger
Joan Mondale
Diane Ravitch
Harriet Pilpel
Robert Coles, M.D.
Dr. W. Andrew Achenbaum
Dr. Mary Catherine Bateson
Stephen Schlesinger
Dr. Estelle Ramey
Dr. Josef Alfredo Antonio ben-Jochannan
Roger Rosenblatt
Eileen Rockefeller Growald
Robert J. White, M.D.
Doris Rapp, M.D.
Charles E. Horton, M.D.
Robert P. Nirschi, M.D.
Mario M. Cuomo, Governor of New York
Stanley Lundine, Congressman, NY
Cal Thomas
Bella Abzug
Professor William W. Leuchtenburg
Richard Lamm, Governor of Colorado
Frances Lappe
Dr. Douglas Bennett
Professor James David Barber
Dr. Stephen Jay Gould

Chaplains
Dr. David H. C. Read
Dr. Ralph W. Loew
Bishop John T. Walker
Dr. Ernest G. Schmidt
Dr. Gordon MacDonald
Dr. John W. Vannorsdall
Dr. Reed M. Stewart
The Rev. Joan Salmon Campbell
Dr. Maurice Boyd, Toronto
Dr. William N. Jackson
Bishop Forrest Stith

Additional speakers at Morning Devotionals
The Rev. George Wirth
Dr. Daniel L. Bratton
The Rev. William Meyer
Barry Vaughn
Dr. Charles Ten Eyck

Religion Department Lecturers
Dr. Michael J. Lavelle
Dr. Kenneth Van Wyk
Dr. Thomas Gillespie
Dr. Leroy T. Howe
Richard G. Watts
Dr. Victor F. Leanza
Dr. Robert J. White
Rabbi Bradley N. Bleefeld
The Rev. Tim Fairman
Rabbi Arthur J. Lelyveld
The Rev. Robert Hoover
The Rev. Gary Cook

Operas
Cynthia Auerbach, Artistic Director

Guys and Dolls
 Anton Coppola, Conductor
 Dorothy Danner, Director
Madame Butterfly
 Anton Coppola, Conductor
 Patrick Bakman, Director
Carmen
 John DeMain, Conductor
 Cynthia Auerbach, Director
Street Scene
 John DeMain, Conductor
 Cynthia Auerbach, Director
Street Scene
 John DeMain, Conductor
 Cynthia Auerbach, Director
 Franco Colavecchia, Designer

Dance
Chautauqua Dance Festival Company
 Jean-Pierre Bonnefoux, Director
 Patricia McBride, Ib Anderson, William Stolar, Soloists
Chautauqua Dance Festival Company, Modern Dance with Martha Graham students. Kevin Keenan, Director, Choreographer
Sleeping Beauty
 Stolar, soloist with CSO

Theater
Conservatory Theater Company
Michael Kahn, Artistic Director
Opening year

Play in Norton Hall
The Glass Menagerie
Roles by Teresa Wright, Tom Hulce, Melissa Gilbert and Mark Arnott

Four productions in Normal Hall

Music School Festival Orchestra
Nathan Gottschalk, Conductor

Soloists
Barbara Kilduff
Chautauqua Dance Festival Company
Laura Ardan
Sae-Kyung Park
Chai-Lun Yueh
Combined concert with Chautauqua Youth Orchestra Anthony Milograno, Conductor
Chautauqua Youth Orchestra Jennifer Wion, Soloist,

Maria Fortune, Sigma Alpha Iota winner

CAA
Dr. Evan H. Turner, Juror
 Chautauqua Art Association, National Exibition of American Art

1986 PROGRAM FIGURES

Musicians
Barry Snyder
William Riley—NFMC Winner
Emanuel Ax
William Stolar
Eugene Fodor
CSO FOUR
  Jan Eberle
  Roger Hiller
  William Scribner
  Rebecca Root Davis
Carolann Page
Douglas Ahlstedt
Nathaniel Rosen
Joseph Silverstein
Jeffrey Campbell
Cleo Laine
James Van Demark
Andre-Michel Schub
The Mendelssohn Choir
  of Pittsburgh
Gary Lakes
Arnold Voketaitis
Louise Russell
Janice Meyerson
Pre Season—The Golden Boys of
  Bandstand
Dinah Shore with The Nelson
  Riddle Orchestra
Blood, Sweat & Tears with David
  Clayton Thomas
Pete Seeger in Concert
Dave Brubeck & Quartet
Roy Clark
The Monkees/Hermans
  Hermits/Gary Punkett
  The Union Gap/Grass Roots
Chautauqua Chamber Singers
Ferrante & Teicher
Peter, Paul & Mary
The Phoenix Boys Choir

Emanuel Ax has been
appearing frequently at
Chautauqua.

Cranberry Lake Jug Band
Roger Miller
New Arts Trio
Spyro Gyra
Bobby Vinton
Butch Thompson & The Butch
  Thompson Trio
The Miami Sound Machine
Air Force Band of the East
The Barbershop Harmony Parade
Jamestown High School Jazz
  Ensemble
"Ain't Misbehavin"—The Fats
  Waller Musical Show in Concert
Miles Davis
Neil Sedaka
Glen Campbell

Conductors
Franz Allers
Jahja Ling
Yoel Levi
Hugo Fiorato
Cal Stewart Kellogg
Uri Segal
Paul Gemignani
Michel Tabachnik
Joseph Silverstein
Kazuyoshi Akiyama
Hugh Wolff
Newton Wayland
Theo Alcantara

Other Programs in the Amphitheater
The Murray Lewis Dance Company
Kevin McCarthy in "Give 'em Hell
  Harry"
Documentary Film—"From Mao to
  Mozart,"
  Walter Scheuer-commentary
The American Dance Machine
Harry Blackstone, Jr.

Platform Lectures
Suzanne Levine
Gloria Steinem
Elizabeth Kubler-Ross
Francine Klagsbrun
Eleanor Holmes Norton
Fred Rogers (seminar)
Elaine Brody
John Wallach
Wang Li
Dr. Harry Harding
Dr. Zhao Jinglun
Yang Jiechi
Harrison Salisbury
James Watt (seminar)
William F. Blair
David Burge
Roger Kennedy
John W. Leggett
Mel Gussow
Amory Houghton, Jr.
Douglas Fraser
Edward T. Hall
The Hon. Donald S. Macdonald
The Hon. Edmund S. Muskie

John Kenneth Galbraith
Albert Shanker
Glenn Loury
James Scamman
Shirley Chisholm
Chester E. Finn, Jr.
Jeremy Rifkin
Pamela McCorduck
The Hon. William G. Davis
Lynn Ray Sykes
Craig Covault
Stanley T. Crooke, M.D.
Michael Romansky
Robert Coles, M.D.
Donald Vickery, M.D.
Roger Rosenblatt
Richard Viguerie
James David Barber
Alfred Schneider
Elliot Richardson
Gus Tyler
Virginia Yans-McLaughlin
David McCullough
Sol Linowitz

Chaplains
Dr. Bruce Thielemann
Dr. H. Maurice Boyd
Dr. Frederick H. Borsch
Dr. Robert L. Hock
Dr. Daniel L. Bratton
Dr. James A. Forbes, Jr.
Dr. Nancy Hardesty
Dr. Leonard Griffith
The Rev. Thomas G. Long
Dr. H. Pat Albright
Dr. Samuel Moffett

Religion Department Lecturers
Dr. Roger & Verna Barrett
Dr. Peter Macky
Howard Fish
Mark Harvey
Henry Smith
Rabbi Mark Loeb
Sister Joan Chittister
Dr. R. H. Bell
Dr. Richard Vieth
Rev. Jeb Magruder
John B. Anderson

Religion Department Seminars
Judge John Milligan
Moorhead Kennedy

Operas
Cynthia Auerbach, Artistic Director

The Rake's Progress
  Cynthia Auerbach, Director
  John DeMain, Conductor
The Mikado
  Harry Danner, Director
  Paul Nadler, Conductor

Il Trovatore
  Cal Stewart Kellogg, Conductor
  David Kneuss, Stage Director
The Daughter of the Regiment
  Dorothy Danner, Director
  John DeMain, Conductor

Dance
Chautauqua Dance Festival
Company

Soloists
Merrill Ashley, Sean Lavery
  New York City Ballet Principals
Serge Lavoie
Modern Dance Department
  Guests from Martha Graham
  Center, New York City

Theater
Conservatory Theater Company
Michael Kahn, Artistic Director

Plays in Normal Hall
Three By Thornton Wilder
USA John Dos Passos
  Adapted by Paul Shyre
Uncommon Women and Others
  Wendy Wasserstein
Love, The Best Doctor
  Moliére

Plays in Norton Hall
Key Exchange Kevin Wade
The Four Poster Jan de Hartog

Music School Festival Orchestra
Nathan Gottschalk, Conductor

Soloists
Sandra Park
Barbara Harbach
Rebecca Penneys
David Burge
Chautauqua Dance Festival
  Company
Lee Wilkins
David Hult

Soprano Ai-Lanzhu, Sigma Alpha
  Iota Winner Artist

Chautauqua Youth Orchestra
Anthony Milograno, Conductor
One concert
Festival and Youth Orchestra
  Combined Concert

CAA
Charles Clough, an artist from New
  York City, Juror for the Chautau-
  qua Art Association's National
  Exhibition of American Art

HISTORICAL LIST OF TRUSTEES

MEMBERS OF THE BOARD OF TRUSTEES

FOOTNOTES

THREE TAPS OF THE GAVEL

1. Scrapbook I, Mrs. Adelaide L. Westcott, page 1. Thumbnail sketches written by John H. Vincent.

2. Scrapbook II, Mrs. Adelaide L. Westcott, page 7. Lewis Miller's speech on opening night, 1888.

3. *Ibid.,* page 25. Dr. Vincent's Recognition Day Address, 1888.

4. Scrapbook III, Adelaide L. Westcott, page 117.

5. Address of Dr. Curtis W. Haug, August 24, 1969, on file in the Chautauqua Historical Collection.

6. Chautauqua Institution Charter, 1902, granted by the State Legislature of New York.

7. Chautauqua Lake Morphometry, Table IV-1, addendum to "A Report to the Public on Chautauqua Lake Studies, Part I."

8. *A Biological Survey of the Allegheny and Chemung Watersheds,* Supplement to Twenty-seventh Annual Report (1937) of the State of New York Conservation Department, page 196, 197. Some lake statistics also taken from this survey.

9. Samuel M. Gray, "well-known expert," is quoted.

10. Vincent, *op. cit.,* page 257, 258.

11. *Ibid,* page 277.

12. Different sources fail to agree on the year of the Miller Cottage construction; the author has chosen to give credence to those who use the 1875 date, although there is some evidence that supports the earlier date of 1874.

13. Vincent, *op. cit.,* page 24.

14. *A History of the Music Festival at Chautauqua Institution from 1874-1957,* L. Jeanette L. Wells, Pages 154-160.

15. Vincent, *op. cit.,* page 75.

16. *Ibid,* page 75.

17. *Ibid,* page 81.

18. *The Story of Chautauqua,* Jesse L. Hurlbut, page 208.

19. *Chautauqua Year-Book for 1895,* page 17.

20. *Ibid,* page 16.

21. *Ibid,* page 15.

22. Hurlbut, *op. cit.,* page 112.

23. Actual amount of debt difficult to determine now. This figure received from Almet N. Broadhead, treasurer of the Institution in 1970. Mrs. Richmond in *Chautauqua, An American Place* uses "approximately $800,000." David Starr's account of the saving of Chautauqua puts the figure over $800,000.

24. *Chautauqua, An American Place,* Rebecca Richmond, page 149.

25. *Ibid.,* page 151.

26. *Ibid.,* page 152.

27. The Chautauquan DAILY, August 28, 1936.

28. The Chautauquan DAILY, August 3, 1937.

29. Notebook of Rebecca Richmond in The Historical Collection.

30. *The History of Eighty-Five Years, 1889-1974. Chautauqua Women's Club,* page 6. (Mrs. Norman G. Jacobs, chairman of the history committee.)

PLEDGE TO THE FUTURE

1. Continuity through Change

1. Copy of Lewis Miller letter to Dr. William Rainey Harper in Margaret Miller Newman's Papers, Box I, Folder 6, Chautauqua Historical Collection. Dr. Harper's reply dated Dec. 22, 1896, though not quoted here, is in the Presidential Papers of William Rainey Harper, Box III, Folder 7, Department of Special Collections, The Joseph Regenstein Library, The University of Chicago. Lewis Miller's letter contains a reaction to an article by Dr. Harper in The Outlook, September, 1896, Vol. 54, Page 551.

2. Vincent, op. cit., page 19.

3. Miller, op. cit., page 7.

4. Hurlbut, op. cit. page 28.

5. Vincent, op. cit., page 24.

6. Hurlbut, op. cit. page 141.

7. Arthur E. Bestor, Jr., "Chautauqua Publications, An Historical and Bibliographical Guide," Chautauqua, New York: Chautauqua Press, 1934, Page 11.

8. Harper, William R., D.D., "John H. Vincent, The Founder of the Chautauqua Movement," The Outlook, September, 1896, Volume 54, Page 551.

9. The Chautauquan, March, 1885, Vol. V, Pages 358, 359.

10. The Chautauquan, March, 1889, Vol. IX, Pages 381, 382.

11. "The Chautauqua Movement," Joseph E. Gould. Albany: State University of New York Press, 1961. Page 24.

12. The Chautauquan, April. 1886, Vol. VI, Page 415.

13. The Assembly Herald, July 26, 1889, Page 1.

14. The Chautauquan, March, 1889, Op. cit., Page 382.

15. "CLSC, 1878-1914, An Historical Interpretation of Education Piety in America" Charles R. Kniker, Ph. D., From the Abstract, Page 3; from Chapter 6, Page 363.

16. Chautauqua Propositions, Box 13, Folder 22, Harper Presidential Papers.

17. Ibid, Box 13, Folder 22.

18. Ibid, Box 13, Folder 22.

19. The University of Chicago seemed to be slated for at least a fringe relationship with the proposed Chautauqua Institute, according to Harper's explanation of his plan.

20. John H. Vincent Letter in Miller-Vincent Letters File Box, Folder 1, Chautauqua Historical Collection.

21. Harper Presidential Papers, op. cit., Box 13, Folder 23.

22. Ibid, Box 13, Folder 23.

23. Ibid, Box 13, Folder 23.

24. Ibid, Box 13, Folder 23.

25. Ibid, Box 13, Folder 23.

26. Ibid, Box 13, Folder 23.

27. Ibid, Box IV, Folder 11.

28. Ibid, Box 13, Folder 23.

29. Ibid, Box 13, Folder 23.

30. Ibid, Box 13, Folder 23.

31. Ibid, Box V, Folder 1.

32. Ibid, Box V, Folder 1.

33. Ibid, Box IV, Folder 29.

34. Ibid, Box V, Folder 11.

35. Chautauqua Historical Collection.

36. Gould, Op. Cit., Page 72. Gould opens Chapter Five, The Tents of Righteousness, with this sentence: "It is a curious fact of history that William Rainey Harper, who borrowed so freely from Chautauqua, never acknowledged any debt, nor did he ever name any of the buildings, quadrangles, branches or subdivisions of the University in honor of the institution to which he owed so much." From "The Chautauqua Movement" by Joseph E. Gould, Albany: State University of New York Press. 1961.

37. Harper Presidential Papers, Op. Cit., Box V, Folder 2.

38. Ibid, Box 67, Folder 11.

39. Annual Meeting, Chautauqua Board of Trustees, Jan. 11, 1900, Trustees Minutes 1892-1903, Chautauqua Press, page 4.

40. In the files of the Chautauqua Historical Collection, N2.

41. Op. Cit., Annual Meeting, Jan. 11, 1900, Page 30, 31.

42. Op. Cit., Annual Meeting, Oct. 14, 15, 1904, Page 8.

43. The Independent, Vol. 82, June 21, 1915, Page 505.

44. Chautauqua Institution Circulars, 1919, Pages 3-12.

45. From Controller's Report, 1921, Circulars, 1921: "At the time of the Comprehensive Campaign in the year 1919 the following commitment was made by the Trustees and confirmed at the close of the campaign at the meeting of Aug. 3, 1921.

"That no commitment will be made by the Board of Trustees involving a capital expenditure in excess of $25,000 for any purpose, and no issue of bonds authorized in any amount, unless and until a vote of the cottage owners as to the same shall have first been taken..."

Trustee action under date of August 3, 1921: "That... each year's deficit, if any, shall be the first charge upon the budget of the ensuing year."

46. Chautauqua Institution Bound Circulars. 1927. Dr. Bestor met with the cottage owners to present the problem of the filtration plant. The cottage owners endorsed the project of the new plant with a two-year subscription plan to help defray the costs.

47. Arthur E. Bestor Memorial in The Chautauquan Daily, August 4, 1944.

48. Letter from Ralph McCallister to the author concerning the Chautauqua years, now part of the McCallister File

in the Chautauqua Historical Collection.

49. In his telegram of resignation to Board Chairman Hough, Mr. McCallister referred to "managerial bureaucracy" which was interfering with his professional duties. The vice president was in Washington as a special guest at the White House Conference on Aging when a telephone conversation with President Carothers decided him against continuing at Chautauqua. His resignation was thus reported by the Washington correspondent of the Buffalo Courier-Express, Lucian Warren, Jan. 12, 1961. Warren had been editor of The Chautauquan Daily earlier in his career.

50. The Chautauquan Daily, July 1, 1963.

51. Ibid, July 31, 1971.

52. Ibid., August 2, 1971.

2. Search for a Successor

1. Theodore Morrison, "Chautauqua, A Center for Education, Religion and the Arts in America," Chicago. The University of Chicago Press, 1974. Epilogue, Pages 243-252.

2. Ibid, Page 251.

3. The Chautauquan Daily, July 8, 1977.

4. Ibid. June 24, 1978.

5. The Reverend Kenneth D. Harvey, Minister, McCracken Memorial Presbyterian Church, Belfast, Ireland. Chaplain for the final Sunday of the 1977 season.

3. Listening Year

1. The Chautauquan Daily, June 24, 1978, Page 4.

2. Ibid, June 29, 1978, Page 8.

3. "Weeping in the Playtime of Others" by Kenneth Wooden was a 1977 CLSC Book Selection.

4. "Letters from the Field" by Margaret Mead was a 1978 CLSC Book Selection.

5. Vincent descendents who attended the Centennial Vesper Service July 30, 1978, were: Sally Vincent McGrath, great-granddaughter of Bishop Vincent; Elizabeth Vincent Foster, granddaughter of Bishop Vincent; Jane Harper Overton, great-grandaughter of both Bishop Vincent and William Rainey Harper and daughter of Isabel Vincent Harper; Maxweil Foster, Jr., great-grandson of Bishop Vincent, son of Elizabeth Vincent Foster; John Vincent, grandson of Bishop Vincent; also Susan McGrath and David McGrath.

6. Beverly Dame Esch is a former member of the Chautauqua Opera Company. Her brother, Donald Dame, was a favorite principal performer in Chautauqua Opera for a number of years.

7. Mrs. Rappole's home was originally the home of Clement Studebaker, Jr., a distinguished Chautauqua trustee and son of President Studebaker. The Chautauqua home of Dr. Jesse L. Hurlbut occupied the site of the Studebaker home and was moved to make way for the new 1902 construction. In 1916 the Studebaker home was purchased by C.T. Terrill, father of Mrs. Nina Wensley. Mrs. Wensley was also to give valuable service on the Board of Trustees, as has Mrs. Rappole, the present owner. The Rappoles acquired this historic property in 1963.

4. New Strategies; Alarms Sounded

1. The Chautauquan Daily, June 23, 1979, Page 10.

2. Ibid, July 11, 1979, Page 4.

3. Ibid, June 28, 1930, Page 8.

4. This article, written by The Chautauquan Daily Editor for the County Office of Historic Preservation, had been published shortly before in newspapers within the county.

5. Second Century Campaign Launched

1. The Chautauquan Daily, June 24, 1980, Page 2.

2. Extensive repairs had been made in 1971 to Kellogg Hall's foundation, but complete renewal was made between 1979 and 1980.

3. Golfview is the small house located on the Chautauqua Golf Course near the highway.

4. The estimate that 10,000 people are resident on the Grounds at the height of the season has been revised downward since many multiple-family residencees have become single family units and some hotels have either ceased or reduced their operations.

5. Col. Vic Richardson, a professional auctioneer, had donated his time and talents to further the Capital Campaign.

6. When the new sewerage treatment plant was built, it was expected that the rehabilitation of the sanitary sewer lines would follow so that rain water inflow could be reduced, and possibly the construction of an overflow retention facility would be necessary.

7. Chautauquans have never tired of saying "Thank you" to Dr. Hanson who has contributed so much to American music.

8. At the May 10, 1980 Board meeting, Dr. Hesse pointed out that if the quality of the orchestra is improved, grants from the N.Y.S.C.A. and N.E.A. will be made more available to Chautauqua and that approval of N.Y.S.C.A. and N.E.A. does affect other donors to the Institution.

9. In an allied matter, the separation of the Symphony Patron Drive from the Annual Fund was approved at the January Executive Committee meeting. A fifty-dollar donation, rather than twenty-five, would provide preferred seating.

6. 'Nothing Succeeds Like Success'

1. At the Annual Meeting in 1980, Mr. Gibbs, Mr. Miller and Mr. Wilder had been designateed by the Board to join Dr. Hesse and Labor Attorney Ray Anderson in the negotiations. Participating on behalf of the Orchestra were two Union officials, Allan Swanson and Vincent Mollare, chairman of the orchestra committee, Jason Weintraub, and two other orchestra members, Denton Williamson and Stephen Smith.

2. Mr. Erdle was assistant professor of painting at North Texas University and a former director of the Chautauqua Art Association Galleries.

3. The Institution's computer was already functioning in the areas of financial applications, mailing list and ticket format, and development-donor program.

4. During the 1980 season, the Play House played at a forty per cent capacity with some evenings as low as five per cent. According to the agreement with the Play House, the Institution cannot choose its plays but are obligated to take what the Play House wishes to present. Furthermore, the Institution must pay for eight performances per week when eight performances cannot be given. More than $100,000 in indirect costs plus a subsidy of over $50,000 is estimated as the impact on the Chautauqua budget.

5. Ms. O'Connor became Dr. Marie O'Connor in 1981. Her dissertation was "Personal Enrichment Through the Arts: Description of Four Curriculum Models in Aesthetic Appreciation"; her degree from the State University of New York at Buffalo.

6. Funded by Mrs. Helen Temple Logan.

7. While good maintenance is its own reward, the 1981 improvements to the cluster of practice cabins or shacks near the highway had public relations value, some argue. Motorists on Route 394 who may be strangers to the Institution might judge the whole Institution by these unique little structures they see as they go whizzing by.

8. Dr. Hesse had made this recommendation.

9. Most organizations similar to Chautauqua function on a 60-40 per cent ratio.

7. Renaissance of Buildings and Spirit

1. Subsequently, at a meeting of the Exeecutive Committee of the Board of Trustees in June, the property was conveyed to Chautauqua Enterprises, Inc., by the Institution.

2. From Jane Mead's first editorial, "Celebrating Chautauqua," in the opening issue of The Daily. She connected The Daily's new graphics with the other dramatic changes that were taking place at Chautauqua.

8. New Directions in Rhythm With the Past

1. But the NEA Challenge Grant Match still needed $265,000 in cash for the performing arts endowment by the June 30, 1983 deadline. The completion of the Match would assure a $250,000 NEA Grant for Chautauqua's endowment.

2. Christine Vaughan and Jennifer Willcock. Ms. Vaughan was head of the art department at the Abby Cross School outside London; Ms. Willcock, principal of a school in London, and both an actress and director in amateur theater.

3. The Ralph W. Loew Endowment Fund now contains in excess of $30,000.

4. Vincent, op.cit., page 242.

BIBLIOGRAPHY

Amiss, Mrs. Bettie D. "Five Weeks at Chautauqua for $50.00." The Chautauqua Historical Collection, 1885.

Ahlstrom, Harold J., ed. "Chautauqua Lake Steamboats." Jamestown, New York: The Fenton Historical Society, 1971.

Bailey, William S., "The Role of Chautauqua in Adult Education",1948. Manuscript in Chautauqua Historical Collection.

Bestor, Arthur E. "A Look Ahead." Written in Chautauqua's 50th anniversary year. Chautauqua's bound volume of 1924

Circulars. In the Chautauqua Historical Collection.

Bestor, Arthur Eugene, Jr. "Chautauqua-Chautauqua Institution," section in "The Historic Annals of Southwestern New York," William J. Doty, editor-in-chief. New York, N. Y.: Lewis Publishing Co., Inc. 1940.

Bestor, Arthur Eugene, Jr., "Chautauqua Publications: An Historical and Bibliographical Guide." Chautauqua, N. Y.: Chautauqua Press, 1934.

Bond, Susan. "I've Seen Chautauqua." Newark, N. Y.: Bond Features, 1946.

Bray, Frank Chapin. "A Reading Journey Through Chautauqua." Chicago: The Lakeside Press, R. R. Donnelley and Sons Co., 1905.

Bruch, Mrs. Kate P. "Early Days of Chautauqua." 1897. The Chautauqua Historical Collection.

Campen, Richard N. "Chautauqua Impressions." West Summit Press, Chagrin Falls, Ohio 1983.

The Chautauquan. Vols. I-LXXII. October, 1880-October, 1889, ten monthly issues per year; Dr. T.L. Flood, Editor Publisher, Meadville, Pa.; publication extended to 12 issues per year from October, 1889 to September, 1899. Chautauqua Assembly purchased the magazine with issues beginning October, 1899 to March, 1902 printed by the Chautauqua Press in Cleveland, Ohio; April, 1902 to September, 1904 in Springfield, Ohio; after September, 1904 and until May 23, 1914, in Chautauqua. After May 23, 1914, The Chautauquan, merged with The Independent. The Chautauquan became The Chautauquan Weekly Newsmagazine between May, 1913 and May 23, 1914. Frank Chapin Bray was editor of The Chautauquan following Dr. Flood's retirement.

The Chautauqua Assembly Daily Herald,1876-1878, Dr. Theodore L. Flood Editor, Mr. Milton Bailey, Publisher.

The Chautauquan Assembly Herald, 1879-1906, Dr. Flood, Editor and Publisher through 1899.

The Chautauquan Daily, published by Chautauqua Institution, 1906 to present. (For a period of approximately 20 years, beginning at the time of Chautauqua's financial crisis in the mid-thirties, The Daily was produced by private investor-craftsmen. It returned to full Institution management in 1960.)

Chautauqua Institution Half Million Dollar Campaign. Pamphlet in Bound Institution Circulars, 1919 and 1920.

Chautauqua Institution, Survey of Seasons (1874-1907). Chautauqua. 1908. Bound Institution Circulars 1908-1912.

Chautauqua LAKE Journal, Vol. 1, No. 1 Fair Point, N.Y.: The Chautauqua Lake Camp Meeting Association, July, 1873.

Chautauqua Pamphlets, Year Books and Reports of the Board Meetings. Trustees Meetings, 1889-1903. The Chautauqua Press. After 1903, annual meeting included in Bound Circulars until 1931. Now filed in Historical Collection.

Clarkson, Eleanor Preston. "The Tiger of Lake Chautauqua." Motor Boating. July, 1963.

Cowden, Robert H. "The Chautauqua Opera Association 1929-1958. An Interpretive History." Part of The Monograph Series of the National Opera Association. Leland Fox, general editor. 1974.

Edson, Obed and Merrill, Georgia Drew. "History of Chautauqua County." Boston: W.A. Ferguson and Co., 1894.

Edwards, James T., D.D.L.L.D., "Pen and Picture, A Chautauqua Sketch-Book." Meadville, Pa.; The Chautauqua-Century Press, 1896.

Fancher, Pauline, "Chautauqua: Its Architecture and Its People." Banyan Books, Inc. Miami, Florida, 1978.

Gerwig, George William, "Chautauqua." East Aurora, N.Y.: Roycrofters, 1924.

Gould, Joseph E., "The Chautauqua Movement." The University of New York Press, Albany, 1961.

Harper's New Monthly Magazine, Vol. LIX, No. CCCLI, August 1879.

Harper's Presidential Papers, 1889-1925, Department of Special Collections, The Joseph Regenstein Library, The University of Chicago.

Hazlett, Samuel M.,"Chautauqua Through the Years, Diamond Jubilee Pageant." Chautauqua, New York: Pri-Ad Corporation, Chadakoin Press, Lafayette Press, Inc.,1948.

Hendrick, Ellwood, "Lewis Miller, A Biographical Essay," New York, London: G.P. Putnam's Sons, 1925.

History, Legislation, By-Laws, Rules and Regulations, of the Chautauqua Assembly, 1889. Syracuse: Courier Printing Company, 1888.

Hurlbut, Jesse Lyman, "The Story of Chautauqua." New York and London: G.P. Putnam's Sons, 1921.

James, William, "Talks to Teachers." New York: Henry Holt, 1899.

Kipling, Rudyard, "Abaft the Funnel." B.W. Dodge, 1909.

Kniker, Charles R.,"The Chautauqua Literary and Scientific Circle, 1878-1914: An Historical Interpretation of an Educational Piety in Industrial America." Ann Arbor, Mich.: University Microfilms. 1969.

Mathews, Shailer, "New Faith from Old," An Autobiography. New York: The Macmillan Company, 1936.

Morrison, Theodore. "Chautauqua, a Center for Education, Religion, and the Arts in America." Chicago and London: The University of Chicago Press, 1974.

Mosedale, John, "Chautauqua In Its 85th Year." Feature for North American Newspaper Alliance. 1959.

Orchard, Hugh A. "Fifty Years of Chautauqua." Cedar Rapids, Iowa: The Torch Press, 1923.

Raymond, Emily, "About Chautauqua." Toledo, Ohio: Blade Printing and Paper Co. 1886.

Raynor, George R., "The Aims, Past, Present and Future of Chautauqua Institution." Paper to be read before the Chautauqua County Historical Society, October 7, 1950. The Chautauqua Historical Collection.

Raynor, George R., "Fish and Fishing in Chautauqua Lake." The Chautauqua Historical Collection.

Richmond, Rebecca, "Chautauqua, An American Place." New York, N. Y.: Duell, Sloane and Pearce, 1943.

Richmond, Rebecca and June Kirkpatrick, "The Chautauqua Jubilee Sketchbook." New York, N. Y.: Brookside Press, 1948.

Richmond, Rebecca, "Invitation to Chautauqua," New York, N. Y., 1953.

"Report to the Public on Chautauqua Lake Studies, Part I, summary of observation, data and research carried on from 1971-1976, issued jointly by State University College at Fredonia, Jamestown Community College and Chautauqua Lake Association. Also Chautauqua Lake Morphometry, Table lV-I.

Rules and Regulations, By-Laws of Board of Trustees, Legislation Affecting Chautauqua, Chautauqua, N.Y., 1930.

Tarbell, Ida M., "All In The Day's Work," An Autobiography. New York: The Macmillan Company, 1935.

Thornton, Harrison John, "Chautauqua—Adventure in Popular Education," two volumes. Manuscript in Chautauqua Historical Collection. Dr. Thornton was a Professor of History at the State University of Iowa, 1929-1952.

Vincent, Dr. George, "Chautauqua,"A Radio address,1930.

Vincent, John H., "The Chautauqua Movement." Boston: Chautauqua Press, 1886.

Vincent, Leon H., "John Heyl Vincent, A Biographical Sketch." New York, N. Y. The Macmillan Company. 1925.

Warren, R. M. "Chautauqua Sketches: Fair Point and the Sunday School Assembly." Buffalo: H.H. Otis, 1878.

Wells, L. Jeanette, "A History of the Music Festival at Chautauqua Institution from 1874 to 1957." Washington, D.C. : The Catholic University of America Press, 1958.

Westcott, Adelaide L., Scrapbooks I, II, and III (1874-1887, 1888-1895, and 1896-1907, respectively). Holley, N. Y. The Chautauqua Historical Collection.

Westgate, The Rev. G. L., "Official Report of the National Sunday School Teachers' Assembly held at Fair Point, Chautauqua County, New York, on the borders of Lake Chautauqua, Aug. 4-18, 1874." New York: Printed for the "Sunday School Union," 805 Broadway, 1875.

Woollcott, Alexander. "The Letters of Alexander Woollcott." The Chautauqua Historical Collection.

INDEX

These cottages on South Avenue are close enough to the Hall of Philosophy to be in the *Quiet* zone during lectures.